TODAY'S HANDBOOK FOR SOLVING BIBLE DIFFICULTIES

TODAY'S HANDBOOK
FOR
SOLVING
BIBLE
DIFFICULTIES

David E.O'Brien

BETHANY HOUSE PUBLISHERS
MINNEAPOLIS, MINNESOTA 55438

Published by Bethany House Publishers
A Ministry of Bethany Fellowship, Inc.
6820 Auto Club Road, Minneapolis, Minnesota 55438

Library of Congress Cataloging-in-Publication Data

O'Brien, David E.
Today's handbook for solving Bible difficulties / David E. O'Brien.
p. cm.
ISBN 0-87123-814-4
1. Bible—Hermeneutics. 2. Bible. O.T. Genesis I–XI—Criticism,
interpretation, etc. I. Title.
BS476.037 1990
220.6'1—dc20   90-30954
                                                               CIP

Printed in the United States of America

TO THREE MEN
WHO SHAPED MY LIFE

The Reverend H. S. Thomasson,
my grandfather,
whose faith and life
drew me to Christ more
surely than any sermon.

The Reverend Gordon K. Peterson, Sr.,
whose ministry and friendship
provided me with a strong example
of a virile Christianity lived hilariously
at full speed at a time in my life when
nothing less would have helped.

The Reverend Dr. Sidney B. Nelson,
whose love for the Lord, love of learning,
and love for a dying world were so perfectly joined
they will always be both a model
and a reproach to me.

CONTENTS

PREFACE

This is a long book so I'll keep this short, but I do want you to know how the questions I've attempted to answer came to be selected.

Both in teaching and in the pastorate I discovered that the number of questions people have about the Bible is surprisingly limited. If I heard a question once I could count on hearing it again, and often.

When I decided to write this book, I decided to go to the people who seemed to be best at asking hard questions: my students. I asked for three questions apiece from a total of about two hundred students in my Old Testament history classes at St. Paul Bible College and a similar number of questions from a similar number of students in Bible classes at Bethany Fellowship.

The result was a folder of questions that weighed about two pounds. Many of the approximately 1300 questions I received were repeated more than once. I assigned these top priority. Others, while asked only once or twice, seemed to touch on interpretive problems that had implications for larger issues within the church. Some questions were included because I didn't think they had been addressed adequately in available literature.

I discarded questions that didn't have a strong textual component. This is, after all, a book about understanding the Bible, not systematic theology. I combined and rewrote questions to say what I thought the students were actually asking. When I was done, I had about 350 questions. I grouped those topically and began to write.

Obviously there were a lot more questions asked than have been answered. I tried to cover as much ground, both biblically and hermeneutically, as I could. There were enough questions about the end times, or predestination, or the place of tongues, or the role of women in the church to write separate books on each topic, but that wasn't my purpose. What I've tried to do is add a small bit of Bible understanding to the lives of ordinary Christians and a larger bit of instruction on how they can find answers for themselves.

ACKNOWLEDGMENTS

My spiritual life and my intellectual life have grown in tandem. The Lord has spoken to me most often through my studies, and in that area He has used a succession of mentors whose teaching has contributed more to me than can be gauged by grade points or degrees.

I may have registered for more classes with Dr. Ronald F. Youngblood than any student in his illustrious teaching career. I greatly valued his high standards, encyclopedic knowledge, warm encouragement, and appreciation of a good pun through my fitful academic career. While I fall far short of his example in every area except the last, he taught me as much about what it is to be a Christian scholar as he did about the Bible

If I know anything at all about the life and teachings of Paul, it is because of the teaching and influence of Dr. George Cannon, a friend whose passionate commitment to Paul and his message has opened those thirteen epistles to me in a way I could never repay.

The wisdom books of the Old Testament have become some of my favorites, thanks to Dr. C. Hassell Bullock. His teaching is filled with reverence for the texts and reverence for a holy God.

The two quarters I spent as teaching assistant for Dr. Samuel Schultz were as valuable as any I ever spent as a student. It was he who taught me that the grace of God is as much at home in the Old Testament as the New.

INTRODUCTION

THIS IS PROBABLY
A DUMB QUESTION, BUT . . .

Most parents are totally unprepared for the volume and complexity of questions that emerge from the innocent mouths of their firstborn children: "Where does God live?" "Why did Papa have to die?" "Will we have to go to church all the time when we get to heaven?" "Can I give Jesus some of my ice cream?"

I enjoy children's questions because they're always sincere. Children aren't afraid to ask what they don't know. Unintimidated by theological jargon, they keep asking until they get a straight answer in language they can understand. How else can ones so young learn what life is all about?

What I don't enjoy is that the questions stop coming far too soon. As kids get older it becomes harder and harder for them to admit that they don't know or don't understand. Perhaps they have learned from adults that not knowing is disgraceful and that asking reveals weakness. Maybe we've treated their questions as "cute" once too often. Or maybe we've answered "Because I said so" enough times to convince them that asking is pointless.

Sooner or later their questions are tucked away with other childhood toys and replaced with the inadequate adult facade of self-sufficiency. The simple questions of childhood that opened up the world for all of us are locked shut with pat answers.

Sincere childlike questions may be as much a part of becoming like little children as the childlike faith we hear so much about. Asking questions is the first step toward understanding. Without questions no way exists to check our understanding against the understanding of others. We have no way of knowing if our question was raised and put to rest years ago.

Somehow adults learn not to ask, or to apologize first if they do ask. I could probably retire at fifty, and that's getting closer every day, if I had banked a dollar every time a student or parishioner has apologized to me for asking a question. "This is probably a dumb question, but . . ." they say before voicing what are often very perceptive and searching questions. The tragedy of this is not the questions and doubts we never express but the answers we never get. In many cases all we need is the confirmation that our own common sense, energized by the Holy Spirit, is valid. In other cases, a simple bit of information about the history, culture, or language of the Bible is enough to clarify meaning.

A few questions have troubled the faithful since the first century. In those cases, the knowledge that our perplexity is shared is a comfort of sorts. At least we know that our questions are genuine and the text is indeed difficult.

EARTHEN VESSELS AND CRACKED POTS

It is arrogant for teachers or preachers to believe that every word they say is understood as they intend, and listeners are grossly misled if they assume their difficulty in understanding is always due to some weakness in themselves.

My first semester of teaching a historical introduction to the Old Testament taught me that. I had lectured at length and with great passion to debunk an approach to the books of Moses known as the Documentary Hypothesis. I was trying to prepare my students for their inevitable first encounter with scholarship that admits no hint of inspiration to the writing of Scripture. Forewarned is forearmed, I thought.

Then came the first exam. I quickly discovered that the majority of my freshmen thought I was teaching my own theory. It didn't matter that I had handed out at least two pages of critique and carefully pointed out all the flaws in the position. Somehow I had made them think that I believed the whole Old Testament had been slapped together out of old Jewish legends and political motivations some time after the Babylonian exile.

What started out as a lesson to teach freshmen how to deal with a threadbare theory ended up teaching me an important lesson about communication. People who preach, teach, or write should never assume that listeners understand their carefully reasoned and eloquently stated positions. It's better to repeat yourself once too often than to leave people as confused as that class of freshmen obviously was.

I accept most of the blame, but some fault lay on the side of the students as well. Over 200 of them listened to the lectures, but not one questioned my presentation of a theory that ran counter to everything they believed about the Bible. Unquestioning acceptance of what you think you've heard can be disastrous.

I once worked at a camp where the speaker for a week was an evangelist who'd spent a lifetime preaching on prophecy. His messages were based on Revelation and related passages. This man's ministry had spanned decades and had touched thousands of lives, but he was in the twilight of that ministry. He tired easily, and fatigue sometimes played tricks with his memory. In the ebb and flow of end-time armies, he'd lose his direction. But his years of pulpit experience had taught him how to execute a homiletical U-turn and press on in a new direction. When he did, even the apostle John might have gotten lost in the traffic. Those sermons never lacked for meaningful nuggets of truth and inspiration, but they were short on coherence.

As sad as his predicament was, explaining it to my high school campers concerned me the most.

I needn't have worried about finding an explanation for the preacher's confusion. I did, however, discover that there was a more profound cause for concern.

Leaving the chapel after one of the more bewildering sessions, I heard two young people discussing the morning's message.

"What did you think of that?" asked the first.

"Oh, he was really deep," answered the second. "I didn't understand a word he said."

They couldn't believe the speaker had been confused, so they readily assumed they were too slow to follow.

As a speaker, it's sometimes a comfort to know that people will often blame their confusion on themselves and not on me. But at a deeper level, it's profoundly unsettling to know that the flock I've been entrusted with might lose out on the riches of the Word because I've been unclear.

This is where the lay person must shoulder some responsibility and not let questions lie fallow. Teachers and pastors who are committed to the ministry of the Word aren't offended by honest questions. In fact, to have someone ask for clarification, or even challenge a point, is a valuable opportunity for Christian leaders. They get a chance to redo something they may not have done well the first time through. One of the great ministries lay people can perform for their pastors is to question. "As iron sharpens iron, so one man sharpens another" (Proverbs 27:17). Sincere questions hone the pastor's understanding as well as our own.

Asking questions also helps us realize we're not alone in our confusion. From the time we start school we're conditioned to feel that knowing is the road to success and approval, and not knowing is the way to failure. To avoid the feeling of failure, a lot of us bluff when we don't understand.

I spent months preparing to buy my computer. First I had to convince myself, and my wife, that the rather sizable expenditure was justifiable. Then I had to figure out which of many available brands and models would do what I wanted it to do at a price I could afford to pay. I attended computer shows, read books and magazine articles, talked to computer owners, and tried to make sense out of a subject that I became convinced couldn't be understood without learning a second language.

I finally bought one, but I barely know the difference between RAM and ROM, bits and bytes, and, for the life of me, I can't figure out what's BASIC about programming. The depth of my computer illiteracy continues to be mind-boggling.

Yet when I go into a computer store to look at a new program or some gadget that will get more out of my computer, I sling what little jargon I know to make myself feel as if I belong there. I'm like the Christians who speak theologese without understanding it; I'm afraid to show my ignorance by asking what all that stuff really means. If I dared to ask someone who would take the time to answer in English, I would probably learn something.

Until we are willing to admit our confusion or ignorance, we can never go beyond what we already know. Before we can learn we have to realize we need to learn.

Fear of being wrong isn't the only reason for letting our questions remain unanswered. In too many conservative circles questions equal unbelief. If we understand faith as the absence of doubt, faith cannot exist if we have questions. However, when we understand faith as a total commitment to obedience to God, the honest questions of a searching believer are an indication of faith's presence, not its absence.

Christians whose faith can't stand questioning should question their faith!

The unreasoned rejection of honest doubts is the mark of a cultist. Cults grow out of the flawed reasoning of human leaders who often have a psychotic need for power. They do not tolerate questions because to answer them honestly would be to risk losing control.

Skillful debaters know that valid questions will weaken their case, so they head them off with an aggressive assault. Debaters look for the elements of their own position that won't stand attack and defend their position with a two-part strategy: to emphasize the strong points of their side and to expose the weaknesses of their opponent's side. Debate propositions are set up to allow clever arguments and manipulation of facts to win. They're concerned with victory, not truth.

Because our message is true, we need not fear questions. But too often we act as if we're debating a proposition and not proclaiming truth. We avoid questions as if their very existence carries seeds that will discredit the gospel.

We need not market the gospel like another product with fanciful claims and unspoken limitations that *Consumer's Report* might uncover. No honest question or doubt can ever harm the truth of the gospel of Jesus Christ.

The Bible is filled with stories of people whose faith was forged in the heat of doubt.

Abraham, the prototype for all who follow God in faith, is so well known for his faith that we sometimes overlook his doubt. Yet Genesis 15 begins with an implicit statement of Abraham's doubt. In verse 1, God identified himself as Abraham's shield and great reward. In verse 2 Abraham voiced the question: "What can you give me since I remain childless and the one who will inherit my estate is Eliezer of Damascus?"

Abraham had already given up everything to obey God. He believed Him so thoroughly in fact that he left one of the most advanced and cultured cities in the ancient world and became a wanderer in a region that the world powers of his day considered a backwater. It would be like asking a city executive to move to the desert and live in a tent with his animals.

That's how thoroughly Abraham had allowed his faith to shape his life. But he couldn't see how a couple as old as he and Sarah could possibly have the son that God had promised.

Yet Abraham didn't try to hide his doubts. He went to God with them instead, and God reassured him. For the first time in God's dealing with Abraham, God made his promise specific. He could have fulfilled the promise through Eliezer, as Abraham obviously thought he would. But God specified that the promise would be fulfilled through a son of Abraham's own body (15:4). Abraham responded with a deepened faith. The promise still seemed an impossibility (17:17), but Moses wrote that Abraham "believed the LORD, and [God] credited it to him as righteousness" (15:6).

Faith can't get much stronger than that. In fact, Paul quoted that verse twice (Galatians 3:6; Romans 4:3) as proof that salvation is by faith.

But there's more. Abraham, whose faith has just been rewarded by God and whose trust in the Lord has since become a symbol for all believers, asks God to confirm His promise with something a little more tangible. "Sovereign LORD, how can I know that I will gain possession of it?" (15:8) Abraham asked, almost demanding that the Lord put it in writing.

And that's just what He did.

How many of us can imagine ourselves in Abraham's place? After accepting God's promise of a natural son and descendants as numberless as the stars in the sky by faith, he asked how he could be sure God would come through on his promise of the land.

The strange story that follows (Genesis 15:9–21) describes the signing of a contract as it would have been done in Abraham's day. We might not recognize it because we think of contracts as pieces of paper signed in paneled rooms with a gaggle of lawyers looking on. For Abraham and his contemporaries though, I suspect that our contract form would lack punch.

In the ancient world, contracts were made by sacrificing animals. Their carcasses were cut into pieces and laid on the ground on both sides of a path. The people agreeing to the contract walked between the severed halves of the sacrificial animals. By doing this they accepted the fate of the animals for themselves if they ever went back on their part of the deal. God, in response to Abraham's question, sealed His covenant by participating in this binding ceremony. More than likely, Abraham would have missed this amazing experience with the living God if he had quietly swallowed his question.

WHEN JOB'S PATIENCE RAN OUT

Job is another example of the faithful doubter. His patience is proverbial, but even he was able to stay patient only through the first two chapters of his story. Beginning in chapter 3, he aimed increasingly pointed accusations at God. These accusations were worse than mere questions! They were insults, taunts, even charges of wrong-doing. Job had no inkling that Satan was the author of his suffering. We know the real villain in this affair, but poor Job's only explanation for his sorry state was that God had turned on him.

Job's complaints against God begin in 3:23: "Why is light given to a man whose way is hidden, *whom God has hedged in?*"

Then, after listening to the fruitless half-truths of Eliphaz, Job replied by wishing the burden of his suffering could be weighed against his sin (6:2). He was convinced that his suffering was out of proportion to any wrong-doing he had committed. He interpreted his suffering as the result of God's vindictiveness. "The arrows of the Almighty are in me, my spirit drinks in their poison" (6:4). Here we see the full extent of Job's doubt as he argued that God had acted unjustly toward him.[1]

Job's final cry for justice was a challenge to God:

I cry out to you, O God, but you do not answer; I stand up, but you merely look at me. You turn on me ruthlessly; with the might of your hand you attack me (Job 30:20–21).

Then Job said, "Oh, that I had someone to hear me! I sign now my defense—let the Almighty answer me; let my accuser put his indictment in writing" (Job 31:35).

Job contended that God was treating him unfairly because He was punishing Job without first telling him what he had done

---

[1]
We will take a closer look at Job, his suffering, and whether or not it was justified, in chapter 8. For now, let's rely on God's own evaluation: "And he still maintains his integrity, though you incited me against him to ruin him without any reason" (2:3).

wrong. Job's complaints and accusations during the cycle of speeches between himself and his friends came frequently and fervently. If any modern Christian were to speak publicly about God as Job did he'd be consigned to the outer darkness reserved for heretics and infidels.

But in all Job's questioning, he never doubted God's existence or power. What Job couldn't understand was how his lifelong friend could turn against him. Job didn't doubt God; he doubted his own intellectualized framework for understanding God.

I would paraphrase and condense Job's argument like this: "If everything I believe about God is true, then what does He think He's doing?"

To understand Job, we need to focus on the incomplete and sometimes inaccurate understanding of God that Job shared with his friends. There was no disagreement among them over the commonly held theology of the day. The difference between Job and his friends was that they had not suffered (16:4–5). Their theology worked in the ivory tower, but not in the misfortunes of life. Job loved God and called out to Him as a bewildered friend (10:8–13), but received no answer.

Job's friends spoke only from the limited wisdom of their sterile lives, which reduced God and all His creation to predictable equations that they could manipulate for their own interests.

When all the arguing had ended and Job had hurled all his questions heavenward like javelins, God appeared. As Job had affirmed, his redeemer did indeed live and came to take His stand on the earth (19:25) to utter His ringing vindication of His friend's righteousness (42:7–9). Imagine the chagrin of Eliphaz when his theoretical, theological God appeared before him and said, "I am angry with you and your friends, because you have not spoken of me what is right, as my servant Job has."

At first, Job's friends had all the answers and Job had all the questions. But when God appeared it was in response to questions, not to unthinking certainty.

George MacDonald wrote some time ago, "true and good and reverent doubts, springing from devoutness and aspiration—are far more precious in the sight of God than many so-called beliefs."

In the throes of his agony, Job intuitively turned to the only one with the answer to his questions. As the answer, God offered himself. As with Abraham, Job's doubts were the building blocks of deepened faith. Without the profound questioning that makes up so much of Job's story, would he ever have been able to say, "My ears had heard of you, but now my eyes have seen you"?

WHEN IT WALKS LIKE A DUCK

I don't want to canonize doubt any more than I want to encourage continued silence. Just as we need to be free to ask genuine questions, we need to learn to recognize an answer when we see it.

For many who call themselves Christians but reject the authority of biblical revelation, the perpetual quest for some spiritually impossible dream is the only goal of their faith. If it looks like a duck, walks like a duck, and quacks like a duck, it's probably a duck, they tell us. In the search for solutions to biblical problems the same holds true. If it looks like a solution, it probably is.

Just as it dishonors the Lord for Christians to remain in continual ignorance because they are afraid to ask questions, so it dishonors Him when we ask questions for which we really don't want answers.

When we get to the place where we don't want to be confused with any more information because our minds are made up and we are comfortable, we mire ourselves in spiritual mediocrity.

GOING FOR THE GROWTH

Runners who finish a day's run dripping with sweat, exhausted, and with their joints aching also feel exhilarated and strangely fulfilled. The Christian's quest for more of the Lord, a quest that has to be undertaken with both heart and mind, can be like that.

The habit of pushing ourselves to the limit of our mental endurance is missing from our American brand of Christianity. The most neglected of spiritual disciplines is the serious study of God's Word.

Answers follow questions. Growth follows struggle. Our goal in approaching Scripture is to seek and to find, to ask and to have opened. Christians who fear study and questioning remain in darkness, but those who refuse answers are more profoundly darkened because their darkness is self-imposed.

The goal of questioning in the Christian life is not to come to answers, but to conformity with the image of Christ.

George MacDonald captured the essence of this quest when he said: "A man may be haunted with doubts, and only grow thereby in faith. Doubts are the messengers of the Living One to the honest. They are the first knock at our door of things that are not yet, but have to be, understood. . . . Doubt must precede every deeper assurance; for uncertainties are what we first see when we look into a region hitherto unknown, unexplored, unannexed."

We all bring to our reading the doctrines we've been taught, assumptions we've made, and pet ideas we've nurtured. As a result, we often see what we expect to find whether it's there or not.

PROLOGUE

IF IT'S BEEN REVEALED, WHY CAN'T I SEE IT?

I t was a Sunday morning, and I was away from my home church filling in for a pastor on vacation. My sermon was a garden variety stewardship sermon that stressed the superiority of God's eternal rewards over this world's material ones.

As I shook hands with the departing worshipers, I spotted a man about fifteen feet away who was thumbing furiously through his Bible. Having preached often in churches where I was a stranger, I had learned to recognize this as a sign that I had stepped on someone's theological bunions and was about to hear the howl.

When the other worshipers had left, he took aim and let me have it with a barrage of "God-wants-you-rich" proof texts. He finished and I took my turn, trying to explain why the carefully selected, out-of-context verses he quoted didn't really support the position he was defending. Through the whole proceedings, I felt the deadening certainty that his opinions, unsupported as they were by Scripture, were ones that he wanted to hold and wouldn't allow to be shaken loose.

True to my expectations, when it was all over, I wasn't convinced that God pays off in Cadillacs, Kruggerands, and condominiums, and he wasn't convinced that He doesn't. His parting salvo seemed calculated to blow my contrary opinions out of the water.

"You can interpret it any way you want," he said, "but I'll just read it the way it's written."

That kind of remark is almost impossible to answer, not because it's true, but because it signals an attitude that's almost unassailable. In the darkest, most reprobate outpost of my old nature, I wanted to squash his glib assertion by asking if he'd read the Sermon on the Mount in Greek and the Ten Commandments in Hebrew, but I didn't. I couldn't, because I understood exactly what he was trying to say, even though it wasn't precisely true.

The claim to simply "read the Word the way it's written" sounds good. It clothes its users with a mantle of spiritual insight and implies that they bring nothing of themselves to Scripture. They simply allow God to speak to them as they read, uncontaminated by human intellect or interpretation.

Sadly, though we might all make the claim from time to time, none of us can accomplish it. We all bring to our reading the doctrines we've been taught, assumptions we've made, and pet ideas we've nurtured. As a result, we often see what we expect to find whether it's there or not.

But assumptions and preconceptions aside, three monumental obstacles keep us from reading Scripture the way it's written. They are history, language, and culture.

People of the biblical world were as thoroughly immersed in their culture as we are. The books of the Bible, written in specific linguistic, historical, and cultural surroundings, reflect those surroundings. As modern Christians our task is to learn enough about these three elements of the total biblical picture to be able to identify them and use them to enhance our understanding.

Most Christians could recite from memory all the stories believers have always told their children, but few have taken the time to learn the history that ties those stories together into a narrative.

Part 1 HISTORY

THE ASSYRIAN CAME DOWN LIKE THE WOLF ON THE FOLD[1]

T he first question I asked students in my Old Testament history class every semester was how many of them loved history. I always insisted that they indicate their answers by raising their hands. I'm glad enrollment in the class wasn't determined by that show of hands. If it had been, I'd have spent most of my time speaking to empty chairs.

Most of us, regardless of age or background, lose our appetites for history somewhere between the signing of the Magna Carta and Sherman's march to the sea. The deadening litany of names, dates, and places drowns out the music of God's underlying activity in the flow of world events. Most of us don't even care to listen any more.

This is tragic because Judaism and Christianity are the only great religions of the world in which it matters whether the stories of their founding really took place as recorded. God revealed himself to real people, at real times and places, in real historical events. To eliminate these events is to eliminate the revelation.

It matters that Israel had a king named Omri, who built his capital city, which he named Samaria, and founded a dynasty, or ruling family, that would be remembered by the Assyrians some 200 years later.

It matters that an obscure Roman official named Pontius Pilate condemned an even more obscure Jewish carpenter to death by crucifixion.

It matters that a young man named Eutychus fell asleep during an over-long sermon that came at the end of a too-full day and fell out a window to his death and miraculous revival.

---

[1]
Taken from Lord Byron's "The Destruction of Sennacherib." In the nineteenth century even unbelievers knew their Bible history and turned to it for their themes and inspiration.

Great paintings are the sum of small details. If the details don't ring true, then the painting itself is open to question. The understanding of these details of the biblical story gives us the background we need to frame the main characters in the portrait.

Most Christians know the biblical story in its broadest out-lines and could recite from memory all the stories believers have always told their children. But few have taken the time to learn the history that ties those stories together into a narrative. This keeps Christians from being able to put their biblical stories together in a cohesive, understandable unit.

Just for fun, here's a quiz. Number the following biblical characters in the order they appear in Scripture.[2]

☐ Moses   ☐ Nehemiah

☐ David   ☐ Deborah

☐ Abraham   ☐ Amos

☐ Malachi   ☐ Solomon

☐ Noah   ☐ Josiah

How did you do? Was it harder than you expected? If you've done well, congratulations. If you got five correct you were average. A perfect score of ten puts you in a very select company.

If a grasp of simple biblical chronology is rare, imagine how unusual knowledge of the history of the ancient world around Israel must be. The names Sennacherib, Nebuchadnezzar, Ramses II, or Cyrus may mean something to us, but what? What were their countries? What roles did they fill? How did their lives affect the lives of God's people?

These may seem like insignificant questions, but the people I've named were all rulers of world powers that had a major impact on Israel. Knowing who they were and what they did

---

[2]
Answers: 3-Moses; 5-David; 2-Abraham; 10-Malachi; 1-Noah; 9-Nehemiah; 4-Deborah; 7-Amos; 6-Solomon; 8-Josiah.

opens a whole new dimension to our understanding of the Bible. The Bible makes much more sense when we make the effort to learn the history it records. The more we know about the world in which the Bible was written, the better we understand the Bible itself. One of the reasons people tend to avoid most of the Old Testament is the obscurity of its historical references. Even the New Testament acquires new meaning when we spend the necessary time to understand its historical setting.

The Wednesday night study group at our church recently researched the historical background of Peter's second letter and then applied that information to gain a deeper understanding of one of the most familiar verses from that letter.

Most Christians can probably quote 2 Peter 1:21 from memory: "For prophecy never had its origin in the will of man, but men spoke from God as they were carried along by the Holy Spirit."

With our modern concern about the inspiration of Scripture, we focus on that issue when we read 2 Peter. But first-century Christians wouldn't have questioned inspiration the same way a twentieth-century skeptic would. Peter's readers would have faced the opposite problem: a world in which gods were everywhere and people needed to be shown the true God and the truth of His revelation as opposed to the numerous other options available.

Second Peter attacks false teachers who were lawless, libertine, and motivated by greed. But who were they? Why did the Lord lead Peter, and not one of the other writers of the New Testament, to make that particular point? An answer to the first question helps to answer the second.

GNOBODY GNOWS THE TROUBLE THEY'VE CAUSED

In the first decades after Jesus' resurrection, the church was troubled by a harmful system of thought known as *Gnosticism*. Its adherents, called Gnostics, were condemned as heretics early in church history, but they remained Christianity's most potent and insidious rival for over three centuries. They believed that they had received special spiritual knowledge, or *gnosis*, from God, which was a special gift for them alone. They had a mystical faith concocted of unequal parts of Greek philosophy, pagan religion, and Christian teaching.

One of the stranger elements of gnostic teaching involved its understanding of God. Gnostics taught that *all* matter was evil, including the earth and its inhabitants. Since God is good, and a spirit, He couldn't have created this evil universe. Therefore the god of the Old Testament, who was the creator, must have been Satan rather than the God and Father of our Lord Jesus Christ!

If the false teachers that Peter combated held to an early form of this Gnostic teaching, you can see how important it was for Peter's readers to know that the God of the Christians was also the God of the Old Testament. God wanted the readers of Peter's letter, who were troubled by the insidious doctrines of the early Gnostics, to know that the Scriptures He'd inspired, the Scriptures to which Peter turned to support the message of salvation in Christ, stood on the firmest possible foundation.

Second Peter was not just a doctrinal pronouncement to affirm the inspiration of Scripture. It was also a condemnation of all that was *not* written under God's direction. The massive body of gnostic writings that has come to light recently confirms the importance of this warning. Peter's second letter was an encouragement to those whose faith had stood firm in the face of a deadly theological assault. And it was correction for those who may have come to doubt.

Scripture wasn't written as a sourcebook of prooftexts for twentieth century theological debaters. It was written as a detailed, integrated statement of the coming of God's grace to men and women living in a fallen antagonistic world. Although our understanding of most verses is generally correct without the historical background, knowing something about the history of the problems they address adds greater depth to their meanings.

As we look at specific problem passages in both Testaments, we'll see that a knowledge of history removes many problems. But it's not just a problem-solving device. Knowledge of history is a learning tool we can use to come to a greater appreciation of the ways of the Author of history.

The forgotten world of the past is important to Christians because history is the canvas on which God is painting the story of His plan of redemption.

CHAPTER 1

PRINCIPLES

1 The more ancient manuscripts we have, the more certainty we have about the true nature of the text.

2 The more ancient the text is, the closer it is to the original; and the closer it is to the original, the more accurate it is likely to be.

3 The quality of the text is as important as the age of the text.

QUESTIONS

1 Why does the Bible number 66 books and not 45 or 110? And why these particular books? What happened to all the books written during Israel's history? How can we know that the Bible we use today isn't different from the Bible Jesus read? Why are there different Bibles? The Catholic Bible has a lot of books the Protestant Bible doesn't have. Why don't we accept them as part of the Bible too?

2 How did the books of the Bible come to be brought together into a single book?

3 How do we know there aren't places where the Bible has been changed over the years to promote some false doctrine?

4 There are places in the Old Testament where numbers don't agree from one book to another. Does this mean there are mistakes in Scripture?

5 Ecclesiastes is a depressing book. Why is it in the Bible?

6 Why does the King James Version mention the Trinity in 1 John 5:8 and the newer translations don't?

7 Why did David work for the Philistines (1 Samuel 27:1–7)?

THE PAST IMPERFECTLY

4 The more we know about the world in which the Bible was written, the better we understand the Bible itself.

5 The Bible may accurately record sinful acts without wholeheartedly applauding them.

8 Where was Tarshish and why did Jonah want to go there (Jonah 1:3)?

9 Why was Jesus so angry when he drove the money changers out of the temple? What was so wrong about what they were doing (Matthew 21:12–13; Mark 11:15–17; Luke 19:45–46; John 2:12–17)?

10 Why was the Samaritan woman so surprised that Jesus talked with her? Why didn't the Jews associate with the Samaritans? (John 4).

11 Did Jewish leaders threaten Pilate when he wanted to free Jesus? If so, why would a Roman governor give in to their pressure so easily (John 19:12–13)?

12 Jesus was supposed to have been thirty-three when He was crucified, but I can't find that anywhere in the Bible. How do we know how old He was?

13 What was Paul's thorn in the flesh (2 Corinthians 12:7–9)?

14 Why was David in Jerusalem when his army was out fighting? Was he just being lazy (2 Samuel 11:1)?

Both children and college students often say and write the strangest things. Almost every parent or teacher has a few wacky and wonderful stories about some weird utterings or writings. Anders Henriksson, a modern and medieval history professor, received the following gems from college freshmen on test papers:

> History, as we know, is always bias, because human beings have to be studied by other human beings, not by independent observers of another species.
>
> History, a record of things left behind by past generations, started in 1815. Throughout the comparatively radical years 1815–1870 the western European continent was undergoing a Rampant period of economic modification. Industrialization was precipitating in England. Problems were so complexicated that in Paris, out of a city population of 1 million people, 2 million able bodies were on the loose.
>
> According to Fromm, individuation began historically in medieval times. This was a period of small childhood. There is increasing experience as adolescence experiences its life development. The last stage is us (from "The All New Past," *Washington Post*).

As a former teacher of Old Testament, I could add a few examples of my own. On one essay question I asked students to identify two important archeological discoveries that helped our understanding of the Old Testament. The discoveries I had in mind were those at Mari (MAH-ree) and Nuzi (NEW-zee), cities in ancient Iraq where documents that shed light on the customs and political picture of the patriarchs' world had been found.

In typical freshman fashion, one student pulled out bits and pieces of not necessarily related information and put them together in an answer that began, "Mary and Suzy were archeological sights."

Agatha Christie, who was married to British archeologist Sir Max Mallowan, once said that it was wonderful to have an archeologist husband because the older she got the more fascinating she became to him!

I doubt if the Mary and Suzy my student had in mind were married to archeologists, but if they were, their husbands must have found the 3,500 year old charmers irresistible.

Most of us aren't archeologists or the spouse of one, and for us there is nothing as uninteresting as yesterday's news. Today's headlines are tomorrow's fish wrappers. If you don't believe me, ask someone under twenty-five about Vietnam. To today's college students, Vietnam is a country about which they know little and care less. It's not that they are stupid, unfeeling, or poorly educated. They just didn't live through the turmoil of the Vietnam era. My Lai, Ho Chi Minh Trail, Tet Offensive, and Khe Sanh mean practically nothing to them.

And why should they? For most people, a sense of history begins somewhere in their early teens. Anything that happened before they emerged from the insular world of their immediate families into the larger world of global events seems ancient, unreal, and irrelevant.

The chaos of the Vietnam years had to be experienced to be understood. For those of us alive then, the events of that period shaped our perception of the world just as the Great Depression and two World Wars shaped the perceptions of earlier generations. But the new generation only knows about it second-hand. And in another twenty years, only the history buffs and the elderly will know what happened and what it meant.

And if the events of the past few decades have such little impact on our collective consciousness, how can we expect people to know or care about the history of a world so long vanished that its great leaders and cities only flicker on the edges of our awareness?

The forgotten world of the past is important to Christians because history is the canvas on which God is painting the story of His plan of redemption. It started when He made the first man. From that moment until now the flow of history has had meaning.

The events of our world show of humanity's slide into rebellion. But those events also point forward to the triumph of God over human rebellion.

The study of the ancient Mediterranean world opens windows on the world of the Bible, so it is an important element in every Christian's understanding of Scripture. It helps us in our quest to know God's Word and God's will, so it's not just yesterday's news.

History relates to the Bible in two ways: (1) specific events that related to the writing and preservation of the Bible, or the history of the Bible itself; (2) general events that happened during Bible times.

THE BOOK WITH A PAST

It may seem odd to speak of the history of the Bible. But parts of it were already ancient when the last books were written. We think of it as a book because it comes to us nicely bound in one cover, but the Bible is more like a library than a single book.

Its first book was written before 1200 B.C. and its last probably about A.D. 96. That's well over a thousand years of history.

The Bible is also a highly selective library. Its 66 books are a careful distillation of the entire literature of the Jewish people for many of those centuries.

 uestion 1   Why does the Bible number 66 books and not 45 or 110? And why these particular books? What happened to all the books written during Israel's history? How can we know that the Bible we use today isn't different from the Bible Jesus read? Why are there different Bibles? The Catholic Bible has a lot of books the Protestant Bible doesn't have. Why don't we accept them as part of the Bible too?

I've been asked all these questions, and they all relate to the history of the Bible, not just the history of biblical times. The process that gave us two different collections of books stretches over as many as 1800 years, a span of time longer than it took to write the Bible.

During the inter-testamental period, a 400-year block of time stretching from Malachi to Mark, Israel's world changed dramatically and forever. These four centuries were also crucial for the history of the Bible.

During the time from Moses to Jeremiah the Israelite population was concentrated in the Promised Land. That began to change in 721 B.C. when Assyria completely defeated the Northern Kingdom and deported the people. Then, in 586 B.C., Nebuchadnezzar conquered Jerusalem, destroyed the temple, and deported everybody but the poor to Babylon, hundreds of miles away.

This process, begun so cruelly by foreign conquerors, eventually created an immense population of Jews outside Palestine that came to be known as the *diaspora*, or the dispersion. During Jeremiah's lifetime a rather large contingent of Judahites sought refuge in Egypt, which would become home for countless Jews in later centuries. And the number of Jews who stayed in Babylon even after Ezra led the return to Jerusalem was greater than the number of Jews who left.

By the time of the Jewish historian Josephus, a contemporary of the apostle Paul, Jews beyond the Euphrates were "beyond counting." In Egypt, the Jewish population in Alexandria alone was estimated between 500,000 and 1,000,000.

The long process by which the Apocrypha (uh-POCK-riff-uh), those books not included in the Protestant Bible, came to be included in the Catholic version of the Bible began with that large colony.

The Jews of Alexandria faced a problem. Over the generations they'd become so at home in their new country that they forgot how to speak their native language, Hebrew. This meant that they could no longer read the Hebrew Scriptures.

Approximately 250 B.C. the problem became so serious that a sort of "Living Bible" of Judaism began to take shape. Originally it was a Greek translation of the five books of Moses. Over the years that collection grew to include the books of history, poetry, and prophecy. In its final form, it was known as the Septuagint (sep-TWO-a-jint). It contained all the books of our Protestant Old Testament, plus other books written during the inter-testamental period.

Since Hebrew was no longer the principle language, even in Israel, this Greek translation became popular. When the church began to spread outside of Israel, the Septuagint was the Bible it read.

In A.D. 70, when the Romans conquered Jerusalem and destroyed the temple again, the break between Judaism and Christianity became complete. In the aftermath of these events, Jewish leaders began to shore up the remnants of their faith. With the temple and its ritual gone, the focus of Judaism shifted to the Law, the synagogue, and personal piety.

Deciding what books would be authoritative for Judaism was an important part of this shoring up. There was very little disagreement about the books we presently find in our Protestant Bibles. Those books had already been in general use as Scripture for centuries.

Most evangelical scholars would say that the Holy Spirit supervised this usage as part of the process of inspiration. The debate that raged at Jamnia was over the new books, written originally in Greek, and added to the Septuagint during the 400-year period during which no prophet spoke to Israel for God. These, written in primarily Greek during the inter-testamental period, eventually became suspect.

Around A.D. 90, Judaism determined that only those books written originally in Hebrew and associated with the great heroes of the Jewish faith would be accepted as authoritative. The books of the Protestant Old Testament were the only ones that met those standards.

The early church, on the other hand, continued to use the Septuagint, which included both the Old Testament books and the later Greek books we now call the Apocrypha.

A few hundred years later, Jerome translated the Septuagint into the Latin of the common people. His translation, the Vulgate, included the Apocrypha, but only because the books were popular among his readers. He denied that they should have any status as Scripture. His assessment of the Apocrypha was ignored, however, and in time the Vulgate became the official Catholic text on which all other translations were based until this century.

The story goes on hold at that point. No real change took place until the Protestant Reformation in the 1500s. The Catholic church had used the Vulgate translation of the Septuagint for 1400 years, but the reformers believed they should go back to the original source, the Hebrew Old Testament. When the reformers rejected the Vulgate and the Septuagint, its source, the Apocrypha, went with them.

As you might expect, the Roman church didn't take the Reformation lying down. As part of the Counter Reformation (Catholics call it the Catholic Reformation), the Council of Trent resolutely affirmed the Apocrypha as Scripture and proclaimed it authoritative for Catholics. From that day to this, the Catholic church has followed that ancient tradition and included fourteen books, or additions to books, in their Bible.

The Protestant churches, on the other hand, following the Jewish assessment of the worth of the Apocrypha, rejected it and made the Protestant Bible the same as the original thirty-nine books of the Jewish Bible.

"So what?" you might ask. "Isn't it enough to know that God inspired the Bible. Why bother with historical process when we know what God wanted all along?"

Historical process is God's chosen method of communication.

The Old Testament is God's record of His use of historical process to reveal himself to Israel in preparation for the coming of Christ. If historical process doesn't matter, the Old Testament is irrelevant.

Christianity and Judaism are the only religions in which the record of their founding (history) and their holy writings (law and prophecy) are one and the same.

In the Jewish Bible, the books we call history are called prophecy. When Jews refer to the former prophets, they're not talking about Isaiah, Amos, Hosea, and the other prophets who ministered during the eighth century B.C. The former prophets are Joshua, Judges, Samuel, and Kings. They are rightly considered prophetic because God is proclaimed (the real meaning of prophecy) in those books through the record of historical process—divinely ordained historical process.

If we believe that God is the God of history, we must also believe that there is divine providence at work in historical processes.

It's important to our faith that Israel was enslaved in Egypt and led out by Moses. It's important that Jesus suffered under Pontius Pilate. And it's important that Jesus was born in Bethlehem, during the reign of Caesar Augustus while Herod was king.

Galatians 4:4 speaks of the "time . . . fully come" in which God sent His Son. That's as clear a statement as Scripture contains that the timeless and eternal God, for the sake of His timebound and finite children, has chosen to work within our framework and not His own.

The canonicity decision made by a Jewish council at Jamnia about A.D. 90 was as much an act of divine providence as was the choice of a man, Abraham, at a place called Ur, about 2000 B.C.

The historical process here is subject to the same kind of theological interpretation as the invasions of Sennacherib or the conquests of Cyrus the Great or the call of Abraham.

If the work of the Holy Spirit in inspiration doesn't extend to the process by which our canon was formed, then we have no Bible. It makes no difference that a book was inspired if, by oversight, it was excluded from the canon. We have no certainty about Scripture if non-inspired books were included.

The Protestant reformers' rejection of the traditional Greek Old Testament in favor of the Hebrew original can be seen in the same light. Through all the history of the Bible, God has been at work preserving, protecting, and passing on what has been handed down from the first. God, as the God of history, is as interested in the labors of copyists as He is in the wars of kings.

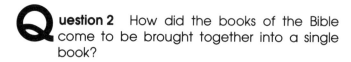

Question 2   How did the books of the Bible come to be brought together into a single book?

The list of 66 books that we consider Scripture is called the canon of Scripture, and sayings from them are said to be canonical.The canon is the official, authoritative list of inspired books that make up the Bible.

The Old Testament was written during a period of 850 to 1,000 years. During that time period Israelites wrote stories, prophecies, history, poetry, and proverbs. They also recorded business transactions, kept almanacs that told farmers what to plant when, wrote letters to one another, and so on. But of the thousands of documents that must have been produced, only 39 were directed by the Spirit to be chosen as Scriptures of Israel and the early church.

In the same way, the New Testament is a residue of the works produced in the decades after Christ. The New Testament itself bears witness to the existence of additional books written by members of the early church.

For example, there's a strong possibility that Paul wrote at least four letters to Corinth alone. Second Corinthians refers to other letters he wrote that many students of Scripture believe couldn't have been 1 Corinthians (2 Corinthians 2:3–4; 7:8–9).

We know that Luke was familiar with many accounts of the life of Jesus when he wrote his gospel (Luke 1:1–4), and yet, of the canonical gospels, only Mark and Matthew could have come earlier.

Scholars know of dozens of letters, Apocalypses (books that describe the events of the end time as Revelation does), acts of the various apostles, collections of the sayings of Jesus, and other gospels. Out of all these, only the 27 books of the New Testament have been preserved by God as the canonical Scriptures of the church.

The process of inspiration must extend to the collection of the authoritative Scriptures as well as to their writing. In that process, the witness of the Holy Spirit in the lives of God's people plays a large role. In fact, while church councils have put their stamps of approval on the canon of Scripture, that canon was in place before they ever thought of meeting to approve it.

The first books of the Old Testament accepted as Scripture were the five books of Moses. All the references to the Law of God in later books prove this. Without those five books, none of the rest of the Old Testament makes any sense at all. So the acceptance of the Pentateuch (PENT-uh-tewk) as Scripture is so ancient that it predates Israel's history in Palestine. The Pentateuch is the foundation in the discussion of Old Testament canonicity.

The collection of the Prophets and Histories came later, but we have no clear biblical statement as to when. We do know, though, that later prophets used the writings of earlier prophets, sometimes quoting them exactly and sometimes paraphrasing them.

We can say, with some certainty, that an authoritative collection of Old Testament books was in use by about 190 B.C. In the foreword to the apocryphal book known as either Ecclesiasticus or The Wisdom of Jesus ben Sirach, the translator says:

> . . . my grandfather Jesus[ben Sirach], after devoting himself especially to the reading of the law and the prophets and the other books of our fathers, and after acquiring considerable proficiency in them, was himself also led to write. . . .

The author of this statement is the first to refer to the traditional three-part division of the Hebrew Bible: the Law, the Prophets, and the Writings. Jesus himself used that description when He reminded the disciples hiding in the upper room that "This is what I told you while I was still with you: Everything must be fulfilled that is written about me in the Law of Moses, the Prophets, and the Psalms." (Because Psalms is the first book in the collection called the Writings it is sometimes called the *Psalms*, or *David*.)

This tells us that by the time of Jesus there was a fixed body of literature that Jews looked to as Scripture. (Decades after Jesus used that description, the council of Jamnia [c. A.D. 90] made their official pronouncement about the humanly authorized content of the Old Testament.)

The same is true with the New Testament. In the first generation after the apostles died, the leaders of the church were already quoting the writings of the apostles as authoritative. By the middle of the second century A.D. people were referring to a list of the letters of Paul as authoritative. The first complete list of the 27 of the canonical New Testament was written about A.D. 360, but most of the books had been accepted long before.

Church leaders determined that to be accepted a book had to have been written by, or associated with, one of the apostles. But more important for both Old and New Testaments was the witness of the Spirit that made them, to use Paul's words, "useful for teaching, rebuking, correcting and training in righteousness" (2 Timothy 3:16).

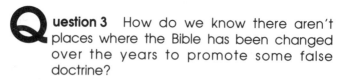

Question 3   How do we know there aren't places where the Bible has been changed over the years to promote some false doctrine?

It amazes me how people who have no use for the clear teaching of the Bible like to use it for their own purposes. They either appeal to some twisted "spiritual" reading of the text or they claim that Christians or Jews have changed the text to suit their purposes.

The first method is easy to beat if we stick to the clearest possible meaning of the text as the original readers would have understood it. The second method requires a bit more work.

A special breed of Bible student has made answering that accusation their life's work. These are the people who figured out the answer to the question about 1 John 5:7–8. Their task is tedious, technical, and trying. I could never do it. But thanks to them we can have certainty that no doctrine of Scripture has been damaged by tampering.

Textual critics compare all the available copies and track the occurrence of variations all the way back to the very earliest manuscripts. By doing this, they discover both where and when variations began to appear.

They go about their work with a few rules of the road.

P **rinciple 1**   The more ancient manuscripts we have, the more certainty we have about the true nature of the text.

In other words, when it comes to determining the most accurate text of the Bible, their rule is, "The more the merrier."

Some breeds of dog are considered more attractive if their ears or tails are surgically altered while they're puppies. Dobermans, for example, are almost always seen with little stubs of tails and sharp, pointed ears. People who have only seen a handful of adult dobermans might reasonably assume they are born that way.

But if they visit a kennel where the dogs are bred, they discover that doberman puppies have fairly normal tails and slightly droopy ears. Only by comparing the adult animal with a large number of puppies can you prove that all dobermans are born one way and, somewhere along the line, changed to look the way we're used to seeing them. The more puppies we look at, the greater our certainty of their original condition. And the younger the puppies are, the less likelihood that they've been changed.

But suppose we run across a litter of puppies fathered by a bassett hound? We could be looking at a mutt with the floppiest ears since Dumbo. No matter how soon after birth we look at him, he won't have the marks of a new-born doberman. In that case, we look at the evidence and determine that he, no matter how young, represents less than a perfect copy of the doberman ideal. How does this canine nonsense apply to the biblical text?

Principle 2   The more ancient the text is, the closer it is to the original; and the closer it is to the original, the more accurate it is likely to be.

In the case of 1 John 5:7, the closer the text got to the original the less likely that the addition, which we will discuss later, was in it. Old Latin texts show the new portion appearing during the seventh century. And before 1400, we can't find any example of the addition in Greek texts. If 1 John were a doberman puppy, we'd conclude that the ears and tail had been altered sometime in the seventh century.

The Old Latin texts I referred to are, for the textual critic, mutts. While they do have value, they are not strong witnesses for the original wording of most texts. It would take a whole truckload of texts of this sort to equal the value of the better Greek manuscripts.

So, for the New Testament, the age of a text is important. But equally important is the quality of the text.

Principle 3   The quality of the text is as important as the age of the text.

There are only a few places in the whole New Testament where additions have been made. In every instance, textual criticism has been able to identify those additions. More important, none of the additions would have changed a single major doctrine of Scripture.

The textual picture is less clear when it comes to the text of the Old Testament, but the evidence that does exist argues strongly for a faithful and accurate transmission of the text.

Ancient copies of Old Testament books are separated from the original manuscripts by over a thousand years in some cases. Our most ancient texts date from the first or second century B.C. But by comparing these texts with those from a later period, we find that the variations within a given text are so slight as to be of no consequence.

The consensus of scholars, both liberal and conservative, is that the text of our twentieth-century translations is as accurate a copy of the originals as any careful and reasonable person would demand. We can be confident that the Bible we read is unchanged in all but the most insignificant ways since the times when the prophets and apostles first wrote it.

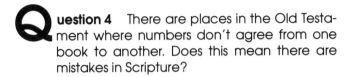

Q **uestion 4**   There are places in the Old Testament where numbers don't agree from one book to another. Does this mean there are mistakes in Scripture?

It's common for writers to point to these discrepancies as proof of the Bible's fallibility. "Aha," they cry, "we knew the Bible was full of mistakes and here's the proof!" Sincere believers have been troubled by these inconsistencies because a comparison of the texts will demonstrate that numbers in parallel passages do sometimes disagree.

If the question is, do our present versions of the Bible contain mistakes, I'm afraid the answer is a qualified yes. When it comes to numbers, the ancient texts have suffered a great deal. And if the ancient texts have been damaged in transmission, the modern translations can't help but reflect that damage. I could list numerous places where numbers have gotten changed, omitted, enlarged, or shrunk. But does that mean the Bible is in error? No. Most evangelicals say that the Bible is inerrant in the original autographs. For those who think of baseball players and pop singers when they hear the word *autograph*, in biblical studies it refers to the original text as it came from the hand of the first writer. In other words, the book as it was first written is without error.

I've tried to show how the modern text of the Bible is reliable, but no one I'm aware of would argue that the NIV is inerrant. The original autograph was inerrant. The text we have today is reliable because the comparison of ancient texts and versions has shown that no copyist's error or scribal gloss has changed the meaning of any doctrine or teaching. There are numerous places, however, where the precise reading of a particular text is uncertain.

That's particularly true when it comes to numbers. We can't always prove that the numbers in the original autographs were different from the numbers we have in the available manuscripts. But there's enough evidence that numbers fared very poorly over the centuries that it is a plausible explanation for most of the variant numbers we find in the text.

For example, 1 Samuel 13:1, in the Hebrew text, reads, "Saul was [___] years old when he became king, and he reigned over Israel [___] two years."

You read it right. Saul's age isn't given in the Hebrew text. Bible translators have figured it out from the Septuagint. And the Hebrew gives the length of his reign as 2 years. We get the round number "40" from Acts 13:21. That's a good example of numbers that have been so damaged in the transmission of the text that they have to be pieced together from other sources.

Later in the same chapter, the number of chariots used by the Philistines is given as "thirty thousand chariots, six thousand charioteers, and soldiers as numerous as the sands on the seashore" (13:5). Anyone with a smattering of mathematical sense can figure out that there were five chariots for every charioteer. Even if the Philistines had abnormally long legs, one man would have had a terrible time straddling five chariots. Since we know that the Philistines used chariots that held two men, and since the Septuagint reads *three thousand chariots,* most recent translations read "three thousand chariots, six thousand charioteers."

What's the point I'm trying to make here? Simply this. Anyone who has ever dialed a wrong number on the telephone, or has trouble remembering numbers larger than three digits, should be able to understand how easily copyists could garble numbers.

The fact that the Septuagint preserves the more plausible reading in these two cases probably points back to an earlier Hebrew text that hasn't survived the centuries. This means that the Septuagint translator of 1 Samuel had access to a text older than the one containing the copyist's error.

We find another example of conflicting numbers in Genesis 46:27, which says that Jacob's household of seventy went down to Egypt. Acts 7:14 says seventy-five. The culprit here is probably the Septuagint.

By Christ's time, this Greek translation of the Old Testament had become the accepted text of the Bible for most of the world's Greek-speaking Jews. The problem arises out of a quotation in Acts 7:14, the part of Stephen's sermon for which he was martyred.

To clear up this problem we need to know a little more about this powerful preacher. We first met him in Acts 6:5. A dispute had arisen in the Jerusalem church over a fund for the care for widows and orphans. The Greek-speaking believers complained that the Hebrew-speaking believers were unfairly overlooking their widows in the distribution of food. In an act of inspired wisdom, the church appointed seven men to oversee the distribution; all seven were from the Greek-speaking, or Hellenistic, community. Stephen is mentioned first in this group. Even his name, which is Greek, attests to the fact that he or his family had come from the Jewish world outside Palestine. This means that Stephen, when he preached in Acts 7, used the Greek Septuagint of the Diaspora, not the Hebrew Bible of Palestine.

The Septuagint, in its translation of Genesis 46:27, adds two sons of Manasseh, two sons of Ephraim, and one of Ephraim's grandsons to the patriarchal census. With these five added to the list, the number in Stephen's Bible totaled seventy-five. And so, in quoting from the Septuagint, Stephen gave the number of Jacob's family as seventy-five.

Does that mean Acts is wrong?

Absolutely not. In fact, Acts 7:14 records Stephen's statement with great accuracy.

I've grown accustomed to using the newer translations of the Bible. I preach from the NIV or NASB, I read the NIV or NEB, and I study from the NASB. But after years of that, when I quote Scripture in a sermon I almost invariably fall back into the wording of the King James. I can't help it. That's the version I memorized as a boy.

Knowing that Stephen was raised in the Diaspora and educated in Scriptures from the Septuagint, what version would we expect him to quote when surrounded by a potential lynch mob? If Acts 7:14 was a quotation from the Hebrew, I might be inclined to doubt its accuracy, even if it did agree with Genesis. A Greek-speaking Jew would be expected to quote from the Greek Old Testament!

Then is Genesis wrong?

Again, absolutely not. Genesis, using the list of people it does, accurately numbers seventy.

On Sunday mornings at the church I previously served, our head usher counted the congregation and entered the count in a record book. I never changed his number, but he took his count early in the service and our congregation tended to be very relaxed about the clock. Therefore, there were frequently more people when we dismissed than when he made his count.

Does that mean he had counted incorrectly? Of course it doesn't. He counted everyone who was there when he counted. The fact that another six or seven people came after he finished counting doesn't render his count inaccurate.

The list of family members Moses chose to count numbered seventy. The Septuagint, translated a thousand years later, took the liberty of adding members of the lines of Ephraim and Manasseh. For them, apparently it was important to extend the count to include two of the dominant tribes in later history.

While the numbers in the two books disagree, both are accurate in what they record. Moses provided us with the biological building blocks for the greatly multiplied people of Israel.

I don't mean to imply that every number problem in the Old Testament can be dealt with simply by blaming a ham-handed stenographer. But the frequency of copyist's error in the transmission of numbers makes it foolish to think that numerical problems in the text are proof that the Bible is riddled with errors.

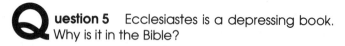 **uestion 5**   Ecclesiastes is a depressing book. Why is it in the Bible?

There is no Scripture passage to which we may refer to answer this question. In a way it violates my plan to restrict myself to questions on specific texts. But the question is important and frequently asked, and Ecclesiastes is a specific text, though a little longer than most.

Ecclesiastes *is* a depressing book. Several years ago after going through Ecclesiastes with an adult Sunday School class, I asked for questions or comments at the end of the session. One of the men remarked that it reminded him of much of modern literature. He taught English at the college level, and he knew what he was talking about. He was right about Ecclesiastes. It does sound like a lot of modern literature.

Tradition says Ecclesiastes was written by Solomon as an old, jaded, cynical man. The text doesn't actually identify its author, but the description offered by tradition fits Solomon. He had observed life. He had tried life. And he had more opportunities to test his answers to life's great questions than most of us would have in ten lifetimes.

The author knows some things for certain. He knows that God exists and that serving Him is better than not serving Him. He knows it is better to be wise than foolish. He knows that the pleasures of life are given in their own time as a gift from God and that they should be enjoyed. He knows that it's better to be loved by a wife and by friends than to be lonely. And he knows that it's all vanity.

The theme he chose for his book is "Meaningless! Meaningless! Everything is meaningless!" After all his searching, he's still painfully aware that everyone dies (2:16; 3:19; 6:12; 7:2; 9:1–6). Every time he offers an answer to one of life's questions, the reality of death pops up like a frightening figure in a carnival funhouse. But no one laughs.

Solomon writes without the certainty of the resurrection, so he stands in terror of death, which will reduce to nothing the wisdom of the wise, the power of princes, and the wealth of the richest. From that limited viewpoint, all is vanity indeed. Death, the great leveler, is to be feared because it robs people of every accomplishment (2:17–24). Hope is found in the enjoyment of life as God gives it.

Even serving God is something to be done in youth before the "days of trouble" come and "you will say, 'I find no pleasure in them'" (12:1). No wonder the teacher concludes that "a live dog is better off than a dead lion" (9:4). "Who knows if the spirit of man rises upward and if the spirit of the animal goes down into the earth?" (3:21). With all his wisdom, the mystery of mortality is one question he cannot answer.

Sadly, it's the most important question of all. Despite all the knowledge that his unaided human observation and deduction can produce, he doesn't know the purpose for his existence (3:11) or what difference it makes that God exists (7:13–14; 8:16–17).

The writer of Ecclesiastes speaks to us from that place in human experience where we feel totally alone. He is the spokesman for all of humanity, who, aware that there is a God, doesn't know where to find Him or how to please Him.

Solomon's fear of death reveals why Satan can use that fear to hold humanity in bondage (Hebrews 2:14–15). Solomon's recurring cry that all of life is meaningless points to the futility of non-theistic attempts to explain the meaning of life.

Without the sure knowledge of the personal God who redeems His wayward children, the best the intellect can come up with is despair.

If there is a biblical book that's ideally suited to open discussion with the cynical, hopeless, pleasure seekers of our day, it's Ecclesiastes. Everything they're trying has been tried. It didn't work then, and it won't work now.

And that, to me, is a good reason for including it in Scripture. It's God's bridge from the inevitable despair of humanity to the hope available only in Christ.

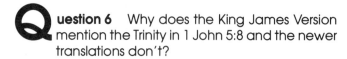

Q **uestion 6** Why does the King James Version mention the Trinity in 1 John 5:8 and the newer translations don't?

Once the canon of Scripture had been set, the history of the text seemingly should have ended. But that's not the case. The continuing history of the biblical text comes through the pens of generations of copyists, men who laboriously hand-copied the Scriptures.

The Chinese developed moveable type in the eleventh century, but it wasn't until the fifteenth century that it was discovered in Europe. In 1454, or thereabouts, Johann Gutenberg used his "new" invention to print the first Bible that wasn't handwritten. Before that time, making a book was a costly, time-consuming process with immeasurable opportunity for copyists to make mistakes.

Even the Bible, which was copied carefully and reverently over the centuries, had thousands of copyists' errors that crept into the text. Not every copyist was as accurate as the next. Some were terrible spellers. Some were inclined to drop words. Others would repeat whole lines without realizing it.

These tiny variations have given rise to a class of scholarship called textual criticism. The work of the textual critic is to compare all the existing ancient copies of the Bible and attempt to eliminate the copyists' errors. Most of this work has had little bearing on the meaning of the text, but occasionally they have to deal with the kind of thing that happened in 1 John 5.

Modern Christians are not the first people to write notes in the margins of their Bibles. Apparently copyists through the centuries made notes of a devotional or explanatory nature in the margins of texts they were copying. The evidence of the ancient manuscripts suggests strongly that this is what happened with 1 John 5:8. Of the approximately 5,000 Greek manuscripts of the New Testament, only eight contain the words "testify in heaven: the Father, the Word and the Holy Spirit, and these three are one. And there are three that testify on earth."

Of those eight manuscripts, only four contain the passage in the text itself. The other four show it as a note in the margin. What's more, none of these can be dated earlier than A.D. 1500. Moving closer to the time the letter was written, we find that some Old Latin texts from as early as the 600s have the Trinitarian statement. Most of these texts came from North Africa, where the church was very large but was also torn by controversies over the Trinity! Perhaps the words were in the original but were deleted by someone who didn't agree with the doctrine of the Trinity. We can never eliminate that possibility entirely, but the available evidence points in the other direction. This is the most convincing argument that this passage was a late addition to the text.

The absence of the passage from ancient Greek texts may not prove anything. But the absence of the passage from the writings of the ancient church fathers lends powerful evidence against the existence of this sentence in the original autograph. Even when the early church writers quoted 1 John 5:7–8, they quoted it without the addition. And the post-apostolic fathers who quote the verse could have used the addition to strengthen their Trinitarian position, had it existed.

The phrase does appear in several non-biblical Latin manuscripts, but even there it doesn't make its appearance until after A.D. 600. Probably written originally as a meditation on the text of 1 John 5:7–8, it found its way into the margins of Old Latin manuscripts and eventually into the text itself.

The text used in the translation of the King James Version was one influenced by this line of Old Latin texts. More recent translations, aware of the history of the phrase, have either left it out altogether or made a note of it in the margin.

I think that's appropriate. What began as a devotional commentary on the puzzling statement about the Spirit, the water, and the blood, has been returned to its rightful place in the margin.

BIBLE HISTORY

Q **uestion 7**   Why did David work for the Philistines (1 Samuel 27:1-7)?

One of the major question marks about David and his checkered career is his willingness to serve as a mercenary soldier for Achish, the king of Gath. In today's world, where nations maintain large standing armies, the work of mercenaries is considered dishonorable.

What David did, however, was ordinary in his day. Service in the army of a powerful king was a profession many able men chose. Being a mercenary soldier was a dirty job, but in a day when there were few standing armies, somebody had to do it. And it paid.

Soldiers in the ancient world were given a small wage, and if they survived they were free to take anything they could carry away. So although soldiering was a high risk profession, it was lucrative for those who were good at it. So David, like many others, probably did it because it paid well.

While David was in the wilderness hiding from Saul a force of men made up of economic and political outcasts gathered around him. He had a sizable following, 600 men and their families, and had to support them or lose them. He could either become a robber king or take employment as a commander of mercenary soldiers.

The second reason is even more basic. Service with the Philistines was necessary for his survival. "One of these days I will be destroyed by the hand of Saul. The best thing I can do is escape to the land of the Philistines. Then Saul will give up searching for me anywhere in Israel, and I will slip out of his hand" (1 Samuel 27:1).

From the time Saul chased David from his court (1 Samuel 19:10) until Saul's death (31:4), Saul's obsession was to catch and kill David.

Principle 4   The more we know about the world in which the Bible was written, the better we understand the Bible itself.

During those years the military pressure of the war with the Philistines kept Saul so occupied with his own survival that he was never able to eliminate his rival (1 Samuel 24:16–19). But from David's point of view, the military pressure had a negative side. Engaged in warfare with the Philistines, Saul's militia developed into a formidable fighting force.

When Saul mounted his first military strike against Nahash, the Ammonite, he led a loosely connected bunch of farmers who had to be threatened with the destruction of their oxen to get them away from their plowing (1 Samuel 11:1–8).

When he made his first military move against the Philistines at the outpost of Geba (1 Samuel 13:3–4), he led an army that apparently fought with the farm implements they had at hand (1 Samuel 13:19–22).

By the time David took up with Achish, Saul had built an effective unity between the tribes. Their early success against the Philistines (1 Samuel 13:23–14:23) gave them control of a military post and, presumably, its armory.

Although Saul was unable to stand against the Philistines and their chariots in a pitched battle, his organization was more than a match for David and his small force.

With the Israelites watching him from one side and the Philistines from the other, David had to walk a tightrope to avoid alienating either. If he didn't perform as a mercenary, he faced the wrath of the Philistines. If he once fought against the Israelites he would never be accepted as king by Israel. To achieve this balancing act, he raided Israelite enemies and told Achish he was plundering Israelite cities (1 Samuel 27:6–12). While keeping his boss happy, he was also winning the allegiance of the Israelite people by defeating their enemies.

When the Philistines gathered for an all-out battle against Saul, David was in a situation where he could conceivably be killed by either side. He was saved by the Philistines' mistrust. Ancient Israelite readers must have laughed at how the wily David had so completely duped his Philistine master.

When the other lords of the Philistines insisted that David not be allowed to march into battle with them, Achish returned to David apologetically. He comforted him with the knowledge that the other lords didn't know David the way he did. David acted the loyal retainer, angered at the mistrust of his master's allies.

Was David right to lie in that way?

No, he wasn't, and the Bible doesn't applaud David's deceit. It merely records it.

P **rinciple 5**   The Bible may accurately record sinful acts without wholeheartedly applauding them.

David's lies, wars, and adulteries are recorded with as much accuracy as his piety and his triumphs. He was a man after God's own heart, not because he never sinned, but because, having sinned, he repented.

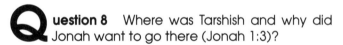

Q **uestion 8**   Where was Tarshish and why did Jonah want to go there (Jonah 1:3)?

Biblical geography is not as simple and as clear cut as we might expect it to be. Yes, Tarshish was a place, possibly a city, but the precise location is open to debate. Many authorities conclude that Tarshish was located in Spain, while others favor the island of Sardinia to the west of Italy. Either of these fits well in the story of Jonah, who took a ship from Joppa on the east coast of Israel and, presumably, sailed westward into the Mediterranean.

The Tarshish to which Solomon sent his ships for "gold, silver and ivory, and apes and baboons" (1 Kings 10:22) could not have been the same place. To begin with, the cargo is inconsistent with a destination in Spain. Besides, it shouldn't have taken three years for a round trip to Spain.

Because Hiram of Tyre provided Solomon's shipping in the Mediterranean, the ships Solomon owned probably had their home port at Ezion-Geber (1 Kings 9:26). That probably means that the "Tarshish ships" mentioned in 1 Kings 10 sailed the east coast of Africa and, possibly as far away as India. This leads many to conclude that Tarshish was, in addition to being a place, also a concept. Tarshish was as far away as anyone could go.

Because ships were clumsy and hard to control, they usually sailed as close to shore as possible. Hence, the effective western limit of Mediterranean trade would have been the Straits of Gibraltar, where Spain and Africa reach out to shake hands. Jonah headed for Tarshish because it was the farthest regularly visited port that people in his world were aware of.

I remember Ralph Kramden saying to Alice, his long-suffering wife on the Jackie Gleason show, "One of these days, Alice— Pow—To the moon." In Jonah's day, they probably would have said, "Pow—To Tarshish!"

Apparently Jonah didn't understand the omnipresence of God. It was a common belief in the ancient world that gods were territorial. The power of the gods, people thought, decreased in proportion to the distance one travelled from their temples.

This is why Ezekiel's book opened with the majestic vision of the transcendent God who goes where He chooses and sees what He likes. Before the promise of redemption and return could be understood, the Israelites had to be told that God had jurisdiction all the way into Babylon.

Jonah probably felt that if he got far enough away from Jerusalem, God wouldn't be able to find him. This sounds rather primitive and theologically naive, but so does Jonah's pouting spell in chapter 4.

After all, the New Testament tells us that the prophets longed to know what we know about salvation (1 Peter 1:10). I think they also would have liked to know more about the God they served. The Old Testament prophets did not have the completed revelation of the New Testament, nor did they live up to everything they did know. Jonah, for example, knew that God would forgive the Assyrians if they repented, and he wanted no part of that.

Jonah set sail for Tarshish, probably a city in Spain, but to him a symbol for the ends of the earth. He wanted to go there because he was running away from God. And yes, he probably did think he could get away with it.

uestion 9   Why was Jesus so angry when He drove the money changers out of the temple? What was so wrong about what they were doing (Matthew 21:12–13; Mark 11:15–17; Luke 19:45–46; John 2:12–17)?

In light of today's church, where we can buy everything from handcrafts to concert tickets in the lobby following the morning service, it does seem a bit excessive. But Jesus wasn't dealing with anything as harmless as the women's circle raising money to redecorate the nursery.

For over a century the temple high priest had been a political appointee of the ruling classes. The position was a plum that could be, and was, bought by the highest bidder or plucked by the most politically powerful. The rich and powerful didn't vie for the position out of piety. Generally, what the rich and powerful want more than anything else is more riches and more power. The high priesthood offered an effective means to both.

Every Jewish man over the age of twenty was expected to contribute half a shekel every year to the temple. The tax could only be paid in silver coins from Tyre. Changing the coinage of the world for the acceptable coin of the temple was one of the functions of the temple money changers.

Since Jesus himself paid the temple tax, and since the money changers served the useful purpose of making it possible for others to pay theirs as well, the existence of money changers in the outer court of the temple couldn't have been what excited His wrath.

Another wrinkle may play a part here. The Law of God required that the animals offered for sacrifice be without spot or blemish. Whether people were offering the poor person's sacrifice of a sparrow or the rich person's sacrifice of a bullock, the priests had to inspect and approve the animal.

The high priests wanted to insure a steady flow of income from their positions, so what better way than to provide approved sacrificial animals bearing the high priest's seal of approval.

Since Tyrian silver coins were the official money of the temple, purchases from this convenient source would have to be made with the assistance of the money changers. Yet even this would not account for Jesus' behavior, since the temple was merely providing a service to make the prescribed worship more convenient.

But what if the priests set the price sky high? Many of the people coming to make a sacrifice were pilgrims from far away or city dwellers who had no livestock of their own to bring. So the priests had a captive audience and could charge as much as they wanted. The Mishna, an ancient Jewish holy book that records incidents of price-gouging for the animals, supports this idea.

If the temple charged exorbitant rates for the sacrificial animals, and then charged exorbitant rates for the exchange of secular money for temple money, the poor would be excluded from worship. This justifies Jesus' accusation that they were turning God's house into a den of thieves (Matthew 21:13) and is a suitable explanation for His anger. A religious establishment that turned the act of worship into a device for wringing money out of the devout deserved God's wrath. Although it isn't a certainty, this scenario may explain the violence of Jesus' response.

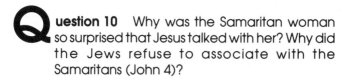

Question 10   Why was the Samaritan woman so surprised that Jesus talked with her? Why did the Jews refuse to associate with the Samaritans (John 4)?

The origins of hostility between Jews and Samaritans go back to 721 B.C., the year the ten northern tribes were deported by the Assyrians. The Assyrians took them far from their homelands, split them up, and resettled them in small groups. They reasoned that the Israelites would be less likely to rebel if they were uprooted, separated from home and kinsmen, and made to pay Assyrian tribute out of the ruins of their new homeland. The surviving upper classes were deported and resettled at scattered locations throughout the Assyrian empire.

The Assyrian emperor Sargon, in his account of the conquest, brags of deporting a total of 27,290 people. That figure shows how devastated Israel was when the Assyrians had finished with them. Of all the government officials, artisans, merchants, and royalty in Israel, there were only 27,000 left to deport after the conquest.

The common people who survived were left on the land. Hebrew talks about "the people of the land." In Jesus' day, it wasn't a very nice description. These people weren't considered important enough to take as hostages or dangerous enough to remove.

After this deportation the historical sense of unity that had existed, even in bad times, between the northern and southern kingdoms was disregarded by a long sequence of conquerors and overlords.

History is unclear concerning the next stage in the process. Jewish sources outside the Bible blame the separation between the Samaritans and Jews on foreign upper class who settled in Israel to replace the deported Israelites and who brought their foreign gods with them. They also adopted the worship of Yahweh, who would have been a valuable addition to their already sizable stable of deities. For polytheists, if one god is good, a dozen are better.

To further compound their negative impact, they also intermarried with the children of the native Israelites. According to this interpretation, it was religious apostasy and intermarriage that made the Samaritans, named for the fallen capital, Samaria, so hated by the residents of Judah.

Yet Jeremiah and Ezekiel, who both prophesied more than one hundred years after the fall of Samaria, considered the Northern Kingdom a continuing part of God's nation. For their part, the northern tribes of Ephraim and Manasseh were orthodox enough to be allowed to contribute to the rebuilding of the temple under King Josiah (640–609 B.C.). The Samaritans themselves have left religious writings that show no evidence of pagan intermingling.

Because of this, some commentators suggest a different reason for the hostility. They point to an incident that took place during the time of Nehemiah.

During Nehemiah's work on the city walls, Sanballat, the governor of the Persian province of Samaria, provided the chief opposition (Nehemiah 2:10; 19–20; 4:1–3; 7–8; 6:1–14). The rebuilding of Jerusalem created a new political unit in the area, which Sanballat must have seen as a threat to his position and security.

The hostility between Sanballat and Nehemiah, therefore, was probably political, but it may have spilled over into the religious sphere.

When the Samaritans built their own temple on Mount Gerizim, probably between the time of Nehemiah and Alexander's conquest, the theological rift widened.

The hostility between Jews and Samaritans continued during the latter half of the inter-testamental period until, by the time of Jesus, a good Jew would detour around the province of Samaria in a journey from Judea to Galilee.

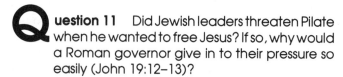

Q **uestion 11** Did Jewish leaders threaten Pilate when he wanted to free Jesus? If so, why would a Roman governor give in to their pressure so easily (John 19:12–13)?

No figure in the New Testament is more widely debated than Pilate. Some consider him a weak, expedient, violent man. The Jewish historian Philo described him in the most uncomplimentary terms, and traditions have made him a suicide in exile. Others make him more a victim than a villain.

I'm inclined to side with those who see him as a victim. If I had been looking for a job as a Roman procurator, I wouldn't have sent my resume to Judea.

Pilate must have been a career military man to have gotten the post in the first place. The New Testament invariably describes centurions as honorable, dedicated men. Putting these together, it's reasonable to deduce that Pilate was once that kind of man.

But Tiberius, the emperor who appointed him and under whom he served for the full ten years of his procuratorship, was a man of paranoid suspicion whose rule was marred by numerous treason trials and executions. Hardly the kind of boss a young man on the way up would want to work under. To make matters worse, the Near Eastern people of Judea didn't think at all like Romans. They were known as a particularly difficult people to govern. The Jewish commitment to one God, for example, was incomprehensible to any citizen of the empire and the source of frequent trouble. Concessions made to the religious sensibilities of the Jews were unheard of in the rest of the empire. Pilate's ten years of service in Judea certainly suggest that he was a reasonably able administrator. What went wrong?

When the Roman legions entered Jerusalem, they usually left their standards outside the wall because the insignia on them prominently featured the imperial eagle, which the Jews considered a graven image. No one knows his reasons, but Pilate decided to ignore the custom and march into the city in full regalia. The people of Jerusalem rioted. Pilate threatened to have them killed if they didn't disperse, and they said they would rather die than allow this blasphemy. Pilate backed down.

Then, in what he probably thought was a well conceived plan to lighten the burden of water shortages in the over-populated city of Jerusalem, he appropriated the temple tax to build an aqueduct. The Jews considered this a sacrilege and once again rioted. This time Pilate deployed his troops and killed many of the rioters, desecrating the city in a way the Jewish people couldn't forgive. This may be the incident referred to in Luke 13:1–2.

By the time of Jesus' trial, Pilate was on pretty thin ice. He had already made two serious mistakes in governing Judea. Perhaps the Jews were waiting for just the right moment to use his blunders to their advantage.

Tiberius, by this time weary of opposition and criticism, had withdrawn into a self-imposed exile on the island of Capri. His paranoia had grown and he'd already had numerous officials executed for treason.

When Pilate tried to free Jesus, the Jewish leadership had him right where they wanted him. They had been very careful to charge Jesus with subversion, opposition to taxation, and claiming to be king. Any one of these charges was enough to make the suspicious Tiberius think that Pilate was participating in a plot against him.

So they shouted their threat, "If you let this man go, you are no friend of Caesar!" If that message got to Rome, Pilate knew he was a dead man. Given the choice of executing an innocent man or being executed himself, he chose the more pleasant of the two options.

uestion 12 Jesus was supposed to have been thirty-three when He was crucified, but I can't find that anywhere in the Bible. How do we know how old He was?

This question demonstrates how historical method is used to answer biblical questions.

Jesus' age at crucifixion is traditionally given as thirty-three. That number is deduced from two bits of biblical information. Luke 3:23 tells us that Jesus began his public ministry at "about thirty years old." Luke's use of the word *about* implies that he didn't intend that age to be a precise statement, but we usually take the age of thirty as a starting point.

John begins his story of Jesus' ministry with Christ's visit to the temple (John 2:14–22) and then mentions two more temple visits (John 6:4; 12:1). Mark talks about two springtimes (Mark 2:23; Mark 6:39) prior to the last Passover visit to Jerusalem. From these passages we deduce that Christ's public ministry spanned three years. If we add three years of public ministry to his age when it began, thirty, we come up with an age of thirty-three.

Is it accurate? Well, it comes close.

The problem is that the ancient world had no set way of saying what year anything happened. Luke 3:1 gives a good example of how years were reckoned in Jesus' day. There we learn John the Baptist began his ministry in the "fifteenth year of the reign of Tiberius Caesar—when Pontius Pilate was governor of Judea, Herod, tetrarch of Galilee; his brother Philip, tetrarch of Iturea and Traconitis; and Lysanias, tetrarch of Abilene. . . ."

This establishes an important synchronism with secular history. Through a careful historical note such as the one Luke has given us, we can establish the date of a biblical event by tying it to events in the world at large. In this case, we can find out the year in which John the Baptist began his ministry.

We know that Tiberius Caesar took the throne in A.D. 14. His fifteenth year, then, would have begun in A.D. 28. That gives us an important starting point. If Jesus followed John the Baptist, His public ministry must have begun some time after A.D. 28. We also know that Herod the Great died in 4 B.C. Since he was the king when Jesus was born, we know Jesus must have been born before

4 B.C. To eliminate Jesus, Herod, when he heard about Christ's birth, ordered that baby boys two years old or younger be killed (Matthew 2:16). So apparently Jesus was born about two years before Herod's death.

Let's put those together. If Jesus was born in 6 B.C., and John the Baptist began his public ministry in A.D. 28, Jesus would have been thirty-four in A.D. 28, probably a year or two before He began His public ministry.

That same year would have been the third year of Pontius Pilate's governorship over Judea. He governed until A.D. 36. From that we know that Jesus couldn't have been older than forty-two when He died.

Everything from here on out has to be educated guesswork, but it will give us a ball park number for Jesus' age.

If we allow one year from the beginning of John's ministry to the beginning of Jesus', He would have been thirty-five when He was baptized. If we accept the three-year public ministry, and there's no good reason not to, Jesus would have been about thirty-eight at His crucifixion. As you can see, we should probably pay more attention to the "about" in Luke's statement. But Jesus' age at death isn't what really matters. What really matters is that His life and death are carefully placed in human history. His work of redemption isn't some legendary tale that took place "once upon a time."

And He was raised from the dead in real space and real time so that people like us, who live in this real world, can have our faith grounded in a historical reality that looks forward to the reality of eternity with Him.

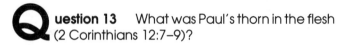

Question 13   What was Paul's thorn in the flesh (2 Corinthians 12:7–9)?

Students of Paul's writings have devoted a great deal of energy to coming up with a theory to explain this cryptic remark. Here are a few of their attempts.

Since the Middle Ages, many commentators have argued that Paul's thorn was some form of spiritual weakness or temptation. Candidates for the specific form of weakness are numerous. Everything from spiritual pride to carnal longings has been suggested. This approach still has occasional champions, but they are becoming as rare as alligator shoes at a Sierra Club convention.

Others have proposed that the thorn may be the persecution he experienced so frequently, especially at the hands of his own people, the Jews. Paul's approach to his persecutors and detractors was well documented in his own writings, however, so his complaint about a thorn in the flesh seems unnecessarily vague in light of his usual candor about persecution.

These are both plausible explanations, despite my own misgivings about them, and in the absence of more detailed information either would serve. There is, however, a third idea that has won the acceptance of the vast majority of modern commentators. They reckon that Paul's thorn in the flesh was a physical ailment or disability. Even though most students today agree on the category, there's little agreement as to the kind of ailment Paul suffered from.

Some have suggested epilepsy, which, while disabling at times, lies dormant between episodes. This would have allowed Paul to carry out an active ministry for over two decades, even though it would have struck him down unexpectedly from time to time. The weakness in this is that epilepsy would have marked Paul, in the minds of the superstitious, as a man possessed. With all the opposition Paul faced, surely his opponents would have taken advantage of this weakness. Yet nothing in his writings hints at this kind of slander.

Others, based on Paul's remark in Galatians 4:15, have theorized an eye ailment. Paul reminded the Galatians that, were it possible, they would have torn out their own eyes and given them to him. That kind of statement implies that Paul may have needed a better set of eyes. Also, the note in Galatians 6:11 allows for the possibility that Paul wrote in large letters because his eyes were weak.

It may be that the blindness Paul suffered following his Damascus Road experience had a longer lasting effect than is usually thought. Given the apparent support offered by these texts and the prominence of eye diseases in the ancient world, we can't discount the possibility of eye problems as Paul's thorn in the flesh.

I prefer another option, though. Malaria accounts for the cryptic references to his problem as well as any of the speculations available. Malaria can lie dormant and allow for periods of normal activity. Then when the blood parasite that causes the disease reaches an active stage in its life cycle, it throws its victim into violent cycles of chills and fever. It troubles its victims for a lifetime but probably wouldn't cause death unless some other disease strikes while the sufferer is weakened from it. Malaria would have been as common in the marshy lowlands of Galatia as the mosquitoes that tormented travellers there. If Paul were stricken with malaria during his first missionary journey, that might offer a partial explanation for John Mark's defection (Acts 13:13). It would also fit well with his statement that he first preached the gospel in Galatia because of illness (Galatians 4:12–15).

Because Paul never actually described the thorn in the flesh, any attempt to identify it must rely on a lot of deduction and will never establish its identity with certainty.

Human nature being what it is, we're always more interested in what we can't know than in what is clearly seen. Since Paul chose not to tell us what his thorn was, we're frantic to know. But Paul didn't mention the subject to pique our curiosities. He introduced it to lead us to a profound spiritual truth.

God's answer to his entreaties was a fatherly, "My grace is sufficient for you, for my power is made perfect in weakness" (2 Corinthians 12:9).

The truth of this may speak louder to us than it did to Paul. In an age that values power, competence, security, health, and financial stability above everything, God's message is that His power is seen in times and places of weakness, not strength. Paul grasped that truth and was able to say, "Therefore I will boast all the more gladly about my weaknesses, so that Christ's power may rest on me" (v. 9).

My daughter Erin has a poster on her wall that I gave her for Christmas a few years ago. It's a picture of a teenage girl executing a handstand on a balance beam. Her muscles are stretched as taut and thick as ropes while she holds her precarious position. The caption reads: "Don't pray for an easy life. Pray to be a strong person."

Paul's thorn, whatever it was, did not make his life easy, but it did teach him that his strength came from Christ, and it came most powerfully when he needed it the most. That alone is strong medicine for the sharpest thorn.

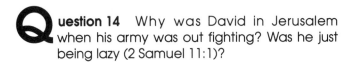

Q **uestion 14**   Why was David in Jerusalem when his army was out fighting? Was he just being lazy (2 Samuel 11:1)?

David's army was out roughing it, risking life and limb at the siege of Rabbah, while the king lolled about Jerusalem, occasionally casting a wandering eye over the back fence. What sloth. What moral turpitude. What a lot of reading into the text.

The text here is very sparse. It outlines the time of year, the activity common to that time of year, and the fact that David was in Jerusalem. Commentators don't agree on the understanding of this verse. Some wax eloquent on the dangers of idleness, while others note that David had already sent Joab and the army against Ammon once (2 Samuel 10:7) and nothing bad had happened to them. Joab and his army routed the Ammonites and their mercenary cohorts (10:13–14).

David's presence in Jerusalem is mentioned as a part of the introduction to the story that follows. If the writer had wanted to make the point that David was derelict in his duty by being there, he would have done so. The writer of 2 Samuel is not bashful about pointing out David's short-comings, and yet there isn't the hint of criticism in this verse.

A verse tucked into the final chapters of 2 Samuel may explain why David stayed behind. The latter chapters of 2 Samuel (21–24) contain a collection of miscellaneous events and writings that were placed there because they were important details that didn't fit naturally into the earlier narratives. They aren't presented in any discernable chronological order. Some commentators refer to this section as an appendix.

In a section recording incidents related to wars with the Philistines is a battle in which David was actively involved as a combatant (21:15–17). In the course of the battle he became exhausted, and a Philistine giant with a new sword set his sights on him. If it hadn't been for the bravery and strength of Abishai, David's nephew, the Philistine would have killed the helpless king.

When the battle was over, the leaders of David's army got together and gave him an ultimatum. In essence, they said, "David, you're a good king, but you're getting in our way. We can't afford to tie up good fighting men to watch you. Face it, you're not as young as you used to be, and war is a young man's game. Here's what we're going to do. You let us fight the battles. We'll let you rule the country."

That's a loose paraphrase, but I think it gets at the meaning. Since the wars with the Philistines are recorded in 2 Samuel 5, and the war with the Ammonites begins in 2 Samuel 10, it seems reasonable to conclude that a significant period of time intervened between the two. David was probably well into his forties by the time Joab went out to do war with Ammon.

If he were a modern executive, we might suggest he was going into mid-life crisis, but I don't like to saddle ancients with modern concepts. Let's just say that David had probably earned the right to remain in Jerusalem and administer a growing kingdom.

Was he being lazy? I think the text answers that question with a no. He was more valuable as a king than as a swordsman. His younger nephew Joab handled the army with skill and ruthless aggressiveness. David had the God-given skill to hold the hard-won kingdom together.

While David had not yet gotten old, he was probably in his late thirties or early forties. The event recorded took place at some time during the wars with the Philistines. Those wars didn't begin until after David was about thirty-seven and a half years old (2 Samuel 5:4–5)!

That verse tells us that David became king over Judah at Hebron when he was thirty. He ruled over Judah alone for seven and a half years. Since there's no evidence that the Philistines ever opposed him during those years, he was probably treated as a tame king acting under their control. It wasn't until the whole nation of Israel anointed David that the Philistines saw him as a threat.

Immediately after all Israel anointed David king (2 Samuel 5:1–5), he led a campaign against Jebus, as it was known at the time, or Jerusalem.

By the time that campaign was over and the Philistines became aware of David as a threat, he must have been at least thirty-eight, not old but definitely approaching middle age.

By coincidence, I was just a little older than thirty-eight when I decided to hang up my wrestling shoes. I'd been working out with a muscular eighteen-year-old 185 pounder. After a few minutes, I collapsed on the side of the mat and tried to remember what it was like to breathe.

The head coach I was working with, a man of infinite sensitivity, ambled over with a grin on his face, looked down at my semi-conscious form, and said, "O'Brien, you'd have to die to get better."

I don't suppose a general would talk to his king that way, but I'm sure that's what Joab and his men had on their minds.

CHAPTER 2

PRINCIPLES

6 An understanding of the prophetic prototype can help open up some of the more troublesome prophetic passages. Looking back at the known biblical world can help us gain a better appreciation for the shape of unknown things to come.

7 To understand apocalyptic literature we need to understand that it is symbolic and that it has its own rules.

8 To understand apocalyptic literature we need to determine what the text meant to the people it was written to.

QUESTIONS

15 Did Ezekiel really predict that Russia would invade Israel in the end time (Ezekiel 38–39)?

16 What does the image of Nebuchadnezzar's dream mean and how does it apply to the end time (Daniel 2)?

17 Daniel 7 seems to repeat Daniel 2. If it's a repetition, what purpose does it serve? If it's not, what does Daniel 7 mean?

18 What is the "sign of the fig tree"? If it's the rebirth of Israel as a nation, how could Jesus say that "this generation will certainly not pass away until all these things have happened" (Matthew 24:34)?

REVELATION, REPLOGLE, AND RAND MCNALLY

9 The most straightforward interpretation of a passage is probably the best interpretation.

10 When reading the Bible, focus on God's activity, not on human activity.

11 To understand the meaning of a parable, we need to look at its context.

19 Why did Jesus refer to "the days of Noah" as a sign of the Second Coming (Matthew 24:37–39)?

20 Who are the 144,000 sealed in heaven (Revelation 7)?

21 What purpose does the Millennium fulfill? It seems strange that there would still be people opposed to the Lord after 1,000 years of His righteous rule (Revelation 20).

Replogle. Not your basic household word. But if you like the earth, you're going to love Replogle. Replogle, you see, is a company that makes scale model copies of this planet. We call them globes.

Globes have always fascinated me. I used them to good advantage back in Miss Anderson's room. (If you went to first grade in Minnesota, you were almost certain to have been taught by a Miss Anderson.) Not a spare minute went by that didn't find me hovering over that mini-earth like a malevolent alien picking a likely continent to invade.

For all that time spent staring, I don't remember much about the shape of the world in those days. In fact, I don't even think I knew what I was looking at. At the age of five I still hadn't figured out that Minnesota wasn't a country, or that my home town Sandstone wasn't the focal point of human history. Even though I wasn't learning much about geography, I did learn that globes are a wonderful tool for getting the feel of the expanses of our world, for land masses and oceans, for continents and watersheds, for the big picture of the shapes, heights, and depths of our world.

But I wouldn't want to plot a course for Madagascar on one. I suppose when Columbus sailed from Spain to the New World a good Replogle globe would have been a marvelous improvement over his flat-earth navigational maps with their warnings that "here there be dragons." But navigation isn't what globes are for. If I want to travel from Wisconsin to South Dakota, I don't want Replogle. I want Rand McNally. He will answer the question, "Where in the world is Wall, South Dakota, and how do I get there?"

A nice ornate globe makes an attractive addition to office decor or to a library lobby. But what if I'm lost and finding a place to stop for the night ranks a lot higher on my priority list than pondering the current shape of the planet? I would rather unfold a plain old road map.

Globes give us outlines, but without detail. They identify mountain ranges, but not cities. Good road maps, on the other hand, give us all the detail we need to arrive at a destination. The natural features of the country, state, or county are there, but only as background for the towns, roads, and other manmade intrusions.

GOD'S MAP OF THE FUTURE?

Has God given us Rand McNally or Replogle in the prophetic books of the Bible? Are these books road maps to give us detailed direction into the world of tomorrow or globes to show us broad outlines of things to come?

I say Replogle. In fact, I think many of our problems in understanding biblical prophecy materialize when we try to use the Bible as a road map into the future. In our quest for detailed information about the day after tomorrow, we search Scripture feverishly for the next historical landmark, but in doing so we treat God's Word like a *Future on $5.00 a Day* traveler's guide. Bibles in one hand and newspapers in the other, we compare them like travellers checking road signs against maps. And every time we glimpse something happening in Russia, China, Egypt, or Israel that seems to fit, we look back to Scripture like children on a long vacation whining, "Are we there yet?"

This is what I call the Rand McNally approach to prophecy, and it's been very popular among conservative Christians for a long time. It assumes that God has given us a detailed map of the end times, which, with the help of a sizable crew of expositors and commentators, will let us track our day-to-day progress to Armageddon.

But popular doesn't necessarily mean right.

NO MATTER WHAT SHAPE YOUR FUTURE'S IN

A growing number of Christians are rediscovering another way of looking at the issue, though. I call this the Replogle view of biblical prophecy. It says that God is less concerned with showing us the details of the future than He is with reminding us of a more timeless message.

No matter what specific events the future may hold for any believer at any point in history, God is still the Lord of it all. We can use Scripture to look into the future, but when we do, we see through a glass darkly. God has given us global shapes, not specific landmarks.

Sadly, this approach lacks pizzazz. Those of us who use it can't flip open a news magazine and demonstrate how the bombing of an Afghan village is a fulfillment straight out of Zechariah or claim to have unearthed secret Soviet plans for the disruption of the Free World's computer networks somewhere in Revelation.

Our natural human curiosity about the future and our less respectable desire to be on the inside sharing classified information find no ally here. But our need for the unchanging message of God's Word does.

Long after that Israeli fighter plane, Arab leader, Russian hydro-electric project, or ten-nation Common Market have ended up in the dustbin with a thousand other, earlier, mistaken attempts to identify some prophetic mystery, the enduring spiritual message of Scripture will continue to encourage, warn, console, and predict.

It will predict, unchangeably and unshakably, God's ongoing sovereignty over the affairs of nations and its ultimate attainment before an astonished world.

This more global approach to prophecy has the advantage of dealing with one nagging question that the Rand McNally approach creates.

WE FOUR AND NO MORE

How can we understand Daniel and Revelation in a way that would make them intelligible, and a blessing, for our day as well as for people alive during the first nineteen hundred years of church history? Revelation 1:3 pronounces a blessing on anyone who reads, hears, or heeds the message contained in the Revelation. But what a select group of readers that blessing applies to if the Rand McNally approach is correct.

Pick up almost any of the dozens of popular books on Revelation available today and ask yourself how anyone born before the latter half of the twentieth century could receive a blessing from Revelation based on their interpretation. Most of them require a detailed knowledge of the political map of this century. If that knowledge is a prerequisite for understanding these books, only the select few of us born into the modern age have any chance at all of understanding John's message, or Daniel's.

No one in biblical times could even begin to understand the detailed descriptions of current events found in most popular prophecy books. In fact, most Christians have lived and died in ignorance of the most basic historical, geographical, and political realities assumed by this approach. Paul said that *all* Scripture is valuable for teaching, rebuking, correcting and training in righteousness (2 Timothy 3:16). If so, how did all previous generations of Christians benefit from these books?

To me, this is a major failing in the Rand McNally approach. I need to find a way to understand prophecy that all Christians since the first century could have understood. If a method of interpretation makes that impossible, I have to reject it.

In spite of our natural curiosity about the future, God never gave His prophets glimpses of the future merely to satisfy their curiosity, or that of their readers.

THE MEDIUM, NOT THE MESSAGE

In biblical prophecy, prediction is always the handmaiden of proclamation. Predictions by God through the prophets were given to encourage or to warn, to comfort or to frighten. And the ultimate purpose was always to awaken God's people to repentance or renewed commitment. To do this, He invariably kept his predictions open-ended.

God used people, places, and events that the prophets' original readers would have recognized and understood to create an outline, a global view of the future that following generations of believers could understand and apply to their own time.

Some will argue that all prophecies have only one possible meaning. Therefore, if Daniel's abomination can point to more than one person, it has no linguistic meaning. Words must have only one meaning. I've said some things like that myself in this very book. But there are always exceptions.

The pun is a good example. In a pun, the meaning of a sentence depends on one word playing against another, so the sound and intention of the sentence depends on a subtle working with multiple meanings.

A variation on this device can be seen in the way Jesus used a double meaning to challenge His enemies: "Destroy this temple and I will raise it again in three days" (John 2:19).

We have an advantage over the Pharisees on this one because we have John's explanation that Jesus was speaking about himself, not Herod's temple. But John would not have explained the saying if he hadn't thought it would confuse people. It obviously confused the Jewish leadership. When they brought Jesus to trial, they accused Jesus of threatening to destroy Herod's temple (Matthew 26:61).

I suggest that biblical prophecy uses this kind of double meaning to convey a message that can take on deeper levels of truth. A caution is in order here. Whatever the fuller meaning of a prophetic text might be, it must be grounded in the historical, grammatical text. It must be a clearer manifestation of something already made manifest.

We are not at liberty to begin with the present day and read it into the text. Rather we need to look at the text and read it forward into our time.

PROPHETIC PROTOTYPES

I use the phrase *prophetic prototypes* to help explain how this works. The dictionary defines prototype as "the first thing or being of its kind." By adding the word prophetic, I'm saying that the Bible shows us the first in a long line of people, things, or events that will recur and develop until, finally, the ultimate fulfillment arrives.

A good example of this is the blessing of Jacob (Genesis 49:10). The dying Jacob prophesied that "The scepter will not depart from Judah, nor the ruler's staff from between his feet, until he comes to whom it belongs and the obedience of the nations is his."

Judah made a good prophetic prototype because his tribe dominated Israel from the time of Jacob to the time of David. When David, Judah's descendant, came, I'm sure the wisemen of his day were certain that Jacob's prediction was being fulfilled in him.

The leaders of Judah in the time of Hezekiah must have seen a fulfillment in the glorious reign of their king. After decades under bad or mediocre kings, this righteous ruler, who was just like his father David (2 Kings 18:3), came to claim the scepter of his righteous ancestor and put things right in God's land.

It wasn't until Jesus came that the first half of that verse was really fulfilled, though. With our knowledge of Jesus we can look back through Israel's history and see how each step along the way brought us closer to Him.

But would the nation of Israel have recognized Him as the promised "Shiloh" without the forerunners who helped shape Israel's expectations? I doubt it.

We easily forget that Jesus himself, in some ways, was a prophetic prototype. In His first coming, He spoke often of the kingdom He came to found. But the obedience of the nations still hasn't been given to Him. His final kingdom is yet to come.

And so we can look back at His first advent and reach conclusions about the second. When He returns in glory, the promise uttered thousands of years ago finally will have been accomplished.

The idea of the prophetic prototype stands out clearly in this prediction. The promise to Judah was expanded and clarified in David, revived in Hezekiah, Zerubbabel, and some would say, Judas Maccabeus.

Each of these leaders was a more advanced prototype of Christ than his predecessor; each added his own part to the whole picture. But it was two thousand years before the King of kings appeared to give Jacob's promise a human face.

The essence of the prophetic prototype as I see it is that the prediction is purposely left vague to keep people looking back at it. Because the outline was fuzzy, no generation in the 1800 years between Jacob and Christ could be certain it applied to them in all its facets.

CLOSING AN OPEN BOOK

So far in this chapter I've talked about *prophetic* writings, which is how people usually classify Daniel and Revelation. But that term isn't technically correct. Daniel and Revelation are a kind of literature without exact parallel elsewhere in the Bible. Daniel is so different from the writings of the other prophets that the Jewish people didn't even include Daniel among them. It is grouped with a section of the Hebrew Bible called *Writings*, which is where we find everything from Esther and Ruth to Job and Ecclesiastes. It is as close as Scripture comes to a category we might call *miscellaneous*.

Principle 6   An understanding of the prophetic prototype can help open up some of the more troublesome prophetic passages. Looking back at the known biblical world can help us gain a better appreciation for the shape of unknown things to come.

Daniel is the only Old Testament example of the literary form called *apocalyptic*. That title comes to us from the New Testament's only example, Revelation, or, in Greek, *apokalupsis (ah-pock-ah-LOOP-sis)*. With the exception of a few chapters in Isaiah, Zechariah, and Ezekiel, very little in the rest of the Old Testament even sounds like Daniel. Scattered passages in the New Testament deal specifically with the end times, but John's book is the only pure example of New Testament apocalyptic writing. Everyone senses the differences between these two books and the rest of the Bible, but when it comes to interpretation we often ignore those differences.

LET'S NOT CALL A SPADE A SHOVEL

Principle 7   To understand apocalyptic literature we need to understand that it is symbolic and that it has its own rules.

To ignore the rules of apocalyptic literature is to wallow in confusion. The first important difference between apocalyptic and other forms of writing lies in its language. Apocalyptic language refuses to be bound by the conventions of every day speech. It is aggressively symbolic. One mistake we make in reading this kind of language is to concentrate on details. I used the phrase *aggressively symbolic* because apocalyptic assails our senses with images that build and grow to create a perception of demonic bestiality or divine beatification.

Although each detail is important in the creation of the perception, the overall impact is usually more important than the sum of its details. Although it's possible to interpret or identify individual elements in the visions of Daniel and John, we can't allow the minutiae to overwhelm us. The closer we can come to the thought worlds of Daniel and John the clearer they're apt to become. And contrary to what some popular writers would have us believe, modern news magazines won't help.

Apocalyptic writing uses numbers, animals, hybrid creatures, and Old Testament quotations and references in ways that would be unthinkable anywhere else. In Revelation, these symbols may be drawn from the Old Testament, especially Ezekiel, but John's vision gives them a new life of their own. This nightmarish imagery tells us we are reading apocalyptic literature. We can't expect words or numbers in Daniel or Revelation to always mean what we expect them to mean. They may have that meaning, but they are more likely to mean something else.

Apocalyptic literature talks much more about the unseen spiritual world than does any other biblical literature. We meet the angelic and the demonic face-to-face. We see the thrones of God and His people set in heavenly courts and the menace of satanic forces boiling out of the abyss. The normal flow of history that generally holds center stage in the writings of the prophets is submerged in apocalyptic literature's overflow from heavenly places. The prophets are apt to talk about the reestablishment of Israel as an earthly kingdom among other earthly kingdoms, but apocalyptic envisions the culmination of earthly kingdoms as we know them.

For Daniel and John the history of humanity is a continual downward spiral to damnation. The only thing that can possibly stop that terrible fall is God's direct intervention, which will end this age.

Scholars often cite pessimism as a characteristic of this literature. I doubt that John and Daniel thought of themselves as pessimists, though. Their murky record of humanity in its flight to damnation allows the luster of God's future to glow with greater radiance.

THAT WAS THEN; THIS IS NOW

One of the most important elements of apocalyptic literature is its doctrine of two ages. God gave this to Daniel as a radical new revelation. Without it, very little of the New Testament's understanding of God's plan of redemption is intelligible.

This age is evil, irredeemably so. The full horror of its corruption can be seen in the beasts of Daniel 7 or the Beast of

Revelation 13. Sin works incessantly, perverting the good, twisting the truth, tempting the pure. Fallen and hopelessly marred, this age can be redeemed only through destruction.

Although believers live in this present evil age (Galatians 1:4), we live also in the power of the age to come, the new age when God's power finally will be present in all its fullness, when the Messiah will reign and God's will shall be done on earth as it is in heaven.

When we grasp this apocalyptic division at the heart of God's eternal plan for earth, it jumps out at us from every book of the New Testament. And the idea has its fullest development in apocalyptic literature.

Apocalyptic literature offers hope and encouragement. Its message is aimed at suffering believers. Perhaps the relative absence of suffering in our western world has caused us to pay too much attention to minutiae. Its most powerful message won't be found in speculation about the date for the Second Coming or the dimensions of the rebuilt temple.

Apocalyptic sees two related truths. First, the church will suffer at the hands of the satanic powers that rule this present evil age. There have been martyrs. There will be more.

Second, judgment is sure, and with judgment will come the vindication of the faith of the saints. In some respects the whole book of Revelation is commentary on Jesus' admonition to fear the one whose powers extend to the soul, rather than the one who can kill the body (Matthew 10:28).

Boiled down to their simplest meaning, all the confusing images of apocalyptic literature teach a single message: *our God reigns!*

This message has sustained believers through centuries of martyrdom and persecution. It's a message we rediscover periodically in the recurring chaos of politics and wars. The world may seem out of control, but our God reigns.

It speaks in the most uncomplimentary terms about the true character of human power and government, and the language is dense and obscure. This is one reason why the symbolism is so disturbing today. It was written to reveal God's plan to those who had ears to hear, but to conceal it from the villains glimpsed by John and Daniel. This originally intended obscurity has been intensified by twenty centuries or more of cultural changes.

A more important reason for the obscurity of the language, though, is the difficulty of describing events outside the scope of human experience. There is no direct correspondence between the end of the world and any other disaster. We may imagine a cataclysm that sweeps the stars from the sky, but we've never seen one.

John and Daniel were called on to see the unseen and to report it in language people of their day could understand. This doesn't mean jet fighters and high-tech artillery are hiding behind descriptions of horses with heads like scorpions and a sting in their tails. It means that the power of language, stretched to its limit, can give us only a rough semblance of things to come.

Volumes have been written on the subject of apocalyptic literature (or apocalyptic) and its theology, meaning, and use of imagery. To do justice to a subject as deep and broad as this one requires more space than the constraints of this book allow. For information to supplement this sketchy introduction, refer to books that devote their entire contents to the subject.

P **rinciple 8**   To understand apocalyptic literature we need to determine what the text meant to the people it was written to.

For each apocalyptic passage we discuss we will ask a single question: "What did the text mean to the people alive when it was written, e.g., the Jews in Persia or the Christians in Ephesus?" They did not know anything about twentieth century political maneuverings, so what did they see in these perplexing images?

Q **uestion 15**   Did Ezekiel really predict that Russia would invade Israel in the end time (Ezekiel 38–39)?

Ezekiel delivered a divine revelation of staggering importance and revolutionary content. He broke the geographical chains that had bound God, in Israelite thought, to Mount Zion (Ezekiel 1:10). He proclaimed the responsibility of the individual for his own sin (Ezekiel 18) and the responsibility of those called by God to warn the sinner (Ezekiel 3:16–27). He saw the humiliation of exile first hand (Ezekiel 12, 19), but saw beyond exile to a new nation made holy by God's presence (Ezekiel 37, 40–48). And yet all we remember about his lengthy book is the wheel in a wheel, the valley of dry bones, and Gog and Magog. Poor Ezekiel!

If Gog and Magog really refer to Russia, we have an advantage over most of Ezekiel's interpreters because Russia, until the nineteenth century, was not a power to be reckoned with. Not a power at all, really.

There was no Russia when Ezekiel wrote. This doesn't mean God couldn't have revealed its future existence to the prophet. Before we make that conclusion, however, we need to examine the means some commentators have used to identify these references in Ezekiel with the modern-day state of Russia.

They use several textual elements to accomplish this. Some, impressed with the similarity of sound between Meshech with Moscow, Tubal and Tobolsk, and Rosh and Russia, simply point to the biblical words as if that were enough. Others try to identify Gog and Magog with ancient peoples who lived in the territory now known as Russia. We need to examine these attempts to see if they stand up to scrutiny.

A lot of writers say that Tobolsk and Moscow are mentioned by Ezekiel as Tubal and Meshech. But remember the principal with which we began this excursion into prophetic writings: The prophecy must have had some meaning for its original readers. If Tubal and Meshech could be located in Ezekiel's day, they would mean more to Ezekiel's readers than cities not founded until over a millennium later. Assyrian records do in fact talk about tribes named the Mushku and the Tabal. As early as the twelfth century B.C. Assyrian kings were in conflict with these people. They keep appearing in Assyrian records until just before the collapse of Assyria at the end of the seventh century B.C.

These were not shadowy, mythical people residing in the indefinite north. They were tribes that opposed Assyria, paid tribute when conquered, made alliances with Assyria's enemies, and suffered horrible deaths when Assyria retaliated. They were not Russians. They didn't even inhabit a piece of real estate now known as Russia. They lived in the area we call Turkey. That they were never truly subdued by the Assyrians suggests that they possessed fearsome military strength. And the Bible says they were a source of slaves and had something to do with metal vessels.

Linguistically, the association of Meshech with Moscow depends on the fact that both words contain the letters *m*, *s*, and *c* in English. The English letters, however, aren't even close to the Hebrew. Since Hebrew was originally written without vowels, the consonants are what matter for this kind of discussion. There are four of them in English: *m*, *s*, *c*, and *w*, and only the English *m* has a parallel in the Hebrew.

Hebrew uses a single letter that combines the sounds of the English *s* and *h*, so there is no parallel between the *s* of Moscow and the *sh* of Meshech. The letter *c* doesn't even exist in Hebrew. The *ch* of Meschech is actually a *k* pronounced as if the speaker were clearing his throat. There's no single English letter to parallel either Hebrew letter. The identification of Meshech with Moscow might look good in English but it wouldn't have any sense at all to Ezekiel and his readers.

Rosh presents another problem. Some versions understand Ezekiel 38:2 to say: "Son of man, set thy face against Gog, the land of Magog, the prince of Rosh, Meshech and Tubal, and prophesy against him."

This translation makes *Rosh* a country, or region, along with Meshech and Tubal. Grammatically, the translation is possible. It's unnecessary, though. The regions of Meshech and Tubal are a common pair in both biblical and ancient non-biblical literature. They go together like a horse and carriage. Most Bible readers could name at least two more sets of names that almost always go together: Sodom and Gomorrah and Tyre and Sidon. It would be odd for Ezekiel to add a third name, Rosh, to that traditional pair.

What makes it even more odd is that the word *Rosh* is not known to represent a country or region anywhere in the Bible or outside the Bible. I wouldn't let that trouble me if *rosh* wasn't such a common Hebrew word. If it was rare, I might argue that it points to some lost locality familiar to Ezekiel but unheard of for over 2,000 years.

But *rosh* is far from rare. Those who live in an area with a large Jewish population may have heard it used in the term *Rosh Ha-Shannah*, which means "Head of the year" or, as we'd say in English, New Year. Rosh is the common Hebrew word for head. Used metaphorically, it often means "chief." The KJV and NIV are right to translate the phrase as *chief prince*.

The language of the text, more than just the etymology of the word, argues against the common identification of Gog and Magog with Russia. If not Russia, who?

Gog may refer to one of two ancient names. A king named Gyges ruled in western Turkey in the seventh century. Ezekiel probably knew the name. A lot of Bible students say Gog refers to Gyges. The Assyrian records that mention him use the name, don't laugh now, *Gugu,* pronounced just the way it's spelled. His country was called *Mat-Gugu,* or "The Land of Gyges." That interpretation fits the prophecy. The oracle would be addressed to *Gugu* of the *Land of Gugu.*

Another ancient word also might work here, although it preceeds Ezekiel by almost a thousand years. Letters found at *Tell-el-Amarna*, in Egypt, mention *Gagaia,* the land of barbarians. If the word survived until Ezekiel's time and retained its meaning over all those centuries, it might work in this passage.

I'm inclined to use Gyges as the historical model, however. Because of the way Ezekiel used language, and because of the rest of the chapter, I don't think he intended his readers to think of this man in a literal sense. Yes, another prophetic prototype is coming. Gog, whether Gyges, Gagaia, or just plain Gog, represents something. He will come as the leader of a coalition of forces from the ends of the earth, all hostile to Israel. They will strike at Jerusalem after its regathering, during a time of such peace that the city has no walls.

Some suggest that this is an oracle against the nations, as found in chapters 25–32, where judgments were announced to the nations that surrounded and threatened Israel. Here, the archetypal enemy rises up with his forces drawn from the outer edges of Israel's world, threatening its peace once again. Some see a heavily veiled oracle of doom for Babylon itself in this.

It may well be. No other word is spoken against Babylon in this book that brackets the destruction of the temple in Jerusalem and chronicles the spiritual state of its exiles. It could well be that God led Ezekiel to pronounce the doom of the Babylonian oppressor, but to do it in language so obscure that it has become one of the most clouded portions of biblical revelation.

The identity of Gog and Magog has been sought and found in countless places throughout the history of biblical interpretation. The early Jewish interpreters saw them as figures representing all the forces in opposition to God. Ambrose (339–397) identified them with the barbarian Goths who lurked at the shrinking perimeter of the Roman Empire and eventually sacked Rome in 410 A.D. Medieval writers, troubled by the Moslem Moors in Spain, saw the liberation of that country prefigured in Ezekiel. Other possible identifications of Gog and Magog included the Huns, Mongols, Arabians, Magyars, and Turks.[1]

The complex history of interpretation of this passage warns us to be careful in our approach and not force this oracle into a predetermined system, which is a common mistake.

From Ezekiel's vantage point, this is a glimpse into the far future, and it resembles Revelation's description of the Battle of Armageddon. Notice I said it *resembles*. John wrote almost 700 years after Ezekiel. By that time, Ezekiel's thoughts, ideas, and images had been passed on to dozens of generations of Jews.

John's record of his vision is filled with language from Ezekiel. But he didn't just quote Ezekiel. He customized. He took the language of the prophet and invested it with new knowledge accessible only to those who had encountered the risen Christ. Ezekiel's vision did not include the doctrine of two ages. It contained no reference to the messianic king. "Son of man," the title God used to stress Ezekiel's humanity in contrast to God's deity, had not yet been given its surprising new twist at Daniel's hand. It was, in other words, the prototype on which God built a fuller meaning for John. When John updated Ezekiel, he did it with the authority of God himself who filled Ezekiel's visions with newer, broader content.

In Revelation, John talked about Gog and Magog as two men. The obscurity of Ezekiel's meaning probably had led interpreters of John's day to see them as symbols for the ultimate evil that stood against God. Their specific historical identification had been forgotten, but their purpose, already present in Ezekiel, remained fixed.

The temptation to fine-tune the interpretation of this kind of writing by identifying the nationality of the villain in this end-time drama is strong, but we can understand Ezekiel's message with-

---

[1]
See Edwin Yamacuhi. *Foes from the Northern Border*. (Grand Rapids: Baker Book House, 1982), 22–23.

out doing so. The vision points our attention to the Millennium, even though the full development of that idea was still centuries in the future.

Occasionally I hear people say that if Jesus were around today performing miracles, things would be a lot different. It would be easier to live as a Christian. It would be easier to witness. It would be easier to believe.

The nature of the Millennium and its grisly aftermath, as described by Ezekiel, reveal the lie behind that glib notion. Every knee will bow, and every tongue will confess that Jesus Christ is Lord, but much of that confession will contain no praise. Bent knees will be signs of servitude, not worship. People will grind their teeth in frustration under the rule of righteousness.

Ezekiel's picture is a dark, surreal image, drawn like some nightmare scene from a Steven Spielberg production, inhabited with grotesque creatures. God's people will be living in peace, but the nations will continue their raging. Opposition will come, not from isolated pockets of evil, but from the mass of hostile humanity drawn from the ends of the world, from the rancor that lies at the core of human rebellion.

This underscores the justice of God's judgment. When the birds of the air gather for their final macabre feast, it will not be because God unfairly consigned so many to perdition. As repulsive as the end of Gog and his allies will be, it is their decisions and sin that brought them to it.

Their depravity illuminates the breadth of God's grace. Prepared to forgive, not willing that any perish, desiring that everyone be saved, God's grace is grand enough to include Gog, if Gog would.

This prophecy opens the eyes of Israel to a reality not yet seen. The mighty promises of God—promises of land, peace, return, and restoration—are not the end of God's plan.

Beyond the purely historical realities of Israel's national life, God laid the groundwork for a far greater, ultimate victory. The heritage of Israel would not be complete when God recalled them from the lands of exile. The restoration of Israel to a place of global dominance does not complete God's plan. Only the total eradication of evil would do that. In the annihilation of Gog's vast, seemingly invincible army we see the first glimpse of Armageddon and its aftermath. For the Prince of Peace to reign among His free people, the world must be brought to the true peace that can come only when people's hearts are pure, and that will happen only when Gog is defeated by the sanctified power of God's justice.

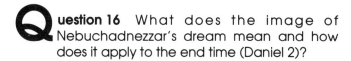

Q **uestion 16** What does the image of Nebuchadnezzar's dream mean and how does it apply to the end time (Daniel 2)?

In Daniel's day, Nebuchadnezzar was BMOE (Big Man On Earth). He had created the New Babylonian empire out of his own drive for power and the strength of his person and vision, and he held it together the same way he won it. He ruled the world, at least the world he knew.

Nebuchadnezzar had a whole staff of wise men, of which Daniel was a part, who were supposed to be able to tell him the meaning of mysterious things. So after his nightmare he sent for them and made them an offer they didn't dare refuse.

"Tell me what I dreamed and what it means, or I'll convert you all to mincemeat," he promised (Daniel 2:5).

No human power could deal with that challenge, and the wisemen knew it. But Daniel's God, who gave the dream to the King, could, and did, give the solution to Daniel. When Daniel told the king the Spirit-led interpretation of the dream, Nebuchadnezzar was forced to acknowledge Daniel's God as "God of gods" (2:47).

As Daniel explained it, the dream was simple and uncluttered. It included specific indications of the passage of time. Nebuchadnezzar himself, with no knowledge of events and kingdoms beyond his own day, accepted Daniel's interpretation with no apparent need to have its details explained.

Unlike Nebuchadnezzar, modern commentators haven't always been satisfied with such a simple approach. The bulk of today's popular interpretations begin with Daniel's simple explanation and go on from there.

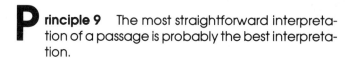

P **rinciple 9** The most straightforward interpretation of a passage is probably the best interpretation.

Most of the questions we ask about chapter 2 come from our attempts to fine-tune the text, not from the text itself. Forgetting all the interpretations we have heard, let's look at the dream using a basic principle of interpretation that almost everyone applauds: *the most straightforward interpretation of a passage is probably the best interpretation.*

The more human ingenuity we use to flesh out our understanding, the more likely we are to stray from the simplest meaning of the text.

When I was teaching Old Testament, I continually challenged my students to look for the *minimum required interpretation.* By those words I meant that they should look for what the text *had* to say, not what it *might* say. What is the minimum required meaning of Nebuchadnezzar's dream?

The statue had four parts, each part a different metal. Each metal stood for a different kingdom, which are usually identified as Babylon, Persia, the Greek empire of Alexander and his successors, and the Roman Empire.

The names we give the four kingdoms aren't as important as some people think, though. Most popular attempts to build a historical case for particular empires have been historically naive at best. For example, the fact that the image has two legs and ten toes is altogether unremarkable. It was, after all, a human figure. In an image of a man, the presence of two legs and ten toes is to be expected.

To interpret the two legs as a reference to the division of the Roman Empire and the ten toes as a ten-nation revival of the Roman Empire is to fall victim to over-interpretation of the worst kind.

When a simple, straightforward explanation for some element in the text makes sense, it's better to adopt it than to search for a hidden, mysterious meaning. The biblical interpretation of this image mentions toes and legs but doesn't elaborate on them. Let's leave it at that.

Daniel was not interested in specific identifications or a top twenty list of human governments. He had bigger fish to fry, or idols to cast. In fact, the interpretation given to Daniel by the Holy Spirit seems more concerned with the everlasting nature of God's kingdom than with the fading, fluctuating fortunes of human domains.

Another clue suggesting that this dream represents human history in general and not just the histories of these four kingdoms is found in Daniel 2:35, which says they were all destroyed simultaneously. Although the dream appears to begin with Babylon and end with Rome, that sequence stands for all government. Daniel's explanation tells us the vision stood for every government since the first one set out to storm heaven from the top of a tower (Genesis 11:4). God wasn't giving a course on history in advance. He was showing the meaning of human history.

Although Nebuchadnezzar's empire was the greatest of his day, it was not the first nor the largest. The Assyrians before him and the Persians after him both commanded more territory and more wealth than he. And Rome, which was not the last empire, has been surpassed in modern times. From a historical perspective, the vision ignores China, the Mali empire in Africa, the United States, the British Empire, on which "the sun never set," and others.

None of this really matters, though, because we can understand Daniel 2 without having to rewrite history to make it suit us. God used a slice of history to stand for all of history. It's as simple as that.

Daniel 2 tells us that human greats give way to greater humans and that nothing human lasts.

P rinciple 10   When reading the Bible, focus on God's activity, not on human activity.

Although the Bible is filled with supporting characters, the real hero is God. Attention in this passage is riveted on God and His plan, not on human government and its passing.

If we were to look for an explanation that would focus on God's activity, not man's, what would it be?

The image depicts the massive complex of human activity in government and conquest. It is enormous and dazzling (2:31), but it deteriorates quickly from gold at the head to a mixture of iron and clay at the feet.

Human governments stand on feet of clay, regardless of how dazzling and impressive they may appear. Their golden tops draw attention away from their unstable foundations. God, who

sees the end from the beginning, knows this and tells Nebuchadnezzar and all his followers that this is so.

To concentrate on the kingdoms represented by the image,
and not on the Stone that brings them all down, is to miss the
point of this chapter. There isn't much argument over the meaning of the stone that smashed the whole thing to scrap because
Daniel identified it as God's kingdom.

Do we begin our histories with a golden age?

That's fine. The past is always more beautiful than the present because time blurs imperfections until they completely disappear, blended into the vague impression of better times gone
by. But if the past was golden, what does the image say about the
present? And worse yet, about the future?

Daniel dashes all our romantic notions about the ascent of
humanity and the superiority of our age. History is headed in one
direction. Down. We have better machines, chemicals, and techniques than we had even a hundred years ago, but for all their
good, they also have enabled us to kill more people at once and
to gratify our fallen desires in more ways. Our civilization may be
more technically "advanced," but it's populated with the same
fallen people as all the rest.

Nebuchadnezzar's dream tells us that we do not become
better, but worse. We do not evolve; we degenerate. There is no
climbing out of the mud to a golden future in this dream. There
is only the stark reminder that people made to walk in God's
garden in the cool of the evening, during the only genuine "golden
age" in human history, have inevitable judgment to anticipate.

When God's kingdom thunders down from the heights, all the
kingdoms of the earth will be crushed to fine powder. Persia
followed Babylon only to be replaced by Alexander the Great's
Greece, which then was crushed under the iron heel of Rome.

The truth of Nebuchadnezzar's dream was that as it has
always been, so shall it ever be. These things will continue to
happen. The monotonous, deadening cycle of rising and falling,
conquering and being conquered, will play itself out like some
awful script whose ending we know and hate but must watch to
the bitter end.

That's the bad news.

The good news is that God will not let it continue forever. He
has already acted, and the Stone from God, not made by human

hands, has already come. It has struck the colossus on its feet, and wherever Christ is Lord the structure has begun its fall. We still await its final destruction, but we can take courage in the knowledge that it will come as surely as morning follows the night.

The message of Daniel 2 should never be limited to specific times or seasons, places or boundaries. It has meaning to God's people in all times and all places. To those outside Daniel's world it speaks of the timeless truth that our God reigns.

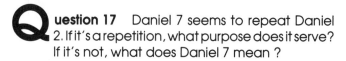

Q **uestion 17** Daniel 7 seems to repeat Daniel 2. If it's a repetition, what purpose does it serve? If it's not, what does Daniel 7 mean ?

The visions are alike in their general historical interest, but they differ most significantly in that Daniel 7 presents greater detail, which can be explained by two factors.

First, Nebuchadnezzar's dream came in his second year of rule, or 604 B.C. (2:1), and Daniel's vision came about fifty years later, in the first year of Belshazzar, or 552–1 B.C. (7:1).

Daniel had over fifty years to reflect on Nebuchadnezzar's dream, and the fuller revelation he received in the second vision left him pale and deeply troubled (7:28). Imagine how it might have affected him without the earlier dream. God often prepared His people with a portion of the truth before He opened the books completely. This is an interesting example of progressive revelation taking place within the boundaries of a single book.

Second, God gave Nebuchadnezzar, an unbelieving Gentile, a sketchy picture of realities to come. He took the king far enough into the future to let him see his kingdom endure throughout his own lifetime. Beyond that, he probably didn't care.

For God's own, though, He saved one of the most marvelous messianic prophecies in the Old Testament. I don't know if Daniel understood the significance of what he had seen, but the "Son of Man" section of this vision (7:9–14) gave New Testament audiences the background to understand what Jesus meant when He called himself *Son of Man*.

As with chapter 2, the real action in chapter 7 unfolds far from the doings of earth's kingdoms. The stone that shattered them in chapter 2 is magnified majestically by Daniel's glimpse into heaven in chapter 7. This vision doesn't focus on the progression of powers seen by Nebuchadnezzar but on the transcendant affairs of heaven. This is a believer's vision. Set amid the praise and worship of heaven's hallowed courts, high above the sordid strivings of Adam's offspring, its message rises to a crescendo of hope and promise.

Let's see how Daniel reported that message.

The image in Nebuchadnezzar's dream had dignity. Made of precious metal (even iron was precious in Daniel's day), it stood cool and implacable above the press of enslaved humankind. It had the brutal dignity of unrestrained power. We see the character of that power in chapter 7, where the nations are depicted as panting, drooling beasts, horrid hybrid monsters stirred up out of the cauldron of the sea. The ancients thought of the sea as the source of all evil. Any illusions about the glories of any empire were laid to rest for Daniel and his readers in this nightmare vision.

IT'S A LION, IT'S A BIRD, IT MUST BE BABYLON

The first beast, like the head of the statue, was noble, after a fashion. It blended the body of a lion, the king of beasts, with the wings of an eagle, the king of birds. It must be Babylon.

Jeremiah used both creatures to describe Nebuchadnezzar (49:19–22). More than that, it recalls his humbling (Daniel 4). The soaring beast had its wings plucked off. The once proud beast was made to stand on the earth as any other creature.

The great bear, a transparent depiction of the Medo-Persia empire, came second. It was a coalition of two related peoples, the Medes and the Persians, which the Persians dominated from the time of Cyrus the Great. The elevation of one side over the other shows this dominance.

The bear gnaws three ribs just as Cyrus chewed up three allies who stood together against him: Egypt, Babylon, and Lydia, the kingdom of the legendary Croesus.

The third beast, the winged, four-headed leopard, with its meteoric ferocity, makes us think of conquests of the Macedonian Alexander. Like a bird of prey, he flew from one end of the ancient Near East to the other in an unprecedented ten-year frenzy of conquest. Like a leopard, he mounted his assault with a ferocity and speed unheard of in ancient warfare. When he died in Babylon at age 33, four generals parceled out Alexander's conquest. The leopard's four heads symbolize the general's part in the Greek domination of the ancient world.

The fourth beast is of a different sort altogether. Unlike the first three, it's not described in terms of any natural animal. Its only identifiable features are large iron teeth and ten horns.

Up to this point Daniel has related his vision without comment, but the fourth beast captures his interest. Especially his "little" horn. So, he asks his heavenly interpreter for "the true meaning of the fourth beast" (7:19).

The writer is using the literary technique of end stress. The first three kingdoms set the stage for the fourth, which holds the substance of this part of the vision.

This beast wasn't like anything before it. Both terrible and awe-inspiring beyond description, it devoured and trampled everything in its way. Likewise, the Roman Empire was different from other ancient kingdoms in size and ferocity. It wielded iron-fisted control over its conquered territories. Earlier empires demanded allegiance and burdensome taxes from conquered territories, but they usually appointed members of the conquered royal family to rule as vassal kings. They returned in force only to punish rebellion. Even the Assyrians hadn't bothered to occupy their subject countries. Rome, on the other hand, sent Roman civil servants to administer and Roman procurators and proconsuls to rule.[2] Roman law and peace were enforced by the iron teeth and brazen claws of the empire.

The Romans were also different in that later emperors demanded worship. Other empires considered their kings gods or as spokesmen of the gods, but the Romans required emperor worship as a kind of loyalty oath. The two deranged emperors, Caligula and Nero, were the first to claim deity. Their precedent

---

[2] During the early period of empire, the emperors dominated, but shared power with the Senate. In the power-sharing arrangement some provinces were governed by the emperor, some by the Senate. Militarily troublesome provinces were under the control of the emperor, who assigned procurators, while the more easily governed provinces were under the Senate, which assigned proconsuls.

was followed by Domitian, the emperor who sent John into exile on Patmos.

Of these three, only Domitian made worship of himself mandatory throughout the empire. When Christians refused to worship the "divine" Domitian, the first systematic persecution from Roman authorities began.

The identification of the first three beasts is almost inescapable, but the description of the fourth, though easily applied to Rome, is vague. Throughout the last nineteen centuries, the fourth beast has been identified with every government that threatened the order of life.

This shouldn't alarm us. The beast is described incompletely because God wanted it that way. If He had wanted to tell us more He could have told us the Antichrist's zipcode and blood type. But if He had, centuries of believers would have ignored everything that didn't apply directly to them and their century.

The fourth beast gives us a glimpse of the Roman Empire, but it may also apply to other world empires.

A regional empire that fit part of the description of the fourth beast ruled over Palestine before the rise of the Romans. Known as the Selucid dynasty, it ravaged Palestine toward the close of the intertestamental period. Their most infamous representative, Antiochus IV (called *Epiphanes*), provided an earlier identification for the beast.

Antiochus displaced other men to gain the throne, spoke vehemently against the Most High, and oppressed His saints with violence as fierce as they'd ever encountered (Daniel 7:24–25). He outlawed the practice of Judaism and erected a statue of Zeus with his own face on it in the temple at Jerusalem. He persecuted any Jew who stood firm in the faith. As world rulers go, he made a very good beast.

The Roman emperor Vespasian fit the description even more closely than Antiochus. On the death of Nero a great struggle for the throne erupted, with three men sitting on the throne in rapid succession, all in A.D. 69. By the end of that year, all three had been killed and Vespasian, the old soldier, became emperor.

His armies besieged the handful of patriots on Masada. His son Titus assumed command of the Roman forces who put down the First Jewish Revolt. Titus has gone down in history as the man responsible for the destruction of Herod's Temple.

Some see similarities between the little horn of Daniel 7 and the emperor Vespasian. While the picture is almost a perfect fit, there are discrepancies here, too. Daniel's "little horn" comes up after the original ten horns, making him number eleven. Counting Roman emperors from Julius Caesar to Vespasian, Vespasian makes the eleventh. That part fits with Daniel's description of the little horn. When the smoke cleared in A.D. 69, Vespasian held the throne after dispatching three other claimants to the emperorship. While these three men, Otho, Vitellius, and Galba, all made claims to be emperor, none ruled and it's questionable whether they actually deserve to be counted. What's more damaging to this identification is the fact that Titus, not Vespasian, sacked the temple and destroyed Jerusalem. Titus was neither the tenth nor eleventh emperor. There's simply no good way to fit him into Daniel's picture of ten horns. The parallel with Vespasian and Titus is closer than the one we might draw with Antiochus but still too imprecise.

God gave the vision with enough clarity and detail to convey His message but omitted enough to leave it open-ended. We can find partial fulfillments at several points in early church history if we're willing to bend the details to fit.

This makes the fourth beast a good example of the prophetic prototype. The final kingdom and its king will be a type we have seen before. And we'll see them again and again until the final curtain comes down on the tragic drama of human history.

We've seen this beast foreshadowed with disastrous regularity throughout the ages, and the current world situation offers no optimistic prospects that anything has changed. Governments that oppress and leaders who place themselves above the God of heaven are the rule, not the exception.

Daniel's vision of Antichrist is like a picture taken against the sun. The outline is visible, but the features are lost in darkness. Believers can hold world rulers up to the light to see if their general shape fits the Antichrist, but we won't recognize him until God himself steps forward to unmask and dethrone him.

Even though the New Testament adds some detail to the image, a positive identification is still all but impossible. These ancient rulers provide a glimpse of the final abomination, a glimpse that has flashed into focus repeatedly around the world and throughout time.

The atrocities of Antiochus pale into insignificance when compared with the atrocities of Adolph Hitler, who some thought might be the Antichrist. The antagonism of Titus to the God of Abraham, Isaac, and Jacob seems almost amiable in light of the hostility of Karl Marx.

Christians in China during the first years of the Communist government of Mao Tse Tung wondered if the Tribulation had come in their lifetimes. Idi Amin set his sights on Christians in Uganda with a special fury that must have made them think of the predictions of the Beast. Who knows what new and worse dictator lurks around the next historical corner?

No matter who he is, he will display the same characteristics as Antiochus, Nero, Domitian, and any of the others who have appeared since. He will try to supplant God. He will oppress God's people. His support will arise from a mixture of military might and the world's ever-present hatred of those who are not quite of this world.

Realizing that evil leaders throughout history have committed ever greater atrocities with ever greater intensity, think of the horror of unregenerate humanity's future.

But that's not the the message God gave Daniel! Although we're fascinated with the dark prediction of Daniel 7, the most important revelation in this vision has nothing to do with the plots of satanic adversaries. The key event of the vision doesn't even take place on earth, but in heaven (7:9–14). The principal figure is neither horn nor beast. It's the Son of Man.

Whenever I read this chapter, I'm struck by the stark contrast between the frenzy of earth and the calm of heaven. While beasts tear one another on earth, the Ancient of Days sits enthroned in majesty and dignity amid His people. In this holy assembly, not in the unholy throes of human rulers fighting for supremacy on rebel earth, the books are opened and the beast is judged.

Although the search for Antichrist appeals to our curiosity, I'm convinced that the great teaching of Daniel 7 is that rulers may run roughshod over God's earth but that thrones are set up in heaven.

Men who are beasts may oppress the elect and blaspheme God, but the kingdom that will never be destroyed does not and cannot belong to them. The peoples of the world may suffer at such men's hands, but ultimately they will watch as judgment flows out like a river of fire to purify the earth.

Do we really need to know more?

Q **uestion 18**   What is the "sign of the fig tree"? If it's the rebirth of Israel as a nation, how could Jesus say that "this generation will certainly not pass away until all these things have happened" (Matthew 24:34)?

The usual interpretation is that the fig tree is the symbol for Israel in biblical prophecy, and Israel is God's prophetic time clock. But I find that idea hard to defend from the text.

Jesus identified what he was about to say as a parable, and the purpose of a parable is to illustrate a spiritual point by using an element from everyday life.

P **rinciple 11**   To understand the meaning of a parable, we need to look at its context.

What many interpreters overlook in the Olivet Discourse (Matthew 24–25) is that Jesus was answering two questions, not one. Most interpretations aim at the answer to the second set of questions: "What will be the sign of your coming, and of the end of the age?" (24:3).

The important first question, so often ignored, was prompted by Jesus' remark about the destruction of the temple (24:2). The disciples were small town boys visiting the city. They had probably seen the temple before, but still they were dazzled by its immensity and splendor. They pointed out to Jesus what a wonder it was, almost like children eager to share a new experience.

Jesus took the occasion to tell them that its future was bleak and certain. The day would come, he said, when there wouldn't be two stones of that magnificent edifice left standing together.

Shocked, the disciples awaited an opportunity to ask what Jesus meant by that. After He had left the temple and had reached the Mount of Olives they asked, "when will this [the destruction of the temple] happen?" To that, they added their question about His coming and the end of the age.

Jesus answered both questions, but we read the answer as if it all pertained to the end time. The problem lies in discerning which verses apply to which answer.

Jesus began (v. 4) with His answer to the question about the end. He warned the disciples against the many false messiahs who would proclaim themselves the answer to God's promises. Then He warned the disciples *not to be alarmed* by wars and rumors of wars nor by famines and earthquakes because they would *not* be the sign of the end (v. 6). In fact, they would be just the beginnings of the birth pains that would rack the earth until His return (v. 8).

Usual interpretation places these things at the very end of this age and point to the increasing number of wars and earthquakes as signs that the Second Coming is at hand. This flies in the face of what Jesus said here. His answer to the disciples told them, and us, that His coming would not be heralded by natural disasters or political upheavals.

The spread of the gospel would be accompanied by the persecution of Christians. Forces would pull at believers, and false prophets would beseech them on behalf of new gospels. Wickedness would grow to such an extent that believers would fall away. But He promised the faithful they would endure (vv. 9–13).

The only verse in this section that gives any kind of information about the time of the Second Coming is Matthew 24:14, "And this gospel of the kingdom will be preached in the whole world as a testimony to all nations, and then the end will come." This verse was a prime motivator in the early days of the modern missions movement.

Even here, I think some of the interest in seeing to it that every language and people group hear the gospel is slightly off target. Not that I think the missions movement is misguided. The real purpose of the church, from day one, has been the fulfillment of this condition for the Second Coming. What I find slightly off is the notion that when the first person in the last language group hears the gospel the end will automatically come.

To me, that places the Second Coming on a legalistic time line similar to games I played as a kid. The person who was IT would shout out a time limit, begin a count down, and everyone else would race like rabbits for the goal, hoping to reach it before the last number fell from ITS lips.

God's mercy and love, not human evangelistic efforts, will keep history in motion until judgment is inevitable.

There is little in verses 4–14 to give any indication of a time for the Second Coming. Verse 15 begins the answer to question one. I suppose we could push all these events into the future and presuppose a reconstructed temple in Jerusalem that carries on the renewed sacrificial system, but I cannot accept that notion without cutting Hebrews 10 out of my Bible. To insist on a return to the sacrificial system is to trivialize the death of Christ by making it apply only for an interim period.

The simple fact is that these events took place in A.D. 70, as Jesus predicted. More importantly, Jewish Christians who remained in Judea heeded Jesus' warning and fled the city in time to escape the destruction. Commentators who understand the passage in this way see the *abomination that causes desolation* in the Roman armies moving against Mount Zion. In A.D. 70, the Roman general Titus breached the walls of Jerusalem, sacked the city, scattered the inhabitants, and obliterated the temple. The only graphic depiction we have today of the furniture of the temple comes from the triumphal arch the Romans erected to celebrate this great "victory".

It may be that this historical event is another prophetic prototype. If so, it would look into the future to a day when the Antichrist would, in the manner of Antiochus Ephiphanes, erect an idol of himself in the holy of holies of the rebuilt temple.

I don't think the text itself supports that idea, however. Too much has been made of attempts to reconstruct a history of the end time from passages like this.

Jesus warned that, in connection with the desolation He described, false Christs and prophets would arise and, if possible, deceive even the elect. Then He warned the disciples not to be among the deceived because "I have told you ahead of time. So if anyone tells you, 'There he is, out in the desert,' do not go out; or 'Here he is, in the inner rooms,' do not believe it. For as lightning that comes from the east is visible even in the west, so will be the coming of the Son of Man" (Matthew 24:26–27).

Jesus knew that the devastation of Jerusalem would be seen by many as an apocalyptic event. Even the Roman historian

Tacitus described it in those terms. He talked about angelic forces seen warring in the heavens and a great voice from heaven crying that "The gods are departed."

Both Adam Clarke (1762–1832) and Matthew Henry (1662– 1774), in their classic commentaries, adopted the point of view that the destruction of Jerusalem was the apocalyptic event Jesus spoke of in Matthew 24. It will probably come as a great surprise to many modern readers to discover that the usual explanation of the passage up to this point is absent from the works of these two classic expositors.

Both saw the spiritual deadness of Israel in the enigmatic reference to "the carcass" and "the vultures gathering" (Matthew 24:28). Both saw the spread of the gospel and the growth of Christ's spiritual kingdom in verse 27.

The word *immediately*, which introduces verse 29, seems to link these preceding events to the Second Coming. Some say this proves that these verses refer to the Tribulation prior to the Second Coming. I suggest, however, that this is a good example of *prophetic foreshortening.*

The predictive writings of the Bible take little note of chronology. It is not unusual to read in the same biblical passage predictions of events that are separated by centuries in fulfillment. For example, Isaiah 9:6–7 speaks of both a baby and a king; Christ came as a baby two thousand years ago but has yet to come as a king.

Here Jesus moves from the initial question about the destruction of the temple to the second question about the end of all things. The word *immediately* functions as a transition. What follows is a brief description, in apocalyptic language, of this same time.

Advocates of other positions will probably propose counterarguments and ask the ultimate question, "What do you do with verse. . . ?"

I admit that there are elements in this that I'm not satisfied with. But commentators often call this the most difficult passage in the book of Matthew, so it's not surprising that I'm not totally satisfied with every jot and tittle of my understanding.

What this interpretation accomplishes, though, is a resolution of the problem of Jesus' own words: "this generation will certainly not pass away until all these things have happened."

This statement is more than a jot or a tittle. It is a straightforward, prosaic statement of our Lord. Other statements are more open to interpretation than this simple declarative sentence.

The inescapable declarative statements of Jesus in this Discourse say that no one knows the hour of the Second Coming. The statement would be less imposing if He had not included himself in the group that doesn't know (24:36)! Verse 42 says that His disciples will not know when He'll return, but cautions them to be ready.

If we find in this passage clear-cut signs that the Second Coming is at hand, it seems that we've also uncovered a contradiction in Jesus' teaching. Could He possibly be saying He doesn't know when He will return and yet be giving signs so we will know?

I've always felt that the "signs of the times" some readers find here are too common to be any good. Preachers are fond of telling us what an awful world this is. They give current box scores on the number of wars, earthquakes, and famines in a given number of years. But their arguments belie an ignorance of history.

The ideal the prophets held forth for the messianic kingdom was that every man would be able to enjoy the vines and trees he'd planted. That shows us a previous world in which stability didn't exist. The entire Bible was written in a world where warfare was so much a part of life that every reader knew that kings went out to war in the spring of the year.

How do we know that earthquakes are more common now than ever?

Who, before the middle of this century, would know about an earthquake in Armenia, Afghanistan, or Indonesia unless he lived there?

What makes us think our generation is the first to experience famines? According to biblical references, famine was a way of life in the ancient world.

Is AIDS the worst epidemic ever? How does it even qualify as an epidemic when compared with the Plague that killed half the population of Europe in a matter of years? So what if AIDS is incurable? There was no cure for the plague either. And it's only been in my lifetime that we have conquered polio, smallpox, and other killer diseases.

What I'm saying is that these things must happen, as Jesus pointed out, but they are not the sign of the end (24:6–7).

The lesson of the fig tree must be seen in light of all this.

Jesus talked about one thing for which there will be a sign: the Roman destruction of Jerusalem. For his Second Coming, there is no sign. He will come as a thief, and those who know a thief is coming will stand watch to catch him.

We know Jesus is coming. We should be as prepared for Him as we would be for a thief.

I don't think Israel is God's time clock for the Second Coming. The main thrust of these two chapters is "Be prepared." When Jesus comes, we'll know. If we live each day as if it were earth's last, the world will feel the impact.

A preacher I know talked to a person who had been involved in a minor accident. The policeman called to the scene wrote up his report and then challenged both individuals to give their lives to Christ. He thought the Second Coming was scheduled for the following weekend and he was working fervently to warn everyone he came into contact with that their time was short!

What would our world be like next year at this time if we were as motivated by Christ's truthful warning to be prepared as that police officer was by someone's erroneous attempt to predict the Second Coming?

"So you also must be ready, because the Son of Man will come at an hour when you do not expect him" (Matthew 24:44).

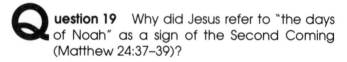

Q **uestion 19**   Why did Jesus refer to "the days of Noah" as a sign of the Second Coming (Matthew 24:37–39)?

We don't actually have a biblical description of life in the days of Noah. The repeated statement in Genesis 6 that men were corrupt is the only concrete reference to behavior. It talks about "wickedness" and the continual evil inclinations of the thoughts of humankind (Genesis 6:5), but it doesn't get any more specific. There's room for almost any interpretation of those words, but corruptness is what we keep hearing about when we get into the story.

Corruptness is mentioned three times in Genesis 6:11–13. In 9:5, God established the death penalty for murder, which argues that murder must have had something to do with the wickedness that brought the flood.

Yet when preachers talk about this text, they always refer to the rise of immorality in the modern age. I've heard too many times that there was "eating and drinking, marrying and giving in marriage" in Noah's day, and that our day is remarkable for its similarity.

As a pastor, I can vouch for the frequency of marriage in our day. It's almost reached epidemic proportions! And as for eating and drinking, look out for those church pot-luck dinners.

Unfortunately, when we read Jesus' statement we look for meanings behind His words and see more than He said. We read eating and think gluttony, drinking becomes drunkenness, and marriage becomes a synonym for sexual immorality.

None of this is what Jesus had in mind. It may well be that immorality is rampant in our day. It probably will be when Christ returns, too. Nevertheless, He wasn't talking about immorality any more than He was talking about drunkenness and gluttony. He was talking about things we do every day to preserve our lives for the next one. He was talking about marriage, which has its fullest meaning when viewed as the prelude to a shared lifetime ahead, a lifetime that implies children and future generations.

In other words, when the Lord returns, people's attention will be riveted on tomorrow. They will be living as if they will continue uninterrupted through their allotted three score and ten.

This whole long section (Matthew 24:36–25:13) focuses on the unexpectedness of the Second Coming.

Jesus began by stating that no one knows when the day will come. To amplify that statement he recalled the pre-flood world when men and women went about their business as if the world would last forever, right up to the moment the rain came. He described two sets of people going about their business only to be brought up short, each in different ways, by the Rapture.

Then He admonished watchfulness. Not the kind that predicts the day, but the kind that is ready no matter when it arrives. The parables of the servant left in charge and the ten virgins are both cautionary, with watchfulness as their theme.

In this context, the warning in Jesus' reference to the days of Noah refers to the unexpectedness of His return. Any search for "signs of the times" here is misplaced.

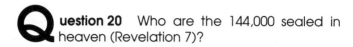

Question 20   Who are the 144,000 sealed in heaven (Revelation 7)?

The text says quite specifically that this is "the number of those who were sealed: 144,000 from all the tribes of Israel."

The real challenge in explaining this passage lies in the meaning of the *tribes of Israel.*

A common interpretation of Revelation says that this is the number of the Jewish martyrs from the Great Tribulation. The number in this case derives from the number of the tribes, twelve, multiplied by 12,000: *12 X 1,000 X 12 = 144,000.*

In Bible times, 1,000 was the largest number for which there was a special word. They had no need for the word *million* because they knew of nothing that numerous, except perhaps grains of sand, and they were considered countless.

The Old Testament used the word *thousand* the way we might use *million,* or one of the larger words our national debt has forced on our collective consciousness.

When God told Israel that He would, "keep[ing] his covenant of love to a thousand generations of those who love him and keep his commands" (Deuteronomy 7:9). He wanted them to know that His faithfulness was everlasting.

Think about it. We frequently use such words as *trillions* or *billions* as if they meant infinity or eternity. And that's the use the Bible makes of its largest number word. When the Bible uses 1,000 in a symbolic sense, it means all there is or all there could be.

The first twelve in our equation is simple to understand. Twelve is used throughout Scripture as the number for Israel, and it comes from the twelve patriarchs. That gets us up to 12,000. We could stop there, since the text tells us there were 12,000 from each of the tribes. Many commentators do. They're the ones who identify these as the Jewish martyrs. They do this because their larger interpretive framework views all of Revelation, after chapter 3, as relating to Israel.

I disagree. Revelation gives pretty clear indication as to its attitude toward ethnic Israel. Christ spoke to the church at Smyrna and encouraged them in the face of "the slander of those who say they are Jews and are not, but are a synagogue of Satan" (Revelation 2:9). This slander went beyond gossip and backbiting. It eventaully led to persecution and imprisonment. The church at Philadelphia received an even more direct statement about those who claimed to be Jews. Revelation 3:9 said they were liars.

In addition to the twelve tribes of Israel, another group of twelve figured prominently in the Bible, this time in the New Testament. That's right. There were twelve disciples, later called apostles, who were known in the early church simply as "the Twelve." Revelation includes the Apostles with the twelve tribes. The New Jerusalem bears the names of the tribes on its gates, and the twelve foundations bear the names of the apostles.

The New Testament doesn't completely ignore Israel in a biological, ethnic sense. But often biological descent from the patriarchs was de-emphasized.

Paul talked about those who had Abraham for a forefather, "as pertaining to the flesh" (Romans 4:1, KJV). He talked about Israelites who were his kinsmen "according to the flesh" (Romans 9:3).

This qualifier is important in light of what Paul said in Romans 9:6–8. Paul's intention here should be clear. Not all who are descended from Israel, that is, Israel after the flesh, are Israel. Not everyone who is Abraham's descendant is his child. It is the children of promise, Paul said, who are Israel! He talked about the "Israel of God" at the end of Galatians (6:16), which is a particularly telling verse, because it comes at the conclusion of a book aimed at the heresy of Judaizing.

The Galatians had been told they must become observant Jews to be Christians. Paul attacked the idea in the most forceful way throughout the book. He ended by reminding them that the new creation which is in Christ was what really counted, not circumcision or uncircumcision (6:15). In other words circumcision, considered vital by Judaizers and the mark of the orthodox Jew, was irrelevant.

What mattered was that the Galatians had been made new creatures in Christ, the act that abolished the dividing wall between Jew and Gentile (Ephesians 2:14) and made the two one, so Paul could say that in Christ there is neither Jew nor Greek (Galatians 3:28). After negating the importance of biological descent, Paul showed the positive side: "If you belong to Christ, then you are Abraham's seed, and heirs according to the promise" (Galatians 3:29). He couldn't have said it much more plainly. For many Christians the idea of the Church as spiritual Israel and heir to all the promises of God is anathema. But I am convinced that this is what the Bible teaches.

The problem with interpreting the 144,000 as Jewish martyrs lies in the assumption that Revelation uses Israel in a strictly literal sense. Those who take this literal view interpret other nations symbolically, but not Israel. Why insist that Israel must be ethnic Israel when Babylon has become Rome and then some ten-nation European super-state?

Why must Israel be ethnic Israel when so many places in the New Testament say that we are now under new terms of agreement between God and humanity. Under those terms, Israel is free to share with everyone else, but has no priority. If the Gentiles are now the seed of Abraham, and heirs according to the promise, why must we see Israel in Revelation?

In fact, there's no hint whatsoever that the church has been removed at the beginning of Revelation. Some will argue that the call of John to come through the door into heaven is the Rapture. It takes some very inventive interpretation to make a case for that idea.

The speaker clearly identifies this vision as "what must take place after this" (Revelation 4:1). John records his observations as his own first-person-singular experiences. There's no hint anywhere in the text that he represents the church.

Where has the church disappeared to in this book?

I suggest they haven't disappeared at all. They make their appearance in the 144,000 of chapters 7 and 14.

We've established that the number is 12 X 12 X 1,000. We've also established that twelve is the number of Israel. Twelve times twelve is a number that signifies the perfection of itself. It stands for the perfect, ideal Israel.

That number may come from the multiplication of twelve tribes times twelve apostles. We see that combination in 21:12–14. One thousand is the number of completion. In other words, it stands for the totality of God's people, Jew and Gentile, brought together under the banner of the Lamb in that last terrible, climactic moment when the forces of evil rise up in the violence of their death throes.

In the 144,000 we find the fulfillment of God's eternal plan of redemption, the calling out of a people for His name, the creation of a kingdom of priests and a holy nation. The number is the symbolic representation of what Paul described in Ephesians. It's the body in which race, gender, and social status are all irrelevant (Galatians 3:28). It includes the full number of those who will be saved, set aside for protection by the seal of God. The Body of Christ, in that generation, will stand complete.

Although the nations continue to rage against Christ and His bride, they have the assurance that they have been marked with God's seal of ownership, and that "neither death nor life, angels, nor demons, neither the present nor the future, nor any powers, neither height nor depth, nor anything else in all creation will be able to separate us from the love of God that is in Christ Jesus our Lord" (Romans 8:38–39).

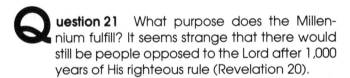 **uestion 21**   What purpose does the Millennium fulfill? It seems strange that there would still be people opposed to the Lord after 1,000 years of His righteous rule (Revelation 20).

Most discussions of the Millennium revolve around whether it's literal or figurative. Christians are divided into three camps on this issue, premillennial, postmillennial, and amillennial. Most evangelicals fall into the premillennial classification, but many call themselves amillennial as well.

Very briefly, amillennialism interprets the thousand-year period as a symbol for the invisible Kingdom of God present in the lives of believers. Postmillennialism is practically a dead issue these days. It was rooted in an unrealistic view of history that saw the progress of the church resulting in the age of justice on earth. premillennialism believes that the earthly reign of Christ and His people is yet to come. It will be preceded by the Great Tribulation, the Rapture, and the Second Coming of Christ. Following the battle of Armageddon, in which the power of the nations of the world will be shattered, the righteous rule of God will be introduced on the earth.

To those who favor the premillennial view, I pose this question: What is the purpose of holding Satan captive for a thousand years and then letting him loose for one last rampage before finally consigning him to the Lake of Fire?

The reason for taking this position is plain. God made all sorts of promises to Israel in the Old Testament. These involved Jerusalem, the Promised Land, and the people of Israel. To fulfill these promises, God, they believe, will re-establish the nation as the pivot point of the world political system. I find this position unsatisfactory. The Old Testament is filled to overflowing with material promises and commands that are given spiritual expression in the New Testament.

Not least of these is the promise of the Messiah. The expectations of Jewish people in Jesus' day were for a king like David to break the Roman yoke, but Jesus came saying His kingdom was not of this world. Even in the Old Testament, Jeremiah spiritualized the most central of Jewish practices: circumcision. Speaking for God, he grouped Judah with Edom, Moab, Ammon, and Egypt because all Judah was "uncircumcised in heart" (Romans 9:25). Yet premillennialists consider it a sin like idolatry to "spiritualize" the land promised to Israel.

I propose another purpose the Millennium might fulfill.

Since the beginning of church history, universalism, the idea that Christ died for all so therefore all must be saved, won the allegiance of some who called themselves Christian. In our age, universalism has gained new strength in combination with the spreading popularity of pluralism. Its plainest modern statement is: *There are many ways to God. Christianity is just one of them.*

Universalism is an idea whose time will never come. It cheapens the doctrine of the Fall and makes the death of Christ an empty charade enacted only for the benefit of the minority who believe it.

The Millennium is the part of God's plan for the ages that unmasks the persistent and virulent notion that we'll make it because God is so loving and we're so good. The fact of the matter is that the mass of humanity has never, and will never, accept Christ as Lord. To do so is too restrictive. It requires that we acknowledge the claim of God on our wills and our lives.

After more than thirty years among His own people, only a handful acknowledged Him as Lord. After a thousand years of a righteous reign in which justice, peace, and prosperity are unrestrained, the mass of humanity will rise up in a final, military version of the first sin.

This time it will do no good to blame rebellion on the Devil. He'll be chained and helpless. But the unrelenting sinfulness of human hearts, restrained only by the powerful presence of Christ in His just rule, will churn out spiritual sedition.

How like God, at the consummation of the age, to rule in justice and peace over people who might still yield in faith to the Lordship of Christ! And how like humanity, offered forgiveness for its continuing opposition to God and to His Christ, to reject it all! In one last vain attempt to snatch deity, humanity will instead snatch defeat from the jaws of victory, turning once again to believe the serpent's original lie.

I can't help thinking of a scene in the seventh book of The Chronicles of Narnia by C. S. Lewis. *The Last Battle* pictures Narnia wracked by the evil of the Beast and his prophet, a donkey dressed in lion skins, and a chattering ape.

After what seemed to be the defeat of Narnia at the hands of the armies of the false god, King Tirian was thrust into the door of a stable that ushered him and his party into an Edenic world. It was a place where the fruit was so sweet that "all the nicest things in the world would taste like medicines after that."

In that wonderful world, they found a band of dwarfs who had shouted the time-honored cry of sinners everywhere: "The dwarfs are for the dwarfs!"

Thrust through the same door, into the same Eden, these sinful creatures sat huddled together, cursing the darkness and filth of the stable they believed they were in.

Lucy, one of the queens of Narnia, was moved by the sadness of their plight. She tried to convince them they were sitting in a beautiful grove of trees, but they insisted, in the pride of their ignorance, that they were all shut up in a stable. They accused her of trying to trick them.

She moved to show them the truth of what she could see and they could not. She stooped and picked some wild violets. "Listen, Dwarf," she said. "Even if your eyes are wrong, perhaps your nose is all right: can you smell that?" She leaned across and held the fresh, damp flowers to Diggle's ugly nose. But she had to jump back quickly in order to avoid a blow from his hard little fist.

"None of that!" he shouted. "How dare you! What do you mean by shoving a lot of filthy stable litter in my face? There was a thistle in it, too."

In spite of Lucy's good intentions and best efforts, the dwarfs clung to their belief that they'd been battered and imprisoned and were sitting in darkness and filth, awaiting their doom.

When Aslan came back from the land of his Father, the Emperor-Over-Sea, Lucy went to him. Grieved that the dwarfs would not see, she asked him to do something for them.

Aslan growled close to the dwarfs, but they cautioned one another not to believe in the sound because it was a hoax. He set a feast before them.

They ate and drank, but they could only taste things found in a stable. For them Aslan's feast was hay, an old turnip, raw cabbage leaves, and "dirty water out of a trough that a donkey's been at!"

Their feast ended in a brawl, as each fought the other to get what little he had. When it was all over, they who had been in the presence of the Lion and could have had everything, were left with nothing more than their boastful cry, "The dwarfs are for the dwarfs."

"You see," said Aslan. "They will not let us help them. They have chosen cunning instead of belief. Their prison is only in their own minds, yet they are in that prison; and so afraid of being taken in that they can not be taken out."

There's no more powerful description in literature of the condition of the men and women who refuse the rule of Christ in the Millennium. I've read it a hundred times, and it always moves me to tears: not for the fictional dwarfs of Lewis's tale, but for the hosts of earth who are so convinced of the reality of their prison they won't let Christ take them out.

The Millennium is the final unmasking of the deceitfulness of the human heart and the ultimate evil of sin. We who bray about peace and fairness, who want a "better world" for our children, who pontificate on the ascent of man, will prefer our lie to God's truth.

Is the Millennium a divine charade acted out to vindicate God's plan?

Is it a thousand years in which the faithful are allowed to play-act at sovereignty and reward?

No.

It's the time when the bride of Christ is present on earth, revealed as the queen who will rule. She will offer bunches of violets to the masses of fallen humanity and have them rejected violently in the last battle.

It's the time when the Son of Man shall return in power and spread a table for His people in the presence of their enemies: a table that even enemies might share . . . if they would.

ALL'S WELL THAT ENDS WELL

There is pain and tribulation aplenty in these passages. But promises shine brightest in the dark. When Daniel's fourth beast rises up out of the fetid and roiling seas, the darkness of earth will reach its zenith. Then the Sun of Righteousness will arise with healing in His wings and the darkness that knew Him not will be scattered in His light.

It ends well, no matter how we get to the end. Or when.

God wants us to know that no matter what horrors of men might arise before, and what sufferings God's people might endure, we are sealed and kept by Him who was, is, and is to come.

Part 2 LANGUAGE

I KNOW YOU KNOW
WHAT YOU THINK I SAID . . .

The most recent books of the Bible are almost 2,000 years old. Therefore, the customs, ideas, and common everyday knowledge that was shared by the apostles and their first-century readers are as foreign to us as the rhythm of village life in Indonesia's remotest valleys.

Even if we could come to the text with intimate knowledge of the history and folkways of biblical times, to read the Bible the way it was written would require an understanding of three ancient languages that only a few scholars can claim. The Bible I read is an English translation, and all of us who read our Bibles in translation stand one step removed from reading it the way it was written.

Every translation, no matter how literally the translators intended to duplicate the original, is to some extent an interpretation because no two languages are alike in vocabulary, grammar, or thought.

A missionary friend of mine is fond of reminding me that English has no decent word for "worship." Although we think we know what *worship* means, it's not because our English word for it tells us. If it did, we wouldn't hear so many sermons, see so many articles, or have such heated disagreements over worship in the Christian community.

Some things that can be said easily in one language, can hardly be said at all in another.

I served as an intern under a remarkable man who is both a brilliant scholar and a godly pastor. One of his multitude of talents is the ability to preach in Swedish as well as English. This ability stood him in good stead in the community his church served, because many people there had grown up speaking Swedish (the way they knew the Lord intended). Every year or so he'd be called to conduct a Swedish service where they could sing, pray, and hear some good preaching, all in Swedish. On occasion, when Dr. Nelson was preaching to his regular, largely

English-speaking congregation, he'd stop in mid-sentence, assume a characteristically pensive look, and then say, "I can't think of a good way to say this in English, but in Swedish it would be. . . ," and then favor us with a phrase or two in that language.

All we transplanted Irishmen, Germans, and assorted Anglo-Saxons would scratch our heads in bewilderment at this, but those old Swedes would beam with new understanding, certain they'd heard the Word exactly the way the apostles had written it!

Translators are faced with Dr. Nelson's predicament on every page of the Bible. A word or phrase that makes perfect sense in Greek or Hebrew may have no English equivalent, but only rarely do they dare say, "I can't think of a way to say it in English, but in Hebrew it would be . . ."

The chance of there being any Hebrews or Greeks from the old country to understand that word are zilch. The translator needs to make an informed judgment on what English word, or group of words, comes closest to the meaning of the original. As any comparison of English translations will show, there are many places on almost every page where the informed judgment of different translators is simply not the same.

The first verse of the Bible offers a good illustration. The KJV reads, "In the beginning God created the *heaven* and the earth." The NIV, along with most contemporary translations, translates the same Hebrew word as *heavens*. The difference that one letter can make in the way we understand the verse is profound.

For us, the word *heaven* overflows with theological meaning. Heaven is the dwelling place of God. It is the home that all believers look forward to some day. It's the place that is as high above the earth in splendor, majesty, peace, and holiness, as God is above humanity. The word *heaven* rings with the anthems of angelic choruses and the shouts of adoration rising from the throats of God's people gathered around His throne. It would be hard for most of us to read Genesis 1:1 and not hear the echoes of that sound.

With the single letter *s* added, however, those overtones are hushed. Moses wrote not about heaven, but about the heavens, not about pearly gates and golden streets, but about the vast expanses of the universe. The reason there is a difference in the two translations is that translation work involves far more than looking up Hebrew words in a Hebrew/English dictionary and finding their English equivalents.

In this case, although the words themselves are among the first learned by beginning Hebrew students, Genesis 1:1 uses them in a figure of speech.

Scholars call it *hendiadys* (hen-DIE-a-dees). In *hendiadys* a writer will use two words, linked by the conjunction *and*, to convey a single concept. *Flesh and blood* is a good example of hendiadys. When we speak of flesh and blood we usually mean natural, material, human life, as opposed to supernatural, immaterial, or non-human.

The KJV translators rendered Matthew 18:17, "Blessed art thou, Simon-Barjona, for *flesh and blood* hath not revealed it unto thee, but my father which is in heaven." If we read the same verse in the NIV, we see that the translators recognized the figure of speech and translated it using the single word *man.*

Both translations are accurate, although in this instance I prefer the King James because it retains the figure of speech Jesus used to make his statement more colorful and memorable. That's what figures of speech are for. In reducing the hendiadys to its ultimate meaning, the NIV translators were accurate but they robbed Jesus' statement of its poetry.

Understanding Genesis 1:1 as an example of hendiadys yields the meaning: "In the beginning God made everything that is, without exception." Moses opened the recorded revelation of God's activity with the magisterial pronouncement, so vital in the polytheistic world of ancient Israel, that nothing existed without the creative Word of God. To today's non-theistic world it says that God's creative act included everything the eye of humanity could see and the mind of humanity could imagine. Every new scientific discovery has already been explained as merely another fragment of God's handiwork.

THE GREEKS HAD A PARTICIPLE FOR IT

No one who has struggled with the first year of a language will ever forget the frustration of translating every word in an exercise perfectly, according to the dictionary, learning exactly what every word meant, and coming up with a sentence that might have been composed by an orangutan pounding on a typewriter with a ball-peen hammer. As slippery as the meaning of words can be, however, understanding their meaning is the easiest part of translation. Words are only the building blocks of language. Without the mortar of grammar to hold them together, they have about as much meaning as the barking of dogs or the cackling of chickens.

Knowing how difficult it is to translate words directly from Hebrew to English, think how much more difficult it is to translate the grammar of Greek or Hebrew into English. In Hebrew, for example, there are not tenses as we think of them in English. Struggle with that for a minute. Hebrew tenses have more to do with kinds of action than time. Hebrew verbs are concerned with such questions as:

Is an act completed?

Is it ongoing?

Is it intensified or turned back on the one who did it?

So how do we get Hebrew verbs into English, where sense of time is so important?

The two Hebrew "tenses" are called "perfect" and "imperfect." The Hebrew perfect tense is usually translated into the English past or perfect tenses. It isn't always precise, but it gets the job done. What it really tells us is that an action has already been completed in the past, or is so certain that it can be spoken of as complete even though it won't actually take place until some time in the future.

Prophets used the perfect tense in this latter sense, so it's called the "prophetic perfect." An event can be far in the future from the perspective of the prophet, but since the act is promised by God it can be spoken of as if it had already happened. The time sense of the tense is past, but the action is still future.

When God promised Abraham, "To your descendants I *give this land*" (Genesis 15:18), He spoke in the perfect tense. Even though He spoke to Abraham 600 to 800 years before the promise was fulfilled, it could be spoken of as a fact of human history because it was already accomplished in the mind of God.

Translation is an incredibly complicated process. That beloved phrase of some preachers, "If you could only read it in the original language. . . ," contains a kernel of truth. (Most of us preachers can't actually *read* it in the original language, either, but we like our congregations to think we can!) But if we can't read it in the original language, we'll never actually read it "the way it's written."

OF THE MAKING OF TRANSLATIONS THERE IS NO END

As difficult as translation is, however, godly scholars through the ages have labored diligently to bring the Word of God to His people in languages they can read and understand. Even before the time of Jesus, devout Jews in Alexandria had translated the Old Testament into Greek for the growing number of people who no longer spoke, or read, Hebrew. The Roman scholar Jerome rendered the Greek and Hebrew into the Latin of the common people in the fourth century A.D. Wycliffe and Tyndale performed the same service for the English-speaking world. The German translation of Martin Luther has held the same place of honor among German speakers as the Authorized, or King James Version has among English speakers.

Through the work of translators on the committees that gave us the New American Standard Bible, the New King James Version, Today's English Version (Good News Bible), and the New International Version, believers today have access to God's revelation in language they can understand and trust. Beyond our English-speaking world, numerous Bible Societies, teams of Bible translators, and men and women from a multitude of mission boards strive to reduce non-written languages to written forms so that residents of the Third World can also read the words of God.

In many ways, the process of Bible translation testifies to one of God's great, on-going miracles. He not only inspired Scripture, but He continues to oversee the faithful transmission of His Word. An infallible original would be of little value if the copy we read is riddled with error. Our Bibles are so faithfully preserved that we can read our English translations with nearly the same confidence and reverence as the first century church read its personal letters from the apostles. No important doctrine or teaching of Scripture is subject to question because of the problems with translation that I've mentioned earlier. The ideas that God taught His prophets and apostles are accessible to us today, even though we are sometimes unable to fine-tune our interpretation the way we'd like.

Problems in interpretation usually arise out of isolated passages dealing with obscure issues. When it comes to knowing how to be saved, how to live the Christian life, or what God requires of us, we need have no doubts about the reliability of our Bibles.

Think of it! God's self-revelation took place over thousands of years, to people who spoke at least three different languages, and lived lives as foreign to us as the lives of an Afghan nomad or a Vietnamese rice farmer. Yet we and others from all over the world can read that revelation, learn from it, grow by it, and meet the God whose book it is!

LITTLE PIECES OF KITTY, AND OTHER MYSTERIES

The problems in translation aren't all on the side of biblical languages. The English language also places a barrier between us and the Bible. The language we speak both shapes and limits our understanding. We interpret the unfamiliar in terms of what we already know.

When my wife was about two and one-half years of age she was introduced to her first litter of kittens. Peering into the box and seeing those tiny, squirming creatures, she exclaimed, "Look, Mommy! Little pieces of kitty!"

No one today, including my wife, knows exactly what reasoning process was going on in her young mind. Perhaps she thought someone very naughty had dropped the cat and it had shattered into "little pieces of kitty."

The sayings of children, filtered as they are through such limited experiences, are filled with examples like this. To understand sights, experiences, and ideas far beyond their powers of comprehension children translate them into terms of their familiar world. We find their statements amusing and adorable. We treasure them because they outgrow that sort of thing so quickly. Or do they?

In the late 60's or early 70's some ingenious graphic artist devised that maddening bumper sticker that said JESUS in large white, block letters on a black background. It sounded straightforward, but it was a visual riddle. The artist ran his white letters to the limit of the page, eliminating their outer edges. To read block letters, our minds depend on those dark borders. Without them, we are forced to interpret the word from outside our usual experience.

Almost everyone I knew tried to find letters in the black shapes because experience teaches us that letters are printed black on white. That led quickly to frustration. Only after we learned to read the white spaces and allow the black to recede into the background did the name of Jesus become visible.

We can almost hear Him saying, "If you have eyes to see, then see."

Our problem was perceptual. We were not used to seeing letters presented that way and our minds refused to process the otherwise obvious information. Even today, knowing what the sign says, I have to struggle when I see it to make my mind overcome the conventions it's used to working with.

This illustrates, in a trivial way, a problem that sometimes obscures our understanding of Scripture. Our known world limits our abilities to understand what is unknown. Our use of language is one of the most subtle forces at work in shaping our perceptions.

In recent works on decision making, its effect would be called "framing." We "frame" an issue when we start out with assumptions of what can and can't be. Because we think in words, we will usually perceive reality in forms for which our language has words and ignore realities for which we have no language.

Because words are arbitrary symbols, they take on whatever meaning we give them. For instance, near Wausau, Wisconsin, stands a hill named "Rib Mountain." To people from Colorado, the word *mountain* conjures up images of the majestic Rockies, so they would laugh at Rib Mountain. It rises out of the north woods to the lofty height of 1,950 feet. It's not Mount McKinley, or even Long's Peak, but for those who live in the flatlands of northern Wisconsin, it's the closest thing to a mountain they've got.

One of my favorite students was a bright young woman who'd come from Hawaii to attend school among God's frozen people. After the first mild snow fall in November, I asked her how she liked it. She'd never seen snow before and thought it was beautiful and fun.

The following spring, after five months of living the semi-snowbound life of a Minnesotan, I asked her whether or not she still thought winter was fun. As I'd expected, the fun had worn pretty thin by that time.

Prior to her experience, how could I have explained adequately to Vicki what living through that winter would be like? She had never even seen frost, let alone 19 inches of snow in one day.

I had a seminary classmate from Nagaland, India. He had grown up in a village that probably hadn't changed much in hundreds of years. One day shortly before we graduated and he returned to minister among his people, I invited him to speak at the church I was working in. On the way home we stopped at a fried chicken place for lunch. As we ate, he began to laugh, thinking about the problem he'd have explaining Colonel Sanders to his people. In his village, if you wanted a chicken dinner you first had to catch the chicken. Depending on the comparative athletic abilities of the catcher and the catchee, that procedure alone might take longer than it took us to order, eat, wash our hands on the packaged towelettes, and leave. He finally decided it would be better not to mention it because they'd never believe him.

People from his village might understand "chicken dinner," but there was no way to convey the image of a red-and-white striped box filled with pre-caught, pre-killed, pre-cleaned, pre-cooked chicken.

The Bible often presents us with similar perception problems. Psalm 1 was written from the semi-arid climate of southern Palestine. In most of that country, wild trees are rare. Yearly rainfall barely supports scrub vegetation, and in some places the deserts are as desolate as any in the world.

When the psalmist wrote of "a tree planted by the streams of water, which yields its fruit in season and whose leaf does not wither," he knew that trees growing away from the steady water supply of canal, river, or oasis were doomed to fruitlessness, if not death. When the burning desert winds blew from the east, the trees whose roots had no constant source of water, withered, lost their leaves, and struggled to survive.

Readers from the American southwest understand the power of that image better than I do. As I look out my dining room window at a grove of trees in their spring foliage, I have to struggle to see trees as the psalmist saw them.

When the woman with the issue of blood touched the hem of Jesus' robe, Jesus said, "I perceive that virtue is gone out of me" (Luke 8:46, KJV). Today, virtue is a feminine word, often a synonym for chastity. Generations of preachers have struggled to make sense of what it meant for Jesus to lose virtue. But virtue had a different meaning in Elizabethan England when the KJV was translated. The word in the Greek text was *dunamis* (DUNE-a-miss), and it meant power. How different the verse is in the NIV, where we hear Jesus saying, "Power has gone out of me."

What meaning fills our mind when we read the word *church* in Scripture? Biblically, it never refers to a building, nor to an organization. Yet in our world confusion exists between the building, the organizational structure, and the true church. To avoid this damaging confusion the Pilgrims, when they landed in Plymouth in 1620, built a "meeting house," not a church. They understood, as the writers of the New Testament had, that they themselves were the church. Now, after centuries of intermingling meanings, the word needs to be qualified very carefully to avoid confusion.

Even when dealing with words in our own language, the meanings intended by the translator and the meaning our background has taught us may not be the same.

How loaded with meanings words can be! Whether Greek or German, Hebrew or English, they all carry burdens of meaning far beyond our casual understanding. The fullness of language is a great gift, but when it comes to precise understanding of Scripture, it can be a great stumbling block in the way of "reading it the way it's written."

CHAPTER 3

PRINCIPLES

12 Do not interpret figures of speech literally.

13 In dealing with types, look for one or two points of correspondence between a real, literal, historical Old Testament phenomenon and its greater New Testament fulfillment.

QUESTIONS

22 The Bible says Jacob was born grasping Esau's heel. Does Jacob really mean "heel-grasper" and "supplanter" (Genesis 25:26)?

23 Why did God tell Jeremiah to look at an almond tree so He could tell him that He was watching (Jeremiah 1:12)?

24 Why did Jesus say He was going to build His church on Peter (Matthew 16:18)?

25 When the psalmist said that God is with us in the heavens and in the depths, does that mean God is in hell too (Psalm 139:8)?

26 Did Jesus put a limit on the number of times we should forgive somone's sin against us (Matthew 18:22)?

27 How can a God who loves the whole world say "I have loved Jacob, but Esau I have hated" (Malachi 1:2–3)? How could Jesus say that people couldn't be His disciples unless they hated their fathers and mothers (Luke 14:26)?

28 A camel can't go through a needle's eye, so was Jesus saying that a rich person can't be saved (Luke 18:23–25)?

29 Jesus told His disciples to ask Him anything and He would do it. That can't mean anything! What if we ask for something wicked (John 14:14)?

TO BE OR NOT TO BE, THAT IS THE GZORNENPLATT

14 Let Scripture interpret Scripture.

30 How could people from every nation under heaven have been present in Jerusalem on the day of Pentecost (Acts 2:5)?

31 Why does the Bible call the moon a light when we know it's only a dead globe that reflects the light of the sun (Genesis 1:15–16)?

32 How is it possible to use the same name (Morning Star) to talk about Jesus (Revelation 22:16) and Satan (Isaiah 14:12)?

33 I've been told Song of Songs (Song of Solomon) is a picture of Christ and the church, but it doesn't sound like that to me. What is the book about and why is it in the Bible?

34 When John the Baptist said that Jesus would baptize with the Holy Spirit and with fire, I understand what he means by the Holy Spirit. What is the fire he promises (Matthew 3:11)?

35 Why would anyone want to graft a branch from a wild olive onto the trunk of a domestic tree? Would that give good olives (Romans 11:17–24)?

36 What does it mean that with the Lord a day is like a thousand years and a thousand years is like a day (2 Peter 3:8)?

37 Why is Christ called the "Son of Man"? What does it mean?

38 Why did John use the number 666 as a sign for the Antichrist (Revelation 13:18)?

True comedians can get laughs without being obscene, and Bob Newhart is one of the best. He has a "button-down mind." One of his routines I remember best was called "An Infinite Number of Monkeys."

Newhart imagined an immense building filled with monkeys and typewriters. There they sat, day in and day out, like some simian secretarial pool, typing gibberish while human monitors watched for signs of genius.

Two chimp checkers, bored with their work, began comparing notes. Like workers everywhere they complained about the job. They griped about the poor dumb apes and their failure to produce anything that even remotely resembled human communication. Then, with a note of excitement, one monitor called his co-worker over to inspect the work of a particularly precocious ape who almost, but not quite, achieved greatness.

"Hey Pete! I think this one's got something! This sounds famous or something. ' To be or not to be, that is the—gzornenplatt?'"

Twenty-five years ago everyone laughed at Newhart's joke because we all knew the last word should have been "question." No other set of English letters would work. But at that level of linguistic theory, why not *gzornenplatt?* Or for that matter, why not *elbow?*

Although our mental furniture includes countless words that have absolute connection with things, places, and ideas, there is nothing about those words that requires them to mean anything at all. Words are only arbitrary sounds that we agree stand for a particular idea.

Most of us think of language as a fixed and serious thing, but in fact it is a very slippery and frolicsome creature. Under the right circumstances, Newhart's *gzornenplatt* could easily become a usable word along with *malaprop, gargantuan,* and *quixotic,* all the product of gifted writers' imaginations.

Our language is full of words that sound just as funny and have taken on their meanings in ways that aren't much less silly. For example, people talk about *bugs* in computers. Back in the primitive days of computer development, a moth got caught in a mechanical switch that made the first computers work. Once the technicians had gotten the *bug* out of the system, it worked fine. Problems in computers have been bugs ever since.

A writer may make up a new word if none of those available suit his purpose. Lewis Carroll gave us *chortling*, a laugh caught somewhere between a chuckle and a snort.

Edgar Allan Poe invented *tintinnabulation* to try to capture the sound silver bells might make.

A hundred years ago, who knew the word *television*? And who today would think of calling a bicycle a *velocipede*.

Because we use language to give orders to employees, instruct children, pass on news of world disasters, project rockets into space, and talk customers into buying, we forget how much pleasure there can be in the use of language.

Words like *bop, tinkle, crash, rumble*, and *roar* all sound like the action they express. English teachers call this phenomena, *onomatopoeia*. Such words add color and zest to language.

Whenever I think of masters of colorful language, I remember Reverend Gordon K. Peterson, Sr., the man I will always think of as my pastor. He may not have known *onomatopoeia* if it bopped him on the head, but he put words together in a way that made my scalp tingle and my belly laugh, depending on his purpose.

He'd talk about "things so exciting they'd make an Egyptian mummy shout," or "people so sour they walked around with faces as long as trombone cases." He once described the early life of a missionary friend who'd been saved from alchoholism and a lot of other things: "His life was so bad, it made a black mark on tarpaper."

He told about having dinner with a non-Christian businessman. During the conversation, Reverend Peterson started talking about the Lord. The businessman started to choke and sputter and spit green beans. Reverend Peterson's summation of that dinner? "I just about got a stucco job defending the faith!"

And then he'd laugh. Not just a genteel little chuckle, but great peals of laughter. How he loved his Lord and how he loved to talk about him in joyful, funny, colorful language.

What I miss more than anything about the way most commentaries and preachers treat the Bible is the lack of color in their language. The Bible is a book people have loved and enjoyed for thousands of years, and we treat it as if it were as lifeless and colorless as last week's mashed potatoes.

Jesus came from a long line of Hebrew speakers who peppered their inspired messages with the most colorful and imaginative language. He talked in technicolor. His teachings stuck in the mind with the tenacity of sand burrs in a wool sock. His language and characters throbbed with life.

It's almost impossible to speak English today and not rely on centuries-old expressions, many biblical, that still add life to our language. We all know what a *prodigal son* is. *Whited sepulchres* are hypocrites. People today are still *weighed in the balance.* Young romantics dream of finding the *apple(s) of (their) eye(s).* And as we get older, we prepare to deal with an assortment of *thorn(s) in the flesh.*

Images like these make concepts memorable. God didn't inspire a Bible that reads like the annual report of Acme Buggywhip and Paper Clip, Inc. He wanted His word to be memorable. And to make it that way, He used every stylistic twist available in a Greek or Hebrew writer's arsenal.

Some Christians write as if figures of speech are for children, as if the real meat lies in the statement of theological propositions. What a shame they didn't tell God before He wrote the Bible. He probably would have inspired a vastly different book if they had.

Don't get me wrong. Theological propositions are fine, as far as they go. But sadly, no matter how gifted or profound the theological insight, the work will lack vividness and life unless the writer follows in the path God himself blazed when He chose to speak in living color.

Saying that God is *omniscient* is essentially the same as saying that "the eyes of the LORD range throughout the earth" (2 Chronicles 16:9). Both need interpretation, but which one will stick with you longer?

We can say that the Lord protects the righteous, or we can say, "The Lord is my rock my fortress and my deliverer . . . my rock, in whom I take refuge . . . my shield and the horn of my salvation" (Psalm 18:2).

We can proclaim Christ as the vicarious atonement for the sins of humanity or we can call him the *Lamb of God, who takes away the sin of the world* (John 1:29).

Who would want to exchange the vital, resonant language of Scripture for the lifeless, technical propositions favored by some theologians? This isn't to say those propositions aren't important or that those theologians aren't doing important work. Nor do I believe that technical language can't teach us things with a precision that we need at times. It is to say, though, that the reduction of the language of Scripture to the theological propositions of twentieth-century minds will always lose something of the richness and depth of God's own chosen form of revelation. The inspired poets we call prophets and apostles gave us a Word in technicolor, in language and concept so vivid and brilliant that it has, for centuries, drawn even the unbeliever to it.

P **rinciple 12**   Do not interpret figures of speech literally.

As custodians of the Word, we seem frightened by the life we encounter there, frightened by the brilliance of the unfathomable wealth of Word and Thought. In that fear we seem intent on reducing the Word of the World Maker to the words of technicians. In a nutshell, the Bible is filled with colorful figures of speech that are there on purpose. When we let the Bible speak in its own accent, without dulling the impact of the language it uses, it speaks much more clearly and forcefully. To let it do that, we need to know when we're reading a figure of speech, what kind it is, and how to understand it.

Someone, somewhere, is sure to argue that figurative language is less precise and needs to be reduced to a more technical form for proper understanding. But poetic speech and technical speech each have their own purposes. A poem or figure of speech is destroyed when it's "reduced" to technical language. If the speaker or writer had intended the purposes assumed by technical language, they would have used it. The choice of figurative language demands that we look for meaning in the figure, not in some more technical evaluation of it.

The problem with technical language is that the more precise it becomes, the narrower the audience to whom it has meaning. The fact is, the communication of ideas from one person to another by any kind of language at all is one of God's great miracles. One Christian expert in language said that real communication among people who speak the same language, grew up in the same part of the country, and are approximately the same age, takes place only about 75 percent of the time.

And yet human language is the medium God has chosen to speak to us. This has seemed so improbable to students of Scripture that for centuries some thought that the Greek of the New Testament was a special language God had devised just for the use of the writers and readers of the Bible. This idea came about because the Greek of the New Testament is enough different from the classical Greek most older scholars were trained in that it seemed like a special, distinct language. Since it didn't conform to the rules of the classical Greek language of Plato and Aristotle, they thought it was devised especially for the writing of Scripture.

Not until the nineteenth century did it become apparent that the New Testament was written in the everyday tongue of common people. How appropriate. As He did with His Son, God sent us His Word in a uniquely human package. Jesus wasn't some mystic projection of divine principle, and the Bible was not written in some secret, esoteric language that we need to learn to understand Scripture.

Neither the original languages of Scripture nor the English into which it has been translated is a technical specialist's language. We can read it as we would read the morning paper or a letter from a friend. On the other hand, we need to learn to read the Bible the way we would read the morning paper or a letter from a friend.

No. There's no echo in here, and the above paragraph is not an editorial oversight. In this case, the bad news is also the good news. The problem with the way we read the Bible is that we treat it as if it were written in the language of heaven. When we make that mistake, we tend to understand everything we read as if it were delivered at the Midwest Sectional Meeting of the Philosophical Straight Talkers Association. If Jesus speaks, He must intend some special meaning quite apart from our prosaic, everyday understanding. But He didn't speak the language of heaven. He spoke the language of the streets and the common people.

Because we treat the language of Scripture as something above normal human language, we often miss important meanings hidden in the common uses of language. We miss the humor, the poetry, the irony, the anger, and the joy. To read God's word with understanding, we need to recapture its human voice—its puns, exaggerations, and symbolisms.

LIVING IN GRASS HOUSES

Somewhere along the line, some literalistic, English-speaking killjoy concluded that the pun is the lowest form of humor. He probably prepared statistical analyses for some government agency.

The pun is a form of humor that's nearly universal. Any language with words that have similar sounds and different meanings will develop, and delight in, puns.

An island king hid his golden throne in the attic of his grass house to protect it from pirates. Unfortunately for him, the heavy throne came crashing down on his head, killing him.

The moral?

People who live in grass houses shouldn't stow thrones.

I used to tell my Old Testament history students that I was going to make my fortune in a chain of barbeque restaurants with an Assyrian atmosphere. I was going to name it "Sennacheribs." After they thought about it for a few minutes, they groaned just as you are doing.

Hebrew may be the most pun loving language ever. What's more, God himself made puns. Unfortunately, puns are the form of expression most easily lost in translation. What makes a statement funny or profound in one language may have no equivalent in a different language. Reams of meaning are lost when Hebrew puns haven't been translated into English. Yet when puns go untranslated, no one even misses them.

For example, the names *Saul* and *Samuel* work wonderfully to stress the contrasts between God's plan for His peoples' king and their own plan.

Hannah went to the temple to pray for a son who would relieve the burden of her childlessness and silence the taunts of her husband's second wife. When the child was born, she gratefully named him *Samuel*, or "God has heard." The child himself was proof of that. Samuel, as Israel's only prophet/priest/judge, was a constant reminder that God did indeed hear the prayers of His people. The name Saul, on the other hand, was a constant reminder to everyone who read about his troubled reign that he was exactly what Israel had asked for. Israel begged for an earthly king so they could be like other nations (1 Samuel 8:5). In doing so, they rejected God as their king.

God granted their request, but the Israelites suffered the consequences of their foolish request. The name *Saul* is a Hebrew word that means "the one asked for." The two names emphasize God's gracious action in Samuel and Israel's rebellious action in asking for a king. "God has heard" is a frequent Old Testament way of saying someone's prayer has been answered. There was no prayer involved with Saul, only a demand.

Hannah's prayer was answered, and her son was God's answer to Israel's need. Saul was named king at the insistence of a people tired of relying on Him. They wanted a human being they could turn to in time of need, and they got exactly what they asked for, but not exactly what they wanted.

A native reader of Hebrew could not read 1 Samuel without being reminded that when they forgot how God could hear their prayers, they got exactly what they asked for.

Puns can be found on practically every page of the Hebrew Bible. They also come through from time to time in the New Testament. When we don't realize we're reading one, we may be confused because the literal translation of the pun doesn't speak with the authority of the original.

Question 22   The Bible says Jacob was born grasping Esau's heel. Does Jacob really mean "heel-grasper" and "supplanter" (Genesis 25:26)?

Heel-grasper does sound like an odd name for a mother to give her son. And supplanter sounds even worse. But then, my grandmother named my father Loraine. Odd name for a man. He called himself Lee, and he liked to tell about Peggy and Dorothy, two of the linemen who worked for him when he was a foreman for the REA in North Dakota. He insisted those were their given names (and that was in the days before linepersons included women).

When it comes to names, there's no accounting for taste. One way to explain Jacob's odd name is that it is prophetic. God gave Rebekah a message that the older of the twins she was bearing would serve the younger (Genesis 25:23). With this knowledge, she would be able to name Jacob, prophetically, *the supplanter.*

That's one way to understand why such a name might be given to a child, and it makes sense. But that isn't the only way to explain Jacob's odd name. And I don't even think it's the best.

Part of what makes this problem trickier than it first seems is the root word from which Jacob's name is formed. Its meaning isn't at all clear. In fact, it isn't even clear what the root for Jacob is. One of the standard Hebrew dictionaries warns us of this at the beginning of its definition.

But commentators say that the verb was actually formed from the word heel. Somebody overtaking a rival from behind might trip him by grabbing him by the heel (although anyone who has ever played tackle football knows how difficult that is). Even so, it could lead to the development of a word for usurper or supplanter that began with the simple noun *heel.*

But there's another way of looking at it. *Jacob-el* was a common name in those days. It meant something like *God will protect* or *God will follow at your heel* (with the idea that he would protect). A mother might name a child that. Maybe that was the original intent in the name Jacob.

But that name sounds so much like the Hebrew word for heel that even a fine name like *God will protect* would remind people of the noteworthy fact that Jacob was born chasing his brother.

This would form the root of a two-layered pun. Jacob, which is a shortened form of what may have been the full name, sounds remarkably like the word *heel.* It also sounds a lot like a word that means to cheat or deceive. We see that level of the pun in Genesis 27:36.

The tragedy in the story of Jacob's deception is as pathetic a scene as we find in the Old Testament. Jacob's father was on his death bed. His house was divided because he favored the older son and his wife favored the younger. The two brothers were as different as two men could be: the one slick as a greased snake and dominated by his mother; the other a macho man whose world was in the strength of his arm, the aim of his bow, and the gruff power with which he took what he wanted.

The despised younger son and the beloved wife conspired to take away the thing poor old Isaac held most dear—the blessing he had reserved for Esau. The two blessings, as recorded in Genesis 27:27–29, 39–40, gave a clear picture of Isaac's feelings for his two sons. The one intended for Esau used up all the good available to Isaac to pass on to his heir. It was clearly designed to leave nothing of worth for Jacob. We know this from the pitiful, hopeless blessing left over for Esau after Jacob deceived his father into giving him the one reserved for his brother.

When Esau discovered that Jacob had stolen what was rightfully his, he groaned, "Isn't he rightly named *Jacob* [Yah-ah-COVE]? *He has deceived* me [Yah-eh-CAVE]" (Genesis 27:36).[1]

The man who would one day wrestle with God began his life grappling with his brother. While his mother probably named him *God will protect,* he went through his early life giving the lie to that noble prayer, but filling the pun on his name with bitter meaning in his relationship with Esau.

Moses showed us this conflict when he recorded the saying that "his brother came out, with his hand grasping Esau's heel [bah-ah-CAVE]; so he was named *Jacob,* [yah-ah-COVE]" (Genesis 25:26). The full irony of this situation is seen in Hosea (12:3), where the prophet talks about Jacob as the man who "in the womb . . . grasped his brother's heel; as a man he struggled with God."

Until that fear-filled night on the bank of the river Jabbok, Jacob's life shouted "cheater." He had fought with his brother, with his father, and with Laban. That night, he contended with God. In his struggles he became a new man whose old name took on new meaning. He was no longer the cheater, the contender with men of old, but the Man-Who-Wrestled-With-God.

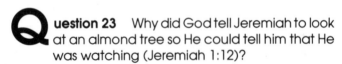

Q **uestion 23** Why did God tell Jeremiah to look at an almond tree so He could tell him that He was watching (Jeremiah 1:12)?

The almond tree is called the "watcher" because it blooms first in the year and therefore is watchful, or wakes up.

Although that's true, it wouldn't mean a hill of almond trees if there weren't more to it than that.

We don't know where Jeremiah's experience took place. We don't know if he saw a real almond tree or a vision of one. But we

---

1

In Hebrew, the word is longer than I show it here. I have taken some liberty to show the pun more clearly.

do know that God used this experience to call Jeremiah to serve Him as a prophet during Judah's last fitful days as an independent kingdom.

It was never easy to be a prophet, but it was doubly difficult when Babylon was beginning its rapid rise to world domination. In that fearsome historical setting, Jeremiah was called, a young and possibly timid man, a man who argued with God about the wisdom of His selection. To put his fears to rest, God gave a sign that would stay with him throughout his long and difficult ministry. That sign was the *almond tree*, the *watcher (shah-KADE)*.

Whenever Jeremiah saw that tree, especially early in the rainy season when it began to bloom long before the other trees, he would be reminded that God, too, was wakeful, watching (*show-KADE*) over His prophet and His promise to see that both came to the end He'd designed for them.

The pun was God's way of sealing His promise to Jeremiah. The sound of the two words was so close that the prophet could never look at the almond tree without remembering that it was God who watched.

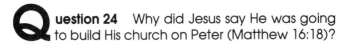 **uestion 24**   Why did Jesus say He was going to build His church on Peter (Matthew 16:18)?

Whenever Protestants tell me they take everything in the Bible literally, I ask how they understand Matthew 16:18. Catholics have interpreted it literally for centuries, and in doing so have defended the papacy.

I believe the statement is a pun, and there's probably not a more trying one in the whole Bible.

The disciples saw no statement of Peter's superiority in this verse. In Matthew 18:18, in fact, they were still debating who would be greatest in the kingdom. In Acts 15, with Peter in attendance, it was James who declared the judgment of the council.

I don't mean to play down Peter's importance in the history of the early church; but although the immediate context seems to favor Peter's elevation, the rest of Scripture seems to argue against it.

In this case, Matthew, working under the guidance of the Holy Spirit, offered us an inspired commentary on the pun. Speaking in Aramaic, Jesus would have used a single word for rock in both places. But writing in Greek, Matthew, who certainly understood what Jesus was getting at, supplied the second word to clarify.

Petros is the Greek for a boulder or rock detached from the bedrock. *Petra* is the bedrock itself. Matthew, as he translated Jesus' statement into Greek, supplied the clue that Peter was indeed the rock, but it would be on the bedrock that the church was built.

What was the bedrock he intended, if not Peter?

Most people point to the confession Peter had just made about the deity and lordship of Christ as the church's bedrock. On that foundation the church is built and will stand firm.

It's no wonder that the Devil, in his efforts to undermine the church, never tires in his attempt to undercut the true nature of our Lord. Once we make Jesus less than "the Christ, the Son of the Living God" we are again helpless and lost. It's the truth and content of Peter's statement, not the statement itself, that are the rock that will withstand the powers of hell.

But Jesus offered the disciples the keys to the kingdom. To some, this is the same as giving authority over the church. And in a way it is. But what we make of that depends on how we view the disciples. If the disciples were a special category of believers, somehow more spiritual, closer to the Lord, of greater worth in the kingdom, then they and their "heirs" were probably the earthly lords of the church.

But if the church is built on the foundation of the prophets and apostles in the sense that their writings are the God-given sourcebook for the life of faith, then that authority is something else again. For all the writing about the meaning of this verse, very little is said about the probable meaning of the keys for a first century reader.

In the affluent ancient household, the master seldom worried about the management of day-to-day affairs. For this they appointed a steward, a slave with training, integrity, intelligence, and loyalty.

The symbol of his office was a set of keys to the storerooms and to the places where the master's treasures were kept. The keys enabled him to deal with merchants and creditors. He was free to open and close, to pay, to contract, to oversee his master's house.

But he was never the lord of the house. He was always the slave who at any moment might be removed from his place if the master found him lazy, incompetent, or worst of all, dishonest.

I see this as the priesthood of the believer rather than the elevation of Peter. Peter stands as the prototype, not the fulfillment, of this promise.

The church, built on the Lordship of Christ, exercises the authority to work out on earth what is decreed in heaven. Rather than a license to run the show, the keys give believers the authority to study, know, and interpret Scripture for themselves, but always under the direction of the Master.

The church, which is a bland foretaste of the real kingdom, is under our control, but only when we operate it under the direction of the Master. The keys teach us that our job is to work in the best interests of the Master, and only under His direction.

I think the keys to the kingdom are talked about in Jeremiah 31:33: "I will put my law in their minds and write it on their hearts. I will be their God and they will be my people."

Or maybe in Joel 2:28, which says He will "Pour out [his] Spirit on all people. Your sons and daughters will prophesy, your old men will dream dreams, your young men will see visions."

The keys had not yet been given. They were promised. I think they were given on the day of Pentecost when, in fulfillment of His ages-old program, God created a people from every nation under heaven to be a people for His name.

So Jesus moved from a simple play on words to a majestic foretaste of the glory of God in His church. Not our church but the Master's. No one may lord it over the rest, for all who are built on the rock of the Lord Jesus have been given the Spirit of God as the mark of authority, and the firstfruits of the greater glory that is to come. With that power, and that promise, we will do what heaven decrees until heaven comes to earth to do for itself.

BIGGER IS MORE COLORFUL

If I had a dollar for every time I've seen a biblical exaggeration misunderstood, I'd be a millionaire.

Well, maybe not a millionaire. But I'd probably be several dollars wealthier.

You didn't believe for a minute that I'd come across a million misunderstandings of exaggeration in the Bible. Instead, you put my obvious exaggeration into your mental computer, checked it out against the way we use that kind of statement, and determined that I was talking about a large number, not a literal million. Even though I said a million, it was obvious to both of us that I intended it to stand for something else.

When it comes to the Bible, though, we shut down that computer. We don't screen for the figure of speech called *hyperbole* (high-PURR-bow-lee) because we know Jesus would never exaggerate. As children, we were all corrected often enough to learn that exaggeration is wrong.

That's where we often miss the point, because Jesus would, and did, exaggerate often. And He did it without lying. Hyperbole is a valid and valuable figure of speech. It's not intended to deceive, but rather to enrich speech by flavoring it with a pinch of humor.

This occurs often in Scripture because it was a favorite of the Hebrew people. If we're alert to it, we'll understand a lot more of the intent of several biblical authors.

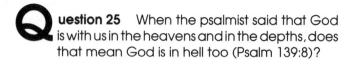

Q **uestion 25**   When the psalmist said that God is with us in the heavens and in the depths, does that mean God is in hell too (Psalm 139:8)?

I might turn that one on its head and ask if it means we are in heaven during our lifetime, or are we able to go both to heaven and to hell when our life is over. Or I might go on to verse 9 and ask if any of us has ever actually flown on the wings of the dawn?

This is poetry, and poetry is supposed to say things like that. Whether it's the timeless, soaring poetry of the Psalms or the relevant, pedestrian verse of today, poetry is characterized by such a density of language that a single line may carry paragraphs of meaning. The good poet is able, with a few well-chosen words, to awaken images in our minds that can take us from the heights to the depths and make all the stops in between.

It's also intended to be *evocative* and not *didactic*. In other words, poets, even biblical poets, use poetry to evoke a sense of dread, awe, and rapture rather than teach the dogmatic content of those senses. Poetry is a type of writing that is supposed to make us feel, not know.

This Psalm evokes the sense of the majesty and omnipresence of God. Although it touches the perimeter of the attribute of omnipresence, it's more concerned with the sense of wonder at the scope of God's interest and presence than it is with the theological delineation of the doctrine.

If asked, the psalmist would probably affirm the idea of omnipresence, at least as an ancient Israelite might put it. But he was swept away by the thought that his God—the God of his fathers and grand-fathers, of Abraham, Isaac, and Jacob—knew him, made him, loved him, and was never far from him.

Does he intend us to believe that God is somehow in hell as well as heaven?

I doubt it. Israel's awareness of life after death was sketchy at best. The Hebrew word *Sheol* used here doesn't mean hell in the New Testament sense. It can mean the grave, or, as in this verse, the depths, as the NIV translates it.

The intent here is to draw a line from the highest to the lowest and then say there's no point on the line where God can't be found, and no point along the line where the psalmist can escape His presence. And the psalmist says it in such a powerful way that we know its truth and feel it with the author when we read with the eye of faith and the heart that pants for God.

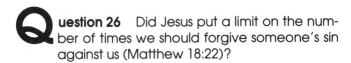

Q **uestion 26**   Did Jesus put a limit on the number of times we should forgive someone's sin against us (Matthew 18:22)?

Of course not. In fact, Jesus used numbers in this verse to say the opposite: that there is no practical limit on forgiveness. He did this by creating a number that means more when it's not literal.

In Genesis 4:15, God's grace toward the murderer Cain was promised using the number seven. If anyone hurt Cain, God said, He himself would insure that Cain would be avenged seven times over. This is one of those places where seven is a good round number meaning "enough." God does the right thing regardless of how often He has to do it.

In Genesis 4:24 the murderous Lamech killed a man in revenge. Flushed with victory he sang a song of triumph for his wives. In his song he mocked the sufficient vengeance of God by boasting that for any harm done him, he would multiply God's seven-fold vengeance by ten and then add another seven.

That's enough times a lot and then some.

Lamech's boast was excessive. The number he concocted, based on a perversion of God's promise, took him into the realm of massive retaliation and mutually assured destruction.

Peter may have had that familiar story in mind when he asked his question. "How many times should we forgive? Seven times? In keeping with God's promise of vengeance should we in this new kingdom forgive that many times?"

Jesus answered, "Not seven times. Not ten times seven times. But Lamech's ten times seven plus seven."

In Jesus' usage, seventy-seven becomes a symbolic reversal of the depths of vengeful violence symbolized by Lamech. It stands as a number that says fullness (seven) times a higher order of fullness (ten) plus fullness.

In other words, the believer is commanded by the Lord to be as forgiving as the non-believer is vindictive. What is the numerical value of our required forgiveness? Literally, we are to forgive seventy-seven times. But the true meaning is that there is no limit to the forgiveness commanded by the Lord.

Q **uestion 27**   How can a God who loves the whole world say "I have loved Jacob, but Esau I have hated" (Malachi 1:2–3)? How could Jesus say that people couldn't be His disciples unless they hated their fathers and mothers (Luke 14:26)?

These two questions can be solved rather simply, once we understand a common characteristic of Hebrew style. Hebrew, and its first cousin Aramaic, the language Jesus probably spoke, are languages that love extremes. They are vigorous, picturesque languages, which, while capable of great subtlety, are also at home with broad and excessive imagery.

That's right. I said excessive. The way Jesus used the words *love* and *hate* seems a little too rough for those of us more comfortable with a "tamer" language. We would paraphrase it by saying something like, "My feeling for Esau seems like hatred when compared with my love for Jacob." The language involved here is vivid, even shocking, but it makes its point memorably.

God chose the nation descended from the younger brother to be the channel for the blessing God promised Abraham. How loved and blessed Jacob (Israel) was! God passed over the nation that would descend from Esau (Edom), which later became the implacable enemy of Israel and was excluded from the development of God's Old Testament redemptive plan. What utter rejection and hatred that must have felt like!

Did God hate Esau? No. But he didn't choose him, either.

Did God love Jacob more than anyone else? Only in the sense that his line would be the line of the Messiah. He was chosen (i.e., loved) to receive the great privilege that went with great responsibility.

The same principle applies to hating our fathers and mothers for Jesus' sake. When compared with our love for Jesus, our love for father and mother is like hatred. The contrast here is between commitments. The Jesus who affirmed that not a jot or tittle of the Law would pass away didn't then command total disregard for one of its laws. He merely intended His hearers to know that their earthly loves and commitments had to be like hatred when compared with their love for and commitment to Him.

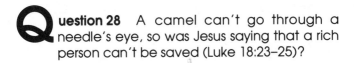

Q **uestion 28** A camel can't go through a needle's eye, so was Jesus saying that a rich person can't be saved (Luke 18:23–25)?

If that's true, poor Joseph of Arimathea, for all his love of Jesus, didn't make it. And Paul was wrong when he said, "God does not show favoritism" (Romans 2:11). So was Peter when he said the same thing in his sermon to the house of Cornelius (Acts 10:34).

Of course rich people can be Christians. But it's hard for people to rely on God when they have so many earthly things to rely on. That was Jesus' melancholy response to the departure of the rich young man who had come to Him for the secret of eternal life. He went away without what he'd sought because he was unwilling to forfeit the short-lived pleasure of wealth for the eternal joy of heaven.

To turn this tragic encounter into an event that would have a positive impact on somebody, Jesus created an image that still grips the imagination and sticks in the mind. His audience was familiar with camels. An indispensable beast of burden in the arid stretches of the ancient Near East, their bad tempers and stubbornness were well known. As was their great size. Jesus put that ungainly creature together with the common sewing needle to teach an important lesson.

Imagine an old Jewish grandmother getting ready to make her favorite grandson a new camel hair robe, and threading her needle with real camelhair, with the camel still in it!

The part of that image I don't care for comes when you put the thread in your mouth and try to lick it into a nice sharp point to fit into the needle's eye.

Yuck!

This is a vivid, graphic illustration of the point, already made, that it's impossible for a rich man to enter the kingdom. Of course we need to remember that, without a miracle of rebirth, it's impossible for any of us to enter the kingdom. Jesus had no intention of excluding the rich from heaven. Instead, he commented sadly on the young man's inability to let go of what he had to get what he couldn't live without.

Jesus used a hilarious image to make that sobering fact stick in people's minds. Maybe some of them were rich.

Some teach that Jesus was talking about the small door in the city gate of Jerusalem called the "needle's eye." This is a common explanation of Jesus' saying. That's not what He was getting at, though. There's a real bite to the expression when we think of it as hyperbole. It goes flat when we reduce the lesson to the level of a Holy Land travelogue.

Besides, there's never been any evidence, either textual or archeological, that such a gate ever existed. There were smaller gates, each with its own name. But none of those names was "the needle's eye."

I suppose someone with a particularly unimaginative streak looked at that image and found it unacceptable. Not recognizing it for what it was, he began to cast about for some logical explanation. In that frame of mind, he probably thought of the small doors beside the city gates in Medieval Europe. Logical, but wrong.

Don't let a humorless and slavish literalism rob this important lesson of its impact. If you're the kind of person who thinks you'll make it through this life and into the next on the strength of your wealth, personality, good looks, or connections, you would do well to remember that Jewish grandmother and her soggy camel.

 uestion 29   Jesus told His disciples to ask Him anything and He would do it. That can't mean anything! What if we ask for something wicked (John 14:14)?

Viewed from a literalistic perspective, this is a troubling statement. It's been perverted by some Christians into a promise of material wealth, physical well-being, and hedonistic happiness.

Jesus wasn't promising a heavenly Visa card with an unlimited line of credit, or a free shopping spree in heaven's treasure house. In fact, this promise of *anything* is severely limited by Jesus himself. This isn't hyperbole, strictly speaking, but it does illustrate how the most universal language can be qualified to become much less than universal.

There are two important qualifications in verses 13 and 14.

First, Jesus promised to do whatever the believer asks *so that the Son may bring glory to the father.* This is an indispensable element in understanding the miraculous working of God in Christ. The signs and wonders performed by Jesus were certainly of great benefit to the people for whom they were done. But the healings and exorcisms had a much greater purpose than to improve the lot of a few suffering Israelites. Those miracles were the signs that the power of God was abroad in the world, and Jesus was His instrument!

Jesus promised He would do whatever His followers asked *so that* the father would be glorified. Next time an investment banker in sheep's clothing tells you that God wants you rich, ask yourself if your elevation to the Fortune 500 will bring glory to God. Then ask yourself if your motivation for acquiring riches is only to bring glory to God.

If you can't honestly answer yes to both questions, I'd suggest He probably doesn't want you rich. He's got something much better for you than wealth that can be eaten by moths, destroyed by rust, or stolen by thieves.

The other qualification is that we're to ask *in His name.* I know, we end every prayer with the formula, "In Jesus name, amen." To our shame, we use that phrase like the magic words "please" and "thank you" we learned as children. We don't have to say the words to appropriate the power of praying in Jesus' name. And using the words won't magically transform selfish, carnal prayers.

To pray in Jesus' name is to pray the way Jesus himself would pray in our situations. It means placing ourselves under His authority and praying as faithful servants whose highest call and greatest joy is to please their Lord.

Will Jesus answer if we pray for something wicked?

Of course not.

Will He give us what we ask if we pray for things that will bring glory to His Father and are in accord with His purpose and person?

Every time. Anything. And that's no exaggeration.

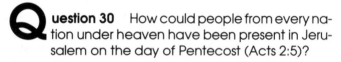

Question 30   How could people from every nation under heaven have been present in Jerusalem on the day of Pentecost (Acts 2:5)?

The text itself tells us where the visitors to Jerusalem had come from. Since they were described as God-fearing Jews, and since they were in Jerusalem for the festival of Pentecost, we know they were pilgrims there for religious reasons. They had come from those nations in the Mediterranean basin where Jews had been found since the dispersion of the nation had begun in 586 B.C.

Were they joined by wild Celts from Ireland, ancestors of the Aztecs from Mexico, and the Incas from Peru? Were there representatives from the forefathers of the Iroquois nation and the Sioux? Not according to verses 8–11.

Luke named representative nations present on that first Christian Pentecost, and they didn't extend beyond the ones known to Jews of Ezra's day.

If there were only people from the Mediterranean world, how could Luke say they were from every nation under heaven?

He could say it by using hyperbole. In this example there's a spiritual truth that outruns the best of Luke's limited human knowledge of the world and its people. First of all, his intention was not to give a census of the world or an anthropologist's catalog of peoples and tribes. He wrote Acts to continue the narrative oɪ *all*.

This is another good example of the use of hyperbole. To try to understand *all* with mathematical precision is a mistake. John records deeds and words of Jesus that Luke omits. If we understand it as hyperbole, meaning an account that includes all the pertinent information, we are closer to Luke's intent.

There's a theological point at stake here, too. To see it, we have to ask why God chose the day of Pentecost to send the Holy Spirit.

Most Christians today understand that God carefully chose the Passover for the death and resurrection of Jesus so people of His day, and every day afterward, would be reminded of the sacrifice of the Passover Lamb. What we don't bother to think about is the significance of Pentecost in the festival calendar of Israel. Passover inaugurates a period of fifty days that culminates in Pentecost. The name *Pentecost* comes from the word fifty.

Passover came at the beginning of the harvest season. In addition to commemorating the passover, it was also the festival at which the first sheaf of barley was presented to God as a wave offering. After fifty days, when the wheat harvest had been finished, two loaves of bread were offered as the first-fruit of the wheat. So the harvest was bracketed by these two festivals.

But Pentecost had other meanings as well. It also commemorated the scattering of the people at the tower of Babel, the place where the descendants of Noah were separated from one another by a confusion of languages. Pentecost was the day on which representatives of those same people were reunited by a momentary reversal of the confusion, making it the perfect day for the descent of the Spirit and the reunion of people from every nation under the sun.

This is why Luke could say, with theological truth, that there were men there from every nation under heaven. They were all there as representatives, as first-fruit, of a universal church that would grow to include men, women, and children from every-where and every time. This group would begin the process of carrying the good news beyond Samaria to the uttermost parts of the world.

A MANNER OF SPEAKING

Q **uestion 31**   Why does the Bible call the moon a light when we know it's only a dead globe that reflects the light of the sun (Genesis 1:15–16)?

This is just *phenomenological language.* In standard English it means that the biblical writers described things as they appeared rather than as they were.

Does the earth have four corners? Does the sun rise and set or move across the sky? Do flying fish and flying squirrels really fly? Do people really "sleep" in death?

No. But we speak as though they do. We use the language of appearance. If I were to go out at night when the moon was full (what would it look like empty?) on a clear autumn evening, I could probably read a newspaper by the light of the moon. I might even comment to someone that the moon is particularly bright.

I know better. I know the moon is a drab, cold rock circling our earth over 200,000 miles away. I know the source of its light is the sun; the moon is only a celestial mirror reflecting the sun's light somewhat inefficiently. Nevertheless, it seems bright.

The Bible does the same thing. It describes the moon, not the way an astronomer would to his colleagues, but the way human beings looking up from a darkened earth have described it ever since we've had a language to describe it.

Q **uestion 32**   How is it possible to use the same name (Morning Star) to talk about Jesus (Revelation 22:16) and Satan (Isaiah 14:12)?

Some preachers are fond of saying things like "Whenever you see the word ____ (you fill in the blank) it always means ____" Such remarks are heard a lot in Christian circles. For example, oil is always a symbol for the Holy Spirit. So is the wind. Leaven is always a symbol for evil. The fig tree is always a symbol of Israel. Darkness is always a symbol for sin. And on and on.

The fact of the matter is that oil is a symbol for the Holy Spirit, sometimes. That's true of the wind, too, sometimes. The fig tree does sometimes stand for Israel, and darkness is sometimes used to depict sin or sinfulness.

But no word always, invariably, without exception, means the same thing in every situation. That's the nature of words. Words are not absolute representations of things. They are only arbitrary symbols that stand for the things we say they stand for. If this were not so, the world would have only one language. Perhaps that was the case before the tower of Babel. When a Babelite said *elbow* maybe there was a direct, one-to-one correlation between the word and the thing. But in our world, with our confusion of languages, no language, not even Hebrew or Greek, uses words as anything more than an arbitrary approximation of the thing represented.

In this sense, all language is symbolic. Words are symbols for things, but only the speaker knows with certainty which things his or her symbol stands for. Some people are better communicators than others because they understand the complex relationship between their thought, the word they've chosen to represent it, and the reality it will waken in the minds of their listeners.

In Revelation 22:16, Jesus described himself as the Morning Star because the figure of speech, *Morning Star*, was filled with meaning for readers of the first century who were looking forward to the return of Messiah.

The prophecy of Balaam in Numbers 24:17 promised that a "star will come out of Jacob." Later history makes it clear that Balaam looked forward to the rise of David. But later Judaism saw more in that star. Jewish apocalyptic literature understood the star as a symbol of the coming Davidic king. The scholars of Qumran, who left us the Dead Sea Scrolls, saw this verse as a promise of the warrior king who would come to overthrow the children of darkness and their ruler. John used a metaphor that was both ancient and filled with meaning when he called Jesus the *star.*

But why the *morning* star?

For lonely shepherds, sailors, or soldiers on night watch, the Morning Star was the sign that dawn was just around the corner. It said to them that the dark, cold night was almost over.

Jesus, the Morning Star, is both the fulfillment of the Davidic promises and the promise that the long night of sin is about to end.

Satan is another matter. Isaiah 14 is difficult. It's so difficult in fact that although it is traditionally regarded as a description of Satan's fall, it is not a reference to Satan at all. Isaiah identifies his subject as the king of Babylon.

The verse that talks about the Morning Star is part of a "taunt song." Considered strange by our standards, it is a song of gloating over the fall of an enemy. It begins in verses 3–4a with an introductory remark that Israel will sing this taunt on the day when God relieves them from the oppression of this arrogant king. Verses 4b–8 contain a stanza describing the end of his reign and the universal celebration it brings.

Verses 9–11 take us into the dank halls of sheol, a word that speaks generally of the grave, not specifically of hell. Here the mighty of the world are gathered to welcome their peer, lamenting that he, like they, has come to the natural end of all men.

The real taunt begins in verse 12. The description of the king of Babylon should be read with a sneer. Isaiah used sarcasm to cast the splendor and pride of the fallen monarch in their true perspective. The one who thought of himself as the greatest and the mightiest, the most magnificent of earth's mighty, has fallen from the heights and his lot, like the lot of all who preceded him, is the grave.

In the eighteenth century, Adam Clarke resisted the temptation to explain this marvelous poetic section as a description of Satan's fall. In the nineteenth century, Keil and Delitszch called that sort of use unwarranted. Matthew Henry didn't even bother to refute the idea, but merely called the king a man who had fallen from the ultimate height of human power.

If we read the passage in its historical context, and allow the text to speak for itself, we see that Isaiah had no thought of Satan when he wrote it. He merely described the Babylonian king in the kind of exaggerated language that was common among the kings of the ancient Near East. If ever there was an effective use of hyperbole, this is it.

Understanding this, the problem disappears. Jesus was the true Morning Star. The king of Babylon thought it within his power to assault the people of God, and indeed the mountain of God, and with that assault declared himself in opposition to God and His plan. He styled himself the Morning Star, but proved, with his death, that the reality fell far short.

For the sake of argument, let's accept the traditional understanding of this verse. Let's say Satan really is the subject here.

There's still no problem. The word star is also used as a metaphor for angels. When a star falls from heaven in Revelation 9:1, it is to be understood as an angel, probably the fallen angel. When the morning stars sang together at creation (Job 38:7), it was probably the same choir that greeted the birth of Christ. If we must have a description of Satan here, it's well within the uses of biblical metaphor.

Even if Satan is the subject of this verse, I think we're still justified in reading it as sarcasm, or at least irony. We know who the real Morning Star is. Wouldn't it be ironic if Satan should be called by that title as he hurtles earthward in punishment for the pride of his rebellion? Think of it. Instead of the Morning Star he wanted to be, he would become the ultimate shooting star.

Biblical symbols must be interpreted according to an individual writer's usage, not with slavish dedication to what they always mean.

 uestion 33   I've been told Song of Songs (Song of Solomon) is a picture of Christ and the church, but it doesn't sound like that to me. What is the book about and why is it in the Bible?

Since before the time of Christ interpreters have struggled to understand what contribution the Song of Songs makes to God's Word. They've developed some ingenious understandings of the book to escape the embarrassment felt by so many at finding a book seemingly devoted to human love in the Bible.

As is so often the case when dealing with problems of language, the first problem in understanding the Song of Songs is determining what it is. Only then can we get down to what it means and what it's doing in the Bible.

There are two approaches we might take.

The first is the easiest. We can understand the book literally, and then try to find the reason such a poem is included in Scripture. But this leaves us with the problem of dealing with a passionate, highly charged love poem.

The other approach has been more popular over the years. It assumes the book cannot be literal and tries to determine what it means symbolically.

The first Jewish interpreters to follow this direction were embarrassed by the book's thinly veiled erotic language. In the Greek world, anything to do with the body was evil. All those magnificent Greek statues and murals of athletes and gods were an effort to escape the "illusion" of this world and to approximate the ideal heavenly form.

Using a technique developed by Philo of Alexandria, the rabbis looked beneath the surface of the literal text and discovered a powerful and uplifting allegory. Here was no love poem of the physical passion between a man and a woman. This was a spiritual song about the love of God for His people Israel.

With the passage of years and the rise of Christianity, the early fathers of the church inherited the Jewish Scriptures and, with them, the problem of the Song of Songs. Being men whose sensibilities were shaped by the same Greek philosophical horror at the physical world as the rabbis, the fathers needed their own technique for keeping the book while shedding its apparent meaning. For them it became an allegory of the love of Christ for His church.

Both of these efforts to slide out from under the burden of a book that no one was willing to accept as literal were based on a single solid biblical truth. Both Israel and the church are described as the bride. Building on this fact, a monumental body of literature grew up with allegorical insights into the real meaning of the book.

In recent years, however, students of the Bible have become uncomfortable with the use of allegorical interpretation. Just as the position is built on a single biblical base, it runs aground on another, equally biblical, fact. There is absolutely no evidence that the Song of Songs is an allegory. Its treatment as such depends on the assumption that it can't be literal.

Matthew Henry warned that it was a book capable of becoming "the savour of death unto death" to those who approached it with a carnal mind. He applauded the rabbis for limiting its use to those over thirty "lest by the abuse of that which is most pure and sacred the flames of lust should be kindled."

With that understanding of the literal sense of the book, it's no wonder that church people through the centuries have insisted on using allegorical interpretation to redeem it.

Don't misunderstand. There's nothing wrong with allegory—when it is allegory. It's a fine literary device for making a point without simply stating the case in straightforward declarative sentences.

Scores of generations of preachers have warned congregations against the smooth and enticing blandishments of the world and encouraged their flocks to persevere in their quest for eternal bliss. But who remembers them?

Pilgrim's Progress, on the other hand, has become an English classic by saying the same thing through the use of allegory.

The Apostle Paul used allegory, sparingly, to make points so troublesome that his usually dazzling logic and argumentation had to be put aside temporarily in favor of a good, illustrative story.

But there's a difference between allegory, a technique used by the author, and *allegorizing*, a technique used by the interpreter.

A skillful allegorist can weave a tale filled with narrative wonder, fearsome and delightful characters, and settings both realistic and outlandish. But underneath it all, he knows what he's getting at, and, if he's done his work well, so do we.

There's no doubt in our minds what Celestial City means. The slough of despond presents no obstacles to our understanding. Vanity Fair has stood through generations as an unequivocal warning against the frivolous but deadly enticements of the world. But the message of *Pilgrim's Progress* was put there by its author, not found there by its readers.

By allegorizing our interpretation, we can make anything say anything.

The great expositor C. H. Spurgeon put his finger, unwittingly, I think, on the Achilles heel of allegorical interpretation while applying it to the Song of Songs. Commenting on 5:3, Spurgeon said, "Such a text as this is very like manna which fell in the wilderness, of which the rabbis say it tasted after each man's liking."

And there's the rub. Such a text, when subjected to the imaginations of allegorizing interpreters, can indeed taste after each man's liking. There is no truth if our understanding is as subjective as that. The form of the text *must* shape the interpretation of the text, or there is no control outside the interpreter for what the text might be made to say.

Most evangelical students of the Old Testament have, for this reason, abandoned the allegorical understanding of the Song of Songs. But that doesn't mean it hasn't cropped up under a different name.

As embarrassed by allegorical interpretation as they are by the literal content of the book, some today call it typology. Like allegory, an understanding of typology is a valid and valuable tool in the hand of the skilled interpreter. But in dealing with the Song of Songs as typology we need to be very careful that the same old intruder hasn't come back with a clean coat on.

Types are Old Testament persons, things, or events that have observable correlations with New Testament persons, things or events.

The word *type* means, in Greek, either a pattern or mold, or the product of that pattern or mold.

We can see how certain elements of the history of the Old Testament people of God might provide a pattern for understanding the experience of the New Testament people of God. But we use this technique only with great caution. It's a tool as open to abuse as allegorization.

Biblical types, like biblical parables, have only a limited number of points of similarity between themselves and the truth they're being used to illuminate.

For example, the serpent raised up in the wilderness to save the people of Israel from snakebite is a type of Christ, who, when raised up on the cross, saved people from their sin. But how much further dare we go in drawing comparisons?

Not much. The serpent in no way partook of the nature of Christ. It was nothing more than an artifact used by God to point the direction toward a much greater salvation. Its salvation was transitory; those who looked on it would one day die. It was saved as a relic and eventually destroyed because a pagan Israel had invested it with deity and worshipped it along with the gods of Canaan.

Principle 13   In dealing with types, look for one or two points of correspondence between a real, literal, historical Old Testament phenomenon and its greater New Testament fulfillment.

I try to limit biblical typology to those areas already marked out by the writers of the New Testament. If they, operating under the inspiration of the Holy Spirit, didn't see a type, I'm reluctant to go where they refused to lead.

This doesn't mean we can't go to the Old Testament to find points of correspondence for our Christian lives today. It means that we're not free to take a New Testament idea back to the Old and reinterpret the Old Testament to teach the New Testament idea.

As a preacher, I've made innumerable forays into the Old Testament to illustrate some theme of the New. As a teacher of Old Testament, I've tried to point out ways in which the Old Testament genuinely pre-figures the New.

But I've never gone to an Old Testament text that seems to say one thing and, using the enlarged vision of New Testament revelation, taught that the Old Testament meant something it didn't say.

Putting the Song of Songs to these simple tests, can we understand it as "typologically" teaching the love of Christ for His church?

The answer is no. Those who call their approach typological find the same things, use the same kind of "this really means that" reasoning, and generally make the literal meaning of the text little more than a screen that obscures the true and spiritual meaning of the book.

This takes us back to the seemingly unanswerable question, if the book is really only a poem about the love between a man and a woman, what business does it have in the Bible?

This question assumes that the love between a husband and wife, even the physical elements of it, isn't a suitable subject for Scripture.

Didn't God make us the way we are, physically drawn together as male and female to be joined in both physical and spiritual union?

Doesn't Paul equate the becoming-one-flesh of Genesis 2:24 with the physical manifestation of love (1 Corinthians 6:16)?

Because this physical relationship between husband and wife was God's plan for us from the beginning, the perversion of this union is reprehensible. Because this physical relationship is a part of the overall plan of God, its sanctity lies at the heart of Jesus' prohibition of divorce.

Why not describe that kind of relationship in langugage both circumspect and beautiful?

Why not celebrate the love between a husband and wife, faithful to one another, joined transcendently in mind, spirit, and body?

What is wrong with finding a model in Scripture for the kind of relationship God intended when He commanded Adam and Eve to be fruitful, multiply, and fill the earth with their descendants?

Q **uestion 34** When John the Baptist said that Jesus would baptize with the Holy Spirit and with fire, I understand what he means by the Holy Spirit. What is the fire he promises (Matthew 3:11)?

This is an example of one of the most critical problems of interpretation in all biblical studies. We've all heard that we should let Scripture interpret Scripture, but we seldom apply that dictum uniformly. All Scripture should be understood *in context.* Almost every preacher, scholar, author, lecturer who takes up the meaning of a specific text will say that. But all too often, after we've said it, we go right ahead and violate it.

P **rinciple 14** Let Scripture interpret Scripture.

Easy to say, hard to do. Interpreting according to context demands scrupulous attention. Sometimes it's easier intellectually to look through the rest of the Bible to find a verse to interpret what we're studying than it is to let the immediate context do the work for us. This verse about being baptized with the Holy Spirit and with fire is one of those places.

For years, I heard that the baptism of the Holy Spirit was what John meant in the first half of his statement. The zeal and power of the Holy Spirit was what he meant by the second half. Time after time I heard that once people had been filled with the Holy Spirit they would be eager to do the Lord's work, to witness, be empowered to win souls and pray for the miraculous.

The proof of that was John's statement that we'd be filled with fire when the Holy Spirit came. Wasn't that what happened on the day of Pentecost? Weren't the disciples filled with a power they'd never known before?

Of course the answer is yes. When we're filled with the Holy Spirit we do receive the presence and power of the living God who indwells us. But that's not what John was talking about. He was preaching a fire-and-brimstone evangelistic sermon.

The good news part of the sermon was that Jesus was coming and He would baptize those who believed in Him with the Holy Spirit. The downside of the message was that He would baptize those who rejected him with the fire of judgment.

How can I say that, when so many have said just the opposite for so long? Actually, I only say it because John said it in the next verse.

Look at the immediate context. John expanded on verse 11 in verse 12. The Lord was already prepared to begin the process of separating the wheat from the chaff, John said. "His winnowing fork is in his hand."

Winnowing was the process of taking the grain, dirty with the process of threshing, and throwing it up into the wind. The wind blew away the lighter dust and chaff, while the heavier grains fell back to the ground. When the winnowing was done, the straw, the chaff, and the weeds were gathered and used for starting fires. The grain was stored for use during the dry season.

John went on to say, "he will clear his threshing floor, gathering his wheat into the barn and burning up the chaff with unquenchable fire." Although it's figurative language, it should be clear what he was saying. Those who are Jesus' own will be gathered in and saved. Those who refuse to respond to the call of the Lord on their lives will be set aside for judgment.

There's nothing wrong with saying that the Holy Spirit confers a zeal for the Lord that we wouldn't have in His absence. The Bible teaches that. But not in this verse.

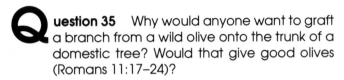

Q **uestion 35**   Why would anyone want to graft a branch from a wild olive onto the trunk of a domestic tree? Would that give good olives (Romans 11:17–24)?

A friend of mine, a horticulturalist, once confided that this passage had caused him real problems as a young Christian. He knew that Paul's description of grafting in Romans 11 made no sense at all. He'd heard people say that such a graft would result in the wild olive branch bearing good olives, but he knew it didn't work like that so he had questioned the accuracy of the Bible.

He knew that genetic programming for olives resides in the branch, not the root. Anyone who has ever read a seed catalog should know that. When an apple tree bears five different varieties of apples it's not the result of grafting a branch into five different types of roots. It's the result of grafting five different kinds of branches into a single trunk.

I think they do that to create a curiosity for the gardener who wants to grow something a little out of the ordinary. (The fruit also makes delicious blended apple sauce.)

Those five-variety apple trees have been grafted onto the root stock of some small, hard, sour, but winter-hardy variety so the trees can survive winters even in the cold climates of northern Minnesota. Each variety brings its positive qualities to the newly grafted tree, but they remain what they were before the graft took place. The desirable qualities of the root stock don't extend beyond its ability to withstand really cold conditions. The desirable qualities of the branch, on the other hand, might not live long enough to come to fruition without the hardiness of the sour apple root.

Paul used the metaphor of pruning to describe how some of Israel had been removed from the root for their hardness of heart. He talked about grafting to explain how Gentiles had become part of the people of God. He warned against complacency because, if the natural branch had been pruned for faithlessness, so could the grafted branch. Then he offered hope for the remnant of Israel by suggesting that, given an awakening of faith, they could be grafted back into the original root. His analogy never extended to the nature of the fruit all this pruning and grafting would produce. That simply wasn't relevant.

Paul's intention was not to teach horticulture. It was to teach theology. Like Jesus, he used agricultural metaphors that people were familiar with. Like any good preacher, he saw the analogy between what happened regularly in daily life and what he had witnessed in history. He used pruning and grafting to illustrate a point, not to teach his readers about pruning and grafting.

Once again, we need to be cautious about pressing the details of metaphoric language. Paul has created a powerful message about the inclusion of the Gentiles among God's people. Let's not insist that he also provide a treatise on plant husbandry.

Q **uestion 36**   What does it mean that with the Lord a day is like a thousand years and a thousand years is like a day (2 Peter 3:8)?

It means there is no relationship between what we think of as time and the schedule God operates under. It doesn't mean that days in heaven last a thousand years.

By using a small number and a large number Peter set up a contrast to warn us against any attempt to concoct time tables for divine activity. We cannot unravel the mystery of the end time and its date by understanding some detail of biblical chronology because God does not use our time scale.

Q **uestion 37**   Why is Christ called the "Son of Man"? What does it mean?

When I was younger I would simply have said that *Son of Man* is the title affirming Jesus' humanity. It's what I had always heard, and it seems logical enough. After all, throughout the book of Ezekiel, God refered to the prophet as *son of man*. There it's clear that the term is used to emphasize Ezekiel's humanity in contrast to the transcendence of God.

And the phrase *son of . . .* means that the person so described has the characteristics of David, or Abraham, or, in the case of Jesus, God.

Since we know that Jesus was both God and man, and since we also know that the divine side of Jesus is covered in the title *Son of God*, it seems reasonable to assume that *Son of Man* is the affirmation of his humanity.

However, during Jesus' lifetime there was no reason to affirm his humanity. Everyone accepted Him as human! In fact it was His obvious humanity that made it hard to accept His deity. It was certainly unnecessary to affirm Jesus' humanity to the people of Nazareth, who exclaimed, "'Isn't this the carpenter's son? Isn't his mother's name Mary, and aren't his brothers James, Joseph, Simon and Judas? Aren't all his sisters with us? Where then did this man get all these things?' And they took offense at him" (Matthew 13:53–57).

Knowing His humanity, knowing His family, living in the same town with His mother, these people needed no reminder that Jesus was human. That was the one thing the citizens of Nazareth knew without even thinking.

By my rough count, the Gospels use the title *Son of Man* eighty-three times, and Acts once. The context of these passages seldom supports the idea that *Son of Man* affirms Jesus' humanity.

In the Gospels, only Jesus used the title for himself. No one else called Him *Son of Man*. He chose the title for himself and no one else in His lifetime adopted it.

Satan called Him Son of God (Matthew 4:3–6). So did the demons (Matthew 8:29).

Ordinary people talking to Jesus tended to call Him Son of David (Matthew 20:30–31; 21:9–15). The voices mocking Jesus on the cross thought it appropriate to use Son of God (27:40). The Sanhedrin also used that title in their interrogation (26:63), and the centurion who stood at the foot of cross gave voice to the certainty that He was indeed the Son of God (27:54).

But none of these titles are found on Jesus' lips. *Son of Man* is the dominant title found in the Gospels, and only He used it. And He used it often. When Jesus called himself the *Son of Man*, I think the Jewish people heard something other than an affirmation of His humanity.

If He called himself *Son of Man* that often, doesn't it stand to reason that it carried enormous weight, not only with Jesus, but with at least some of the people who heard Him say it? To get an idea of what the first century Jewish leaders heard in that simple phrase, read those eighty-three verses in a single sitting. One impression will overwhelm you.

The *Son of Man* is no mere mortal. The offices and activities Jesus described in that title are simply not appropriate for one who labeled himself merely as a fully human individual.

He was Lord of the Sabbath (Matthew 12:8; Mark 2:28; Luke 6:5). Think of the furor that remark must have caused. He had power on earth to forgive sins (Matthew 9:6; Mark 2:10; Luke 5:24). That, of course, was considered blasphemy by some of His hearers (Matthew 9:3). He had angels at His command (Matthew 13:41) who would devote themselves to His service as they ascended and descended at His bidding (John 1:51). In this last verse Nathanael identified Jesus as the Son of God, but Jesus responded by calling himself the *Son of Man*.

To understand this glorified figure that Jesus chose as His own self-description we need to look to Daniel 7:13. This *Son of Man* was not just the representative of humanity. He was a glorified heavenly warrior whose coming would herald the fall of the beasts described earlier. He would be worshipped by all humanity and given a kingdom that would never pass away.

When Jesus stood before the Sanhedrin, undergoing His final confrontation with those religious leaders, He was asked if He was the "Christ, the Son of God" (Matthew 26:63). He answered with a simple "I am" (Mark 14:62). Then He added, "You will see the Son of Man sitting at the right hand of the Mighty One and coming on the clouds of heaven."

Is it conceivable that all the doctors of the Law and all the members of the priesthood who sat in judgment at that moment could have missed the allusion to the power and authority given the Son of Man in Daniel 7:13–14? I don't think so. Having made that connection, is it possible to believe they didn't find it absolutely blasphemous that this weak, tired, soon-to-die human being should equate himself, not only with the Mighty One, but with the glorified being Daniel described?

The High Priest tore his clothes in symbolic mourning at the enormity of the "crime" Jesus had just committed.

Perhaps it was Jesus' simple yes that prompted that response. I'd say my own simple yes if it weren't for the one time in the New Testament when *Son of Man* was uttered by someone other than Jesus.

Stephen stood before the gathered Sanhedrin, accused, like his Lord, of blasphemy. Courageously he retold the story of Israel and its rejection of all God's prophets. He closed his attack with a fiery assault on the current generation which stood responsible for an even greater sin, the betrayal and murder of the one all the prophets had predicted.

How did they respond to this tongue lashing? They were furious and gnashed their teeth. Then Stephen sealed his doom with the Spirit-empowered testimony, "Look, I see heaven open and the *Son of Man* standing at the right hand of God."

When they heard that they covered their ears, shouted to drown out the sound of what he said, and killed him.

No one today is sure what the phrase meant to them. Often scholars fight mini-wars over the literary origins, the specific usages, the dependencies and quotations that fill out the meaning of the phrase. But the Sanhedrin knew what Stephen said, and they killed him for it.

My own opinion is that *Son of Man* spoke of the glorified Jesus who would come one day with power to overthrow all the human pretensions and approximations of true religion, all the human efforts at self-aggrandizement and self-advancement, all the systems human beings have substituted for the rule of God in their lives.

Jesus is not *merely* human. He is ultimately human. Jesus is heaven's perfect man, filled with the glory of God, of which all other men have fallen short.

Q**uestion 38**   Why did John use the number 666 as a sign for the Antichrist (Revelation 13:18)?

Surprisingly, John used the number to let his readers know exactly who was talking about. John told us quite plainly that the number was the number of the beast's name (v. 17). He then continued the discussion in the form of a numerical riddle. Since John seemed to think anyone who had a certain level of insight could crack the code, it must have been a riddle that his contemporaries would have found challenging, but not impossible.

One solution offered frequently by commentators is that 666 is a number that will eternally fall short of the glory of God. If, as is maintained by those who offer this suggestion, 777 is the number of the Trinity, then 666 is a number that aspires to, but never attains, deity.

This is certainly the safest interpretation, and I'd ordinarily be inclined to accept it. It is a relatively sober understanding that doesn't lend itself to extravagant claims or outlandish identifications. But the text does say that the number is the number of *a man's name*, and not just *the number of man*. The NIV translators made a decision between two equally valid understandings of the Greek on verse 18. They chose to say, "it is man's number." They could just as easily have translated it, "the number is that of a man," as does the NASB, which gives the verse a totally different flavor.

The NIV's translation favors the rendering "number of man." The NASB's translation leans toward a specific man.

I'm inclined to agree with the NASB. That doesn't make the solution easy. It just says that I think a specific name, familiar to John's readers, could be identified by working out the numerical value of his name.

There's no certainty about this, but of the candidates for the office, I like Nero. If Nero's name is translated into Hebrew, the numberical value of its letters is 666. In Hebrew there are no numerals. To write numbers you must either write them out using complete words or substitute something shorter. The Hebrew people learned very early to use each letter of their alphabet as numerals as well as letters. Therefore the first letter of the alphabet, *aleph* is also the number one. *Yodh,* the tenth letter of the alphabet, does double duty as the number ten. This is how a numerical value can be assigned to a name. You simply add the value of each letter, and the sum of the letters used to write Nero in Hebrew is 666. Whether or not John's readers could have translated Nero's name into Hebrew is another question, but let's assume, for the sake of argument, that they could and did make that connection.

Nero fits well into the picture presented. He persecuted the church. He proclaimed himself a god and demanded people's worship. He was a monster whose evil stood out in an age of monstrous rulers. He provides an excellent prototype of the beasts to come, which I think is the important part of the vision. I don't think John was identifying the Antichrist who will rise up in the end-time. I doubt that we will know him when we see him. From my understanding of the Bible, he'll probably be lost in the crowd until it's too late. John himself acknowledged that many who taught Jesus hadn't come in the flesh were to be thought of as *the* Antichrist (2 John 7).

But we should be able to see the shape of things to come, if not the face, and be aware that, since the spirit of antichrist was in the world even in New Testament times, church history has been witness to a host of antichrists, preparing the way for the final Antichrist.

The lesson to be learned from this numerical riddle is not as specific as we might like. It challenges us to look back and see what John's model may have been. With that in mind we can look forward and be forewarned. Although the information we have at our disposal is limited, we should know enough to recognize the "false christs and their prophets [who] will appear and perform great signs and miracles to deceive even the elect—if that were possible" (Matthew 24:24).

We have to believe something put us here. If we refuse to acknowledge God, we invent something to replace Him.

CHAPTER 4

PRINCIPLES

15 Do not overstep the purpose of Scripture by reading it as a scientific treatise on creation.

16 Don't build doctrines based on difficult passages.

17 Let clear teachings illuminate unclear passages.

QUESTIONS

39 My Bible translates Genesis 1:1, "In the beginning God created," but I've seen other translations that read "In the beginning of creation, when God made. . . ." What's the difference and is it important?

40 Should Genesis 1:2 read, "the earth *was* formless and empty" or "the earth *became* formless and empty"?

41 Is the word *day* used in Genesis 1 a twenty-four hour day, or does it have some other meaning?

42 Does the word *us* in Genesis 1:26 teach the the Trinity?

43 If God is a spirit (John 4:24) what does it mean that we're made in His image? Is there a difference between image and likeness (Genesis 1:26)?

44 Why did God have to rest after the first six days of creation (Genesis 2:2)?

"THE ELEPHANT'S CHILD" AND OTHER SCIENTIFIC FABLES

18 Keep in mind the "principle of threes." The Bible frequently makes a point by breaking the point into threes.

19 Keep in mind the "principle of end stress," which means that the real emphasis is on the last element. The two that come first are there to set up the third.

45 Does the Bible teach that it never rained until Noah's flood (Genesis 1:6–8; 2:5)?

46 Wasn't the land watered by a mist that took the place of rain (Genesis 2:6)?

47 Did God really make man out of the dust of the ground (Genesis 2:7)?

48 Why is God referred to only as God in chapter 1, but as LORD God in chapter 2?

49 Why didn't Adam and Eve die when they disobeyed God (Genesis 2:18–25)?

50 What does it mean that Eve was a "suitable helper" for Adam (Genesis 2:18–25)?

51 Why was Adam and Eve's simple act of disobedience punished so severely (Genesis 3)?

One of Rudyard Kipling's *Just So Stories* tells the fanciful tale of an elephant's troublesome child who made his way up the "Great grey-green greasy Limpopo River all hung about with fever trees" where he met the armor-plated crocodile. The crocodile, who had a taste for elephant child filet, tried to swallow the tusky tyke beginning with its nose. According to Kipling, before this encounter all elephants had short, bulgy, boot-like noses.

When the crocodile grabbed his nose, the elephant child set his feet in the mud. With the help of a friendly python, he began a colossal tug of war with the crocodile. The elephant child's life was saved, but the strain on his nose was just too much. It was stretched into a fine, long trunk.

When all his elephant relatives saw what a handy thing the trunk was for spraying water, taking tender leaves from the tops of trees, and administering well deserved spankings, they all went off to the crocodile for their own trunks. Ever since, all elephants everywhere have had trunks instead of short, bulgy boot-like noses.

It's a wonderful, light-hearted story, but how could anyone mistake it for a credible scientific theory that explains the elephant's elongated snoot?

Strangely enough, though, this fictitious tale and evolution, the accepted scientific explanation of life, have a lot in common.

THE ZERO FACTOR

There is one main difference between Kipling's story and evolution. The process Kipling assigned to single individuals in a single generation has been stretched by evolutionists over millions of generations and assigned in tiny fractions to billions of individuals. In both cases, however, physical changes experienced by one creature are passed on and become part of the genetic heritage of all subsequent creatures.

What makes Kipling's story as plausible as any of the competing theories of evolution is that he at least begins with an elephant family. Evolution begins with nothing. There's a problem here that most third graders understand when it is pointed out to them.

Not long ago my daughter Erin brought me her math homework to decipher. I dropped out of math not long after third grade, so her homework, which is increasing in complexity, has nearly exhausted my shadowy memories of things mathematical. Fortunately for both of us, though, I remembered the answer to this problem.

What happens when we multiply or divide by zero?

The answer, simply put, is that zero times anything equals zero. Zero cannot be multiplied or divided. This concept demonstrates the magnitude of the miracle of creation and the silliness of naturalistic attempts to explain it. No matter how fancy they make the theory, or how many billions of years they allow it to work, evolutionists are still multiplying by zero: No life times eight billion years equals no life.

THE MISSING LINK

The problem with so many of the naturalistic theories about origins is that they begin with nothing and willfully disregard the one quantity that will let the equation make sense: God times time (any amount we choose) equals all.

Equations that leave God out must explain the universe by multiplying nothing times almost limitless time to explain the development of something.

Yet the spectacle of the universe in all its splendor and life in all its complexity is unthinkable without some intelligence planning it. Without God, even the most devout secularist needs to invent some other force to oversee creation.

E.T. GO HOME

Some scientists, despairing of explaining creation by the increasingly shaky theories of evolution, have looked to the heavens for their answer. But they have not found God. They have found Good Extra-Terrestrial Intelligences. Actually no one has found any extra-terrestrial intelligences, good or bad, but they're looking real hard. Considering the amount of money and effort they're spending, someone must have a lot of faith that they're out there.

Our space program has sent a probe into the galaxy with a message telling these supposed intelligences to give us a call ASAP. They will, these scientists are certain, help us shed the old nature and enter into newness of life. They will proclaim freedom to the captives, declare peace on earth to men of good will, and generally heal all our diseases.

Secularist scientists have taken that a step further. Having conceded finally that life really is too complex to have arisen without a guiding intelligence, they have accepted the idea of creator. But he's not the one you and I know.

"He" is some advanced, intelligent, powerful, good extra–terrestrial civilization who, eons ago, came to earth and planted the seed of life here. Some day representatives of his civilization will return to walk the face of this garden planet in the cool of the evening and fellowship with their creations. Until they do we can't prove they exist, but their priests and theologians have the utmost faith that they do.

The nice thing about them is that they won't make any demands on us. They'll just tell us what we need to know and we will see the error of our ways and change. If we don't, the best that can happen to us is that we'll just keep muddling on the way we do now. The worst is that we will plunge ourselves into a manmade armageddon.

If our creator turns out to be just another creature, as these scientists say he is, we aren't accountable to anyone. If he is just like us, only smarter, we can become like him without admitting our sinfulness or his superiority. And that's the real point to this frantic search for extra-terrestrial intelligence.

More and more scientific research is pointing toward the revolutionary notion that the incredible order and complexity of life demands an intelligence who created it. A growing number of scientists is admitting that life couldn't have gotten here if someone from outside had not put it here. But unfortunately, most of them neither acknowledge God nor thank Him.

Although these theories make good science fiction, they cannot bear the weight of the evidence they've been called on to explain. What's more, they demonstrate my point beautifully. We have to believe *something* put us here. If we refuse to acknowledge God, we invent something to replace Him.

BABY NEEDS A NEW PAIR OF GENES

Most scientists today don't buy the idea that life from somewhere else put us here or will come someday to explain our purpose. Scientists like their god more impersonal than that. If their god had an icon or symbol, it would be a pair of dice or a roulette wheel. In their quest for a higher power to add to that impossible equation we've talked about, they have made blind, dumb chance their god.

James Weldon Johnson imagined God kneeling down on the river bank to shape Adam out of the mud, but a devout scientist would probably picture him kneeling in an alley throwing a pair of dice.

I've been reading books on the debate between secularist science and biblical views of creation for almost thirty years, and the ease with which secularist scientists accept chance as a personal, conscious being always astonishes me. The evidence of the created universe declares so powerfully that it was put here by an intelligence greater than man that when God is refused His rightful place in the equation, chance usually becomes the deity who takes His place. "Chance decided," "chance decreed," "chance planned," are conclusions made by people who reject God as the source of everything.

No matter how distinguished scientists are, how many their degrees, or how impressive their publications, they can look pretty silly when, brought face-to-face with the inescapable reality of God, they have to explain that it really isn't God.

ASKING THE RIGHT QUESTIONS

Christians aren't without fault, either. We confuse truth with right, orthodoxy with infallibility, and ignorance with wisdom. So few of us know anything about the disciplines of science that we often aim our critiques at theories and ideas no scientist would recognize.

The debate over science and creation, for example, is muddied when we assume they're all wrong and we're all right. Because we are ignorant outside our own realm, we ask all the wrong questions.

Scientists, with the tools of scientific inquiry, can ask *what*, *how*, and in some very limited cases, *why*.

What is the structure of the earth's crust?

What forces cause earthquakes and hurricanes?

How does the genetic code in living creatures work to ensure that mother cats don't bear baby mice?

Why do bacteria die in this dish of mold?

Science strays from its calling when it asks the ultimate questions about the purpose of the universe or human life. It can't tell us how to live righteously. Its investigations are strictly limited to the physical world, so it will never answer the questions of the spirit. Science can weigh, analyze, measure, dissect, and then describe and explain physical realities of the most frightening complexity. But it can't weigh truth, measure goodness, or cut through to the heart of God's love for His lost world. The transcendent truths are beyond the scope of its inquiry.

The questions related to the transcendent truths belong to theology. But Christians are not satisified to deal with them. We have been guilty of asking science's questions of a God who's more interested in the condition of our souls than in the weight of a hydrogen atom.

Because we "understand" the Trinity, we think that all lesser secrets lay open before us. If we're right in our theology, we assume we are right about everything else. We often forget that theological orthodoxy doesn't guarantee scientific accuracy any more than advanced knowledge in a scientific field equips the scientist to speak theologically.

THE TALE OF TWO BOOKS

The great battleground between these two opposing views of reality is Genesis 1–3. The war raging there is more like the trench warfare of WWI than it is like the air raids of WWII. The two sides are locked in an unwinnable struggle that will ultimately litter the battlefield with casualties. There's no future in it when both sides insist they have the only truth. To break the deadlock they must recognize that the book the scientist is reading and the book the Christian is reading both belong to God.

When Paul, in Romans 1, described the revelation of God in nature, he prepared the way for an understanding of scientific *truth* as God's truth. That understanding lies at the root of modern science, but it's not commonly admitted in the secular world. God, who is the author of truth, is also the creator of the universe. What He's written in the "book" of creation, when properly understood, doesn't conflict with what He's written in the book of His Word.

When science leafs through the pages of the universe, it is unlocking the grammar of the book of creation. Because the book is written in unknown languages, scientists must read it very tentatively. Their reading is slow and painful, like the homework assignment of first-year language students. They put words and grammar together in a variety of ways that are sometimes right, sometimes wrong, and sometimes a little of both.

The scientific method observes some aspect of the created world, gathers relevant data, proposes an hypothesis, tests it empirically, and, if the testing verifies the hypothesis, accepts it as true. Scientists will hold to the current theory with all the zeal and orthodoxy of the devout believer, but eventually, if the theory proves wrong, the real scientist will reject it. The process may take generations, but truth will win out.

The quest for God's truth in the universe shouldn't be seen as the enemy. It's a tool as neutral as a crescent wrench. Many of the great scientists have been Christians who see their task as cataloging, analyzing, and understanding God's other book.

ALL COULD BE QUIET ON THE CREATION FRONT

The real battle over Genesis 1–3 is between antagonists on both sides of the debate who overstate their case. The scientist who uses God's book in nature to deny His existence, and the Christian who uses God's book in Scripture to deny the genuine truths of science. Both misuse the tool God has provided for our understanding.

In the wrong hands a crescent wrench can become a murder weapon, but it's still the same innocent device that changes the tires on a child's bicycle.

In the hands of men and women committed to the eradication of the very idea of God, science can be misused. When it is used as truth, rather than as a tool to find truth, it is no longer science but Scientism, a faith as blind and irrational as any cult.

Science can be practiced honestly, even by nonbelievers, to unlock the observable mysteries of God's creation. If a non-believer discovers the cure for cancer, it will be because he or she successfully unlocked the truths God has built into His universe.

Scientism, on the other hand, is the empty faith of people who must believe in something but will not believe in the true God. Claiming to be wise it becomes foolish and exchanges the glory of the immortal God for images made to look like mortal man and birds and animals and reptiles (Romans 1:22–23). Paul's phrase is an accurate description of the trend toward pure materialism.

The battle today is between Scientism and human interpretation, not between science and Scripture. There is no conflict between scientific truth and biblical truth.

WE WERE LIKE CHILDREN THEN

Principle 15   Do not overstep the purpose of Scripture by reading it as a scientific treatise on creation.

Genesis 1 is not a twentieth-century science book. I'm not arguing that God couldn't have given us one if He'd wanted to. In fact, if He had chosen to inspire a scientific treatise I have no doubt that He would have given us one that battalions of Einsteins would need millennia to unravel.

Moses, however, wrote his account of creation in an age that didn't even know there were other planets in the sky or other continents on the far side of the globe. The concept of zero was unknown, the germ theory of disease was still three thousand years in the future, and the best doctors of the day mixed magic spells with their nostrums, unsure which was more effective.

In that world, what scientific language would God use to explain creation? It would certainly be different from what He would give us today. And if God used scientific language accurate in the 1980s, how long would it be before that knowledge had gone the way of other older theories and language?

No description of creation in scientific language can be time-less. No timeless description of creation can be scientific. To tell us the timeless truth of creation, the revelation had to be something more than a scientific treatise.

In timeless, nonscientific language, He told us where we came from, what our place in the order of creation was to be, and why our human experience is so ringed by pain and effort. He laid to rest all the false gods of ancient man and undercut the prideful curiosity and the curiously misplaced pride of modern man. He carefully chose not to burden his revelation with scientific language that would rapidly find itself outdated.

BETTER LEFT UNSAID

Genesis tells us God spoke creation into existence, but apart from the creative power of the Word of God, the mechanism of creation is both unexplained and unmentioned. There's no mention of atoms, galaxies, the nature of light, or the laws of genetics. It's important that we know God created, but apparently it's not important that we know how.

In the past hundred years many have tried to establish linkages between the spare, beautiful account of Genesis 1 and the emerging details of what are still infant sciences. The best of these disturb me, for one simple reason. It's been tried before, and the results have always been disastrous.

For centuries the church insisted the Bible taught a *geocentric* (earth-centered) universe. Theologians quoted every verse in the Bible that talked about the sun rising and setting as proof of the "scientific" theory. Today, no informed Christian would argue that the sun revolves around the earth. There have been too many satellites, space probes, and shuttle launches for us to hold on to that outmoded idea.

The theory had to be abandoned in the face of clear-cut evidence against it. Unforunately, when that particular theory had to be abandoned, the biblical passages that "taught" it were abandoned with it.

It's a monumental blunder when we support a questionable biblical interpretation with questionable science, but an even more incredible blunder when we adopt a scientific world view as "biblical" and then use Scripture to support it.

Tragically, that's exactly what the church had done. Because Christians had twisted Scripture to support an untrue scientific worldview, the credibility of Scripture was destroyed for many when the worldview was proven false.

The conflict between the Bible and science was born out of the misguided Christian desire to wed the truth of Scripture to the theories of science. And it continues to be a danger for Christians who rush to find biblical evidence for every new theory or to create new pseudo-scientific theories on the basis of particular schools of interpretation.

The minute we tie Scripture to a particular scientific world view, it shackles the timeless absolutes of God's Word to the changing, uncertain voice of man.

Even when that voice comes from Christianity's most brilliant scientific spokespersons, by the very nature of science it can only speak tentatively, knowing that today's certainty can become tomorrow's old wives' tale.

The task of science is to discover what is, as God's ordered creation defines it. The task of Scripture is to tell us about the truths that lie beyond the reach of scientific experimentation. It's the deeper truths I'm interested in. It's impossible to deal with these chapters without making some passing reference to scientific and interpretive theories, but I intend to avoid scientific speculation as much as possible. I hope to give answers that will have meaning for our day, but that are not confined to our day by the narrowness of a western scientific worldview.

Question 39　　My Bible translates Genesis 1:1, "In the beginning God created," but I've seen other translations that read "In the beginning of creation, when God made. . . ." What's the difference and is it important?

The difference in translation involves a rather technical debate over the grammar of the Hebrew in this sentence. As long ago as the Middle Ages some Jewish scholars were insisting that verses 1 and 2 weren't separate sentences but that verse 1 was a subordinate clause. This would require a translation like, "In the beginning of creation . . ." or "When God began to create."

Some translations today have been influenced by that medieval Jewish argument. This is an honest and genuine attempt to do justice to a difficult grammatical problem.

I'm of the opinion, however, that there's another, less honorable reason for choosing this alternative. I think some critics favor the second translation because it allows a pre-existent earth. "When God began to create, the earth was [already there] formless and empty." The creation myths of the ancient world all begin with pre-existent matter, so these critics seem compelled to find pre-existent matter in Genesis. By using this translation, they're able to read Genesis 1 as just another ancient creation myth.

It would be unfair of me to leave the impression that everyone who favors this translation thinks that way. Only in the last couple of hundred years have some biblical scholars abandoned their belief in divine inspiration and sought the Bible's source in pagan cultures.

Certainly, the Jewish commentators who advanced this idea in the Middle Ages had no such motive, and some modern commentators who are influenced by them are free of that taint.

The Hebrew, as it has come down to us, can be read in this way. This means we can't always tell the orthodoxy of scholars on the basis of their translation of this verse. I know of at least one Christian writer who follows this tradition with no lessening of his commitment to the truth of creation.

On the side of the more familiar translation, all the ancient versions of Genesis favor it. Translators standing much closer to the original than we do saw nothing wrong with the absolute statement that "In the beginning God created. . . ."

The reason a problem exists at all is because our Hebrew Bible was originally written without vowels. To appreciate the importance of that problem, try this on for size: *N th bgnnng Gd crtd th hvns nd th rth. Nd th rth ws wtht frm nd vd, nd drknss ws pn th fc f th dp.*

Once you got over the strangeness of it, you probably recognized Genesis 1:1–2 from the King James Version. If Moses had written in English, Genesis 1:1 might have looked like that. The way I've written it out is probably readable because we know English and know the verse. But what if it had been an unfamiliar sentence written in a foreign language?

For the Jews of the eighth and ninth centuries A.D., Hebrew had become a foreign language. They didn't speak it anymore, and this made it harder and harder for them to read the vowelless Hebrew of their Bibles.

To overcome this, a group of dedicated Jewish scholars known as the *massoretes* invented a system of vowels to make reading easier. The translation of Genesis 1:1 that we read in our Bibles today relies on vowels added to the Hebrew two thousand years after it was written.

This is why I said the Hebrew "as it has come down to us" can be translated, "When God began to create. . . ." translators can argue both sides of this case because there's no way to be certain that the vowels in the Hebrew, which are critical for this translation, are the right ones.

Therefore, the translation of the verse depends on much more than the simple grammatical reading of the Hebrew. It also depends on the rest of the chapter and the rest of Scripture. When the focus is expanded in this way, the clearly preferable translation is the familiar one.

For nonbelievers with a need to eliminate God from their equation, the alternative reading offers some false comfort. For believers the wording doesn't matter. Any of the readings can take us back to the time before there was anything but God, when He, with His word of power, spoke all there is into being.

Does Genesis 1 teach that God created out of nothing?

Like so many doctrines of Scripture, the idea that God created out of nothing is present in Genesis 1 but doesn't appear fully developed until the New Testament. The Old Testament statement, when amplified by further revelation from the New Testament, is fully compatible with the doctrine of creation out of nothing.

It's implied in the statement that God created the heavens and the earth. If "all there is" is what God made, He must have begun with nothing. The fact of the matter is that no account of origins except the biblical one can take us back to a time when nothing but God was.

The Hebrew word, *bara* (bah-RAH), may imply creation out of nothing. It ranges in meaning from "initiating something new" to "bringing into existence." The Bible always uses the word (in its basic tense) with God as its subject. From this, some Old

Testament scholars have concluded that it has a purely theological meaning. Men never *bara*. Only God does.

Other Scripture also helps answer this question. Ephesians 3:9 tells us that God created all things. Revelation 10:6 describes God as the one who created heavens, earth, sea, and all they contain. John 1:3 identifies Christ as present and active in the creation of all things. Most powerfully, Colossians 1:16–17 says: "For by him all things were created: things in heaven and on earth, visible and invisible, whether thrones or powers or rulers or authorities; all things were created by him and for him. He is before all things, and in him all things hold together."

Even though eternity is a commodity that science can't measure or evaluate, something must be eternal. If God didn't give matter existence, matter must have been here forever. But if matter is finite, something, or someone, must have been here first. The Bible says that someone was God. Hard as it has tried, science has been unable to push beyond the veil of silence that shrouds the origin of all things. It may theorize about the time before there was anything, but the only evidence that exists for that time is found in the Word of God.

When faced with such a choice between believing in an eternal God and believing in an eternal cloud of cosmic gas, I'm glad that Scripture teaches that God, who is eternal, created the universe. Our hope for the future isn't built on a cosmic accident leading to ultimate oblivion, but on the grace of the righteous and omnipotent God who made us to be His people. The clear sense of the whole of Genesis and the rest of Scripture argues that God's creation was not restricted to a mere reshaping of already existing matter. All matter originates with the creative word of God.

Although Genesis 1:1 is not the strongest biblical statement of what theologians refer to as creation *ex nihilo*, out of nothing, it fits well into a biblical mosaic that does teach it.

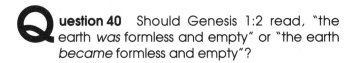

Q **uestion 40** Should Genesis 1:2 read, "the earth *was* formless and empty" or "the earth *became* formless and empty"?

The answer to this question depends on how we read the verb that is the common Hebrew word for "to be." It occurs so

many times in the Hebrew Old Testament that many Bible concordances don't even bother to list it.

In all the Old Testament, the verb is translated "become" or
"became" only twice (2 Samuel 7:24; Deuteronomy 27:9, KJV).
Since it's translated *became* only twice in hundreds of occurren-
ces, we need a very powerful reason for doing so in Genesis 1:2.

That powerful reason doesn't come from the text itself. There
are no textual clues to suggest that the word should be anything
but *was*.

The motivation for this translation comes from a Christian
attempt to create a harmony between modern science and Scripture. This attempt is known as the "gap" theory, and its proponents insist on the translation "became."

When geologists began to argue that the earth was incredibly
old, several theories were proposed to handle the problem an
ancient earth raised for the traditional understanding of Genesis
1. The gap theory was one of these. It provided a limitless amount
of time for all the fossils and rock strata uncovered by the new
science of geology by arguing that Genesis 1:1 described an
original creation that had existed since, as C. I. Scofield put it, the
"dateless past."

This idyllic creation, which may have existed for milions or
even billions of years, was destroyed by the fall of Satan. All this
is covered in Genesis 1:1, with references made to Isaiah 14 and
Ezekiel 28. These two prophetic oracles are read as descriptions
of the fall of Satan and the destruction of the first earth and its
inhabitants. The gap in time between that first creation and the
current one is sought in Genesis 1:2. The formless and empty
earth described there is interpreted as the devastated shell of a
world destroyed in angelic warfare.

To make this interpretation work, the verb in Genesis 1:2 was
translated "became." No current versions that I'm aware of follow
this translation, although the NIV does put "became" in a foot-
note, primarily on the basis of the past strength of this theory. In
spite of the reluctance of translators to adopt the reading, the
popularity of the notes in the Scofield Bible, which adopted the
theory, made this the dominant approach among conservative
Christians until recently.

The weakness of the gap theory lies in its lack of clear biblical
support. Proof sought in Ezekiel 28 and Isaiah 14 depends on a

fanciful interpretation that turns oracles against the King of Tyre (in Ezekiel) and Nebuchadnezzar (in Isaiah) into records of the fall of Satan.

To interpret those passages as descriptions of the fall of Satan, we have to ignore the clear identification the prophets make. Their oracles are both addressed specifically against the kings of Tyre and Babylon (Isaiah 28:4; 28:12). Finding ambiguous references to the fall of Satan and the destruction of the creation over which he ruled takes little notice of context.

Principle 16   Don't build doctrines based on difficult passages.

A basic rule of interpretation is that we shouldn't build doctrines out of difficult passages. The gap theory is built on a secondary, and unlikely, reading of Genesis 1:2 and a forced interpretation of two highly poetic statements in the Old Testament prophets.

The best reading of Genesis 1:2 is the most familiar one. "Now the earth was formless and empty, darkness was over the surface of the deep, and the Spirit of God was hovering over the waters."

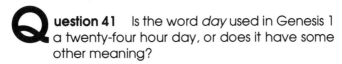

Question 41   Is the word *day* used in Genesis 1 a twenty-four hour day, or does it have some other meaning?

The Hebrew word *yom*, meaning day, can be, and is, used in a number of ways in Scripture. It can mean either a twenty-four hour period or that part of a twenty-four hour period during which the sun is shining. For example, in verse 14 day is contrasted with night, the one being light, the other dark. This alone argues that the word can be used with a degree of flexibility.

The meaning of the word is stretched even further when we read the KJV translation of Genesis 2:4: "These are the generations of the heavens and of the earth when they were created, in the day that the Lord God made the earth and the heavens."

Here the meaning of the word is neither a twenty-four hour period nor the portion of a twenty-four hour period governed by the sun; it is the whole period covered in Genesis 1. In other words, in the creation story alone we find at least two meanings for the Hebrew *yom* (day) that don't speak of a twenty-four hour period.

This shouldn't come as a surprise. Our English word *day* has as many shades of meaning as does the Hebrew word. We understand which meaning applies in English by the context. If I tell you that I'm going to stop for a visit the day after tomorrow, you have no trouble deciding my meaning. If I say that it's been a sunny day, you know I'm not referring to the whole twenty-four hour period. If I'm giving one of my kids a history lecture (which I do from time to time) and talk about what life was like in Jesus' day, my children understand that I mean the whole historical period in which Jesus lived.

That range of meaning is also possible in Hebrew. Our choice of meaning has to consider all these possibilities. The more meanings a word has the harder it is to know its meaning in any single setting. It's like the problem I have when I go into an ice cream shop and have to decide which flavor I want. Being a weakling when it comes to ice cream, I usually wind up getting three scoops, each one different.

With words, though, we can't do that. No word can have more than one meaning in any given sentence. We have to choose one. The following are the most popular choices of meaning for the word *day* in Genesis 1.

A DAY BY ANY OTHER NAME

Literal. The day of Genesis 1 has been taken to mean a twenty-four hour period through much of the text's history. As recently as the 1600s, such leaders of the church as Archbishop James Ussher and the Cambridge Hebrew scholar Bishop Lightfoot felt confident enough of that interpretation to compute the exact week of creation. He assigned it to the week of October 18–24, 4004 B.C. Adam, he said, was created on October 23 at 9:00 A.M., Greenwich Mean Time.

Most contemporary Christian scholars shy away from such precision, but many still hold to a twenty-four hour day. This is the simplest, most straightforward reading of the text and that fact alone has kept this view alive for more than 3,000 years of interpretation. Many Christians assume that the only reason to reject the literal understanding is to accommodate modern geological science.

There are, however, many in the evangelical community who disagree with it. They find the creation story itself at odds with a literal twenty-four hour day.

The events of the sixth day of creation are reported in some detail. On that day, God made the animals and then Adam (1:4–16; 2:15–23). On that same day, he placed Adam in the garden of Eden, where Adam lived long enough to become lonely. To alleviate his loneliness, God brought the animals of the earth before him for naming, and finally created Eve. The description of the events of that day as found in chapter two must certainly have been the work of more than twenty-four hours.

We need to insist on an interpretation that is internally consistent. We need not fear that if creation took longer than six twenty-four hour days God will be demeaned and the magnitude of the miracle of creation diminished.

Look at the heavens on a clear, starry night and realize that all the lights of all the stars are less than a tithe of what's out there. We see only the stars of our galaxy, and not all of them. The scale of the universe stretches beyond our sight and our most extravagant imagining.

Astronomers measure distances in the universe in terms of light years, the distance light travels in a single year. That distance is six trillion miles. By that standard, the nearest star is twenty-four trillion miles away. They measure the universe in millions of light years. That's six trillion times millions.

Estimates say that our galaxy has one hundred billion stars. Our galaxy is part of a cluster containing nineteen galaxies. Over a billion galaxies can be "seen." That gives us a universe made up of approximately 100,000,000,000,000,000,000,000 stars. How does the passage of time, regardless of its amount, diminish the miracle?

The question here isn't what God *could* do, but what He *chose* to do. If it diminishes the miracle of creation to have taken more than six days, what do we make of the miracle of the Exodus? Hundreds of years after God made His promise to Abraham, generations after the descent into Egypt, a full eighty years after the birth of the man God had chosen to be His prophet, God finally brought Israel out.

The record of Scripture is a continuous record of God's patience in waiting for the proper time. In working out his plan of salvation for fallen humanity, He moved at a painfully slow pace. The miracle of the Incarnation was implied in Abraham's time, but how long did it take to fulfill? The miracle of the Second Coming has been laid out in as much detail as we're going to get, but it hasn't happened yet.

In other words, we argue that God must have worked very quickly indeed in His creation of the universe. He must have taken six days and no more. If God had chosen to create the universe in six minutes, I believe it would have been done that way. The question is, what did He choose to do?

It wasn't just the rise of modern geology that made people question this literal view of the days of creation. As long ago as Augustine (372–430), some Christians explained the days of Genesis 1 as figurative. Augustine argued that the days of creation were too sublime to be literal.

Revelatory Day Theory. Some argue that the days of Genesis don't represent creation days at all. They are, according to the argument, a way of describing specific periods in which the revelation of creation took place.

According to this theory, when Genesis mentions the evening and morning of the first day, it's not the day in which light was created, but the day in which God revealed the creation of light. When it refers to the evening and morning of the second day, it isn't describing the span of time it took for God to create the firmament and separate the waters from each other, but the duration of the vision in which Moses saw it happen.

The strength of this view lies in its ability to answer the question, "How did Moses know what he recorded in Genesis 1?" Obviously he was not there to observe, and it's equally unacceptable to contend that he simply reworked the mythology of his day to tell of God's creation. Most evangelicals agree with the idea that Moses' knowledge came through direct, special revelation. If that revelation was received and described in six visionary periods, Genesis 1 answers two questions, not one. It tells us who made everything and how we know.

This, however, is not a reading that recommends itself, even though I find it attractive. My principle complaint with it is that the text itself doesn't give any hints that it should be understood in this way, and there are no other biblical passages that support it. This doesn't necessarily mean it's wrong; I'd just like to see more evidence.

Age-Day Theory. Another approach offered by Christian commentators sees the days of Genesis 1 as geological periods. In very general terms, the Age-Day theory attempts to harmonize the biblical text with the geological evidence. Proponents argue that the account of creation in Genesis 1 is roughly parallel to the currently accepted geological model of origins. This model describes earth in the beginning as an undifferentiated, water-covered globe, shrouded by clouds, and without life. There is light, but no sun, moon, or stars visible. In the course of time God brought the dry land up out of the seas in a way that corresponds with scientific theory.

Using this approach to the interpretation of Genesis 1, the age-day theorist retains the biblical account without having to abandon the scientific. The strength of it lies in its ability to harmonize what some see as conflicting accounts without denying any scientific validity to Scripture. The metaphorical interpretation of the word *day* in this approach is textually valid.

Although some argue against this interpretation, it isn't because Genesis 1 cannot be read metaphorically. Nothing in the text itself prevents us from reading it this way.

The Age-Day theory provides a way to understand Genesis 1 without going to war with science. It defends the authority of Scripture while preserving a description of the age and origin of the earth that is followed by numerous Christian scientists.

Its weakness is that the six days of creation don't follow the geological time scale as closely as its defenders might like. The creation of the sun, moon, and stars follows the creation of light by three days, or ages, if you will. In Genesis, fish and birds are created on day five and reptiles on day six. If this account were to correspond faithfully to current scientific theory, the creation of birds would have to come later than the creation of reptiles.

Some argue that the lights were obscured by banks of cloud enveloping the earth, but the language of verses 14–18 is quite clear in saying that God *made* and *placed* the lights in the vault of the heavens. To argue that they were already there but not yet visible simply doesn't work with the text.

WHEN BROTHERS DISAGREE

Some argue that *day* in Genesis 1 *must* be interpreted as a twenty-four hour period; I'd reply that it *may* be interpreted that way but that Bible-believing scholars have read the text in a number of different ways as well. When I taught Genesis to Bible college seniors, I presented a total of fourteen evangelical approaches, all of which were attempts to understand Genesis 1 by people who love God.

Only people who are committed to the accuracy of Scripture even bother with this sort of thing. Those for whom God's Word has no authority simply ignore Genesis 1 or relegate it to the category of interesting ancient myth. None of those fourteen evangelical positions called into question the *fact* of creation. None of the people who suggested them doubted that God is exactly who the Bible says He is. But all were finite human beings with limited understanding and information. It doesn't matter which position we take, we have to arrive there on the same basis. We are, after all, earthen vessels.

As one who is painfully aware of my status as a cracked pot, I confess that I'm not totally satisfied with any of the suggestions I've offered. For me, the question is too limited. It may be important to decide whether the day of Genesis 1 is twenty-four hours or a geological age, but I suspect the importance of this chapter lies elsewhere. Whether the days are short or long, they record the fact of creation. Whether short or long, they speak of the majesty and sovereignty of God. Whether short or long, they point the mind of modern readers back to before there was an earth or humanity and place us, with all our pretensions, in perspective.

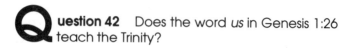

Q **uestion 42**   Does the word *us* in Genesis 1:26 teach the Trinity?

There have been three main answers to that question, and the answer we choose depends on our theological perspective.

Some, searching for an explanation in the mythologies of Israel's neighbors, see this as a consultation between God and His heavenly court. In this case, they look at the Mesopotamian creation stories and see that they talk about a kind of heavenly town meeting.

The Babylonian story called a *Enuma Elish,* or *When On High,* has been heralded as one of the sources of the biblical creation story. It tells of a struggle between the gods. Tiamat, the grandmother of them all, became impatient with her grandchildren, whose noisy parties were disturbing her rest. Like any rational grandmother, her solution to the problem was to kill them all. The younger gods met to figure out what to do. They elected Marduk as their champion to defend them against dear old granny. In his battle with his grandmother he enlisted the aid of the great winds, who blew her up like a balloon. With her mouth held open by the winds, Marduk fired an arrow down her throat and killed her. When it was clear that she was dead, Marduk hacked her in half with his sword. Out of the top half he made the sky and out of the bottom half he crafted the earth.

The bearing this crude story has on Genesis 1:1 is not immediately evident, but negative critics consider it the source of the creation story. In it they see the origin of the idea of the heavenly court, which they believe Genesis 1:26 refers to.

A similar but more biblical approach has been popular with commentators for centuries. Using Job as support, they argue that God is taking counsel with the angelic Host. Job does introduce this idea in chapters 1–2, but the notion that God consulted with the angels over the creation of humanity seems inconsistent with the often repeated biblical teaching that creation was the will of God alone. To make it the kind of decision we might reach in a corporate board room trivializes it.

Some commentators, both Jewish and Christian, have seen the answer in something they call the plural of majesty. God is too great and majestic to be spoken of in the singular, they argue. Therefore, in this passage, his "let us" is the kind of grammatical quirk that allows a single individual to speak of himself in the plural.

The use of this kind of language is widespread. During my days in the Marine Corps Recruit Depot in San Diego, I learned to address my superiors as "the Drill Instructor" and myself as "the private."

"SIR, the Private requests permission to speak with the Drill Instructor, SIR."

We never called the DI *you* because, according to them, a *you* is a female sheep. Marine Drill Instructors are great at discipline but not much at spelling.

Queen Victoria of England is said to have responded to an off-color remark with a cool, and chilling, "*We* are not amused."

Sometimes we use the "editorial we" in writing. Preachers often fall into the habit of saying "we" when they really mean "I." Perhaps God, as we do today, was speaking of himself in the third person. This is a plausible explanation, and it may be true, but it lacks support from Scripture. Although I can find numerous examples of this kind of language all over the world and from almost every period of history, I can't point to any clear biblical examples outside the first eleven chapters of Genesis. This does not disprove that the Lord is speaking of himself in the plural, but it makes the argument less compelling.

THE TRINITY SPEAKS

The interpretation most often adopted among Christians has been the Trinitarian one. In it the persons of the Godhead take counsel over the most important act of creation, the making of humanity.

I am in general agreement with this, but I am careful how far I push it. The Trinity is primarily a New Testament doctrine. That doesn't mean we cannot find support for it in the Old Testament, but it lies a lot farther beneath the surface there.

When God said, "Let us make. . . ," the Christian reader, with the more complete revelation from the New Testament in mind, can hear the voice of the Trinity. I doubt that Israelite readers would have. For them it probably spoke of the majesty of God, a majesty that we know today includes the mystery of three persons in one.

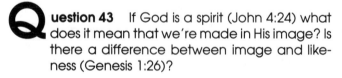 **uestion 43** If God is a spirit (John 4:24) what does it mean that we're made in His image? Is there a difference between image and likeness (Genesis 1:26)?

This verse has led to doctrines or speculations about the physical nature of God. Some early rabbis interpreted it to mean that God has a physical body that is flesh and blood like ours. Mormons also teach this doctrine.

P rinciple 17   Let clear teachings illuminate un-clear passages.

The principle at work in interpreting this passage must be the *analogy of Scripture*. Since the Bible speaks clearly in saying that God is a spirit, this unclear reference must be understood in that light.

The teaching of this verse is that God has made us enough like himself for communication to take place. I can offer some areas in which we, in a small way, are made in God's image.

Human beings are creative. We can take different and unrelated elements and make something that never existed before. We can arrange pigments on canvas to create a picture or molecules to create a plastic. We reflect God in our creativity.

We are called to have dominion over nature. God has made us stewards of His world. Like His sovereignty over us, He has trusted us with limited sovereignty over His world.

Each of us has a personality unlike any other person's. In the expression of that personality, each of us reflects an infinitesimal portion of the person of God. Because God is a person, we reflect that personhood.

In short, what we are as people at our best and most noble is something of what it means to be made in the image of God. If, as Scripture teaches, God is a spirit, it's only reasonable to seek His image in us in those places where we too are spiritual.

Numerous attempts have been made to distinguish the differences between the two words *image* and *likeness*, but those attempts are futile. It's true that the words have their own distinct dictionary definitions. Image is often used of statues, idols, or artistic representations of physical things. Likeness, on the other hand, was a favorite word of Ezekiel, who was very careful never to say that he had seen God and His attendants, but only their likenesses (1:5, 10, 13, 15, 22, 26, 28).

But the use of those two words in verse 26 follows the rules of Hebrew literature, not Hebrew dictionaries. Known as *parallelism*, it is one of the most common and misinterpreted of all biblical literary devices. In the basic form of parallelism two phrases are used as synonyms. For example: "Hear my prayer, O LORD; Let my cry for help come to you" (Psalm 102:1).

The psalmist asked twice for God to hear his prayer. He simply repeated the request in different language to create a poetic effect.

In Genesis 1:26, the simplest understanding of the two words used together is that, in some way, God has made us like himself. To press the language beyond this is to make the text say more than it's intended to say.

Even with this simple understanding of the image and likeness of God, the theological implications are immense. We are stamped with the likeness of God; His ownership is assured. Unbelievers may reject God, but they can no more overthrow God's dominion than they can change the force of gravity.

Because the remnant of that image is still within us, the human being is to be valued. This knowledge lies at the heart of Christian opposition to abortion and euthanasia, at the heart of Christian efforts to lighten the burdens of poverty and homelessness, and at the heart of Christian efforts to evangelize the lost throughout the world.

In our political, social, and evangelistic efforts, we're doing nothing noble. Rather, as fragments of the total image of God, we reach out to men, women, and children whose flawed likenesses cry out to be healed and added to the growing likeness of God's Son.

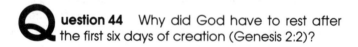

Question 44   Why did God have to rest after the first six days of creation (Genesis 2:2)?

The Hebrew verb translated *rest* can be translated more literally as the word *ceased*. This doesn't mean God withdrew from active involvement in the affairs of the world, but that His work was finished and so He stopped. There was nothing more to do.

Our problem with this statement probably comes from the way we might kick off our shoes and flop on the couch after a particularly hard day at work. We need rest when we've been very active.

But God's "rest" is completely different. God didn't rest because He was worn out; He stopped working when the job was done.

Q **uestion 45**   Does the Bible teach that it never rained until Noah's flood (Genesis 1:6–8; 2:5)?

Two places in Scripture imply that this statement may be true. Genesis 1 describes the separation of the "water under the expanse from the water above it" (1:6). This is said to be the "canopy" of waters that surrounded the earth until God opened the "floodgates of the heavens" (7:11), inundating the earth with the waters that had been stored there since the second day of creation.

Genesis 2:5 adds the other link in this interpretation. "The LORD God had not sent rain on the earth."

The existence of a great canopy of water that filtered out harmful cosmic rays has been used to explain the unusually long lives of the patriarchs who lived before the flood. It has also been argued as the source for the massive amounts of water necessary to flood the earth. But the plainest meaning of the word translated "expanse" in 1:6–8 doesn't give us the picture of a canopy of water.

This notion of a canopy and the idea that it didn't rain until the flood may arise out of a desire to excuse Noah for his drunkenness. Some argue that fermentation never occurred before the flood because of the different atmospheric conditions. Noah, therefore, having never consumed a fermented beverage, drank the wine as if it were grape juice and became drunk.

Nowhere does Scripture teach that fermentation began after the flood or that Noah's drunkenness is the innocent result of drinking what he thought was wholesome grape juice. It does Scripture no honor to invent ways to make offensive events palatable to us when Scripture itself records them and makes no effort to sanitize them.

Paul said, "These things happened to them as examples and are written down as warnings for us" (1 Corinthians 10:11). He was talking about the bad example of the Israelites in the wilderness. One of the many ways that Scripture is different from other ancient writings is that its only real hero is God. The human characters are presented without the least attempt to gloss over their sins or failings. If Noah drank too much the Bible wouldn't cover up that fact.

By ignoring context, Genesis 2:5 might be used to argue that there was no rain until the disastrous downpour that brought the great flood. But in reading the whole passage a much different picture emerges. Chapter 2 backs up and gives a more detailed account of certain aspects of creation. Verse 5 is a summary statement parallel to the summary statement of Genesis 1:1. In this case, though, Adam and Eve are the focus of the whole chapter, so the idea of the emptiness and inhospitality of the earth is developed with reference to them rather than with reference to the cosmos.

The "mist" referred to in the KJV (2:6) is really streams, as a better understanding of Hebrew has demonstrated. The clear biblical picture of life on earth before the flood seems to me to assume that conditions then were very much as they are now. I see nothing in the passage that argues for a water canopy surrounding the earth and much that points away from it. I say that Genesis 1 and 2 give this speculation very little real support.

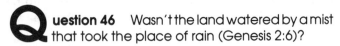

Question 46   Wasn't the land watered by a mist that took the place of rain (Genesis 2:6)?

This is partially true. The earth was watered by some source other than rain, but it wasn't a mist. The word usually translated *mist* by the KJV is better understood today and means streams, as translated in the NIV. The ancient Near East, with the exception of Palestine, depended on rivers. Egypt was known as "The Gift of the Nile" because without the water of the Nile there could be no agriculture, cities, or life as the Egyptians knew it. There was rain in the Tigris-Euphrates valley, but it was seasonal and erratic. The great civilizations of Sumer, Babylonia, and Assyria were impossible without their great rivers.

The picture that emerges from verse 6, then, isn't of a misty, cloud-shrouded earth, but of an earth where the rivers provided enough water for the sparse wild vegetation common in such semi-arid regions. But the intense cultivation of the land necessary after the fall required rainfall plus the added benefit of irrigation from the streams provided by God for that purpose.

Q **uestion 47**   Did God really make man out of
the dust of the ground (Genesis 2:7)?

Did God kneel in the dirt of the Mesopotamian plain and make
a human mudpie? While many conservatives argue forcefully,
and correctly, that the Bible must be interpreted literally, they
demonstrate what they mean by that statement when, without
batting an eye, they treat this verse as a metaphor. I know of no
commentators who insist that Genesis 2:7 is a purely literal
description of God's creative act.

Keil and Delitzsch, in their classic conservative commentary
on Genesis, say:

> The formation of man from dust, and the breathing of the
> breath of life we must not understand in a mechanical sense,
> as if God first of all constructed a human figure from dust, and
> then, by breathing His breath of life into the clod of earth which
> he had shaped into the form of a man, made it into a living
> being.

The theological importance of this verse is foremost. We
learn a tremendous amount about what we are and how we relate
to God in these few words. The purpose isn't to describe the
process by which God made humanity, but to tell about the
stupendous contrasts that He built into us.

Being made of the dust affirms our oneness with creation.
Our stewardship of Earth and its resources, our humble origin,
our frailty and weakness are all there in the word *dust*. Like the
dirt and the earthworms that live in it, like the hyenas and
vultures that scavenge over it, we are of the earth.

Paul said that God made the first man "of the earth, earthy"
(1 Corinthians 15:47, KJV), stressing the contrast between the
man of earth and the Lord from heaven. That contrast is born in
Moses' description of humanity's earthy origins.

Even the name Adam points us back to the dirt. In Hebrew,
Adam is pronounced *Ah-DAHM* and the the word translated
"dust," or "dirt," is pronounced *Ahd-MAH*. Adam, the first man, is
begotten of *admah,* dirt. As is so often the case in Hebrew, the
point is made with a pun.

So we're of the dirt, the common stuff of creation. Our urge
to pride must ever run aground on that fact. Because God wanted

us to be reminded of that common origin, Moses wrote that God made us of the dust of the earth.

But Genesis 2:7 teaches us that God took special, intimate, and personal care in our construction. The crude clay vessels of the early Israelites and the masterfully graceful Grecian pottery were both made of the clay of the earth. Similarly, God made the human being and the mole from the same stuff.

But the artist chose a pattern for us unlike the utilitarian pot that was cranked out in quantity to be used, broken, and thrown away. He made us like an heirloom to be looked at, treasured, and handed down for generations. Unlike the animal, made for our use, He made us to become His companion and friend, entrusting us with the beauties of the Master's estate.

Not through a simple word of command did humanity spring into being. God did not command the earth to bring us forth like a walking cash crop. He formed us. And whatever process He used, the vital truth is that we are the Master Craftsman's masterpiece. How intimately God brought life to Adam.

My family has recently welcomed a dog into our home. He is a beautiful pet, about thirty pounds of curly black and gray fur. His affection for the family that rescued him from the St. Croix Valley Animal Shelter's death row is boundless. Wherever we are, there he is. Duffy sits at our feet, lays his head on our laps, and looks up at us with the most adoring brown eyes a pet owner ever dreamed of seeing.

Before we brought him home, we were given a pamphlet on how to care for him. It includes everything from dietary requirements to separation anxiety. But the section that took me by surprise was the one that told me how, if my new dog should choke, I could save his life with mouth-to-mouth resuscitation! As much as I love our dog, I don't know if I'm up to giving him mouth-to-mouth resuscitation.

"And the Lord God . . . breathed into his nostrils the breath of life." Think of that. Whatever the process, we who are of the earth, creaturely, were animated with divine breath. created in His image, we are stamped with His trademark. The almighty God who spoke the stars into being stooped to breathe life into His human child.

To insist on a literalistic understanding of this verse would be like reading a computer analysis of Mozart's *Requiem* instead of enjoying a virtuoso performance. How sad to reduce a truth so sublime, a music so beautiful, to pallid description. It's enough to know that we who were made of the earth have been lifted to touch heaven. Our need is proclaimed in our earthy origin and our God ordained destiny in the breath of life.

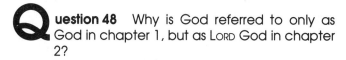

Q **uestion 48**   Why is God referred to only as God in chapter 1, but as LORD God in chapter 2?

The Old Testament uses two principal words for God: *Elohim* and *Yahweh*. *Elohim* is almost always translated God. It is the generic word for god in most Semitic languages (languages related to Hebrew).

Yahweh raises some problems for translators, though. It is God's covenant name, the name by which He made himself known to people from the beginning. It doesn't have a precise translation, unless we want to use "I AM," the one God himself gave Moses in Exodus 3:14–15. But "I AM" is awkward in most of the places where *Yahweh* is used.

To get around this, translators use the word *LORD*. This is because *Yahweh*, when encountered in the Hebrew text, is traditionally read that way. This tradition is older than we know and goes back to the Jewish refusal to pronounce the covenant name for God.

Another word used for God that can be confusing in translation is *Adonai*, the Exodus Hebrew word that actually means lord. To distinguish between the two, most Bible versions will let us know that *Yahweh* is intended by printing LORD in capital and small capital letters. When *Adonai* is intended they use Lord with lower case letters.

When Genesis speaks of the LORD God, it gives the two principal names for God, *Yahweh* and *Elohim*, used together as a compound name. Behind this is a very simple theological motivation. Genesis 1 shows us the transcendent God, distant and powerful, the creator whose mighty acts have to do with stars and planets and near infinite space. What an awesome and fearsome God *Elohim* is.

But Genesis 2 describes God in totally different terms. Here, *Yahweh* bends to create Adam. *Yahweh* lavishes love and care upon His creation. *Yahweh* establishes a relationship between creature and creator, a relationship that is unique in the literature of the ancient world.

In the polytheistic world of the patriarchs and ancient Israel, the danger existed that God's people might misunderstand and see one god in Genesis 1 and another in Genesis 2. At the beginning of God's revelation it's important to make it clear that the transcendent creator God is also the close-at-hand covenant God. So the two names are brought into the narrative as a compound name. *Yahweh Elohim* made us. Not just the God of the inter-galactic spaces, but the God of loving touches and walks in the garden.

The relationship between God and man is built on the most fundamental foundation. As *Elohim*, He created us and owns us. As Jonathan Edwards reminded us, it's a fearsome thing to fall into the hands of that kind of God. But the picture is tempered. As *Yahweh* He loves us. If God were only *Elohim* we might serve him out of dread, and if God were only *Yahweh* we would have no assurance that He could keep His promises. But as *Yahweh Elohim* we know that the God of the covenant is also the God of infinite power. Because our God is *Yahweh Elohim* we know that He can do what He's promised.

Q **uestion 49**   Why didn't Adam and Eve die when they disobeyed God (Genesis 2:15–17)?

They did. God meant spiritual death and Adam and Eve died spiritually when they ate the fruit. But physical death is also meant here, which is what Israelite readers would have thought of. In Paul's discussion of Adam's sin in Romans 5:12–6:10 and 1 Corinthians 15:42–49 it's impossible to separate the grim reality of physical death from the equally grim truth of spiritual death. It's too simplistic to say that God really meant spiritual death without taking into account the clear biblical teaching that we die physically as a result of Adam's sin.

In the garden, God provided access to a tree of life that would enable Adam and Eve to live forever. Without it they were as mortal as we are. God stationed cherubim and a flaming sword at the entrance to the garden after Adam and Eve sinned to keep them from returning to that tree (3:24). In this way, physical death was as much a consequence of the fall as was spiritual death. Spiritually speaking, their relationship with God was shattered by their sin.

From 3:8–11 we conclude that Adam and Eve had an intimate relationship with God, who walked in the garden in the cool of the evening and was accustomed to seeing and talking to Adam.

The image is crystal clear. God planted the garden for the enjoyment of Adam and Eve, but it was also a place where He communed with His creatures during the most pleasant time of the day. In the context of that fellowship, Adam and Eve enjoyed life, both physical and spiritual.

When the fellowship was destroyed, so was the source of life. Without the source of life, neither spiritual nor physical life was possible.

The reason physical death and spiritual death didn't take place simultaneously is, to my way of thinking, a simple matter of grace. If God was unwilling that any should perish in Peter's day (2 Peter 3:9) and we rely on that gracious patience in our day, what makes us think that He was eager to execute judgment in Adam's day?

Separation from God and from His life brought its inevitable result, and Scripture records Adam's physical death. But the Lamb of God was slain from before the foundations of the world (Revelation 13:8), and I believe that God's grace made available to sinners like us was also available to our first father and mother.

If I'm right, God's grace and mercy offered Adam and Eve the opportunity for repentance. Although they, as we, were dead in their trespasses and sin, their physical deaths came as a part of a natural process begun by their expulsion from God's presence. And as He waits for us, the patient father awaited the joyful return of His first prodigal children.

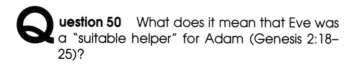 **uestion 50**   What does it mean that Eve was a "suitable helper" for Adam (Genesis 2:18–25)?

Adam Clarke, a godly scholar who died early in the nine-teenth century, long before there was a women's movement or concerns over feminism in the church, wrote concerning verse 18:

> . . . a help, a counterpart of himself, one formed from him, and a perfect resemblance of his person. If the word be rendered scrupulously literally, it signifies one "like," or "as himself," standing opposite to or before him. And this implies that the woman was to be a perfect resemblance of the man, possessing neither inferiority nor superiority, but being in all things like and equal to himself.

In 1:27 we read that both man and woman were made in God's image. In chapter 2 we see a man, alone and made in God's image, who requires a companion suitable to him. There was no other creature in God's creation like him, so to fill that void God created woman.

Adam's response to his first encounter with Eve tells us a lot. She is "bone of my bones and flesh of my flesh," Adam exclaimed. He used a Hebrew expression that could be paraphrased, "This is the very essence of me!" After combing the animal world for a companion suitable for him, Adam exclaims that in the woman he sees an essential part of himself.

The Talmud (the authoritative Jewish commmentary on the Scriptures) says, "He is called Man only if he has a wife." A modern day Jewish commentator, remarking on this, said, "like his rib, she is part of him, part of his structure, and without her he is essentially incomplete."

I think this is an essential teaching of the passage, and it works both ways. God created man and woman to be complementary parts of an indivisible unity. The concluding comment of chapter 2 seems to support this.

We often pass over the statement that they were naked and unashamed, but there's a profound reason that the remark was recorded. It tells us that there was such a unity between Adam and Eve that to see one another unclothed was no more shocking or embarassing than the sight of one's own body. Because they were one flesh they were unashamed.

That oneness was shattered by the fall. After they ate the fruit of the tree of knowledge, they saw one another as naked, separate, threatening beings whose sympathy and support could no longer be taken for granted. Their sexual relationship became

one of exploitation and manipulation, no longer the joyous celebration of divinely ordained oneness, and emotionally they saw
themselves as individuals with different and possibly competing
goals and motives. No longer one flesh, they were bound together
by mutual need and incompleteness, but not by a sense of total
identity.

Adam's petulant, "The woman you put here with me—she
gave me some fruit from the tree, and I ate it" (3:12), is a far cry
from the ecstatic cry of recognition he uttered in 2:23. Nothing
gives stronger proof of the radical change that has taken place
in the relationship between Adam and Eve than this. Here we see
the adversary relationship that characterizes so much of our
modern literature on the subject. The fall and its effects give rise
to notions of subordination and inferiority, not creation.

I see the idea of unity and oneness, not subordination and
inferiority, in this story. God designed man and woman differently
so they complement one another. Their functions, biologically
and to a certain extent socially, are different, but I find very little
support for the notion of subordination or inferiority in this
passage.

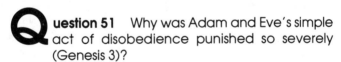

Question 51   Why was Adam and Eve's simple
act of disobedience punished so severely
(Genesis 3)?

When I was a boy stealing apples from the trees on the way
to school I wondered the same thing. It seemed innocent enough:
a boyhood indiscretion to which no one objects but the crabby
tree owners who selfishly horde their precious apples. I used to
hear the story and wonder if God was like the woman who used
to stand on her back porch and wave her broom at me when she
saw me in her tree. But now my checkered past has caught up
with me. Two of the last four houses I've lived in have been across
the alley from elementary schools. I can appreciate the frustration of nurturing a tree, a vine, or strawberry and raspberry
plants only to see the fruit walk off across a ball field to be thrown
at trees, cars, and classmates just for the fun of it.

When we focus on the act of eating the fruit, we make the
common mistake of riveting our attention on the act and not the
spirit. It's the spirit that's weak in this account.

Two related interpretive principles are at work in Genesis 3. Notice that the serpent offers Eve three inducements. He begins by questioning the prohibition against eating the fruit of the tree (v. 1). Then he denies the certainty of punishment (v. 4). Finally he tells Eve she and Adam will be like God if they'll just eat the fruit (v. 5).

P **rinciple 18**   Keep in mind the "principle of threes." The Bible frequently makes a point by breaking the point into threes.

P **rinciple 19**   Keep in mind the "principle of end stress," which means that the real emphasis is on the last element. The two that come first are there to set up the third.

We sometimes miss the point when, in interpreting a parable or a story, we give each of the elements equal weight.

In this case, both principles are at work. The final statement "You will be like God, knowing good and evil" (3:5) shows the true nature of the temptation and sin. Eve rationalized their disobedience by noting how good the fruit was, how beautiful the tree was, but ultimately that it was desirable for gaining wisdom (3:6). Here we have three rationalizations with the weight resting most heavily on the third.

The essence of Adam's sin was that he chose to be like God. In fact, that's the essence of all subsequent sins. Sin is the active replacement of God's standards, will, and commands with our own. Whether it's the decision to steal, murder, commit adultery, or gossip, we follow the lead established by Adam when we seek happiness in places God prohibits.

The clearest contrast between sin and righteousness is probably found in Philippians 2:5–11. In that famous passage, Christ, the second Adam, who is God, refuses to clutch at that status, while the first Adam, who is in God's image, demands more. The obedience of Christ is contrasted with the disobedience of Adam and the glorification of Christ stands out starkly from the depravity Adam willed to his descendants.

God didn't judge Adam, and with him all subsequent humanity, for eating a fruit. He judged Adam and his race for rebellion of the highest order. We want to be God, and we reject the only path open to that goal. Created god-like, we prefer our own version of deity. For that, Paul tells us, we are given over to the consequences of our own rebellion (Romans 1:21–25).

Adam's sin was not the simple indiscretion of a school boy. It was a traitorous thrust at the sovereignty of God. The punishment, tempered as it was with grace, was just and sure. We understand the death penalty for treason, and we understand the role of executive clemency. God could justly condemn and graciously pardon. The fact that Adam's physical death was delayed is evidence that He did both.

IN THE END OF THE BEGINNING

The majesty and purity of Genesis 1 dissipates in the rebellion and exile of Genesis 3. The beginning ends with Adam and his world condemned to futility and frustration (Romans 8:20–22). But it was only the beginning.

As important as the events of these three chapters are, they aren't the focus of Genesis. Like a good foundation, they are strong enough to support the rest of human history and divine revelation but they receive little embellishment. The very brevity of the story of creation and the fall is a clue that when God inspired it he wanted our attention to be drawn further than the account of creation.

More time is spent talking about Adam and Eve and God's relationship with them than about the rest of the physical universe. As the story continues in Genesis 4, Eve conceives and bears sons and daughters. The fallen race goes on, but not without the fatherly eye of God ever watchful over it and the mighty hand of God ever active in redemption. As the playwright said, "Thereby hangs the tale."

CHAPTER 5

PRINCIPLES

20 Interpretation should arise out of a text, fit its purpose, and avoid hypothetical understandings.

21 Where a theological explanation is possible, don't appeal to shaky and unprovable scientific speculation for one.

QUESTIONS

52 Why was Abel's offering acceptable to God when Cain's was rejected (Genesis 4:3–5)?

53 What was the mark of Cain (Genesis 4:13–16)?

54 If Adam and Eve were the first humans, and Cain was their first son, where did his wife come from (Genesis 4:17)?

55 How could the patriarchs before the flood have lived for so many hundreds of years (Genesis 5)?

56 Who were the "sons of God" and the "daughters of men" referred to in Genesis 6:1–4? Were the "Nephilim" their children?

57 What does it mean when God says His spirit will not always contend with man? Is the 120-year period God mentions the life span of man after the flood (Genesis 6:3)?

58 Does the Bible give a specific reason for the flood? What is it?

59 How long is a cubit, and how big was the ark?

ENTER CANAANITES, STAGE LEFT

22 Don't use a difficult passage to explain another difficult passage.

23 When we encounter a genealogy we should ask about its purpose.

60 Why do some Christians argue that the flood didn't cover the whole earth?

61 God gave the rainbow as a sign that He would never flood the earth again. Doesn't that prove that it hadn't rained before the flood?

62 What was Ham's sin? The curse Noah placed on Ham's line seems too severe for simply laughing at him.

63 Why was Canaan cursed when it was Ham who sinned against Noah? Does the curse on Canaan explain the enslavement of blacks by white races (Genesis 9:25–27)?

64 A lot of people around the world aren't included in the genealogy of chapter 10. Why not?

65 The story of the Tower of Babel has always troubled me. What was the terrible sin of the people? Was God afraid that they would succeed and storm heaven (Genesis 11:1–9)?

We need to read Scripture with our hearts open to the spirit, but we also need to read with our minds plugged in. When we ignore the clues the biblical writers give to tell what they're doing, we misunderstand their purpose. Part of our problem today is that we no longer tell stories. We leave storytelling to professional writers. Whether they're script writers for television, or authors who concoct stories in silence to be read in silence, we lose the thrill of participation that the art of storytelling arouses.

Think of Jesus speaking to the crowd and saying, "Now there was a certain rich man" or "Two men owed money to a certain moneylender" or "A man was going down from Jerusalem to Jericho, when he fell into the hands of robbers." His inflection and style tell us we're about to hear a story.

In a world where there was no entertainment for the common people except what they or their neighbors could produce, a good story told by a good storyteller was a real prize.

I can visualize a Jewish family sitting around their evening fire. The sun is setting, supper is finished, and the day's work is done. Before Moses there was no Bible to read, but there were stories to tell, from the dawn of time, handed down faithfully from generation to generation.

I hear the children jostling for position nearest to their father, their voices ringing out requests for favorites.

"Tell us the one about Father Abraham."

"No! Tell us about Joseph in Egypt."

"I want to hear about Noah and the flood."

Father thinks for a moment, then responds, "We haven't heard the story of Noah for a long time."

The chorus of children's voices sings in glorious harmony, "Yes, Noah!"

Father clears his throat, adjusting his voice to that of a storyteller.

"When men began to increase in number on the earth" he begins.

I try to hear that voice when I read the first four verses of Genesis 6. The lines have grabbed the attention of generations beyond number. They've reminded thousands of listeners of a world long vanished. They've reverberated with the solemn words of divine abandonment and throbbed with the menace of the nephilim, great heroes of a bygone day whose exploits surely aroused a thrill of fear and a flush of admiration.

Genesis 6:1–4 are the opening lines of one of earth's great stories. Great not simply because it's true, but because it's told so well. The stage is set by recalling the events that frame Noah's story. In the midst of the events, we get a glimpse into the mind of God, and we see where the story's going.

Historical sections like this are told to be fascinating. Yes, they contain information. But it's the kind of information we might get from reading the headlines as we pass a newsstand. We might speculate about the details of the story, but without reading the story itself, we have no absolute certainty. If God had meant us to have absolute certainty about those events, we'd have more than headlines. A clever interpreter can provide details, but they're the product of the interpreter's informed imagination, not the content of Scripture.

SETTING THE STAGE FOR THE STORY

The first three chapters of Genesis are a prologue that introduces us to the marvelous universe God created. It opens our eyes to our place in God's plan and the tragic fall from grace that explains our lostness.

Looking forward, the heart of Genesis begins to beat in chapter 12, where we meet the patriarch Abraham whose biography lays the cornerstone for God's plan of redemption. The eight chapters that link these two very different sections serve a vital function. Abraham is introduced into a world of cities and cultures, people and politics. To understand Abraham, we need to know where those other people came from, which is what we learn in Genesis 4–11. I think of Genesis 1–11 in terms of drama.

The script for Thornton Wilder's classic play "Our Town" begins like this:

> No curtain. No scenery. The audience, arriving, sees an empty stage in halflight. Presently the STAGE MANAGER, hat on and pipe in mouth, enters and begins placing a table and three chairs downstage left, and a table and three chairs down-stage right.

These are known as stage directions. Sometimes they're much more detailed, but "Our Town" is produced with a minimum of sets and staging. Stage directions are never read aloud in performance, and the audience is only aware of them through what they see when the house lights dim and the curtain rises.

The play can't go on without them. They tell actors where to enter and exit. They dictate the location of action on the stage. They open the playwright's mind to the director and cast and let them see the room or countryside the author envisioned when writing the story. Even a play like "Our Town," which is played on an empty stage with a few scattered tables, chairs, and benches, needs stage directions to get under way.

When I read the opening chapters of Genesis, I think of them as the stage directions. In Genesis 1–11 we're introduced to the cast of characters who will occupy our attention throughout the rest of Scripture and the rest of human history. We meet God, the creator, in chapter 1 and his friends Adam and Eve in chapters 2 and 3. The fallen line of Cain, the godly line of Seth, the peoples of the ancient Near East, and the ancestors of Abraham are all introduced to us here.

The stage itself, with sky, sea, and dry land in place, is brought to life with vegetation, fish, crawling creatures, birds, and land animals. Beyond the realities of the world God has made for us, we learn of His chosen relationship with that world. As creator, He is sovereign. We discover that He has the power to judge, but we also learn that His power is tempered by the desire to redeem. In the story of the Fall we learn why redemption is necessary. In the story of Cain and his descendants we see the tragic deterioration of a lost humanity. In Noah and his family, we're introduced to the first biblical example of God's grace, and in the tower of Babel we see the prototype for all of humanity's organized rebellions against God.

The divine drama of redemption, played out on the stage of human experience, can't begin until chapter eleven completes the stage directions. Then Abraham makes his entrance.

Historically, we don't necessarily need the first eleven chapters of Genesis to understand what follows. But theologically, none of the rest of the Bible makes sense without them. Think of all the biblical teaching that rests on Genesis 1–11.

There would be no doctrine of universal sin without the account of the fatal disobedience of humanity's representative. Without universal sin there is no need for redemption. If sin isn't present in all humanity because of the original sin of the first man, what happens to Paul's explanation of redemption as found in Romans 5 and 6? Without the pure, simple account of creation, any concept of God's sovereignty is hard to support. Even monotheism, the belief in one God, depends on the established truth of creation.

As important as these chapters are, they are as puzzling as any in the Bible. I will give what I've found to be satisfactory solutions to biblical problem passages in Genesis 4–11. But be aware that other believers offer other solutions. This is not the place for arrogance or dogmatism. Christian men and women of unquestionable commitment are divided on interpretation here and, although some do so, these aren't good chapters to set up as tests of orthodoxy. Instead, look at them as sources for truth that will stand us in good stead in our act of God's drama of redemption.

The Canaanites have exited. The stage is ours. Let's pray that when God brings down the curtain at the end of our time on stage, He will be pleased with our performance. We can increase the likelihood by understanding those who preceeded us.

Question 52   Why was Abel's offering acceptable to God when Cain's was rejected (Genesis 4:3–5)?

The traditional answer to this question has been that Abel offered a blood sacrifice while Cain's offering was only grain and vegetables. Since God demands blood sacrifice, the gift of the fruit of the soil was unacceptable.

On the surface this looks like a good answer, but a closer look shows us something more.

To begin with, this event took place thousands of years before the requirement for blood sacrifice was explained in the Law of Moses. In the absence of any mention of that requirement in this passage, I question the validity of applying that Mosaic revelation to the time of Abel.

Furthermore, the Hebrew word translated "offering" is not the usual word for a blood sacrifice. In fact, its most common meaning is "gift." If Abel offers God a gift from his flock, and Cain offers a gift from his field, we're not talking about a sacrifice in the usual sense of the word.

The Hebrew word for that kind of sacrifice contains the idea of the slaughter of an animal. If Cain's offering was a violation of the requirement for blood sacrifice, that would be the word used.

The language of the text offers a different clue. It emphasizes the quality of Abel's offering. Abel offered not only the firstborn of his flock, but the choicest of the firstborn. We probably miss the point when we read that Abel brought "fat portions from some of the first born of his flock" (4:4). In a cholesterol crazed age it's hard to appreciate that the fat of the lamb was considered the best part. It was given to the honored guest at dinner or to God in an offering. Abel's offering was the best part of the best offspring of the flock.

Cain, on the other hand, brought "some of the fruit of the soil." The way it's phrased calls our attention to the contrast. Abel scoured his flock for the best and offered it to God. Cain's offering consisted of just some of his crop. I can see Cain rummaging through his rutabaga bin to find a few bruised, wilted specimens to add to the sour apples and hail damaged wheat.

The language is sparse, but it doesn't take much imagination to see Cain's attitude. In contrast with his righteous brother, who wanted to give God nothing but the best, Cain brought whatever came to hand.

We might also ask if Cain would have become angry at his brother, and at God, if his offering had been brought in the spirit of giving that God honors? If Cain had prepared his gift for God like a gardener preparing an exhibit for the county fair, picking only the best of the best of his produce, I believe God's favor would have rested on him as well as on Abel.

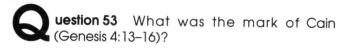

Question 53   What was the mark of Cain (Genesis 4:13–16)?

At its simplest, the mark of Cain was a mark of ownership. Cain feared that when he went into the world anyone he encountered might kill him. In a day before uniform law codes and uniformed police officers, his fear was reasonable. Citizens of a city or region were granted whatever protection their family, village, or town might afford. But for people in a strange place, there was no protection.

A great deal of malicious nonsense has been read into this passage. Some understand the mark as a curse of some sort. In the Middle Ages, Jews were required to wear a mark identifying them as Jews. The "Christians" who decreed this oppressive "mark of Cain" justified it as marking the "murderers of Christ."

Others have interpreted the mark as skin color and have used it as an excuse for enslaving Cain's "descendants." Far from being a curse, though, this is one of the many early examples of God dealing with sin by administering grace. Cain's banishment from the land was his punishment. The mark was just the opposite. It was God's way of showing anyone who encountered Cain that he was under God's protection.

What the actual mark was, Scripture does not say. In not saying, it turns our attention away from the actual physical mark and rivets it on the graciousness of God, which took a man so hardened as to murder his own brother and placed him under divine protection. God marked Cain to protect him. Cain was his, and no man could harm him without the God of all grace taking action.

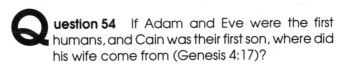 **uestion 54**   If Adam and Eve were the first humans, and Cain was their first son, where did his wife come from (Genesis 4:17)?

This is one of my favorite questions. Every non-believing college sophomore asks it, and I enjoy having it hurled at me. I'll be sitting there talking about the faith with a friend or someone who's interested in Christianity. A stranger will overhear and sit down to listen. After a while he'll clear his throat, squint at me like Clint Eastwood in the hope that I'll make his day, and let me have it with the Cain's wife question.

For people who've never read the Bible, this seems an insurmountable challenge to its credibility. There are two simple answers to the question.

One answer, the one I don't use first, involves an attempt to deal with the problem of very ancient human-like fossils. Some people argue that God initially made a creature that would be nearly indistinguishable from humans.

This creature existed alongside all the other animals, developing some simple culture, making simple tools, burying its dead, and, in all outward appearances, acting human. The difference was that these creatures, as advanced as they appeared to be, were before Adam. They had intelligence, but they lacked the soul that God first breathed into Adam.

Since we understand humanity primarily from a spiritual standpoint, it's not too far-fetched to speculate that there were human-like, soul-less creatures on the earth at the same time as Adam. If they were there, Cain might have married one of them.

I mention this theory, often referred to as the theory of a "pre-Adamic man," simply for information. Although it has some attractive features, it creates as many problems as it solves. It does offer an explanation that harmonizes Scripture and Paleontology, though, and several evangelical students of the Old Testament find it quite plausible.

The other explanation is much simpler. Cain married his sister. The thought horrifies us, but there are some good reasons for adopting it. If God intended the human race to begin with two individuals, He also, of necessity, intended that their children intermarry. The Bible tells us that Adam and Eve had other sons and daughters (5:4). They were children of the wellsprings of all humanity's genetic material, so there was no good genetic reason for them not to marry. Their children would suffer none of the negative effects of intermarriage, and God's laws prohibiting such things were millennia in the future.

In that simpler world, only one command given to the first parents could still be obeyed. God had told them to multiply and populate the earth. The simplest, most biblically supportable answer to the problem of Cain's wife comes from within the apparently numerous daughters of Eve.

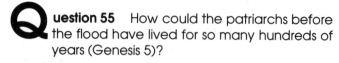

Q **uestion 55**   How could the patriarchs before the flood have lived for so many hundreds of years (Genesis 5)?

It must be very humbling for a modern medico to read Genesis 5 and see the ages of men who, without the benefit of high tech hospital care, organ transplants, and antibiotics, lived to be over 900 years old. Enoch, the baby of the chapter, was translated at the tender age of only 365 years.

Numerous attempts have been made to explain these great ages. Some assume the years are to be read literally; others assume they are symbolic.

In this case, it's argued, the literal is the simplest, most straightforward reading. For those who agree with this, there are a variety of explanations for the advanced ages of the men they call the "antediluvian patriarchs" (forefathers from before the flood). Most of these involve some combination of natural forces that prolonged life before the flood, which were removed after the flood.

The canopy that some suggest was placed around the earth at creation is one explanation. If we accept the idea that a great envelope of water surrounded the earth before the flood, we can assume that it had some impact on life on the earth. The most notable of these would have been the screening of harmful radiation from outer space. Without the harmful affects of cosmic rays, a longer life span would be possible.

Others suggest that a change in diet after the flood accounts for reduced lifespans. It's commonly held that humanity was vegetarian before the flood.

Genesis 9:3 specifically states that Noah and his descendants would be allowed to eat the flesh of animals, with the qualification that the blood not be left in it. The shift from a vegetarian diet to one containing red meat explains the decreased longevity, they argue.

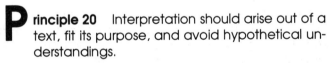

Principle 20   Interpretation should arise out of a text, fit its purpose, and avoid hypothetical understandings.

I believe these explanations are inadequate. As dealt with elsewhere in this book, the notion of a canopy around the earth rests on a rather thin textual foundation. If I could accept the existence of the canopy I might be able to accept the idea that the canopy screened out harmful radiation. Such a canopy, however, would screen out a lot more than harmful radiation. Anyone who has ever seen bright daylight turn to a dusk-like gloom as the clouds of a heavy thunder storm rolled in can imagine how little light would come through an envelope of solid water.

In the same vein, although God specifically allows the eating of meat in the new covenant with Noah, it was never prohibited before the flood.

We might assume that Noah's great-grandfather was a vegetarian, but there's no biblical text that says so. In fact, unless there's been some radical restructuring of human anatomy and physiology since the flood, it can be argued that God designed us to be meat eaters. Our digestive systems are constructed to convert meat to our use just as our teeth are designed to chew a variety of foods, including meat.

A less naturalistic explanation says that the degenerative effects of sin spread slowly through the human race. I'm much more inclined to accept this theological explanation than I am the pseudo-scientific ones we've just looked at. Of the literal understandings of the passage, however, my favorite interpretation would be the one that I think is most in keeping with the theological intent of Scripture.

In the Old Testament, God's favor is expressed by prolonged life. The degenerate line of Cain was described in Genesis 4, concluding with the violent, vindictive Lamech. Chapter 5 presents the stark contrast of the godly line of Seth, culminating in Noah, the man on whom God's favor rested.

In comparing the two chapters, we notice two things: it doesn't mention the ages of any of Cain's descendants, and all seven of their names are echoed in Seth's line. These points are often overlooked when we use these passages for computing the age of the earth.

The ages of Seth and his offspring play a part in the theological function of these chapters. Moses must have had a reason for omitting the ages of Cain's line while going into great detail on the ages of Seth's.

Could it be that the great ages of the "antediluvian patriarchs" were unusual even then, and that the reason they're mentioned is because they were unusual? If so, they're recorded to demonstrate God's blessing and not for purely chronological purposes. This idea is bolstered by the similarities of the names recorded in the two lists.

SETH'S LINE	CAIN'S LINE
Adam	Adam
Seth	Cain
Enosh	Enoch
Kenan	Irad
Mahalalel	Mehujael
Jared	Methushael
Enoch	Lamech
Methusaleh	Jabal, Jubal, Tubal-Cain
Lamech	
Noah	

The transfer of the names from Hebrew to English softens the obvious similarities, but they're still fairly obvious. Each list has a Lamech and an Enoch as well as several names that are similar such as Cain and Kenan, Irad and Jared, Mahalalel and Mehujael, Methusaleh and Methushael.

What a dramatic contrast. And what a graphic demonstration of the difference a godly father makes in the lives of his descendants. Most important is the powerful contrast between the degenerate line of Cain and the godly line of Seth, which alone preserved knowledge and fear of the Lord. How fitting that the representatives of that line should be blessed with exceedingly long lives.

This answer arises out of the text, fits the purpose of the text, and doesn't require some hypothetical natural situation to account for the long lives.

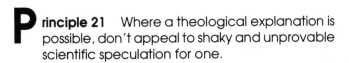

Principle 21   Where a theological explanation is possible, don't appeal to shaky and unprovable scientific speculation for one.

Some evangelicals believe that the symbolic use of numbers is a better explanation than any I've mentioned so far. The barbaric "Song of the Sword" sung by Lamech (Genesis 4:23–24) is an example of this.

Lamech, Cain's descendant, was chosen to demonstrate the outcome of Cain's original sin. He killed a man in retaliation for an injury. Looking back to God's promise of seven-fold vengeance against anyone who harmed Cain (Genesis 4:15), Lamech promised he would avenge himself seventy-seven times. It's hard to ignore the symbolic importance of the fact that the Sethite Lamech lived to the ripe old age of 777.

There are enough elements in the two genealogies to raise the possibility of a metaphorical or literary purpose. The two lines, beginning with Adam, contain seven Cain and ten Seth representatives. With the addition of three sons of Lamech, Jabal, Jubal, and Tubal-Cain, both lists total ten. It may be a coincidence that the number of generations from Noah to Abraham is also ten (Genesis 11:10–26), but I doubt it.

I also doubt that it's a coincidence that Genesis itself is divided into ten sections. Anthropologists studying genealogical records among preliterate people have discovered that the preferred number of generations in any geneaology is ten. To maintain this symmetry, only major representatives of the line are mentioned. It's probable that this is the case in Genesis 5.

A middle ground position assigns the ages to dynasties rather than to individuals. Significant ancient genealogical documents offer parallels to this. In most cases, they record high points rather than completely retell the nation's history.

I favor a theological, possibly symbolic approach. It seems in keeping with the purpose of Scripture to see the ages mentioned in Genesis 5 as a reflection of God's blessing on the righteous sons of Seth. The application of the literalistic approach has yielded much argumentation but not much that's useful for teaching, rebuking, correcting, or training in righteousness.

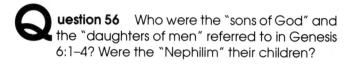

Q **uestion 56**   Who were the "sons of God" and the "daughters of men" referred to in Genesis 6:1–4? Were the "Nephilim" their children?

An answer that has enjoyed wide acceptance among conservative Christians is that the "sons of God" were fallen angels and the "daughters of men" were human women. This was the dominant view in the early church and among ancient Jewish commentators as well. The historian Josephus, writing shortly after the time of Jesus, presented this interpretation as fact. He gave no indication that there was any other possibility.

The phrase "bene elohim" (ben-A EL-o-heem), translated sons of God in verse 2, is used of angels in the Old Testament (Job 1:6; 2:1; 38:7; Daniel 3:25). Further support is found in the reference to spirits who, in the days of the flood, were disobedient and, as a result, were in prison at the time of Christ's death (1 Peter 3:18–20; Jude 5–7).

The "nephilim" (ne-fil-EEM) were the children of this unnatural alliance between fallen spirits and human women. The word "nephilim" itself may be derived from the Hebrew verb *naphal* (na-FALL), which means "to fall." If this understanding is correct, "nephilim" means "the fallen ones."

As popular as this view is among Christians, it suffers from some serious flaws. One that troubles me most is that those who argue most forcefully for this interpretation tend to come from the extremes of Old Testament scholarship. They are either the most conservative or the most liberal of Old Testament commentators.

Those of the liberal persuasion point to the numerous stories from mythology where a great hero is the son of a human mother and one of the gods. They mention Gilgamesh, Hercules, the Greek Titans, and the giants of Nordic myth. This passage in Genesis, they say, is just another example of mythological thinking cropping up in the Bible. Even when they admit that the biblical writer doesn't agree with this mythological thought, they hold to the assumption that it represents some early Hebrew myth.

If the fallen angels/human women understanding is true, they may have a case. But nothing in Scripture suggests that such a bizarre relationship is a possibility. First Peter 3:18–20 and Jude 5–7 offer very weak support.

P **rinciple 22**   Don't use a difficult passage to explain another difficult passage.

One of the most basic of rules of interpretation is don't use a difficult passage to explain another difficult passage. Few New Testament passages are as difficult to interpret as those used to support this idea. The story, as understood by some leading conservatives, seems more at home among the Greeks and Hittites than among the chosen people of God.

The most troubling flaw is that Jesus himself says that angels neither marry nor give in marriage (Matthew 22:30). For fallen angels to marry human women involves a type of physical existence and relationship that contradicts Jesus' specific teaching and the general tone of Scripture.

Most commentators who adopt this position say this union, and its unnatural offspring, caused the flood. God himself told the reason for the flood, however, and it had nothing to do with the presence of demigods on earth. Even if it did, the punishment seems misplaced. If cohabitation between demons and women brought the flood, why was humanity in general the focus of judgment?

Further, if the "nephilim" were the offspring of their union, and the flood was to wipe them out, it failed. The "giants" that later frightened the Israelite spies so badly they wanted to turn back from conquering Canaan were called, in Hebrew, "nephilim." Unless they were stowed away on the ark, they must have been formidable swimmers.

Some commentators get around this problem by moving the fallen angels into the period after the flood. They suggest that the cohabitation is continuing and that whenever it happens a new crop of "nephilim" spring upon the world. If the fallen angels theory is more at home in Greek mythology, this kind of speculation is more at home in a Stephen King horror story.

The list of conservative commentators who reject this idea is long and impressive. Matthew Henry, Adam Clarke, C. I. Scofield, Gleason Archer, E. J. Young, and others all seek another meaning of the text. The position adopted by most of them finds support in the text's immediate context.

First, the fallen angel idea assumes that all four verses (6:1–4) point at the coming of the flood and explain its purpose. I think, however, that these verses are another example of the Hebrew summary statement. Verses 6:1–4 provide a very general picture of conditions before the flood.

The marriage of "daughters of men" with "sons of God" is an important contributing factor, but not because the marriage is an unnatural one between spirit beings and human women. Rather, the joining of the two lines, one godly and the other ungodly, described in chapters 4 and 5, resulted in the apostasy of all humanity, with the exception of Noah.

Principle 23　　When we encounter a genealogy we should ask about its purpose.

Until we know the purpose of a genealogy, we're almost certain to misunderstand and misuse it. We've already established that the line of Cain shows the downward course of human morality. The line of Seth shows what happens when parents hand down the knowledge of the Lord to their children. After the line of Seth reaches its conclusion in Noah, the sons of God and daughters of men married and had children.

Genesis 6:1–2 points to the mingling of God's people with the Devil's people. The descendants of the man who "was not because God took him" have married the daughters of the man who sang that he would avenge himself seventy-seven times. In the context of this dilution of the believing community God said that His spirit would not always strive with humanity (v. 3).

Verse 4, wrapping up some loose ends, introduces us to the "nephilim." Nowhere in the text are the "nephilim" said to be the children mentioned in verse 2. The problem we have with verse 4 comes because we automatically link it with verse 2, when Moses never intended that to happen.

Israel knew about the titans and demigods so popular in ancient mythology. The Hittites and the Mesopotamians both had stories about them. Moses assigned them to this period. They were heroes all right, but only in the sense that other men were heroes. When the events of verses 1–3 were taking place, there were "nephilim" on the earth, the text says, and they were there afterwards as well. They were, it goes on to say, heroes, but the word used is one that is applied to David and his "mighty men" or heroes. These mythical heroes of superhuman stature were certainly men of great renown, but they were men nonetheless.

My answer to the question, then, is that the sons of God were not angels, fallen or otherwise. They were the descendants of the godly line of Seth. The daughters of men were women of the degraded line of the murderous Cain. Their intermarriage gives proof from before the flood of Paul's wisdom in warning against marriage with unbelievers (2 Corinthians 6:14). The "nephilim" were heroes, not the offspring of an unnatural union, but heroes of a sort the Israelites knew from their own experience.

Question 57   What does it mean when God says His spirit will not always contend with man? Is the 120-year period God mentions the life span of man after the flood (Genesis 6:3)?

There are at least two ways of understanding this verse. The RSV translation, "My spirit shall not abide in man forever," implies that the extraordinary life spans of the patriarchs who lived before the flood will be shortened to a mere 120 years.

On the other hand, the NIV translation, "My spirit will not contend with man forever," says that God will place a time limit on His patience. The Holy Spirit will work to convict the depraved humanity of Noah's day for only 120 years; after that comes judgment.

The obscurity of the Hebrew in this verse makes both versions possible. My personal preference, though, is the second. If this was a reference to the average human age limit after the flood, it never took effect in any consistent manner.

Of all the characters in Scripture whose ages we know, only Moses lived 120 years. Joseph lived 110, but came several hundred years before Moses.

In the absence of other biblical evidence that this was intended to be an average life span, support for this approach is hard to find.

My preference for the other interpretation would be a lot easier to defend if there was plenty of support for it, but I have to be honest and say that I don't think there is. The strongest argument I can put forward is that it seems to fit well with the biblical teaching that God isn't willing that any should perish.

This is a theological argument based on the doctrine of grace. From Genesis to Revelation, God never brought judgment without warning and opportunity for repentance. One hundred and twenty years allowed time for the calling of Noah, the construction of the ark, and a long, though fruitless, evangelistic career. The writer of Hebrews said that Noah's faith condemned the world (Hebrews 11:7).

He had the faith to build a boat, the dimensions of which were unequalled until the era of modern shipping, and to build it in a part of the world where it had no place to sail. During the 120-year period of God's forebearance, the ark stood as tangible evidence of the intangible future of the human race, and for the full course of years, brought no one to repentance.

That's my preference, but either approach does justice to the language of the verse. It's a mistake to sink footings and build a skyscraper on the swamp of speculation.

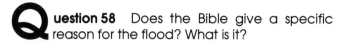

Question 58   Does the Bible give a specific reason for the flood? What is it?

Yes, the Bible states the reason for the flood, and it does so several times in Genesis 6. We tend to read over the Bible's explanation because we have in mind a common misinterpretation of Matthew 24:37.

In Matthew Jesus said that His Second Coming would be as unexpected as the flood was in the days of Noah. Right up to the moment the flood came people were absorbed in the normal pursuits of everyday life. That's the gist of the famous "As it was in the days of Noah" passage.

As we mentioned in an earlier chapter, when we read this passage our eyes are drawn to the practices of eating, drinking, and marrying. That's what Noah's contemporaries were doing when God sent the flood, so we assume those practices are the reason for it. Eating, drinking, and marrying are rather innocent exercises, however, so something more evil must have been going on. So we read the passage in terms of gluttony, drunkenness, and immorality.

But that isn't what Jesus was saying. This whole section speaks of the unexpectedness of the Christ's return. Just as the people of Noah's day went on with the normal activities, so will people alive at the Second Coming. Men will go to work and women will prepare dinner as if the world will always be here. But in the midst of their daily toil, it will all end.

Genesis 6:5 says that humanity's wickedness was great and "that every inclination of the thoughts of his heart was only evil all the time." The concept of evil certainly includes gluttony, drunkenness, and sexual immorality. But verse 5 uses the concept of evil and wickedness without reference to its specific manifestations. The two key words in this verse, wickedness and evil, need an interpretation, which the Bible provides.

Genesis 6:11 says that "the earth was corrupt in God's sight and was full of violence." In Hebrew, this isn't the violence of warfare or the sometimes unavoidable violence of authorities restraining a greater violence. It's the malicious, oppressive, cruel violence that anyone would recognize as sinful.

Jewish sources from centuries past interpreted the "lawlessness" or "violence" (both are possible translations of the Hebrew) as the result of too much ease and affluence. Men and women who had everything, they reasoned, became cruel and impious. They took no thought of God and had no consideration for His creation. This is a shocking thought for twentieth-century Americans.

Verse 11 narrows the possible meanings of wickedness and evil. The specific wickedness and evil of humanity before the flood was a violent, oppressive, and cruel way of life. God repeats the evaluation of verse 11 in verse 13. It was for violence, He says, that He would have to destroy the world.

The Hebrew word translated "corrupt" speaks of destruction. In fact, when God says that "I am surely going to 'destroy' both them and the earth" (v. 13), He uses the same verb.

Sometimes nonbelievers will ask how a loving God could destroy all life for the sake of a little sin. This passage implies that when God decided to flood the earth, humanity had already ruined it and itself. His only choice was to wash the planet clean and start over.

And wash it God did. God accused Cain by saying that his brother's blood cried out for justice (Genesis 4:10). In a world filled with violence, how magnified the crying must have been. The earth that had been a garden for the first inhabitants had become a slaughter house, so soaked with innocent blood that its cry rising to heaven must have been a painful shriek in the ears of a just and loving God. I think that's why God chose water as His instrument of judgment. The waters of destruction were, in a way, also the waters of a new creation. Once cleansed, the earth could become the home of a new humanity with Noah and his sons as the founders.

Q **uestion 59**   How long is a cubit, and how big was the ark?

The word cubit comes from the Latin for "forearm." In the roughest sort of way, that's how long a cubit is. Most non-metric measurements got their start in this imprecise way. An inch is the width of someone's thumb. On average, thirty-six thumb widths are a yard, as is the distance from your nose to the tip of your thumb. A foot was . . . well, you guess.

This concept would work if God had stamped us all with the same mold, but who would want to sell anything by the foot to someone who wears size sixteen shoes? And how would you like to run a fabric store with Kareem Abdul Jabbar measuring yards from his nose to his thumb?

To reach some uniformity a nation usually chose a particular thumb, foot, or forearm as a standard. Usually it belonged to the king. In the case of the biblical cubit, the usual length is 17.5 inches. We don't know whose arm that came from or, for that matter, whether it was the cubit in the time of Noah, but we usually compute the size of the ark using that standard.

That gives us a ship about 450 feet long, 75 feet wide, and 45 feet high. With its three decks it had a cargo area of 101,250 square feet. Not until the late nineteenth century was a larger vessel launched. The largest ocean-going tankers today are in the range of 1,000–1,200 feet. Modern vessels dwarf the ark in size and tonnage, but they're constructed in high-tech shipyards using the best of modern engineering. The *Queen Elizabeth 2,* with an overall length of 963 feet and a beam, or width, of 105 feet, is the second largest passenger vessel in service. It's a bit more than twice the length of the ark and only thirty feet wider.

A more reasonable comparison would be a nineteenth century wooden hulled vessel. The *U.S. Constitution,* that invincible frigate from the heroic era of our country's naval history, measures only 204 feet overall with a width of forty three and one-half feet. In that small area, she carried a crew of 450.

There were larger wooden ships than *Old Ironsides* but, until the 1880s, none matched the ark in length, assuming that the 17.5-inch cubit was the standard in Noah's day.

The standard cubit is arrived at by measuring the Siloam tunnel, built by Hezekiah around 700 B.C., and dividing the length by 1,200 cubits, the dimension given in the inscription carved in the tunnel to celebrate its completion.

If the cubit were longer in the days of Noah, the ark would be proportionally larger. If shorter, the ark would be smaller. Either way, it stands as one of the truly monumental construction projects of the ancient world.

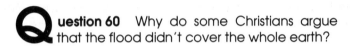

Q **uestion 60**   Why do some Christians argue that the flood didn't cover the whole earth?

This dispute, like the one over creation, is of no interest to unbelievers. For the most part, only those with a high view of Scripture are concerned with the nature and the extent of the flood. Very few nonbelievers accept the historical truth of the biblical flood.

A particular understanding of the flood has become a test of orthodoxy for many Christians in recent years. The arguments of the chief sponsors of the position would have us believe that all real Christians agree with them. Those who don't, they imply, have had their spiritual vision clouded by compromise.

Regardless of the claims made for this position, it's possible to be a spiritually alive, effective Christian and disagree. Far from the image of unassailable scientific certainty we receive from proponents of this flood-geology, no current approach to the question of the great flood is without its problems.

My purpose is to suggest that the idea of a massive, life-eradicating, global flood is not the only possible explanation of the biblical data. In fact, there are some good reasons why many evangelicals have come to accept a localized flood.

They begin with an assessment of the evidence God left in the book of His world. Most Christian geologists argue that there is no evidence of a worldwide cataclysm. Signs of localized catastrophes of unthinkable proportions are found everywhere, but nothing that proves a single, worldwide flood.

This statement does not call into question the truth of Scripture, but it does call into question a particular set of interpretive ideas. I suggest that this is a valid use of nature. In fact, I wonder if God didn't place information in nature to use as a corrective for our sometimes inadequate understanding of the Bible.

Whether we like to admit it or not, for centuries Christian authorities appealed to the Bible as proof that the earth was flat. But hardly anyone alive today insists that Scripture describes a flat earth, even though it was the official understanding for hundreds of years.

The same verses are still there, and nonbelievers still point to them as proof that the Bible is wrong about the nature of the world. But did Scripture ever teach a flat earth? I think not. Bible readers today see poetic imagery in places where Christians of past centuries saw proof of a flat earth.

Do Christians sometimes read their own ideas into Scripture? Of course, but that doesn't mean Scripture is in error. I believe in an infallible Bible, but I don't believe in the infallibility of interpretation.

The realities of the world, as we observe it, have made the flat earth interpretation an impossibility. They have also made a picture of the solar system with the sun revolving around a fixed earth impossible to believe. In these cases, the book of the world, nature, has operated as a very effective corrective to the mistaken reading of the Book of the Word.

The geological evidence that suggests there was no world wide flood is nowhere near as persuasive as the evidence arguing against a flat earth. But it is evidence we should use in assessing our interpretation of Scripture, not the truth of Scripture.

I acknowledge that some Christians with impeccable credentials in science and engineering argue that the whole earth bears witness to a flood so staggering it could only have been the flood of Noah. Nevertheless, in this debatable and highly technical area I've chosen to accept the opinion of Christians whose scientific credentials, also impeccable, bear more directly on the study of earth. In doing so, I have found very few Christian geologists who accept the idea that there is scientific evidence for a global flood.

Christians tend to assume that anyone with a doctoral degree knows everything. But there is some truth to the joke that says doctors are people who narrow the focus of their study so they know more and more about less and less until they know everything about nothing. Joking aside, the truth is that doctorates are earned by devoting intense study to a narrowly defined topic. A friend of once described the topic of his Ph.D. dissertation as "A county in Virginia that I used to be interested in."

Some people are awed by anyone with a Ph.D., but those in the scientific community will listen to geologists only when they speak about geology, not when they pontificate on anatomy. In fact, the author of an article on geology took another author to task because he, as a geophysicist, wasn't qualified to speak authoritativly about historical geology.

My point in all this is that we need to be a little more discerning in our acceptance of authorities. I still believe the flood was universal, but not because of the evidence of creation science. I refuse to let a temporal scientific explanation influence my understanding of God's timeless word.

Other sincere Christians argue that the flood only covered the Mesopotamian river valley. They offer several arguments in favor of the theory of a localized flood.

First, there's what I call the "economy of the miraculous." God seldom does more than is required in a particular situation. For instance, He parted the Jordan River for Joshua and Israel, but there's no record that He leveled the Jordan valley to ease their passage. That would have been a nice touch, and the priests carrying the ark would probably have appreciated it, but it was unnecessary.

Jesus could have healed all the sick of all Israel with a word, but He chose to heal only those who came to Him personally. God sent fire from heaven to prove himself, but He left the elimination of the Baal priests to Elijah. And speaking of Elijah, God sent ravens to feed him instead of providing food directly, as He did later when Elijah was fleeing from Jezebel.

God's demonstration of His power throughout Scripture is rare enough to remain awe-inspiring but always restrained. God doesn't swat mosquitoes with meteorites. If His aim was to eradicate all life, with the exception of Noah and his family, the flood would have been extensive enough to accomplish that goal, but not more extensive.

If, as proponents of the local flood idea argue, the whole human race was contained in the Mesopotamian river valley, it would only have been necessary to flood that portion of the earth.

The second argument involves the word translated "earth" throughout the flood story. It's a common Hebrew word, occuring over 2,500 times in the Old Testament. In over 80 percent of those occurences it is translated "land," not "earth." For example, it describes the "land" of Israel, not the "earth" of Israel. The intended meaning is not always clear, so some argue that in much of the flood story the meaning was "land" and not "earth." That simple change makes a remarkable difference in the way the flood story reads. If English translators had chosen land rather than earth, some key verses would read as follows:

The "land" was corrupt in God's . . . (6:11). God saw how corrupt the "land" had become, for all the people on the "land" had corrupted their ways (6:12). I am going to bring floodwaters on the "land" to destroy all life under the heavens, every creature that has the breath of life in it. Everything on the "land" will perish (6:17). Reading the story this way, do you agree with the idea of a local flood, or do you see a universal flood?

Using information available in Genesis, one Christian scholar calculated the depth of flood waters that covered the earth as 108 feet. On the basis of the numbers from Genesis, he argued that the flood waters decreased at a rate of only four inches per day. At that rate, a water depth of 1,000 feet would take 3,000 days, or nearly nine years, before Noah could depart from the ark at a time when "the water had dried up from the earth" (Genesis 8:13).[1]

According to Genesis, though, the water dried up in time for Noah to leave the ark on the first day of the first month of his 601st year. The flood began on the seventeenth day of the second month of Noah's 600th year. That's less than a year from start to finish.

If the flood was localized, some people argue, God would have had no reason to promise Noah that He would never again destroy all human life with a flood. But, if the intent of the flood was to destroy all life, and not simply cover the globe with water, this covenant poses no problem for the idea of a localized flood.

The clear meaning of the covenant with Noah is seen in Genesis 9:11: "Never again will 'all life' be cut off by the waters of

---

[1]

Arthur C. Custance, *The Flood: Local or Global?* (Grand Rapids, Mich: Zondervan Publishing House, 1979). The specific calculations are found on pages 22–25. Custance's book is the most detailed and, to my mind, convincing presentation of the local flood theory.

a flood; never again will there be a flood to destroy the earth."
The second half of the verse is interpreted by the first. The
destruction of the earth is equated with the judgment of all life.

The ark's size and the effort involved in building it are both
justified even if the flood was local. If the flood devastated an area
several thousand miles square, the animals aboard the ark would
be just as necessary to replenish the land as they would be in a
global flood. The ark itself was certainly used as the focal point
for Noah's witness to his age.

My purpose in giving these arguments for the local flood is
not necessarily because I am convinced they are correct. I give
them because they are, despite the claims of the more vocal
supporters of a global flood, a fair and possible interpretation of
Scripture.

In a world where nearly three billion people have never heard
the name of Christ, there are more important issues at stake for
the evangelical community than the extent of the flood.

And there are more crucial issues at stake within the church.
I hope that we can learn to live together even when we disagree
on this issue.

Q **uestion 61**   God gave the rainbow as a sign
that He would never flood the earth again.
Doesn't that prove that it hadn't rained before
the flood?

If the text said there had never been a rainbow before and
that God created it specifically as a sign to Noah, the answer
might be yes. But it doesn't.

To make this theory convincing it is necessary to show that
God's signs are special creations. The most significant of those
signs in the Old Testament is circumcision. Christians often
assume that circumcision was never practiced outside Israel, but
in fact it was widely practiced throughout the ancient Near East.
The Philistines, who were immigrants from the Greek Islands,
were singled out for disdain by Israel because they didn't practice it. Egyptian art preserves evidence that, before the time of
Abraham, the Egyptians practiced circumcision.

When God established His covenant with Abraham, He took
an existing practice and gave it new meaning. When Christ estab-

lished His New Covenant with the disciples, He also took an established Jewish religious rite and gave it new meaning.

Those who argue that it had never rained before the flood usually argue that the earth was watered by heavy mists before the flood. Mists heavy enough to provide water for the earth's vegetation would have been heavy enough to cause rainbows, which are the result of light filtering through water vapor suspended in the air. Even if there had never been a drop of rain, rainbows would have existed wherever there was a waterfall and whenever light passed through a mist.

Unless God rewrote the laws governing the passage of light through a prism after the flood, Noah and his sons might have seen the rainbow before. But when they saw it after the flood, it had a totally new meaning. The rainbow came at the end of the storm. It reminded them that there would be no more forty-day storms that would leave no survivors. What would be a more natural mark of this new covenant than the sign they associated with the end of the storm?

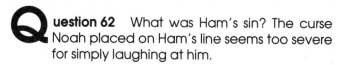

Q **uestion 62**   What was Ham's sin? The curse Noah placed on Ham's line seems too severe for simply laughing at him.

The severity of Canaan's punishment has bothered interpreters since the time of Christ, at least. The Rabbis deduced a sin far greater than simple ridicule. They pointed out that seeing a person's nakedness is often used as a euphemism for sexual relations. If this understanding of the text is correct, then no punishment would be adequate.

Others, also ancient, looked at the frequent stories of ancient peoples involving the emasculation of a father by an upstart son. This too suggests a crime against Noah that warrants the very harshest of punishments.

But modern commentators generally reject these two views in spite of their antiquity. This was a culture in which, according to the later law of Moses, to strike a father was a capital offense. The punishment seems extreme in an age when a drunk driver can wipe out an entire family and receive probation as a sentence. But standing at the headwaters of human history, in a world where survival might depend on respect for parents, Noah's outrage is more plausible. God's plan for humanity called for the elevation of the father role as an example of His own relationship with creation. There's no reason to be surprised at the severity of punishment.

Question 63   Why was Canaan cursed when it was Ham who sinned against Noah? Does the curse on Canaan explain the enslavement of blacks by white races (Genesis 9:25–27)?

This question, as do so many in this chapter, reminds us of how little detail we find in the first eleven chapters of Genesis. I get the impression that the events recorded here are presented only because they have a bearing on what follows.

Were it not for the eventual displacement of the Canaanites by Shem's descendants, Israel, I don't believe we would have been told this story. And the only details we are given are those that have a bearing on later history.

As a result, the story is an outline with only enough information to fill in the background for later biblical events. The number of possible interpretations indicates the difficulty of the passage.

Some suggest that it wasn't Ham who sinned against Noah. Others, under the influence of the clear meaning of the text, admit that Ham was the transgressor but insist that Canaan must have been his accomplice.

Several versions of the Septuagint (the Greek translation of the Old Testament) apparently assumed that the appearance of Canaan's name is a mistake, since they simply replaced it with Ham's name.

An ancient rabbinic interpretation said that Noah cursed Noah's son Canaan because Ham had already been blessed by God and nothing Noah said could harm him. Therefore, the only way to get to Ham was through his son.

A related explanation for cursing Canaan for Ham's sin is seen in numerous biblical statements. For example, we read in Hebrews that Levi offered a tithe to Melchizedek, even though his father was not yet born when Abraham met the priest/king. He was, however, "in the body of his ancestor" (Hebrews 7:10). This means that Levi was present, even though his grandfather, Abraham, was at a stage in his life when he thought God's promise would be fulfilled through the slave, Eliezer of Damascus.

God's repeated warnings against sin in Israel are couched in language that reminds us that we are never far removed from our forefathers. In four places in the Pentateuch (Exodus 20:5, 34:7, Numbers 14:18, and Deuteronomy 5:9) God promises that the iniquity of the fathers will be visited on their children to the third and fourth generations.

Israelites never thought of themselves as individuals disconnected from past or future generations. This sense of connectedness was so total that God sent Jeremiah and Ezekiel to remind Israel that their punishment was for their own sin, not that of their fathers (Jeremiah 31:29–30; Ezekiel 18:2).

I think this is the reason Noah cursed Canaan and not Ham. Ham's hope for a form of redemption through his descendants was eliminated by that curse. Ancient Israelites held onto the hope that their children would succeed where they had failed. The other side of that coin said that a child's failure could negate a father's success.

Derek Kidner put it well: "For his breach of the family, his own family would falter."

As for the idea of basing racial supremacy on this passage, I wish it were too antiquated to need discussion. But it isn't. Ten years ago I thought the old "Curse of Ham" argument had crawled into its hole and died. In the last few years, however, I've run across pamphlets that are doing their best to resurrect it.

Any casual reader of the text can see how untrue it is. Although the three north African nations are included among the sons of Ham, at least two of them, Put (Libya) and Mizraim (Egypt) are not black nations. A third, Cush, probably refers to northern Sudan, not modern Ethiopia.

The fourth son, Canaan, is the one who was cursed and he is most certainly not black.

The only thing I can conclude is that there will always be people who, for whatever reason, will seek ways to elevate themselves by downgrading others. As long as Christians ignore the clear teaching of Scripture, that God himself is no respecter of persons, we can expect them to twist Scripture to support their prejudices.

uestion 64   A lot of people around the world aren't included in the genealogy of chapter 10. Why not?

This genealogy, often known as the "Table of Nations," lists approximately seventy nations, ethnic groups, and linguistic clusters. It is a particular kind of genealogy. It is unlike modern straight line genealogies that anthropologists frequently call "linear genealogies."

A linear genealogy is the kind Norman Rockwell illustrated for the cover of Saturday Evening Post in 1959. A branch twines up from the stump of a tree rooted in the sparse soil of a pirate's island. There, at the very root of the tree, is an evil-looking pirate, black eye-patch and all, and a beautiful Spanish girl.

Moving up the tree, people appear, alternately respectable and disreputable. A colonial couple in powdered wig and bonnet sit above a dour clergyman and his even more dour wife. The tree sprouts both a Union and a Confederate soldier. On one branch is a grizzled mountain man and his Indian wife. Just above them, sit a cowboy and a dancehall girl. At the pinnacle, above the faces of a wholesomely middle-class man and woman is the face of a grinning redhaired boy, who symbolizes the distillation of 200 years of family history. He's been traced back to a pirate and his lady by means of a linear genealogy, which demonstrates the relationship of a living person to a person long since dead by tracing ancestry in a straight line from the one to the other.

That sort of genealogy is very important when it's necessary to determine heirs to thrones or fortunes. We hear a great deal about the British royal family and, although our Constitution prohibits royal titles, a great many Americans pride themselves on having ancestors who came over on the Mayflower or took part in the American revolution.

The genealogies of Jesus in Matthew and Luke are linear genealogies. In Matthew they trace Jesus' descent back to David, and in Luke to Adam.

Just because this is the most familiar kind of family tree doesn't mean it's the only kind, however. Anthropologists have identified another kind that's just as important, but for a very different reason. This type is called a "segmented" genealogy. Instead of tracing a family's history in a straight line, a segmented genealogy takes branches, or segments of the family now in existence, and tries to show how they're related by tracing them back to a common ancestor.

In cultures where they have no writing, these genealogies are kept by memory and can cover great spans of time. But they usually only include three generations. The generation now alive, the generation of the common ancestor, and a linking generation. The linking generation is usually chosen for the importance of its members.

The segmented genealogy is used to create a peaceful relationship between hostile neighbors. Most societies prohibit warfare between family members. Many societies use the segmented genealogy and that prohibition to end conflicts when nothing else seems to work. To bring a war to a close, the wisemen of two opposing tribes will get together to search through their memorized linear genealogies until they come up with a common ancestor. Then they construct a segmented genealogy to show that they're really brothers and shouldn't be fighting.

The "Table of Nations" is a segmented genealogy. At the end of the chapter, a small linear genealogy takes us back to the time of Terah, Abraham's father. Traditionally, segmented genealogies do not mention every single people on earth. Here, a nice round number of seventy nations and peoples are listed, demonstrating their relationship to each other through the sons of Noah.

I think this is one of the most important missionary chapters in the Old Testament. It tells us that God's interest, from the very beginning of the post-flood world, was focused on the tribes, nations, and language groups of a lost world. Indeed, Israel was the medium God used to reach that lost world, but that shouldn't blind us to the fact that this special kind of genealogy underscores the unity of humanity under God's care.

We aren't all the children of God in the special sense that the redeemed are, but we are all brothers and sisters in our need. No cultural or racial chauvinist can look at the world and say, like the Pharisee, that we are not like those sinners. Genesis 10 brings us back to the reality that we are all related by blood and by sin. Traced back to the family of Noah, no people under the sun are out from under the covenant God made with Noah, and no person can claim exemption from God's sovereignty.

Although there are thousands of tribes, nations, and languages not mentioned in this genealogy, they don't have to be mentioned. As we stand on the threshold of the first act in the unfolding drama of redemption, God reminds us that the need is universal.

We who know the gospel and have responded by giving ourselves to Jesus Christ by faith, are still tied to the people of the world by this genealogy. Our obligation to all those billions of lost men and women is fundamental. No matter how distant, they're all relatives.

Question 65   The story of the Tower of Babel has always troubled me. What was the terrible sin of the people? Was God afraid that they would succeed and storm heaven (Genesis 11:1–9)?

Like the other stories in these first eleven chapters, this one is so sparse of details that it gives rise to a bewildering array of interpretations.

The Bible begins and ends with cities called Babylon. In Revelation, Babylon is a code word for Rome. In Genesis, Babel is the Hebrew name for Babylon, which means "The Gate of God."

The tower was very likely a Babylonian "ziggurat." Its description fits such a Mesopotamian temple tower (vv. 3–4). The core was made of sun dried mud brick, and they were faced with fire-hardened ceramic brick, sometimes glazed. The pitch, or tar, that occurs frequently on the surface of the oil-rich land of Iran was a logical, and common, substitute for mortar.

They had a shape like a stack of pyramids with the tops cut off. Stairways along their faces reached the temples always located at the towers' peaks. Some of the most sacred observances of Mesopotamian religion took place in those temples.

The Tower of Babel was in the east. From a biblical orientation, that would mean Mesopotamia. The word "Shinar" is used elsewhere in the Old Testament to refer to the southern part of the Mesopotamian river valley, which included the city of Babylon.

But this isn't a story about geography or ancient temple construction. It's about sin and judgment. What was so sinful about building a city and placing a tower in it? To determine this we need to read between the lines.

The motivation for building the tower is plain. We can't enter their minds and know for certain what they were thinking, but perhaps they were remembering the time when the flood erased humanity from the earth. If so, their motivation for building a tower that would reach to heaven may have been a safeguard against such a thing happening again.

Or maybe they were thinking they would harrass God for erasing humanity from the globe. This is a popular interpretation. Verse 4 seems to point in this direction. Making a name for yourself was no less important then than it is today. Human pride is certainly a possible motivation.

Some suggest that the purpose of the tower was to reach heaven for an attack. Isaiah 14:13 gives some support for this idea. Isaiah addressed a king of Babylon who lived thousands of years after the incident recorded in Genesis. Poetically, Isaiah could have been looking back to the act of rebellion suggested in Genesis and applying the same motives and sinfulness to the last king of the Babyonian empire, who lived almost two hundred years after Isaiah. It seems fairly clear that Isaiah is looking back at the account from Genesis. It also seems clear that he interprets Genesis in terms of an attempt to storm heaven.

Unfortunately, the poetic reinterpretation of the Tower of Babel isn't a strong argument that the original story intended that meaning. Isaiah's purpose was not to explain Genesis but to proclaim the sin and judgment of Babylon in the most powerful terms. Poetry, even prophetic poetry, uses language differently than does narrative and discourse.

An allusion to the king of Babylon storming heaven in this passage speaks eloquently of the arrogant pride and ambition of that empire and its rulers. The rebellious nature of these people is best seen by looking at the context of the story. After the flood (Genesis 9:1, 7), God commanded Noah and his family to multiply and fill the earth. The purpose of the city and tower was to avoid doing that. The builders were afraid they would be scattered. The city and tower were to protect them against that.

The sin of building the tower is in keeping with the dulling litany of sins that preceded it. More than simple pride, it was the violation of a specific command given by God and an attempt to thwart His purpose for the world.

The men got together and decided to build bricks. The bricks were such a success that they decided to build a city with them. They were so proud of their city that they decided to build a tower that would reach to heaven and make a name for themselves. When the work was half done, God noticed that they were up to something and went to inspect it.

It wasn't that God was near-sighted or that they caught him off guard with their construction project; the writer was poking a little fun at their efforts. This heaven-scraping tower, intended to make a great name for them, was of so little consequence, the writer implied, that God had to stoop down to figure out what it was, leaving the reader with the image of a man walking in his garden and getting down on his hands and knees to inspect scurrying ants around an anthill.

Was God afraid that this tower would reach to heaven? Of course not. Is the gardener afraid that the ants will overthrow the house? The concern expressed in verse 6 is the concern of a father, not an opponent.

This reminds me of parents talking to their children: "After all the benefits we've given you, how can you behave this way? If you're going to act like this I'll . . ." I have to admit I've used almost identical wording with my children. God, looking at the descendants of Noah, saw children who had entered into a covenant with Him through their illustrious forefather and who were defying one of the provisions of that covenant. They struggled to maintain the style and quality of their lives that they had become accustomed to, apparently thinking that any change would be disastrous. The people of Babel stubbornly insisted on doing their own will and leaning on their own understanding. But God saw the future and the fulfillment of His plan of redemption that included a planet full of people won back to himself. This centralized, defiant civilization was trying to stop that plan for its own benefit. With a word, God brushed their rebellion aside.

The people of Babel were a lot like churches today that prefer to sit by while the world passes into eternity without Christ rather than upset the comfortable sameness of their fellowship and structure.

A literary device used extensively in this section is "irony," which heightens the drama of a play by using incongruity between the situation and the accompanying words or actions. The audience sees the incongruity, but the characters in the play do not.

Here's the irony. Verse 9 says that the place was called Babel "because there the LORD confused the language of the whole world." The Hebrew plays with the sounds of the two words, *Babel* and *confusion*. "Bab-EL," or Babylon, was arrogantly called the gate of God by its later residents. In their frenzy to make a name for themselves, they built the tower that would reach heaven. But regardless of what they called themselves, the place turned out to be, not the gate of god, "Babel," but "Bal-Al," confused. The pun and irony are obvious in confusion, and it is a mournful reminder of the consequences of rebellious human pride.

When people set out to make a name for themselves in opposition to God's will, the only name that sticks is "Balal," or confusion.

ALL'S WELL THAT BEGINS WELL

Now the stage is set. In one masterful chapter of Genesis, the physical universe and its origin is put into place. In the next we meet the first of a long cast of characters, and then the conflict, which finds its resolution in Christ, begins.

We meet the antagonist whose purpose is to entangle God's people and his line of men. Into the midst of this record of failure and rebellion, the Sons of God emerge as a bright hope, even in the dark judgment of the flood. This marvelous world that God made is peopled with multitudes dazzling in their diversity but unified in their need.

The prologue proper concludes with the statement that all the peoples of the world stand under God's judgment in their divisions. And then the curtain rises with a note of hope. We meet Abraham, the man who, like Adam, was a friend of God and in whose line all men and women of faith are counted. The preparation is over. Now the play can begin.

Part 3 CULTURE

WAYS OF
BEING HUMAN

Father Brown had stopped for a moment, and picked up out of the long grass, where it had been wholly hidden, a queer, crooked Oriental knife, inlaid exquisitely in coloured stones and metal. . . .

"It's very beautiful," said the priest in a low, dreaming voice, "the colours are very beautiful, but it's the wrong shape."

"What for?" asked Flambeau, staring.

"For anything. It's the wrong shape in the abstract. Don't you ever feel that about Eastern art? The colours are intoxicatingly lovely, but the shapes are mean and bad—deliberately mean and bad. I have seen wicked things in a Turkey [sic] carpet."[1]

G. K. Chesterton's clerical sleuth put his finger on the problem we all face when we encounter another culture. Everything in it seems wrong! For Father Brown, not only was the shape of the dagger wrong, but by its wrongness, it spoke of things inherently evil. The variety of ways human beings have of expressing their humanity is so great, and the differences between us so vast, that not even the most sensitive and enlightened can cope with them all. Man, created in the image of God, reflects that image in everything from silvered glass to polished metal to the still surface of water in a clay pot or hollowed gourd. The differences are what we call *culture*. Culture has little to do with curling your pinky when you drink your tea, saying *to-MAH-to* instead of *to-MAY-to*, or raving in hushed tones about the inner energy of some abstract expressionist painting.

At its simplest level, culture is all the things we've learned that make us Americans, Canadians, Germans, Chinese, Lebanese, or Jews. The languages we speak, the utensils we eat with,

---

[1] G. K. Chesterton, "The Wrong Shape," *The Penguin Complete Father Brown* (New York: Penquin Book, 1981).

the houses we live in, the way we celebrate our weddings and mourn our dead are all parts of the complex thing called culture.

Within the United States alone, there are major regional cultures. A Southerner and a Northeasterner will probably find a lot of things in common with one another, but their dialects and their pace of life will be different. Midwesterners will find the ways of the Southwest mystifying, irritating, and beguiling.

Even within a single state, wide variations in culture are possible. The other night my wife and I were eating with friends in a restaurant. As we ate, we saw a wedding party pull up at the curb and emerge from their vehicles. The bride, in her flowing white gown, and the groom, in his tuxedo, were followed by a whole string of richly attired attendants. No sooner had their cars been driven off than another, unrelated wedding party appeared. But their destination was different. They headed for the bowling alley next door.

Several people in our group who hadn't grown up in this part of the country, my wife and I included, were incredulous. We considered it some bizarre tribal ritual, but we learned that it's not uncommon in this region for newlyweds to make a state visit at the local bowling alley. They bowl a line, presumably to assure happiness, prosperity, and the good will of the proprietor, before embarking on the bumpy road of matrimonial bliss.

To some, the shape of that custom seems as wrong as Father Brown's oriental knife, but to others it's as American as the flag and apple pie. Culture provides a "right" pattern for our houses, transportation, utensils, clothing, and family structure. It determines which biologically digestible material is food and which is revolting. Because we grow up in our own culture we assume ours is the right way, indeed the only way, to behave.

How many of you wonder why the British obstinately insist on driving on the wrong side of the road?

Hebrew reads backward, from right to left. Hebrew books open at the back and are read to the front. But to those born and raised in Israel, English reads backward.

And what about oriental languages that read up and down?

There is, of course, no inherently correct side of the road to drive on and no correct direction to read in, but our ingrained culture tells us that someone else's way of doing things is wrong.

Culture dictates whether we look a person in the eye or avert our gaze. Early encounters between American businessmen and their Japanese counterparts sometimes foundered on this cultural difference. For the American, direct eye contact is proof of honesty and square dealings. We describe people who won't look us in the eye as "shifty-eyed" and consider them dishonest. For the Japanese, however, direct eye contact is considered an insult and the averted gaze is a sign of respect. Working from these cultural assumptions, Americans dealing with Japanese label them shifty and deceitful, while the Japanese consider Americans rude and ill-bred.

Increased contact between cultures around the world is diminishing this kind of misunderstanding, yet every missionary who attempts to share the gospel cross-culturally still must deal with what is known as "culture shock." Even within our own country, a move from north to south, or northeast to southwest, or from almost anywhere to southern California will result in a mild form of the same kind of culture shock. The tempo of speech, pace of business, speed of walking, and thousands of other simple, subtle signs will tell others we're a foreigner and remind us that we're far from home.

A SHORT VISIT TO A STRANGE PLANET

Reading the Bible involves a kind of delayed culture shock as we step into a strange and exotic world. At best, some Bible customs confuse us; at worst, they repel us. Part of our difficulty lies in not understanding the culture of the Bible, and another part of our problem lies in not understanding the impact our own has on us. When we read the Bible, we assume that all the great people of Scripture would make wonderful deacons or elders in our American church. But in fact, there's hardly a person in the Old Testament who would even be allowed to join most of our churches without some major modifications in behavior.

The world of the New Testament is much closer to our own, so we would probably accept Peter or Paul into membership, but we might find the behavior of these great Christian heroes a bit strange.

Let's look at a few examples of biblical culture shock that create questions for the modern reader.

TIME MARCHES ON

Westerners are dominated by time. We live by time-tables, schedules, and appointments set up in fifteen-minute blocks. We measure success by how much we can cram into that series of fifteen-minute slots. Few of us ever consider how thoroughly time shapes our view of the world. We no longer begin our day with sunrise, but we know to the microsecond what time it took place. We've imprisoned the sun in a framework of quartz crystals and metal, so now we can "save" daylight every summer by letting the sun out of its artificial prison an hour later every day!

How different time must have been to the farmers of Galilee, who rose when the light awakened them, ate when the sun stood overhead, and turned their tired donkeys toward home when lengthening shadows signalled the departure of day. In the biblical world, time was reckoned in terms of seed time and harvest, watches of the night, and the rising and setting of the sun. Because precision in time keeping was impossible (clocks only began to sprout minute hands in the seventeenth century) it was neither sought nor expected.This imprecision in biblical chronology sometimes causes great consternation for the twentieth century reader, but would have presented no difficulty for the early Christian.

Our western time sense creates a real problem for the biblical record of Christ's time in the tomb. Counting it out from the facts of Scripture, He was buried late Friday afternoon, probably just before sundown. He was in the tomb Friday night, Saturday, and Saturday night. Then, very early on Sunday, He was raised from the dead. His total time in the tomb was about 36 hours. By our way of figuring, this is a mere day and a half!

Why did Jesus say He would be in the tomb "three days and three nights" (Matthew 12:39–40)?

First century Jews did not add hours to come up with days. To them, any part of a day counted as a whole day. Saturday, beginning with sundown Friday and ending with sundown Saturday, counted as the second. Sunday, beginning at sundown Saturday, was almost half over when the women arrived at the tomb at dawn of the third day.

But Matthew 12:39–40 says, quite specifically, three days and three nights. By any reckoning, the night beginning at sundown on Friday and the one beginning on Saturday evening cannot be stretched into three nights. Does this mean the Bible is in error?

Hardly! Jesus was using *days and nights* as a hendiadys, the figure of speech previously mentioned that uses two words or phrases to convey one concept. He used the phrase "three days and three nights" to speak of three days—Friday being the first, Saturday the second, and Sunday the third—and that is the way Matthew's Jewish readers would have understood it in the first century. Nothing more precise was necessary, or intended.

By understanding the culturally conditioned standard of time keeping, what seems to be an insurmountable biblical contradiction becomes perfectly understandable.

PLEASE DON'T SPIT ON THE FURNITURE

Another cultural problem that causes frequent misunderstanding has to do with our twentieth century level of understanding. Just as the Old Testament patriarchs lived with a different perception of time than we have today, they also had a different, and much more basic, understanding of God's truth.

Here again we need to leave the twentieth century behind and take ourselves back to a time when the best scientific knowledge was mixed with a tinge of superstition, to a time before any of the Bible had been written. God was operating under what I call the "Don't spit on the furniture" principle.

A few years ago, when my youngest daughter was just beginning to explore the world and her own capabilities in it, she discovered she could spit. When you're only two, this discovery is on a par with Balboa's encounter with the Pacific Ocean. She was quite proud of herself and practiced her new skill at every opportunity.

One summer afternoon I was babysitting with Meaghan and her older sister, Catie. My attention was on a stack of summer school assignments that needed grading, not on my two-year-old geyser, when Catie, who was almost five, broke my concentration with excited indignation. In a state approaching panic, she announced that Meaghan was spitting on the furniture!

I went to investigate this wonder.

Sure enough, there on an upholstered chair, on a footstool, and on practically every piece of furniture in our living room, I found the moist evidence that Meaghan was, in fact, spitting on the furniture.

I had two choices. I could discuss the ethical ramifications of private ownership, the criminal penalties for vandalism, and the social ostracism that is sure to be the lot of indiscriminate spitters. Or I could simply tell her to stop spitting on the furniture. I chose the latter. Meaghan's stage of development (and my preference for dry furniture over a dry lecture) dictated that decision. She could hardly be expected to understand the concept of other people's property when her vocabulary hadn't moved much beyond an occasional shout of "Mine!" She could, however, understand her father's command, "Don't spit on the furniture!"

As great as the faith of the patriarchs was, they were still at the "Don't spit on the furniture" stage. So God began with the basics: He set out to teach them that He was the only true God, that He alone had created everything, and that they must learn to obey Him. He chose not to deal with the minor superstitions that permeated their culture until after they had learned the first vital lesson. It took God 2,000 years of active, intimate involvement with Abraham and his descendants before even a remnant was ready to accept Christ.

Jacob had not yet become Israel when he used superstition to build up his flock. He was still some years away from his crisis experience on the bank of the river Jabbok. He believed that the production of a sizable herd of black, striped, and spotted sheep was the result of his own cleverness and the spell he had cast on his breeding stock. Everyone in Jacob's world relied on this kind of trick. Sometimes it worked, but not for the reasons they suspected. They believed their world was controlled by spirits and powers whose cooperation they needed to get things to work. In Egypt, for example, doctors would diagnose an ailment and prescribe the best folk medicine available and then prescribe the proper spell to make the medicine work.

The white sheep and goats in Laban's herd would have carried the genes for a wide variety of mottling. So even when white sheep mated, they produced mottled lambs as often as not. After one generation, with about three out of four of Laban's lambs and kids going into Jacob's herd, the "wisdom" of Jacob's spell would have seemed obvious to him.

The text never says God instructed that strategy. In fact, it attributes Jacob's success to God's blessing, not Jacob's spell. Because the wily and devious Jacob was still spitting on the furniture, God's dealings with him were still at a very simple level. God knew the rules of genetics and the foolishness of stripping willow rods, but Jacob needed to come to a living relationship with the God of his father more than he needed to have his harmless tricks debunked.

THE PRINCE ON A DONKEY

The story of David in his later years is tragic, but in the midst of the sad picture of inter-familial murder and immorality is a tiny vignette that is both puzzling and amusing to modern eyes.

Second Samuel 14 chronicles two related crimes. Amnon, David's oldest son, developed a passionate desire for his half-sister Tamar and gave full expression to that desire by raping her. To add to her shame, he then called his servants and had her thrown out of his house, forcing her to walk home through the streets of her father's city in shame and mourning. In addition to the great sin he committed, Amnon made a serious and dangerous tactical mistake in abusing the beloved sister of his younger brother Absalom.

We seldom see Absalom clearly because his rebellion against his father paints our picture of him in the darkest of hues. Absalom, however, was a true son and a worthy successor, to his father. He was handsome, intelligent, loyal, cunning, and fierce in his vengeance. He was very much like his father. Absalom's cold-blooded patience is also notable. When he discovered what Amnon had done to his sister, he immediately took her under his protection and, somewhat cryptically, promised her that things would be taken care of (1 Samuel 13:20).

To David's shame, the Bible contains no record that he made any attempt to punish his lawless son Amnon. After two years of waiting for his father to act, Absalom moved to avenge his sister. He invited David and all the royal sons to attend the festival of the sheep shearing at his country estate. He must have known that David would decline, because when he did, Absalom quickly asked that Amnon be sent in his place. While David questioned this request, he finally agreed, sending his first-born son to his death. When the banquet was far advanced and Amnon was "in high spirits from drinking too much wine," Absalom signaled his servants to fall on Amnon and kill him. When the other royal brothers saw this, they assumed they were caught in a plot to eliminate all the other heirs to the throne and fled in panic.

As sordid and repulsive as this incident may be, the modern reader will see humor in 2 Samuel 13:29, which records that "all the king's sons got up, mounted their mules, and fled."

What a picture! It conjures up images of Laurel and Hardy, or possibly Sancho Panza bouncing along comically behind Don Quixote. Donkeys and mules have comic connotations in our culture. To us, the horse is noble and the donkey a buffoon.

But during David's time, horses were generally considered too wild to ride and were usually used only to pull chariots. Job 39:19–25 describes the fearsomeness of the chariot horse. They were pointed at the enemy, almost like a pair of four-footed projectiles, and given their heads. A chariot horse in full gallop was an awesome sight to a foot soldier. They could be shot with arrows until their chests bristled like pincushions and still keep coming, trampling their master's enemies underfoot while gasping for their last breath.

The animal people rode was usually the donkey, or mule, the horse's more docile cousin. To own an animal for riding implied both wealth and status.

Far from being comical, the picture of David's sons fleeing on the backs of mules speaks of their wealth and status as the sons of a king. While we associate royalty with white chargers, the ancient Israelite would have associated it with a mule.

Could it be that Jesus, when He chose the donkey as His mount for the triumphal entry, was consciously reminding His people that their great king David had himself ridden a donkey and that now David's greater son had come to claim his father's throne?

MEANER THAN A JUNKYARD DOG

People who have been raised on Lassie, Snoopy, Benji, and fluffy little lap dogs have difficulty understanding the depth of abhorrence most residents of ancient Israel felt toward dogs. For them, all dogs were dangerous and disgusting. Dogs weren't kept as pets in Israel.

Dogs roamed wild around the fringes of villages and in city streets. At night they crept in and ate garbage, refuse, or whatever else might be found. If an animal had died in the street, they ate it. If a person had died, or had fallen and was too weak to get up again, the dogs would eat him too.

The most graphic illustration of this in the Old Testament is found in 2 Kings 9:33–36. Jehu had overthrown the kings of both Israel and Judah. He had slaughtered most of the members of the royal families of both nations. In this passage, he had just ridden into Jezreel to confront Jezebel.

News of his slaughters had already reached the palace, and Jezebel came to the window, dressed to die. She shouted a taunt at Jehu, and he called for her servants to throw her out of the window to the street below. Jehu's horses trampled her where she fell, and he left her body there while he went into the palace to eat his dinner. When he finished eating, he sent servants out to retrieve Jezebel's body for burial. Instead of finding the body of their former queen, they found a bit of skull, the palms of her hands and soles of her feet. The rest had been eaten by dogs.

The attitude toward dogs in Bible times is so radically different from our own that we almost always misunderstand biblical references to dogs.

Proverbs 26:17 is one such reference: "Like one who seizes a dog by the ears is a passer-by who meddles in a quarrel not his own."

During the presidency of Lyndon Johnson, a press photographer caught a shot of the president playing with his two dogs. He recorded, to the shock of a dog-loving nation, the President of the United States hoisting his pet into the air by nothing more than the dog's floppy ears. The howls of dog lovers were heard throughout the land. A caption writer paired the picture with the above proverb.

Pulling on the droopy ears of a tame and affectionate household pet can hardly be compared with trying the same stunt with a half-starved, vicious scavenger. The proverb warns us that meddling in someone else's quarrel means taking your life in your hands. Our understanding is weak because we're apt to picture Lyndon Johnson's beagle, not Jezebel's jackals.

SOFT AS A PUPPY'S EAR

Having made the dogs of the ancient world thoroughly repulsive, I now have to warn against applying this background to the incident recorded in Matthew 15:21–28 and Mark 7:24–30, where we read that Jesus said to a Gentile woman, "It is not right to take the children's bread and toss it to their dogs." Jesus' seemingly harsh rebuke of the Gentile woman seeking deliverance for her possessed daughter seems glaringly out of character. Did the Jesus who taught us to love our enemies actually call this suffering woman a dog?

Jesus did not use the usual word for dog here. Instead He used the diminutive form. In English, that would be "doggie." His use of that word indicates that He was talking about a household pet and not the kind of dog we just described.

The Roman world in general had a very different approach to the dog than did Israel. Art has survived from Roman times that shows charming family groups in which the children appear playing with household dogs. Dogs in the Roman world were used in many of the same ways we use them today—as watch dogs, hunting dogs, sheep dogs, and household pets. The woman Jesus compared to a dog was from Phoenicia, which was part of the Roman world. The sting felt by a Jewish listener to Jesus' words would have been largely absent in this Gentile woman.

Jesus, who grew up among people who hated both dogs and Gentiles, spoke to this Gentile woman as her understanding, not His, dictated. The woman's reply supports this. "Yes, Lord, but even the dogs eat the crumbs that fall from their masters' tables." Commentators often call the woman's response witty. They also stress the apparent lightness of the exchange and the delight Jesus obviously felt at her faith and quickness of mind.

It's true that Jews of Jesus' day referred to Gentiles as dogs, and it's possible to see a reflection of that attitude here. But Jesus' choice of words doesn't support that conclusion.

In this account Jesus established a principle that the apostle Paul also used. Paul said that the gospel was preached to the Jew first and then to the Greek. Jesus stressed that He came first to deal with the children of the family, or the household of Israel.

In saying it the way He did, Jesus posed a sort of riddle. Riddles were very popular during Bible times, but not as entertainment for children. In the ancient world riddles were relished as mental exercises for adults. The Phoenician woman, showing an alertness of mind that was commendable, picked up on the light tone of Jesus' words and turned His saying to her advantage, in much the same way Jesus himself had done so many times when sparring with the Pharisees. We could almost say that Jesus set up the woman's answer, providing her with the opportunity to affirm her faith, should she choose to take it. In her jousting with words, she reached out to touch the universal promise of the gospel, and in so doing, became a firstfruit of all Gentile believers.

"FISH GOTTA SWIM"

Like our language, our culture becomes so much a part of us that we hardly notice it. We swim in culture like fish swim in water, and just as fish are unaware of the water around them, we are largely unaware of the culture around us.

CHAPTER 6

PRINCIPLES

24 Approach the Bible with the awareness that beliefs, attitudes, and assumptions about the nature of things will sometimes be radically different from our own.

QUESTIONS

66 Why did Abraham agree to use Hagar to produce a son when his wife Sarah was still alive? Why would Sarah allow it (Genesis 16:1–4)?

67 If the Hittites thought so highly of Abraham, why did they take money for the cave of Machpelah (Genesis 23:1–20)?

68 Why would Laban, who had just been cheated by Jacob, bless him (Genesis 31:41–54)?

69 If Esau was ready to forgive Jacob and live at peace with him, why did he come to meet him with 400 men (Genesis 32:6)?

70 Why are the tabernacle and the sacrifices described in such detail? Why do we need to know these things (Exodus/Leviticus)?

71 It sounds as if Israel threw dice for their inheritances in the Promised Land. Did they just gamble for something so important (Joshua 18:6–8)?

72 Why were the cities of refuge necessary (Joshua 20)?

73 Why did God hold Jephthah to his tragic vow and require him to sacrifice his daughter? Or does the text mean something other than sacrifice (Judges 11)?

74 Israel took the Ark of the Covenant into battle against the Philistines. Why (1 Samuel 4:3)?

75 What made Israel want a human king when God had taken care of them ever since they left Egypt? Why couldn't they just trust God (1 Samuel 8)?

TO SKIN
A CAT

76 Why did God choose Saul to be king? It sounds as if God made a mistake and changed His mind about it (1 Samuel 10–12).

77 If David already had two wives, why was he so insistent on having Saul's daughter, Michal, returned to him (2 Samuel 3:12–16)? What was so awful about Adonijah asking for Abishag as his wife? Why did Solomon have him killed because of it (1 Kings 2:13–25)?

78 How did Joab have the nerve to disobey David and then talk to him the way he did after he killed Absalom (2 Samuel 19:1–7)?

79 What does it mean that David "rested with his fathers" (1 Kings 2:10)?

80 Why did Solomon have so many wives (1 Kings 11:1–3)?

81 God commanded that His temple be built at Jerusalem. So why did Jeroboam think he could get away with building temples at Bethel and Dan (1 Kings 12:25–33)?

82 Knowing God's prohibition against graven images, why would Jeroboam put golden calves in those sanctuaries?

83 What are high places, sacred pillars, and asherim, and why are they so terrible (1 Kings 14:23)?

84 What does it mean that Ben-Hadad will let Ahab build "streets" in Damascus (1 Kings 20:34)?

85 Was Elisha really twice the prophet Elijah was (2 Kings 2:9–14)?

E veryone knows it never rains in Southern California. But for almost the entire three weeks of our family vacation, it did nothing but rain. And hard. People drowned in flash floods. Many businesses closed because nobody could get to them. Houses, without warning or a fond farewell, relocated themselves from the sides of hills to the bottoms. One even found its way onto a freeway just north of San Diego. I kept looking for "Watch for fallen houses" signs but never noticed any.

With devastation on every side, the O'Brien family had one overriding concern—to get the kids into Disneyland before we had to return to Wisconsin. As the days dwindled down to a precious few, it became evident that we would go in the rain or not at all. So we went in the rain. We spent the day soaked to the skin, but we didn't have to wait in line.

In the parking lot we noticed that most of the cars had California license plates on them. We couldn't understand why anybody who lived in California would choose such a day to visit Disneyland.

At the "Small World" ride, we turned to the family in the seat behind us to begin research on the question.

"Are you from California?" we asked.

"No. Why would we be here on a day like this if we were?"

We soon learned that they too were from Wisconsin. Like small town residents everywhere, we identified home by referring to the nearest larger town.

"We live near Platteville."

"Really? We live near Richland Center!"

Both are mid-sized towns in southwest Wisconsin.

"Where near Platteville?" we asked.

"We own a farm just outside of Cobb," they answered.

"Really," we responded. "We have a good friend from Cobb."

And so, on a rainy day at Disneyland, in a boat about to enter a ride called "It's A Small World After All," we met a Christian family who lived about twenty miles from us, on the farm next door to the one where our friend Marc Mueller grew up. Doesn't that prove that it really is a small world after all?

In one sense, yes, it is a small world. We can be almost anywhere and run into someone we know, or someone who knows someone we know. But in the sense intended by the pop anthropologists who presented us with the idea for the ride in the first place, no, it isn't a small world. We may all live on the earth, look essentially alike, and have the same basic needs for food, shelter, and love, but there the similarity ends.

ONCE WE GET TO KNOW EACH OTHER

We have this naive assumption that if we could get all the people of the world into one big room to talk about the things that matter to them, all our differences would disappear.

Except for animal rights activists, we pretty much agree that "there's more than one way to skin a cat," meaning that one problem can have a variety of solutions. We think of all the ways there are to tie a necktie, cook a steak, or get from Sioux Falls to Cuyahoga Falls. Americans love options, and we're committed to keeping them all open.

But people who have skinned a lot more cats than any of us might be horrified if someone suggested an alternate way of accomplishing the task. Considerations unknown to us may make the preservation of their time-honored methodologies more important than efficiency, productivity, or profitability, which we value more highly than tradition.

Consider the proverbs we use to express our vision of reality.

Time is money.

If at first you don't succeed, try, try again.

A man's home is his castle.

May the best man win.

The squeaky wheel gets the grease.

Do you agree with most of these? All of them? If you do, you're a genuine American.

But in much of the third world, they don't make any sense at all.

The idea of making yourself a nuisance to get your own way might work in the States, but in much of the world such behavior marks Americans as rude and inconsiderate.

We ignore a contradictory proverb: "When words are many, sin is not absent, but he who holds his tongue is wise" (Proverbs 10:19).

"May the best man win" makes sense in a culture that values competition, but it offends anyone raised in a part of the world where cooperation is valued more than individual achievement.

And what does "Time is money" say to a culture that has no clocks and operates on a barter economy?

Not long ago someone warned us not to trust anyone over thirty. Americans worship youth. But in countries where life expectancies hover in the upper forties and lower fifties, the older the better. In Liberia, when a man reaches an advanced age he gets a new name: "Old Man." Here that would be a term of derision; there it's a badge of honor.

While traveling as a salesman in the upper midwest one summer I drove the back roads and came across town after little town that bragged, on highway signs, that they were progressive. Nobody wants to be considered old fashioned. Yet for the majority of the world's people, progress threatens their security, which is rooted in the unchanging rhythm of life inherited from their ancestors.

Americans find the continual haggling over price in third world countries either quaint or annoying. Buying and selling for Americans is strictly a financial transaction for us. Money and goods change hands, period. But in other countries, it's a social transaction as much as it is economic.

My wife and I enjoyed one of the most pleasant half hours of our first trip to Liberia while we sat in the sand dickering with three "charlies" (peddlers) over a necklace and some earrings. A good time was had by all, and that may have been as important for all of us as the sale.

AMERICANS, UGLY AND OTHERWISE

We hear the word *chauvinist* a lot. So much so that it seems to have lost its original meaning, which is "the prejudiced belief in the superiority of your own group."

Americans are probably the only people on earth that consider chauvinism a bad thing. It is almost universal to consider your own group better and your own ways best.

To be a true citizen of the world, and, more importantly, a true world Christian, we need to recognize the multiplicity of ways there can be to see the world.

I'll probably always feel, somewhere deep in my soul, that every individual is entitled to a private room to be alone with his thoughts. After all, isn't a man's home his castle? Not necessarily.

In Africa that idea strikes nearly everyone as both selfish and anti-social. And who's to say they're wrong?

WALK TODAY WHERE JESUS WALKED

No matter how many Holy Land tour brochures say otherwise, it's impossible to "walk today where Jesus walked." The Jerusalem of Jesus' day is about thirty feet under ground, and the walls that surround the Old City today were built by Suleiman the Magnificent in the sixteenth century A.D.

No one can ever get inside another culture and understand it the way those born into it do. That includes the biblical culture. One of the greatest barriers to our understanding of the biblical text is our assumption that Jesus, Moses, Abraham, and Paul shared the same views about things as we do.

But they didn't. They lived in a world as foreign to us as modern day Tibet or Indonesia. And the difference is more profound than just the exotic trappings of life in the Middle East. Some of the most basic assumptions of American life are absent from the biblical world.

P rinciple 24   Approach the Bible with the awareness that beliefs, attitudes, and assumptions about the nature of things will sometimes be radically different from our own.

Some argue that the Bible is a capitalist book and others argue that it contains Marxist truths, but the reality is that both are absent from the Bible.

Yes, the Bible speaks about owning property. But it's not the private ownership that we know in this country any more than it's the state ownership championed by Communism.

The biblical concept of ownership is that a proprietor holds title as a steward, mindful of how his actions will affect future generations. In fact, the Law of God commands, in Israel at least, that "privately" owned land could never be sold, only leased until the sabbath year.

The more Greco-Roman view had come into being by Jesus' day, but the early church continued to hold everything in common, harking back to the more Near Eastern approach.

People thought of themselves as individuals and frequently demonstrated the kind of western initiative and independence of thought that we value. But they never did so without knowing, no matter how independently they may have acted, that they were responsible to their family, clan, tribe, and nation. They also knew that their actions had an impact far beyond themselves.

No Israelite would have sung "I've Got To Be Me" or "I Did It My Way" without an occasional, shame-faced glance over his shoulder to be sure none of his family was listening.

The following questions arise out of cultural differences, and in understanding those differences we can find answers.

Question 66   Why did Abraham agree to use Hagar to produce a son when his wife Sarah was still alive? Why would Sarah allow it (Genesis 16:1–4)?

Few incidents in the Old Testament bother modern Christians more than this one, which involves Abraham's adultery and Sarah's unusual involvement in it. What Abraham did was not right. And God did not tell him it was right. But we can learn why Abraham and Sarah *thought* what they did was right.

Fathering a son was the highest value Abraham's culture had for marriage. Abraham loved Sarah, and Sarah loved him in return. As a couple, they had achieved a level of success and affluence few of us expect for ourselves. But their marriage hadn't produced a son, which made all Abraham's accomplishments meaningless to him. The tragedy of having worked his whole life only to turn his estate over to an adopted slave haunted him. In our culture, it's hard to identify with the intensity of that feeling. Abraham would have done anything for a son of his own.

For women in Sarah's time, affirmation came only from motherhood. They had no status in life apart from having children. Sarah could be a good wife, but it wasn't enough to give her life meaning. The same was true when Hannah was barren (1 Samuel 1). Her husband asked her if he wasn't better for her than ten sons, and she answered no. As much as Sarah loved Abraham, and Hannah loved Elkanah, they needed sons to give their lives meaning.

Enter Hagar, an Egyptian handmaid (Genesis 16:1). Hagar offered the opportunity for both Sarah and Abraham to have their dreams fulfilled. As Sarah's servant she could, according to the standards of their society, become a mother in place of her mistress. The arrangement was not unlike surrogate mothers we read about in the news.

A collection of contracts, deeds, personal letters, and other documents discovered in the ancient Mesopotamian city of Nuzi illuminates some of the strange cultural practices of the patriarchs. One contract uncovered was similar to a modern-day pre-nuptial agreement. It didn't establish rules for the division of property in the event of divorce, as modern ones do. Rather, it addressed the much more pressing issue of fertility. What was to be done if the marriage produced no children?

The contract specified that Miss Kelim-ninu was to be given in marriage to Mr. Shenimma. In the event that no children were born, Miss Kelim-ninu had to acquire a slave girl as wife for Mr. Shenimma. The contract also mentioned that the bride-to-be would receive a slave girl as a wedding gift. The custom seems barbaric to people for whom having children is a greater concern than not having them.

At 85 years of age, Abraham was probably not driven by his desire for another woman. But he was driven by the desire for a son. Sons were the ancient world's social security. Without a male heir to inherit the husband's wealth, the wife could only hope she died before her spouse. Without a strong son, neither parent could be assured of a place to stay or hands to care for them when the inevitable disabilities of old age overtook them. This social setting motivated Sarah's decision to offer Hagar to Abraham, and certainly the same setting motivated Abraham to accept the offer. This plan was conceived by Abraham and Sarah, not God. The Bible records the actions of its main characters as they happened, not as they should have happened.

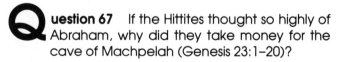 **uestion 67**   If the Hittites thought so highly of Abraham, why did they take money for the cave of Machpelah (Genesis 23:1–20)?

This question comes up every time I teach Old Testament History, and the answer is all wrapped up in our way of doing business. Here in the west, business is strictly a financial trans-action. In the Ancient Near East, however, and in most of the Third World today, business was and is a social transaction as well.

A nineteenth century traveller to the Holy Land once re-corded his exasperation at trying to buy something from an Arab merchant. His greetings, the traveler recorded, were obsequious and fawning, wasting almost forty-five minutes of the traveler's valuable time before beginning to discuss the price. Then the crafty fellow quoted a price that was so obviously excessive that the Victorian gentleman almost broke off the transaction in anger.

Anyone familiar with eastern merchants and the delight they take in the process of the sale has to laugh at the naivete of the western visitor. The Arab merchant, on the other hand, probably shook his head at the man's rudeness.

The transaction between Abraham and Ephron, read in its eastern setting, is a perfect example of the kind of business transaction still common throughout the world.

The speeches of Ephron the Hittite indicate that his dearest desire was to make a gift of the land to his old friend Abraham. Abraham had to find a burial site for Sarah. He knew it, Ephron knew it, and the elders of the Hittites knew it.

Abraham, however, was a resident alien, a class of people who had no legal rights and were usually excluded from the purchase of land. When Abraham approached the Hittite elders for permission to buy land he was asking for something their law and custom didn't ordinarily allow. The reason he did not go first to the owner of the land he wanted (v. 4) was probably because the owner would not have been able to sell to him without the permission of the elders.

Negotiations with Abraham got under way at the city gate (v. 10), which means this was an official meeting of the Kiriath-Arba/Hebron planning commission. The city gate was the equiva-lent of the later town square. Business, both private and civic, was conducted there for all to see.

Part and parcel of the oriental business transaction is to treat the buyer with great respect and flatter him shamelessly. Abra-ham's wealth must have weighed in his favor, but their descrip-tion of him as a "mighty prince" was probably flattery. By their standards he was still a foreigner without land and without standing in their culture. Instead of giving him permission to buy the land, the elders offered him a burial site on property that belonged to any one of them. If they could induce Abraham to accept the simple gift of a burial place for Sarah, he would remain a person without standing, still a landless foreigner under obligation to his hosts.

Abraham had a different idea, though. He saw this land as a foothold into the Land of Promise, and he would not be deterred from purchasing it. He turned his attention to the owner of the field, who apparently had overheard the discussion.

Ephron, like the Hittite leaders, offered Abraham a place to bury Sarah free of charge, but Abraham insisted on paying for the property.

Here the transaction became a little different. Ephron, perhaps thinking that he was beginning a long and spirited session of haggling over price, named a price that may have been more than exorbitant: 400 silver shekels. We don't know the exact size or desirability of the field, but since Abraham wanted a tomb, not acreage, it might not have been anything to shout about.

Not too many years later, Jacob paid 100 pieces of silver for his land (Genesis 33:19), which probably wasn't a hobby farm of a few acres; shepherds take up a lot of space. In a later day, Jeremiah bought a farm field for seventeen shekels (Jeremiah 32:9). In comparison, Ephron's 400 silver shekel price tag seems steep.

The rule of thumb I was given when I visited Africa for the first time was to pay one-half to two-thirds of the asking price for anything I bought from a peddler. I'm sure Abraham had some similar rule of thumb. But he did what was unheard of; he agreed to pay the asking price. The contract was drawn up and the technical language of the bill of sale is recorded in Genesis 23:16–18.

According to tradition the cave and the graves are still there. And the site is still venerated by pilgrims, Christian and Jewish alike, as the first piece of property owned by Abraham in the land God had promised to his descendants. Four hundred shekels of silver as a down payment on the land God would give seems a small enough price to pay.

uestion 68   Why would Laban, who had just been cheated by Jacob, bless him (Genesis 31:41–54)?

The Lord watch between me and thee while we are absent one from the other.

This famous verse, known usually as the "Mizpah blessing," is quoted, stitched on samplers, used as a benediction, and generally misunderstood. Long treated as a warm familial farewell, the well-known words testify instead to the heat of suppressed mistrust and anger that existed between the two men.

The stories in Genesis about Jacob's years with Laban paint a picture of Jacob, whose name is a pun on the word for cheater, as an apprentice under the master scoundrel, Laban. Jacob's twenty years of servitude under his father-in-law were fraught with connivance, hostility, and discord. Jacob, fresh from his cunning victory over his father and brother, found himself playing in the big leagues when he took on Laban. From the initial skirmish, which went to Laban, to the final battle, which Jacob won only because God intervened on his side, the saga of Jacob and Laban is one of familial intrigue and antagonism.

Jacob's flight from his father-in-law, and Laban's enraged pursuit of his larcenous son-in-law, is the discordant prelude to what has come to be called, erroneously, a blessing.

Jacob's time in the bosom of his mother's family was difficult for him. But in spite of the enmity of Laban's own sons and the unwanted marriage Jacob had been tricked into, it was also a time of undreamed of prosperity. He had come to Laban as a fugitive seeking asylum. Twenty years later he had extensive flocks, two wives, eleven sons, and a thinly veiled hostility for his adoptive family (Genesis 31:4–7).

Fearing that Laban might once again change the terms under which he labored, Jacob enlisted Laban's daughters in a plot to desert the regions of Haran for the uncertain security of home, where his brother Esau waited. That Jacob wanted to be with the brother he had so often fought with gives us a clue as to the strength of Jacob's desire to be finished with Laban. Without Laban's knowledge (but, as Laban saw it, with his daughters, grandchildren, and property, Genesis 31:31–32), Jacob set out for his homeland.

Laban found out within three days that his shifty son-in-law had headed west with practically everything he valued: family, herds, and household gods. Without hesitation he gathered his forces and set off in hot pursuit. Before he was able to reclaim what he considered stolen, God intervened. By way of a dream He warned Laban not to pursue the matter with Jacob. Laban was a man robbed, he thought, of everything and constrained from taking his rightful vengeance by the threat of a powerful deity.

Laban recognized the power of God through the dream. If he didn't know God personally, he was at least superstitious enough to know dreams were nothing to trifle with. When he finally confronted Jacob, he was no longer the vengeful man who had left Haran. He was terrified of the God who had sent the dream. Even so, he made a veiled threat against Jacob. "I have the power to harm you," Laban warned Jacob (v. 29).

The two men parted enemies. The stone pillar was a boundary marker between their two territories. It was also to remind them that they had entered into a pact with God himself as witness. Let me paraphrase the so-called "Mizpah Blessing" in this light: "Let God keep an eye on the two of us when we're unable to do that for ourselves. Jacob, you take good care of my daughters. God has not permitted me to take back what is mine but may He himself take vengeance on you if you ever mistreat Rachel or Leah. And heaven help you if you ever think of taking other wives."

Why do we think that a man who had two wives, fathered twelve children by four different women, bought his brother's birthright for a bowl of soup, cheated his elderly father out of the joy of conferring his blessing on the son he loved, and cheated his twin brother out of that blessing would have any compunctions about keeping household gods?

The clearly stated biblical lesson is that the patriarchs were idol worshippers.

Q **uestion 69**   If Esau was ready to forgive Jacob and live at peace with him, why did he come to meet him with 400 men (Genesis 32:6)?

Poor Jacob had just wriggled out of a twenty-year entanglement with his wealth and skin still intact. Now he has to deal with a twenty-year-old grudge held by his big, mean, macho brother. Talk about jumping from the frying pan into the fire.

He sent a message to Esau telling him how he'd prospered and that he was returning from his long exile. Imagine his chagrin when his messengers returned with the news that Esau was on the way with 400 men. Jacob didn't like it. He prepared for the confrontation, but in a different way than he would have twenty years earlier. He began with prayer, reminding the Lord of the promises he was heir to. Knowing what might be awaiting him, Jacob sent an apology to Esau accompanied by a lavish gift.

Esau responded as Jacob would have wished, possibly because of the gifts, certainly because of the prayer. The reconciliation between the two hostile brothers seems warm and genuine.

Isaac had blessed Esau with all there was left. Jacob deceived his father into giving him Esau's blessing, making Jacob the master of the bounty of the field and vine, of the sweetness of heaven's dew and the richness of the earth. That left Esau with the empty expanse of the desert, to be lord of what he could take and hold from the wilderness. He would be a rough and wild man, as fitted his nature, and with nothing but his wits and his wilderness, he would live, when need be, by the sword (Genesis 27:39–40).

People who fit that description were quite common during the patriarchal period. They apparently roamed throughout the ancient Near East from Babylon to Egypt. This doesn't mean that a single wanderer would migrate from one end of the fertile crescent to the other. They seem to have had very limited migratory patterns, usually staying within the jusrisdictions of a few cities, even making treaties with the kings of those cities.

They lived in the shadow of the town and grazed their flocks on the stubble from the farms. They lived in a sometimes uneasy relationship with their more settled neighbors. For the most part, they tried to maintain good relationships with the cities near which they camped. But it was not unheard of, in times of political disruption, for a powerful nomadic chief to move into the city and become its king.

The nomads provided a wilderness for outlaws and outcasts from the city. They could run to these nomadic chiefs and become part of the chieftain's personal army. These small armies were so effective that they provided the mercenary backbone of their neighbors' armies in times of war.

The 400 men were a part of Esau's retinue, as were the 318 trained men who followed Abraham (Genesis 14:14). He was probably never far from them, just as the American president is never without his secret service guards and personal retinue.

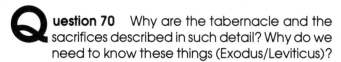

Q **uestion 70**   Why are the tabernacle and the sacrifices described in such detail? Why do we need to know these things (Exodus/Leviticus)?

I'll admit that the descriptions in these books sometimes drive me to distraction. My guess is that very few Christians read every line of these two books during their annual progress through the Bible.

If we were contractors, though, we might not be surprised at what we discover in Exodus. The first thing contractors need when preparing to build a detailed building is detailed instructions. They need to know exactly the sort of information Moses gave us. In reading Exodus, we don't realize that long portions of it were the contractor's blueprint.

When Bezalel and Oholiab began to assign projects to their subcontractors, they needed a materials list, dimensions, and instructions for decorative details before they could proceed. The simplest, most straight-forward reason for the inclusion of all those details about the tabernacle is that they were necessary for its construction.

For most of us, though, this manner of description strikes us as excessive unless there's some profound meaning hidden in it all. In a way, that perception is right, because there is a profound meaning in these detailed descriptions. But it isn't the allegorical kind of typology many of us are familiar with.

For example, you may have heard someone say, "The black curtain of goat's hair is a type of sin. Black is the color of sin, and the goat is the type of sin." They forget that Isaiah talks of sins being of scarlet and ignore that nowhere in Scripture is such an interpretation presented.

For them, the details cry for interpretation. Why would God go into such detail if it weren't somehow more than just the contractor's instructions?

There's good news. All these things did happen for our instruction. We just tend to look in the wrong places for our lessons. We ignore the impact such instructions might have had on people of a totally different culture than our own.

Because we don't offer sacrifices or build that kind of temple, we encounter the biblical examples as unique in human history. But the sacrifices of Israel have their counterparts in the way their neighbors worshiped. Every temple they'd ever been in had been laid out on the same plan as the tabernacle. It was the standard Near Eastern temple pattern with three parts: a court, a holy place, and a holiest place where the deity resided.

Some don't like the idea that Israel's temple was built from a common model. They think it should have been a unique, once in an earth-time design. Yet missionaries today use culturally familiar things to bridge communication gaps. We call it contextualization, and it's generally considered a good way to introduce a new, or even radical, truth in a culturally familiar form. In Israel's case, God used the form of the tabernacle and the structure of the sacrificial system to move the people away from their belief in spirits.

We have this mental image of Israel as a bunch of devout, spiritually mature, theologically sophisticated wanderers roaming from oasis to oasis discussing the finer points of the Council of Chalcedon, but it just wasn't so. These people had no written Scriptures, no trained clergy, no body of theological writings, and no prophetic voices. Their most familiar theological models were Egyptian and possibly Canaanite.

They probably gave allegiance to the God of Abraham, Isaac, and Jacob, but I find no evidence in Scripture that they were monotheistic in the sense that we are today. After 3,000 years of history, experience, and teaching there are still people who call themselves Christian and yet consult their horoscopes, knock on wood, throw salt over their shoulders, and would cross a street to avoid walking under a ladder. But most of us know better.

Even in America, with centuries of Christian teaching behind us, petty superstitions with their roots in spirit worship are with us every day. So we shouldn't be surprised that Israel at Sinai was still centuries away from kicking the spirit habit. In fact, their behavior in the wilderness and during the period of the judges is all but incomprehensible if they'd already risen above it. The biblical picture is much more coherent if we see the Israelites in the wilderness as kindergarteners in their understanding of the faith with which Moses presented them.

The notion that there was only one true God had never been tried before on a national level. Israel had a lot to learn about this Yahweh they followed through the Red Sea. If He was to be worshipped as the only God, it was important to the Israelites that they worship him properly.

Most religions approach their deities with great fear, or at least great respect. In many cultures people don't just walk up to their god and announce their presence willy-nilly and expect to be welcomed with open arms. Animists believe that such behavior will get them struck by lightning, squashed by a falling tree, bitten by a snake, or felled by some particularly loathsome disease.

Maybe there's a piece of truth about worship we can learn even from the animist. Where there's great power, the prudent person treats it with great respect. The Power who controlled the waters of the Red Sea was not to be trifled with.

If God had merely told Israel, "Let's have a house warming and y'all come, y'hear," I doubt if he would have had any takers. It would have seemed far too dangerous. To calm the potential fears of a people who had never had a close personal relationship with this incredibly powerful God, the Lord laid down careful plans for them to follow in getting to know Him.

The sacrifices were important audio-visual devices aimed at teaching Israel about God's nature and its responsibilities toward Him. Israel knew practically nothing. They would learn through the sacrifices and the tabernacle that God is holy and requires the same kind of holiness from His people. They would learn that sin matters, and that only the costly shedding of innocent blood would wash them clean. They would learn to depend on the Lord and to realize that the Lord, not their best efforts, was responsible for their prosperity.

Most importantly, they learned that the sacrifices were not enough. Moses records this frightening information in Numbers 15:22–31. After the Israelites made a golden calf at Sinai, murmured against God's chosen leader, and melted with fear at the prospect of trusting the Lord to keep His word, God gave them their next lesson in responsibility.

In verses 3–31 we learn that willful, defiant sin cannot be atoned within the sacrificial system. In other words, there are sins that the Law can't deal with. This is the first hint that God's dealings with them would be more than just the strictly legal one the Law prescribed.

The sacrifices and the tabernacle teach a great deal more. For the specifics, consult some of the reference books I recommend in the appendix.

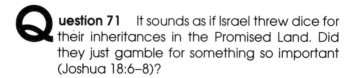

Q **uestion 71** It sounds as if Israel threw dice for their inheritances in the Promised Land. Did they just gamble for something so important (Joshua 18:6–8)?

They did cast lots, sort of. As nearly as we can tell from the Old Testament, the mysterious *Urim* and *Thummim* were lots used when an Israelite wanted direction from the Lord.

If an Old Testament translation of Hebrew words, such as *Urim* and *Thummim,* have to be written in English letters, it probably means they can't be translated satisfactorily.

No one really knows what these were, and that ignorance goes back as far as we know. By the time the Old Testament was first being translated into other languages the meaning of the two words had already been lost.

We know from Scripture that the high priest carried them in his breastplate and used them for discerning God's will (Numbers 27:21; 1 Samuel 14:41; 28:6; Ezra 2:63). They were primitive tools, figuring prominently in the early history of Israel and continuing in use until the book of Acts (1:23–26) when the apostles used something like them to choose Judas' replacement.

There was never a consideration that this was gambling. In Proverbs 16:33 we see a glimpse at Israel's attitude toward the lot. "The lot is cast into the lap, but its every decision is from the Lord." Apparently they were part of the primitive apparatus God used to reveal himself at that early stage to His nation. They were still spiritual babies in their knowledge of what it meant to be adopted by God as His own.

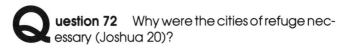

Q **uestion 72**   Why were the cities of refuge necessary (Joshua 20)?

The cities of refuge were a step forward in the administration of justice in Israel. There were shrines and temples where criminals and innocent fugitives might seek the protection of the deity, but no cities. And no provision was made for judging the guilt or innocence of the fugitive.

Unlike the ancient concept of sanctuary, the city of refuge served both as prison and refuge, but only for the one guilty of what we might call involuntary manslaughter. If the elders of the city determined that a person had lain in wait, or committed premeditated murder, the criminal was expelled from the city.

This may not sound like a great deal considering what the cities were like! The cities of the ancient world were packed with houses inside the walls like blocks in a box. It's no surprise that Hebrew has no proper word for *street*; there probably were no streets as we would recognize them. The only place where people might congregate was in the open area surrounding the gate.

According to the biblical regulation, the fugitive was required to stay within the city walls until the death of the current high priest. Today we call that an indeterminate sentence and consider it inhumane.

Usually the murdered person's family caused the murderer to flee to the city of refuge. In the rough and tumble world of the patriarchs, justice was largely a family affair.

Say I get a little hot under the collar and poke you a good one in the nose. Nothing major. Just a little nose bleed, a couple of shiners, and maybe a new lump on your nose. There were no courts. No police. No prisons. Just family. And every family had its designated hitter. An ancient Near Eastern designated hitter had more in common with Big Eddie from Detroit than he did with a declining baseball star.

He would probably come looking for me to blacken both my eyes, break my nose, and, for good measure, maybe knock out a few of my teeth so everybody would know not to mess with his family.

You might think that would be the end of it, but I have a family too. When my designated hitter swings into action, things begin to get serious. It's no longer just two ornery people getting all worked up over some little nothing.

And that kind of clan warfare was what passed for a legal system in the ancient world before God established cities of refuge for those who got into trouble innocently. Such a system of justice may seem crude to us, but it saved the hide of innocent people.

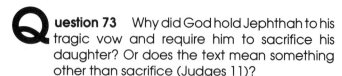

Question 73 Why did God hold Jephthah to his tragic vow and require him to sacrifice his daughter? Or does the text mean something other than sacrifice (Judges 11)?

Like it or not, this story presents one of the rare instances in the history of Israel when they practiced human sacrifice.

Before God's call to be a judge, Jephthah was an outlaw. His value to Israel lay in his hardness and his band of adventurers. He was the son of Gilead and a prostitute, which made him an outcast, but, like Esau, he lived a life made possible by his own strength. He was isolated from whatever may have passed for theological orthodoxy in those days.

But we should also remember that there wasn't much that passed for orthodoxy in those days. "In those days Israel had no king; everyone did as he saw fit" (Judges 21:25). Jephthah's pagan vow, which certainly had to include the people of his house, must be seen in this setting.

He certainly thought that, if the sacrifice of a bull had great power before the Lord, the sacrifice of a daughter would carry even more power. That idea of greater power is always what lies behind human sacrifice. He was in a situation where power mattered.

How could God bless a man who had made such a vow, and then fulfilled it?

Keep in mind the fact that very few of God's chosen instruments were without fault, or even serious sin. Moses was a murderer. David was an adulterer and a murderer. Jacob was a con-man and Abraham was a liar. Jonah was a racist who rebelled at the idea that God would forgive the Assyrians. And what about Peter's impulsiveness and the contentious spirits displayed by James and John?

But God used them all.

God can use whomever He chooses to use. He used Balaam, the Syrian prophet. He used Cyrus, the Persian king. He even used Pharaoh and his hardness of heart to advance His plan.

Jephthah was chosen. He fulfilled his purpose. God's choice of Jephthah for one purpose does not mean that Jephthah was somehow a perfect person.

I find this knowledge encouraging.

I know that sinless perfection is beyond me, but I continue to press on toward that target. Even in the midst of my failings, though, I want God to use me. If He demanded that I achieve sinlessness before I'm usable, there's little hope for me.

But he doesn't demand sinlessness.

What he demands is faithfulness and willingness to do as He commands. That Jephthah could provide. And so can we.

Q **uestion 74**   Israel took the Ark of the Covenant into battle against the Philistines. Why (1 Samuel 4:3)?

Why do baseball players refuse to change their socks when their team is on a winning streak? Why do some actors get furious if you whistle in the dressing room? Why do some hotels in some parts of the world number their floors 11, 12, 14? We forget how high the level of superstition in the supposedly Christian west can get.

Israel's decision to carry the Ark of the Covenant into battle with them is just one example of how high the level of superstition among the ancient Israelites could get. Contrary to all God told them about the care and use of the Ark, when things looked threatening on the battle field, Israel took it with them as a charm to guarantee their victory against the Philistines. The religions of Canaan, which had a tremendous impact on the thinking of ancient Israel, were not much different from the third world religious form we call animism, the belief that spirits inhabit things. To control evil spirits they believed they must possess something inhabited by a more powerful spirit.

This took place at the end of the period of the judges, a time of unremitting apostasy as Israel was seduced, time after time, by the gods of Canaan.

Although they were dealing with Yahweh, they were apparently thinking in spirit terms. This is part of the struggle the major and minor prophets describe.

One of the two major themes of that collection of books is Israel's adultery with other gods.

Jeremiah lamented that Israel dallied with false deities, right in the temple. Yet they called on Yahweh for protection (Jeremiah 7:9–10). The descendants of these Israelites relied on the temple in the same way for protection. The Judahites of Jeremiah's day looked at the rising power of the Babylonians and, instead of listening to Jeremiah's warnings, chanted superstitiously, "The temple of the Lord, the temple of the Lord, the temple of the Lord" (Jeremiah 7:4).

Just as Christians in our day unwittingly mix faith with the ideas and values of the culture in which we live, so the people of Israel incorporated the religious sensibilities of the people of Canaan. When they marched out to fight the Philistines, they did so in the name of Yahweh. But they profaned that name by using it in the same magical way that the Philistines might have used their own gods.

The lesson we must learn from this, and from the other dismal incidents of apostasy recorded throughout the Old Testament, is that of cultural sensitivity. I believe the Israelites were baffled by the criticisms of the prophets and the judgments they suffered for their adulterous behavior. Their behavior was normal for their world, so even if they had had Scripture they probably would have been unable to see how it contradicted the way they were.

Dr. T. Titus Tienou, one of Africa's foremost Christian leaders, explained this when he used the equation, gospel + culture = Christianity.

None of us is free of the taint of our non-Christian culture. But to live in the most Christian way possible we need to look back to Scripture and learn to distinguish between what we do because we were born in the United States and what we do because we've been bought by Christ. If we fail in that, the Christianity we practice will be as tainted with unexamined, unchristian ideas and behaviors as was the religion of the Israelites who carried the ark into battle.

uestion 75 What made Israel want a human king when God had taken care of them ever since they left Egypt? Why couldn't they just trust God (1 Samuel 8)?

A little boy who was having trouble getting to sleep at night made repeated nocturnal visits to his parents' room. His mother finally managed to ferret out the problem: he was afraid of the shadows in his dark room.

Being a good Christian, she prayed with the terrified tyke. Thinking that would take care of his fear, she rolled over to capture what was left of a night's sleep. Unsuccessfully.

"What is it this time?" she grumbled.

"I'm still scared," he whimpered.

"But honey, didn't we pray together?"

"Yes."

"And don't you know that Jesus is there in the room with you?"

"Yes."

"Then what's wrong?"

"I think I'd rather have somebody with some skin on," he replied.

Israel wanted someone with skin on. They wanted somebody who was physically there when they needed him. They wanted a king who could be reached at a moment's notice and whose action they could observe.

They had lived through a long, painful period with God as king, and none of those qualifications fit. All Israel wanted in the time of Samuel was a physical, human redeemer. They asked for a king like the nations had. Samuel explained all the negative aspects of having a human king (1 Samuel 8:10–18), but they wouldn't listen. Their attention was focused on the benefit. It was singular, and it was the same benefit they had received from the judges. In times of danger, there would be a strong, warlike man to come to their rescue.

The Israelite's unwillingness to trust God is at the core of their demand for a king. Why would they trade the God who loved them for a human king who would exploit them? Before we're too hard on those Israelites, though, remember that the same urge rests in all of us. We want a president who will return prayer to the classroom and morality to the streets. We want a banker who will stand ready to step in and smooth out our financial reverses, and the cost in this case is considerably less than the Israelites were willing to pay. We want an insurance agent to pay us back if we lose anything through accident, theft, storm, or flood. We, too, would rather rely on "someone with skin" than put our affairs and our futures in the Lord's hand.

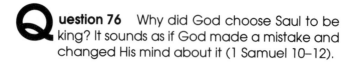

Question 76   Why did God choose Saul to be king? It sounds as if God made a mistake and changed His mind about it (1 Samuel 10–12).

God chose Saul because Saul was a good candidate for the office. He had all the right qualifications. He was big and impressive looking (1 Samuel 10:24). In fact, when all the people shouted "Long live the king," most of them knew about Saul was that he was a head taller than the rest of them. Ours isn't the first nation to pick it's leaders on the basis of image. Saul's first military encounters also confirmed the wisdom of the choice. He warmed up by defeating Nahash the Ammonite (1 Samuel 11:11) and then went on to triumph against overwhelming odds in his first encounters with the Philistines (1 Samuel 13–14).

In spite of the negative image most preachers paint of Saul, he was able to awaken intense and lasting loyalties among the people. Today he is so thoroughly overshadowed by David in most of our minds that we miss the indications of his popularity among the people of Israel. It was probably that loyalty that kept his army behind him in the final, losing confrontation with the Philistines. It was that loyalty that motivated the men of Jabesh Gilead to risk their lives to rescue his body from the walls of Beth Shan and give it a decent burial (1 Samuel 31:11–13). It was that loyalty that kept the northern tribes from giving their allegiance to David until seven years after Saul's death (2 Samuel 5:5).[1]

1
The seven years and six months that David was king in Hebron began about the time of Saul's death (2 Samuel 2:1–4) and ends with his move from Hebron to Jerusalem shortly after the death of Ish-Bosheth, Saul's surviving son.

God's seriousness in choosing Saul may be seen in the judgment Samuel announced against Saul for his impatient offering of sacrifice for the sake of public opinion (1 Samuel 13:13–14). The judgment reveals God's plan for Saul and announces the tragic news that it has been cancelled because of Saul's sin. Instead of establishing Saul's house as the ruling dynasty, God removed His support for Saul and transferred it to another.

Saul was given the opportunity to live up to God's highest call on his life. The fact that Saul was unsuccessful doesn't mean God's choice was a mistake. It means only that Saul lacked commitment to do God's will as well as the humility and true repentance necessary for success. Saul's rejection is a warning to all of us. God's calling is sure, but our response is less sure. I have no question about God's ability to keep us as His children.

I'm a great deal more reserved about our ability to respond properly to God's specific call for service. Saul had been anointed for a job. He was called in the same way a pastor or missionary might be called. He accepted that call, but in the course of his service he began to free-lance, operating as if he were able to perform God's work in his own way. This rejection of God as King over the king led to his fall, not from grace, but from power.

Q **uestion 77**   If David already had two wives, why was he so insistent on having Saul's daughter, Michal, returned to him (2 Samuel 3:12–16)? What was so awful about Adonijah asking for Abishag as his wife? Why did Solomon have him killed because of it (1 Kings 2:13–25)?

These two seemingly unrelated questions have the same answer. In both cases, marriage to the right woman would have cemented their claims to the throne. Although David had been anointed king by Samuel, he still had to deal with the political problem of claiming the throne. Even after Saul's death, some people believed the throne still belonged to Saul and ought to go to one of his sons or grandsons. By reclaiming Michal, David established himself as one of Saul's heirs.

Solomon's response to Adonijah's request for Abishag is triggered by the knowledge that his brother is trying to link himself with the former regime by marriage, just as his father had done in his marriage to Saul's daughter Michal.

When Solomon chastised his mother for even making the request, he said, "You might as well request the kingdom for him—after all he is my older brother—yes, for him and for Abiathar the priest and Joab son of Zeruiah" (1 Kings 2:22).

Solomon saw through the plot of his opponents. We may surmise that Adonijah enjoyed some support within David's own household (1 Kings 1:9–10), and his younger brother knew that his father's concubine was all that Adonijah needed to bring to a full boil the simmering opposition to his reign.

Adonijah, as Solomon's older brother, also had a claim to the throne that many, Solomon among them, would have considered valid. He took advantage of what may have been Bathsheba's political naivete by asking her to use her influence with Solomon to acquire Abishag as his wife.

Abishag was the young girl given to David as a concubine in his advanced old age, and would have added additional legitimacy to Adonijah's burning ambition to be king. This is the same idea that generated the shameful behavior of Absalom when, after he had taken Jerusalem, he erected a tent on the city wall and there entertained David's concubines who had been left behind to look after the house (2 Samuel 16:20–22). We can also explain the falling out between Ish-bosheth and Abner over Rizpah, Saul's concubine, in the same way.

These are unpleasant episodes in the life of Israel, made more unpleasant when we consider the feelings of the women involved. Michal was torn from a husband who obviously loved her deeply (2 Samuel 3:15–16). Abishag's function with David, whatever it was, gave no thought for her as a person and when David died she became a pawn in a deadly game of power politics. Rizpah and the unnamed concubines were used as symbols, and nothing more.

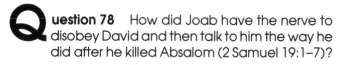

Q **uestion 78**   How did Joab have the nerve to disobey David and then talk to him the way he did after he killed Absalom (2 Samuel 19:1–7)?

The relationship between David and Joab is complex. David's sister Zeruiah was Joab's mother, and while it seems likely that

Joab was younger than David, they were peers, as well as uncle and nephew.

Joab was a man of cold-blooded pragmatism and brutality. Joab murdered Abner (2 Samuel 3:24–26) because Abner had killed his brother Azahel (2 Samuel 2:18–23). But the biblical account tries to show that Abner did what he did out of necessity and not rancor. Joab also hated Abner because it looked like David was interested in ousting him from command of the armies, and Abner was the candidate to replace him.

That would have been a good political move for David if it had succeeded. For seven years Abner had been the power behind the throne of the northern tribes. He was an able man with a loyal following and would have done a great deal to cement David's hold on those fractious tribes.

David's response to the murder tells us a lot about his growing antagonism toward Joab. He uttered a curse upon Joab and all his father's house! And then he ordered Joab to march as chief mourner in Abner's funeral procession.

Whatever David's motivation for this display, we can't have any doubt about the impact it had on his nephew. This was a public humiliation that Joab would not forget.

It was as long as two decades before Joab had the opportunity for revenge. During the difficult years between Absalom's murder of his brother Amnon and Absalom's death at Joab's hand, Joab had been Absalom's primary patron.

It was Joab who intervened with David (2 Samuel 14:1–24) to bring Absalom back from exile. It was Joab who interceded on Absalom's behalf when David allowed him to live in Jerusalem for two solid years without ever seeing him (2 Samuel 14:33). And when it became apparent to Joab that Absalom had become David's implacable enemy, he decided that Absalom had to die.

I think the best explanation for Joab's behavior is that he saw in Absalom a fitting successor to David.

Joab probably would have championed Absalom for the throne with the intention of becoming the power to whom the young king turned for advice. But when it became evident that there would be no peace between David and Absalom as long as both lived. Joab decided that Absalom had to die.

When David gave Joab his orders on the eve of the critical battle, he made it quite clear that Absalom was not to be harmed.

David, his judgment clouded by his flawed love for his rebellious son, didn't see what Joab saw so clearly. If Absalom lived, he would rebel again, and next time he would win.

That's why Joab killed Absalom against David's orders. Joab got revenge against David for earlier humiliation. With a thinly veiled threat, he warned David that if he didn't stop "not a man will be left with you by nightfall. This will be worse for you than all the calamities that have come upon you from your youth until now" (2 Samuel 19:7).

Joab was the general of the army. It had been years since David marched to battle with these men. By mourning Absalom instead of celebrating their triumph, David insulted them. Joab and David both knew that Joab need only say the word and the army would be gone, leaving David alone, friendless, and helpless.

In a touch of poetic justice, Joab, who had been forced to march as chief mourner in his rival's funeral procession, would prevent David, the man who had ordered his humiliation, from mourning the son he loved.

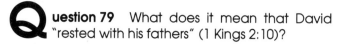

Question 79   What does it mean that David "rested with his fathers" (1 Kings 2:10)?

It's not uncommon for the Old Testament to tell us that one of the kings slept with his fathers or was gathered to his fathers. This is a reference to ancient burial customs. In the days when people were buried in large tombs with niches for several bodies, they were, quite literally, with their ancestors in death.

A body was placed in one of the niches in the family tomb, where it lay until time had reduced it to a skeleton. When the niche was needed for another family member, the bones were gathered and buried. Sometimes the bones were placed in a separate chamber within the tomb and sometimes they were interred in the floor. In any case, to be gathered to the fathers was a poetic way of describing what happened to the body after death.

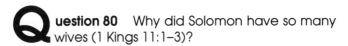

Q **uestion 80**   Why did Solomon have so many wives (1 Kings 11:1–3)?

People who are able to forgive David his eight named wives (2 Samuel 3:2–5 lists six, to which we add Michal and Bathsheba) are invariably offended, if not horrified, by the overwhelming excessiveness of Solomon's unnamed thousand.

Having been through one wedding of my own, I can't imagine how Solomon had time for anything except getting fitted for tuxedos and going to wedding rehearsals. If each wedding took a minimum of two days, that works out to almost six years of his forty-year reign.

Unless we get rid of our cultural image of marriage we'll never understand the problem of Solomon's wives. His multitudinous state marriages are as different from the modern American institution of marriage as Lachish is from Los Angeles.

It's true that polygamy was practiced in ancient Israel. It's just as true that most Israelites had only one wife. God's law prohibited the harem building that we remember Solomon for (Deuteronomy 17:17). In fact, the regulations set down for the king in Deuteronomy make me think that God had Solomon in mind when He revealed them.

Solomon was an ambitious man. Apparently he wanted to make people forget David's greatness by overshadowing his reign in the glory of his own. One characteristic of Solomon's reign was his aggressive foreign policy. He ruled over "all the kingdoms from the River to the land of the Philistines, as far as the border of Egypt" (1 Kings 4:21).

His fame attracted the Queen of Sheba, who made the long trek from the southwestern regions of the Arabian peninsula to test his wisdom and be dazzled by his splendor.

He received 666 talents of gold every year in taxes, and a talent may have been worth as much as 386,880 dollars. This income didn't include the tribute from the Arabian kings and taxes from the governors of the twelve administrative districts he'd established in Israel. Nor did it include the gold from his far-flung mercantile enterprises. With his wide-ranging commercial interests, his empire extended to the limits promised to Abraham (Genesis 15:18–21). Because of his frequent dealings with foreign kings, especially Hiram of Tyre and Egypt's Pharaoh, it is highly probable that he also had extensive treaty relations with his trading partners and his vassals.

That's where the wives come in. To seal such a treaty it was customary for the stronger king to marry the daughter of the weaker king. It was similar to the royal marriages we see in European history, except on a much larger scale. These wives came from all over the ancient Near East, tokens of the official policy of friendship or subservience between the kingdoms of their fathers and their husbands. I wonder if Solomon even knew who most of them were. They may have been married by contract without ever seeing each other at a public ceremony.

This doesn't mean Solomon was right in what he did. It means only that there was some reason behind what to us seems to be a bizarre record of meaningless matrimony.

No matter what the cultural reasons were, Solomon was violating a specific regulation from the Lord. For all his wisdom, for all he accomplished, his obsession with power and wealth apparently led him to disregard God in his quest for more of both. His multitude of wives are the immediate evidence, and his apostasy the ultimate result, for as God warned, they led his heart away from the true God to the worship of others.

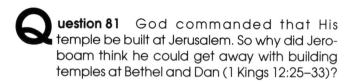

Q **uestion 81** God commanded that His temple be built at Jerusalem. So why did Jeroboam think he could get away with building temples at Bethel and Dan (1 Kings 12:25–33)?

Jeroboam knew that if the people of the northern tribes continued to make religious pilgrimages to the south, he'd never hold their allegiance. He needed to give them temples where they could worship God without leaving home. He chose two cities with ancient, holy connections as sites.

Dan was the place the tribe of Dan conquered for its capital when forced out of its God-given inheritance in the south. The story, as reported in Judges 18, mentions a renegade Levite who the Danites hired as a priest. When he left the household of Micah to assume his new position, he took with him the silver idol that he had worshiped in Micah's household. They established a shrine for the idol at Dan.

That probably happened early in the period of the judges. By the time Jeroboam chose it for his northern temple site, it had a history of at least 300 years as a religious center. Jeroboam gave the people of the north their own shrine that was far older than the newly established temple in Jerusalem.

Bethel had an even longer history. Abraham had stopped there and built an altar when he first entered the land (Genesis 12:8), Bethel was also the site of Jacob's dream of the angelic escalator (Genesis 28:10–22). By the time of Jeroboam, it was a holy place with a history over a millennium long.

Both Dan and Bethel, then, were logical choices for sanctuaries. I can see Jeroboam's marketing directors developing a campaign to convince the citizens of his new country to shift their loyalties from Jerusalem.

"Bethel, First name in sanctuaries."

"Dan, A name you can trust. Same priestly family for ten generations."

 uestion 82 Knowing God's prohibition against graven images, why would Jeroboam put golden calves in those sanctuaries?

They may have been looking back to Aaron's golden calf in the wilderness, but I think there's another possibility that is more likely.

The Ark of the Covenant may have been the inspiration. Part of the Ark was the mercy seat, which was God's throne and was fashioned after thrones common in the ancient Near East.

Baal, the Canaanites god, was sometimes depicted standing on the backs of bull calves. Perhaps someone reasoned, "Why not give the Israelites a focus for their worship. We won't show Yahweh the way we show Baal. We'll just make the calves he'd be standing on—like they had with the mercy seat on the Ark of the Covenant. The people will know that the invisible God of Israel stands tall astride those calves."

The result of this kind of thinking was a combination of orthodox Israelite theology with Canaanite. The motivation may have been to give the people something in place of the Ark of the Covenant in the holy places Jeroboam built to replace Solomon's temple. But whatever the motivation, the result was a disaster.

For the rest of Israel's short history, the writers of scripture would evaluate subsequent kings with the sombre epitaph, "He did evil in the eyes of the Lord, walking in the ways of Jeroboam and in his sin, which he caused Israel to commit" (1 Kings 15:34).

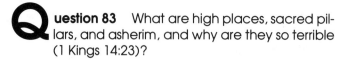

Q **uestion 83**   What are high places, sacred pillars, and asherim, and why are they so terrible (1 Kings 14:23)?

Even today, we tend to think of heaven as up. After 2,000 years of hearing that God is a spirit, how many of us can honestly say we don't visualize Him in some form surrounded by clouds, looking down on the earth. This mental trick allows us to think of God in a tangible way. We know it's incorrect, but we do it anyway.

The theologically unsophisticated people of Canaan had a similar conception. They too considered the abode of their gods as being up high. That being the case, it was logical for them to build their place of worship on the highest hill. The closer they were to where the gods were, the more effective their worship would be.

Some of the "high places" were not, however, located on the tops of high hills. One of the things that seems to connect all of them, though, is an artificial platform built of stones and earth that raised up the worship place.

The high places were often nothing more than an open air shrine with an altar and a few of the other appliances of sacrificial worship. They were the unauthorized places where the false gods were worshipped or where the true God was worshipped falsely.

The *Asherah* and the *sacred pillars* were cult objects. One well-known Israeli archeologist showed a slide of a strangely constructed piece of pottery that he identified as a cult object. He explained that archeologists call anything they don't understand or recognize a cult object. In fact, we don't know with any certainty what these were.

Asherah was the name of the principal female deity of Canaan (1 Kings 18:19). The *Asherah* were objects erected in her honor (1 Kings 15:13). They seem to have been made of wood, because they could be burned (Deuteronomy 12:3) or cut down (Exodus

34:13). We can't say more with certainty. It's common to describe them as wooden poles set up in honor of the goddess. They may have been carved to resemble her, but none has survived, so we don't really know.

The *sacred pillars*, on the other hand, were of stone. They had a long and honorable history that went wrong when Israel began to worship Baal. Earlier in patriarchal times they were merely commemorative stones. Our grave markers are a good modern example.

But the sacred pillars condemned by the prophets were symbols of the god Baal. They were apparently unworked stone, which, in their crude strength called to mind Canaan's principal male god. Together they stood in the high places where the cruel and immoral rites of fertility were celebrated. Together, with their religion that called for no commitment, only sacrifice and lasciviousness, they seduced the hearts of the people of Israel.

Q **uestion 84** What does it mean that Ben-Hadad will let Ahab build "streets" in Damascus (1 Kings 20:34)?

You've heard the adage, "To the victor go the spoils." The streets in Damascus were part of the spoils of Ahab's victory over Syria. These were commercial streets, trade zones, where Israel's merchants were allowed to do business without hindrance or tax in the capital of their traditional enemy. These trade zones were like Japan's tariff-free commerce in the United States today. Israel's trade zones in enemy territory were a graphic demonstration of Ahab's total defeat of Ben-Hadad. They allow us to see Ahab as he really was: a powerful, feared monarch. We focus our attention on his spiritual bankruptcy, but his contemporaries weren't concerned about that. They saw him as an ally to be courted and an enemy to be feared.

Assyrian records tell us that a coalition formed between Ahab, Damascus, and Hamath stood against Shalmaneser III in a battle at Qarqar. Ahab's 2,000 chariots would have been a key element in that force. While Shalmaneser boasted of a great victory, he was actually stopped cold for several years.

Ahab's streets in Damascus are a token of the power he was able to exercise among Israel's neighbors.

Q **uestion 85**   Was Elisha really twice the prophet Elijah was (2 Kings 2:9–14)?

There are far more stories about miraculous deeds connected with Elisha than are attributed to Elijah. This might lead to the conclusion that Elisha's request was honored and that he did in fact receive twice the power that Elijah exercised. But the Jewish people never thought of Elisha's request as being for power. And when God inspired Malachi to talk of the coming Day of the Lord He promised the return of Elijah, not Elisha (Malachi 4:5). Jesus himself validated this expectation when He identified John the Baptist as the fulfillment of that prophecy. And it was Elijah who stood on the Mount of transfiguration with Jesus and Moses as the greatest of the prophets (Matthew 17:3–4).

Besides, the request sounds arrogant when we rephrase it to capture the understanding we often have: "Elijah, you'll be gone soon, but I'm still a young man. I want to be a prophet and I want to be the greatest prophet ever. Ask the Lord to make me twice the prophet you were."

We misunderstand Elisha because the meaning of his request for a double portion of Elijah's spirit can be understood only in light of the Israelite inheritance laws. Their way of dividing estates was simple and straightforward. The oldest son was always chief heir, unless the father changed it. Scripture records a number of examples that show the preference for the oldest son could be overturned (Isaac, Judah, and Manasseh, to name three), but it usually belonged to the firstborn.

Being chief heir had certain responsibilities attached to it, but the benefit that went with the responsibilities was a larger inheritance. Twice as large, in fact. The property and other wealth was divided into one more portion than there were sons. With two sons, there would be three portions. With four sons, five portions. With twelve sons there would be thirteen portions, etc. The chief heir received the extra portion.

Elisha was not asking to be twice the prophet or have twice the power. He was asking Elijah to petition God to allow him the privilege of continuing Elijah's work as his heir. And when the mantle passed from Elijah's flaming chariot to Elisha's shoulders, the world knew his request had been granted.

*Was the Black Death God's plan
for Europe? Did Genghis Khan
ravage a continent at
God's command?*

CHAPTER 7

PRINCIPLES

25 To interpret Scripture correctly, we need to ask the kinds of questions we use subconsciously in more mundane circumstances: "What is the author trying to prove?" "Where does the author's information come from?" "How does that information affect my understanding of what the author has to say?"

QUESTIONS

86 Does God create some people for salvation and heaven and others to go to hell (Romans 9:19–24)?

87 How can people deny predestination when the Bible teaches it so clearly (Ephesians 1:4–12)?

88 If God knows everything, and He's ordained everything, what is the purpose in our prayers? If God's will is going to be done anyway, why do we even have to ask (Ephesians 6:18)?

FREE PEOPLE, SOVEREIGN GOD

---

26 Keep in mind the Old Testament concept of corporate justice. It carried over into the lives of the Jewish writers of the New Testament, so it's important in interpreting all of Scripture.

---

89 How can I know God's will for my life? I'm never certain if what I'm doing is in His will or out of it (Ephesians 5:17).

90 Is it possible for believers to lose their salvation (Hebrews 6:4–12)?

What makes your neighbor mow his lawn at 7:30 in the morning on your day off? What makes people decide they can burglarize a house to finance a drug habit? What makes one person take up arms to end another's life? What makes governments, divinely ordained for the protection of the righteous, imprison, torture, and kill their own people? What makes monsters like Adolph Hitler, Pol Pot, Idi Amin, and Joseph Stalin unleash horrors worse than death on numberless millions? We might answer all those questions by pointing to the unfathomable depths of evil in the heart of fallen humanity. We might talk in terms of subconscious primal hatreds from the dawn of the race. Or we could look outside ourselves and ask, "Is it possible that God decreed all these things?"

Did the loving God we're taught to call Father mandate mass torment and annihilation for multiplied millions throughout the bloodstained history of humanity? Was the Black Death God's plan for Europe? Did Genghis Khan ravage a continent at God's command? Was the "calculated frightfulness" of the Assyrian empire divinely ordained?

All this raises one of theology's most profound and troubling questions. In a world with a surplus of pain and catastrophe, where does the management, or as theologians would say, providence, of a good and loving God fit? Are these the harmonies, counterpoints, and dissonances of some divinely orchestrated symphony called human history? Can these be considered part of the good gifts that come from God (James 1:17)? If they are good in some rarefied theological sense, can we even know what good means? If they're not good, do we accuse God of sending evil?

Skeptics have no problem here. They simply affirm the mindless absurdity of life and chalk it all up as the punchline in some cosmic joke. We who are believers don't have it so easy. Our dilemma dates back to before the time of Christ. The Greek philosopher Epicurus put it into words for us. He proposed that an all-loving God would not abide evil. Since evil exists, God must either be all-good or all-powerful. He couldn't be both.

Christians tend to respond to that charge from within the hermetically sealed safe-house of our theology. From that sanctuary we have no difficulty affirming the truth of both attributes. Of course God is all-powerful. Of course He's all-good. When we leave the refuge of theological discourse to venture into the world around us, though, the answers that flow so freely in the ivory tower drop limply into our discourse with the suffering and bereaved.

In the living of life, it almost seems that Epicurus was right. Following his lead, some modern writers have resolved the difficulty by accepting God's power but rejecting His goodness. Others opt for a nice but ineffectual heavenly grandfather who likes us a lot and sure feels sorry for us, but who is reduced to wringing his hands in impotent concern. The most radical simply deny God's existence.

For the biblical Christian none of these alternatives offer a solution. We worship the God of the Bible, not the fabrications of philosophers. The God of the Bible is both good and powerful. Our challenge is to find a way to understand the relationship between the two. Most of our Christian solutions are attempts to grapple with the question of how God governs His universe. We all accept the biblical metaphor of God as king. We part company over the kind of king He is.

ALL IN ONE AND ONE IN ALL

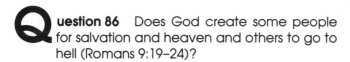 **uestion 86**   Does God create some people for salvation and heaven and others to go to hell (Romans 9:19–24)?

Romans 9 can be a very troubling passage if we read it without careful attention to Paul's purpose. Motivation, or author's intent, is critical to a proper understanding of the message. Few of us do it consciously, but we all evaluate author intent in our everyday reading.

Paul chose Isaac and Jacob to prove a point in Romans 9, but it wasn't a point about predestination. Commentators often get side-tracked because Paul spoke about the freedom of God's choices.

His purpose, however, was not to propose a doctrine of predestination; it was to defend God's decision to include the Gentiles among His people.

To do this, Paul went back to the Old Testament to demonstrate the supremacy of divine promise over physical descent, even among Abraham's children.

Verse 6 helps us see this. He began this important section with the statement, "It is not as though God's word had failed." If God had made all those promises to Israel and then broken them, His promises to the church wouldn't have been worth the breath it took to speak them.

Throughout Romans 9–11 Paul was concerned with demonstrating in as many ways as possible that God had dealt justly with the Jew and could be trusted to deal justly with the church.

P **rinciple 25**   To interpret Scripture correctly, we need to ask the kinds of questions we use subconsciously in more mundane circumstances: "What is the author trying to prove?" "Where does the author's information come from?" "How does that information affect my understanding of what the author has to say?"

As Paul confronted the problem, he used a common literary device called *diatribe*, in which the author sets up an imaginary opponent to raise the questions the author believes need to be answered. I use a little of that technique myself in this book. In Romans, Paul put arguments he'd heard against his teaching into the mouth of this literary opponent.

Apparently this was a question Paul expected to be of major importance to his readers. In at least five other places in Romans he made some specific reference to it (2:2; 3:5; 3:19–20; 9:6; 11:1–2).

Beyond that, a great deal of the general teaching of Romans 1–8 addresses the issue of salvation for the Gentiles in relation to Israel and the Law.

"Have God's promises to Israel failed?" is a searching question that strikes at the heart of the gospel. Has God acted justly with Israel or has He simply turned His back on them and adopted the Gentiles as His own?

If everything is pre-determined, and God has already created us either for glory or perdition, how are we accountable for what we do before Him?

If God arbitrarily loved Jacob and hated Esau, how can Esau be blamed for anything?

If God made Pharaoh to be stubborn, how can he be criticized for his stubbornness?

In other words, if God condemns humans for their sin but makes them unable to choose *not* to sin, how can we talk about God's justice?

There are two directions we can go in interpreting Romans 9. One assumes that verse 20, "But who are you, O man, to talk back to God," is like the answer we give a child who, given a direction she neither understands nor likes, digs in her little heels, sticks out her little chin, and says, "Why?" Adults everywhere respond by saying, "Because I said so."

There are times and circumstances when this is an entirely appropriate response. Sometimes, because of the complexity of the complete answer, it's the only reasonable response. The question is, does that kind of response fit Paul's argument?

It may.

Using one of the basic rules of interpretation, the clearest, simplest reading of Romans 9 is that God predestines and those who are predestined play no active part in the Divine decree. As a lifelong Arminian, it grieves me to admit this, but that's the simplest reading of the text.

Read in this way, Paul is presenting a picture of the sovereign God of the universe making such decisions as please Him, for reasons that only He can know or understand, and carrying out those decisions without the consent, cooperation, or resistance of the people involved.

God chose Isaac before he was born to be the child of promise, and of the yet unborn twins Jacob and Esau, He declared His preference for Jacob.

In both these cases it's clear that God's choice preceded any merit on the part of the chosen. Given this picture, Paul's curt "Because He says so, that's why" is a completely appropriate reply.

Such an answer doesn't answer the question, but it isn't intended to. After all, God's ways aren't our ways and God's thoughts are higher than our thoughts. Where do we get the right to ask those questions in the first place?

The power of this first interpretation lies in its straightforward treatment of the text, and countless Christians since the Reformation have read it this way.

It is not the only way to read the text, however. In fact, there are several reasons why it would be better to consider another interpretation.

I've already maintained that the focus of Paul's teaching in Romans 9 isn't predestination. He's arguing instead for the justice of God.

More importantly, Paul isn't talking about the fate of individuals in this section; he's speaking about the disposition of whole nations and ethnic groups.

If he isn't teaching about predestination, and if he has the fate of nations rather than individuals in mind, it isn't valid to use the passage to argue for individual predestination.

The idea of corporateness must be taken into account here. We also need to look at what biblical interpreters call the "general tenor" of Scripture. In other words, does the traditional view of predestination fit with the general teachings of the Bible and with the teaching of Romans in particular?

In their original context, the Old Testament passages that Paul uses actually argue against the notion of individual predestination.

Paul's concern in Romans 9 is with God's faithfulness to His promises. He has returned to the point he raised in chapter 3, that Israel's historical advantage was great. She had received privileges in the past that were part reward and part preparation for the great responsibility with which God had entrusted her.

But as Paul wrote, he lived with the emotional agony of seeing his own nation, blessed by God as it had been, replaced by a vigorous, growing, increasingly Gentile church. To some, this suggested that the promises to Abraham, Moses, David, and all their heirs had been broken. Paul, better than anyone, recognized the potential disaster this idea presented.

If God had made all those promises to the nation of Israel, had blessed it with all those privileges, and entrusted it with all those responsibilities, how could He leave Israel behind and accept the Gentiles instead?

More important for Paul and his followers, though, was the question that any inquiring person would ask at this point. How could they believe in the faithfulness of God when He appears so fickle? If He would drop Israel like a hot penny, what guarantee could the church have that it wouldn't suffer the same rejection some day?

Don't take this question too lightly. With 2,000 years of Christian teaching and experience behind us, many of us don't even think to ask it. After all, we have the biblical record of God's faithfulness and the apostle's answer to the question.

But for Paul and his readers this was a very disturbing thought, whether raised by a pagan skeptic or a Jewish opponent, and it required a careful response. Romans 9–11 records Paul's inspired, and inspiring, reply.

He began with an affirmation of his personal anguish over the lostness of Israel and a summary of its past glories as God's covenant community (9:1–5). The richness of that heritage was something Paul both loved and lamented. Without a moment's hesitation, however, he left the past behind and, in verse 6, began his assault on the charge of faithlessness that people had leveled against his God.

Have God's promises to His people failed?

Can God be trusted to act justly?

Three times in chapter 9 (vv. 6, 14, 19), Paul responded to these questions as if they had been flung at him by a real antagonist. In each case he issues an emphatic denial and turns to the Old Testament for support.

I wish we could have listened as Paul dictated, "It is not as though God's word had failed" (9:6). Imagine the indignation crackling in the apostle's voice. The very idea! How could the Judge of all the earth do what was unjust? Paul directed his indignation at people who should have known better.

The apostles taught their converts the Old Testament as a foundation for understanding the life and ministry of Jesus and as the unfailing revelation of God. Anyone who had read the Old Testament should have known the answer to that question.

The faith of Israel was totally dependent on the faithfulness of God. And the sure promises of God had found their fulfillment in the redemption provided in Christ Jesus. But those promises had never included all the children of the patriarchs. God's choice had always fallen on some and not on others.

Abraham had numerous children. We usually think only of Ishmael and Isaac, but he had at least six other sons named in Genesis, all by his lawful wife Keturah. He also had sons by his concubines (Genesis 25:1–6), although we don't know how many of either there would have been.

Out of all those children, only Isaac was the son of promise. At least seven other sons had no part in God's promise to Abraham. Paul's point in Romans 9:6–9 is that, from the start, mere physical descent from Abraham meant nothing.

If some Israelites were left out because they refused faith in Jesus, that was nothing new. The Old Testament contained a wealth of evidence that there had always been those who could claim a biological link to Israel who were not Israelites in the true sense of the word (9:6). God's calling in the Old Testament had always been on the basis of faith, not genealogy.

But the historical precedents Paul cited raise a second, and in many ways more troubling, question. The act of choosing Isaac, and then his son Jacob, had a dark side. The choice of these sons required the rejection of their brothers. Paul's argument was that God's choice was His alone, without reference to any merit on the parts of the ones chosen, especially in the case of Jacob and Esau (9:11).

Since Isaac was the son of Sarah, Abraham's half-sister, some might argue that his selection was justified on the basis of parentage. To answer that objection, Paul pointed to the case of the twin brothers Jacob and Esau, who shared the same father and mother.

In their case there was absolutely no reason for God's choice apart from His own divine decision. Paul was illustrating an important point: God wasn't doing anything in the church that He hadn't already done in Israel's lengthy history. Far from being unjust, God was being consistent.

Never in all God's dealing with Israel had there been a time that all of Abraham's descendants were part of the divine promise by virtue of their birth.

A master debater, Paul immediately anticipated an objection. He knew some readers would reply, "How unfair," so he defused the objection by raising it himself.

If God simply decreed and people simply obeyed, I probably would raise the same objection. In fact, if any human ruler or judge acted in the way some understand God to act in this passage, the outrage of oppressed people would eventually lead to his overthrow.

But who could overthrow God? And who are we to question His actions? It is vital to remember that the Bible teaches that God does what is right because it is right. His might doesn't make whatever He does right. His might works to uphold His right.

The fact that He is too powerful to question hardly answers the accusation of injustice. If we want to argue that way, then oppressive leaderships must be right because they are often too powerful to be overthrown, at least for the present.

Nor does it work simply to say that God's ways are mysterious and past knowing, when the very reason Paul wrote this section of Scripture was to explain God's working.

It's also no good to make a distinction, as some do, between fairness and justice. If God expects justice from us, as the Bible makes abundantly clear He does, His idea of justice and ours must have something in common. We must have at least a rudimentary understanding of what is just or fair behavior if we are to live up to the standards laid out for us in Scripture. If Paul argued that God was just in his treatment of His people, there must be some understandable concept of justice involved in his argument.

Which brings me back to the concept of corporateness. While it often escapes modern readers, the ideas of corporate election and judgment were very much a part of the mental furniture of the first century Christian. Notice the Old Testament passage Paul quoted. When Malachi (1:2–3) told his listeners that God loved Jacob and hated Esau, it wasn't the individuals he refered to, but the nations that descended from them. Israel, God's people, was elect. Edom, the enemy of God's people, was not.

As far back as God's prophecy to Rebekah (Genesis 26:23) the promise of a national future for both Jacob and Esau was evident. God told Rebekah there were two nations in her womb, not just two sons. The nation that descended from the older son would serve the nation that descended from the younger son. That prediction certainly did not apply to the individual sons of Isaac, for during their lifetimes Jacob clearly feared Esau, the dominant brother.

Similarly, Paul was talking about the fates of Israel and the Gentiles, not individuals, so it's important to notice these corporate elements in his argument. Paul later stressed the importance of individual response to God's call (e.g., Romans 10:9–17), but here he was concerned with the fate of nations.

God's election, which Paul presented in terms of the call of the nation Israel, had never been a benefit granted automatically to anyone who happened to descend from Abraham. Israel, however, tried to take advantage of that election by calling on God for protection, even while they worshiped other gods. Unfortunately for them, God never intended His promise to be a blank check drawn on the vaults of heaven. Election had a purpose in God's plan and reason in God's grace.

He tells us the reason in Deuteronomy 7:7: *Just because.* "I chose you," God said, "because I loved you." This is where God falls back on the old parental "Because I said so" line of reasoning. Notice, though, that this is not some mushy-headed, sentimental love. God was the first parent who practiced tough love.

He began with the love in verses 7–9, but he got tough in verses 1–11. The first of several warnings comes here: "Those who hate him he will repay to their face by destruction; He will not be slow to repay to their face those who hate him. Therefore, take care to follow the commands, decrees and laws I give you today."

The promises that followed in chapter 7 were wonderful, but they all began with the word *if:* "If you pay attention to these laws . . . then the Lord . . . will keep his covenant of love with you."

He also made it quite clear that even the privilege of the Promised Land was a double-edged sword. God's grace to Israel, in spite of their undeserving natures, was the bright side of God's judgment of the Canaanites: "After the LORD your God has driven them out before you, do not say to yourself, 'The LORD has brought me here to take possession of this land because of my righteousness.' No, it is on account of the wickedness of these nations that the LORD is going to drive them out before you" (9:4).

I think an important biblical principle in this passage is too often overlooked.

Grace is God's choice; judgment is ours.

God's promise of the Land, spoken of in such absolute terms by many, would not come about until the Canaanites, who resided in the land, had reached the point where judgment was God's only option. God himself told Abraham that his family would receive the land only after four hundred years for the "sin of the Amorites has not yet reached its full measure" (Genesis 15:13–16).

God chose stiff-necked Israel (His words in Deuteronomy 9) for no reason other than His grace. His severe punishment of the Amorites (Canaanites) would not come in the same way. God doles out grace for no reason; people must earn His wrath. When their iniquity reached a certain level, judgment could not be turned aside. And even then, God extended grace to Rahab and her family.

When we realize that Paul's point in this chapter isn't predestination at all, but the awful justice and awesome grace of God, our friend Pharaoh is not such a daunting problem after all.

Pharaoh, despite his stubborn resistance to what started out as a simple request from Moses, was *not* hardened for his own damnation. God hardened him so that the name of the LORD might be proclaimed in all the earth.

The missionary God, who chose Israel to receive the benefit of the Law, the prophets, and the temple and its service, wanted the world to know who He was. Pharaoh, representative of the nation of Egypt, was the instrument. This Pharaoh, whoever he was, sat upon the throne of Egypt during the New Kingdom, the Age of Empire. Whether he was Thutmose III, as some contend, or Ramses II, as others insist, he was one of the greatest conquerors in a history that stretched back at least a millennium and a half. Regardless of which Pharaoh watched his invincible armies drown in the waters of the Sea, his humbling was a sign any willing heart would recognize. In fact, it was the very sign cited by Rahab as the reason for her belief in Israel's God (Joshua 2:11).

There's no question that God hardened Pharaoh's heart, but we can't ignore the fact that Exodus assigns a gracious purpose to this hardening. This leaves us with two questions: How did God do it, and why?

The understanding that God simply hardened Pharaoh by divine decree with no reference to Pharaoh and his role neglects part of the textual evidence. Although the Bible records nine separate statements about God's intention to harden Pharaoh's heart, it also records three in which we're told that Pharaoh hardened his own heart. These don't imply in any way that God was doing it for him

The only way to make sense of these two apparently opposing statements is to see God's power working with Pharaoh's own decision-making process. Pharaoh's pride would not let him free the Israelites. He had resolved to resist Moses and his God. The early plagues moved him only to resist, not repent. God gave him the strength to continue his resistance throughout the full course of the ten plagues.

I don't know what God would have done had Pharaoh caved in under the first demonstration of His power, but I'm sure He could have handled that as well. What did happen is that God strengthened Pharaoh's resolve to resist.

That brings us to the second question. Why?

God told us why before Moses ever confronted Pharaoh's court with Aaron's writhing rod. He said, "I will harden Pharaoh's heart, and . . . he will not listen to you. Then I will lay my hand on Egypt and with mighty acts of judgment I will bring out my divisions, my people the Israelites. And the Egyptians will know that I am the LORD" (Exodus 7:3–5).

Moses was instructed to tell Pharaoh that the plague of blood, which turned the life-giving Nile to a stinking stream of pollution, was to make him "know that I am the LORD" (Exodus 7:17).

God announced the same thing through Moses in Exodus 9:14–16, but with a noteworthy difference. The demonstration of God's power was still intended to show the Egyptians that "there is no one like me in all the earth." Then God added: "But I have raised you up for this very purpose, that I might show you my power and that my name might be proclaimed in all the earth."

A final purpose is revealed in 10:2. The demonstration of God's power was also to be a witness to the people of Israel and to their children and grandchildren that God was God. As we read the rest of the Old Testament, we see that whatever else they may have done or believed, they continued to look back to the time of the Exodus with wonder.

The purpose of all this misery, then, was to demonstrate the person and nature of God to a watching world. Each new plague was an opportunity for repentance and faith. The fact that a "mixed multitude" left Egypt with the natural children of Jacob may attest to the effectiveness of that demonstration.

There is, then, a biblical reason for looking at the hardening of Pharaoh's heart with slightly different eyes. He who in sinful rebellion would not acknowledge God willingly, was brought to the point where he had no recourse. In that humbling, I believe the potential existed for Pharaoh's repentance as well, not just his capitulation. People in Egypt must have gotten the message, or they would not have cast their lot with a band of helpless slaves fleeing the power of one of the mightiest empires on earth.

The harvest among the Gentiles seems slim enough, with Rahab and her family as the only recorded converts. Nevertheless, the purpose of God was fulfilled.

After his discussion of Pharaoh, Paul made a brief allusion to Jeremiah 19, where, once again, the Old Testament text argues against the kind of predestinarian interpretation usually offered for Romans 9. In this passage we learn that God told Jeremiah to go to the potter's house. There he watched the potter at work and saw that any piece of work that failed to measure up to the potter's plan was reduced to a lump of workable clay and redone. It was the potter who controlled the process.

When God explained the spiritual meaning of what Jeremiah had seen, He first affirmed His sovereignty over the affairs of *nations*. Then He went on to say that if He announced judgment on one of those nations, and that nation repented, He was free to forgive and turn the judgment away. It seems, at least for Jeremiah, that God was free in His sovereignty to change the destiny of the vessels, or nations, fit for destruction. Just as free as He was to reconsider the destiny of nations made for better things (Jeremiah 18:1–12).

If Paul intended his allusion to Jeremiah to teach predestination to hell or heaven, he couldn't have picked a worse source. What the visit to the potter's house proved was that God's plan could be revised on the basis of the response of nations.

To this point, then, the whole chapter deals with the fate of nations, not individuals. Nowhere does it deal with predestination to heaven or hell. If there is any sense of predestination so far, it's within the flow of earth's history, not beyond it.

Now to the crux of the matter. Didn't Paul say God made some vessels for wrath and others for mercy?

Yes, but not in the way we usually understand that statement. To fathom his argument in Romans 9 we have to keep Romans 11 in mind. That, after all, is where he is headed. He's building a case for the justice of God in His dealings with Israel. It's intriguing that Paul then raises the question, *"What if* God chose to make some for honor and some for wrath."* I'm sure he knew his imaginary antagonist would immediately leap to the same conclusion many of us have: God has somehow, unjustly, created a part of the human race for destruction in hell. But that wasn't Paul's point.

I think I hear a note of irony in verse 22. He seems to agree that God might have created some for wrath just to show His power. But in the same sentence it's clear that those prepared for destruction had also been the recipients of God's patience.

Then, in verse 23, he takes us back to the main theme. Those who believe in Christ are objects of mercy prepared in advance for glory. In that context, who are the objects of wrath? They can only be unbelieving Israel. Many Jewish religious leaders of Paul's day would have assigned the Gentiles to that sorry state. But Paul saw things more clearly, for in verse 25 he fired a volley of Old Testament texts to prove that the Gentiles would one day be called God's people. In doing this he drove home the point that Israel, as a nation, would be represented only by the remnant.

He ended the chapter with a summary of his argument so far. There's nothing about individual predestination in this summary. There's only the solemn evaluation of Israel's unbelief and the faith of Gentiles. Since Paul summarizes at this point, so will I.

Romans 9 is a chapter about the destiny of Israel. The emphasis on predestination in the chapter is aimed at explaining, as Paul does in greater detail in chapter 11, that the apostasy of Israel had been prophesied throughout the Old Testament. With that apostasy, according to Paul, would come the salvation of the Gentiles. Paul argues that God is just in doing all this. Israel deserved their treatment because of their faithlessness. This is not some new idea on God's part. He'd warned from the beginning that disregard for the conditions of the Covenant would result in destruction. What's more, God had also made His desire known to bless the nations through Israel from His first contact with Abraham. All that, determined in the eternal counsels of God, was taking place in Paul's day. But not a word of it pertains to individual election or perdition.

TOGETHER IN THE HEAVENLY PLACES

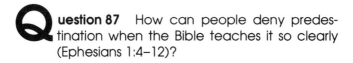 **uestion 87**   How can people deny predestination when the Bible teaches it so clearly (Ephesians 1:4–12)?

Ephesians 1:4–12 is one of the two linchpins of the doctrine of predestination. I don't think I've ever read a predestinarian book or article that didn't lean heavily on Paul's statements in Ephesians 1.

The mistake commentators make in their discussions of this passage is starting with word studies of *predestined, chose, purpose,* and *will.* That's not to say word studies are unimportant, but Paul's meaning of these words can't be determined by looking in a dictionary. We can't understand what he meant by *predestined* without looking carefully at the entire chapter, the line of Paul's argument, and the use he makes of predestination in the development of that argument.

To do this, we have to make a brief detour into the thought world of Bible times. It'll be a bumpy detour, because the way Westerners think and the way the biblical writers thought sometimes differs markedly. Those who read the Bible as if a twentieth century American wrote it from a table in a seminary library may experience a severe case of cultural vertigo on this detour.

The difference lies in the way we understand ourselves. Europeans in general and Americans in particular take the idea of individualism for granted. As we practice it in the latter part of the twentieth century, individualism is the idea that the needs and interests of the individual count for more than the needs and interests of the group to which the individual belongs.

The pop-culture heroes in novels, movies, and television are all ruggedly individualistic and "street smart" loners who scoff at the conventions of society and opinions of others. A Rambo or Dirty Harry is the ultimate in individualism. Their popularity confirms the power individualism holds over us.

At a philosophical level, of course we value the individual. In fact, the reason the nations of the west value the individual is because Jesus taught them to. That's the truth at the core of a rotten apple.

Each of us was important enough for Christ to die for. But His death was supposed to liberate us from our isolated individuality and incorporate us into His body. Instead, we've turned the Christian idea of individual value into an excuse for running our own course regardless of the consequences to anyone else. Over the past three or four decades, we've seen that scenario played and replayed dismally across the stage of our national life.

I graduated from college in 1968, the era of the hippie. In 1988 I pastored a church in an affluent suburb, where the yuppie era was still in full swing. Due to its emphasis on conspicuous consumption and shallow self-interest, no one is lamenting its passing, but it's bound to be replaced by another, equally individualistic, age yet to be christened by the media. No matter what name we give it, the next movement of mass culture will define itself with the same narrow focus on ME.

Hippies and yuppies were all on the typically western search for their own identities in protest and Perrier.

An Israelite never needed to search for his identity. It was one thing he never lost. He might not know anything else, but he knew exactly who he was: the son of his father, the grandson of his grandfather, a member of his tribe and a bit player in the age-old story of his people. In our self-oriented age, that seems oppressive, but actually it's a liberated way of living.

This doesn't mean that people in Bible times lost their individuality in group consciousness. Not at all.

People were always individuals, but they were individuals with a well-defined place in the world. Their responsibilities, duties, benefits, and prerogatives were all determined by that place. Their decisions and behavior affected others, and that had to be considered.

Achan (Joshua 7:15–26) is a good example of how the actions of a single person affect the nation and the family. Achan exercised the fighting man's right in the ancient world to take plunder from the ruins of a conquered city. But in exercising that right, he disobeyed God's command to suspend that right and to dedicate the city as an offering to the Lord.

That individual decision cost the nation a humiliating defeat in the battle of Ai. Thirty-six men met their deaths in that attack. Because our awareness of sin is so conditioned by our western individualism, it's hard for us to imagine how God could allow those innocent soldiers to die for the sin of one man.

And when the Lord revealed that Achan, son of Carmi, was the guilty party and thereby responsible for the defeat at Ai, it wasn't just Achan who received punishment. Because he was head of a household, his family shared his guilt, even though they hadn't participated in his action. Because he sinned, his entire family died.

The sin of the individual does affect those around him. There are no victimless crimes, no private sins. Knowledge of sin may be kept secret, but the impact of sin never can be. That's an important element in understanding the oneness among the individuals of the Bible.

All of us need to be reminded of this biblical idea from time to time. I don't advocate stoning whole families when one member sins, but it's good to consider how devastating the sin of one person can be to the well-being of a family or a church body.

P **rinciple 26**   Keep in mind the Old Testament concept of corporate justice. It carried over into the lives of the Jewish writers of the New Testament, so it's important in interpreting all of Scripture.

When we give ourselves to Christ to be made into new creatures we become a part in the body of Christ. We can't ever think of ourselves in purely individualistic terms again. We belong to a spiritual community in which our every action, both public and private, has potential for great good or great harm.

Leaving behind some of the aggressive individualism that characterizes American Christianity and biblical interpretation since Augustine may help us understand what Paul was getting at in Ephesians 1.

When the Old Testament discusses predestination, it almost always stresses the trustworthiness of God over the fickleness of humanity. There's an important element of this contrast in Ephesians.

People who write books on Ephesians say that it's a letter intended for the church at large, not just the church at Ephesus. There are two reasons for saying that.

First, the words *in Ephesus* don't appear in some of the best and earliest manuscripts of the book. One ancient writer refers to it as the letter to the Laodiceans. Origen and Jerome, church fathers of the third and fourth centuries, both said the phrase was absent from the best copies they had access to.

Second, we would have expected Paul to write some personal greetings to a church where he had spent three years, but there are none.

It seems that Paul wrote a form letter, one intended to be copied and sent to several churches, probably in Asia Minor. Each copy would be addressed to the church intended; except for the address, they would have been identical. We don't know how many were sent, but there is good evidence that at least two existed at one time. I suspect there were several more.

I like that view. When we read Ephesians we're in touch with revelation addressed to the church at large, not to some specific church with its specific problems. Although there is a problem addressed in Ephesians, it's one we all face in the same way.

The churches with which I'm familiar are often less than perfect. Often a lot less. In my pastoral ministry I've enjoyed taking people to Ephesians and looking past the frailities of Christians to the eternal plan of God for people who, in Christ, would be holy and blameless before Him.

Ephesians is the book of life *in Christ*, a book in which the view of the church is so lofty and exalted that some people can't believe Paul could have written it. After all, Paul was the man whose letters were dragged out of him by the sins and shortcomings of sinners who were now saints, but saints whose life-time habits died hard.

What people could be more appropriate, I ask, to tell us about God's plan to seat us in the heavenly realm *in Christ?*

The letter opens with a doxology that must be one of the longest and most complicated sentences in literature. Verses 3–14 cover three quarters of a page in my Greek New Testament with only commas and colons to break the flow of Paul's torrent of praise. In the midst of this verbal flood, one thought surfaces three times to give shape to the stream. Verses 6 (to the praise of his glorious grace), 12 (for the praise of his glory), and 14 (to the praise of his glory) bring us back to the grandeur of the Blessed, "the God and Father of our Lord Jesus Christ."

This letter to the church begins, then, with its Founder, with the One who ordained, before the foundations of the world, that there should be a Redeemer and that He should have a body made holy through participation in Him.

This doxology rushes out three times from the person of God, to describe what He's done, and then returns to Him in the phrase, *to the praise of his glory.* There's a structure here that I can show you by setting out the passage as I see it.

> **Praise be to the God and Father.** . . (v. 3)
> > who has blessed us. . . (v. 3)
> > for he chose us . . . (v. 4)
> > he predestined us . . . (v. 5)
> > > *to the praise of his glorious grace* . . . (v. 6)
>
> **In him** . . . (Christ) (v. 7)
> > we have redemption . . . (v. 7)
> > he made known . . . the mystery of his will (v. 9)
> > we were also chosen . . . (v. 11)
> > > *for the praise of his glory* . . . (v. 12)
>
> **In Christ** . . . (v. 12)
> > you were . . . included when you heard . . . (v. 13)
> > you were marked in him with a seal . . . (v. 13)
> > > *to the praise of his glory* (v. 14)

This doesn't account for every jot and tittle of the doxology, but it gives an outline that provides an easy way to study its structure. It takes us from the magisterial mind of God, through the work of Christ, to the outworking of God's plan in the church through the power of Holy Spirit. Paul returns to this structure at the end of the chapter as well. He prayed that the Spirit would bring his readers to a deeper knowledge and understanding of their hope and inheritance, and the power that guaranteed both. Then he described the might of God in terms of the resurrection and glorification of Christ, themes he obviously intended as encouragement to his readers.

Finally, in what I consider one of the most potent of all biblical statements about the church, he said, "And God placed all things under his feet and appointed him to be head over everything for the church, which is his body, the fulness of him who fills everything in every way" (vv. 22–23).

Paul didn't come to this point by chance. He began, even in his salutation, to talk about the church, faithful *in Christ Jesus.* Although this is a fairly common phrase in Paul's greetings (see 1 Corinthians 1:2; Philippians 1:1; Colossians 1:1) it isn't used here simply as a form of greeting. The frequency of the idea throughout the doxology and the conclusion he reaches in verses 22–23 make me think that *in Christ* is a major theme in this chapter.

What does Paul mean by these two simple words? We think of it, if we think of it at all, from our individualistic perspective, as a kind of metaphor that just means to be a Christian. But I think he's talking about much more: the believer's participation in the ongoing life of Christ as a part of His body.

Paul talks elsewhere about the two Men, the First Adam and the Second Adam (Romans 5:12–6:14; 1 Corinthians 15:21–22, 42–49), who divide all of humanity between them. The first Adam, through his disobedience, brought death to all who participate in him. The Second Adam, through His obedience, brought life to all who are *in Christ.* Paul explained this idea fully in Romans and used it less extensively in 1 Corinthians to explain the resurrection. Most Christians treat this as an interesting literary device. I think it's much more.

According to Paul in Romans 5, we are all participants in Adam. In Adam the human race is dead spiritually and will be dead physically as part of its participation in him. To be in Christ, on the other hand, means to take part in the resurrection to eternal life (1 Corinthians 15:22). To be in Adam means to be carnal, or of the flesh, as in Galatians 5:17, 19. To be led by the Spirit is to be *in Christ.*

When we become participants *in Christ* we share in the newness of life in a body that has not sinned and not been brought to death for sin (1 Corinthians 5:17; Galatians 6:15; Ephesians 2:15, 4:24; Colossians 3:10). Our old nature has been crucified (Romans 6:6; Galatians 2:20). It's not just a pious fiction that the believer is crucified in Christ. Rather, *in Christ* we become participants with him in His death, burial, and resurrection.

The subject of the Second Adam, and our participation in Him, would fill a heavy volume, and I'm not up to writing one of those. But all these ideas, and more, are involved in Paul's simple phrase *in Christ.*

I think this phrase is the key to understanding all the talk in this passage about predestination, election, and the like.

We have received every *in-Christ* blessing, blessings available only in those heavenly places to which the Heavenly Man has ascended.

If all died through their participation in the First Adam, and the elect all live through their participation in the Second Adam, and the status of *in Christ* is at the heart of all Paul says in Ephesians 1, then we need to look at predestination and election from a totally different perspective.

Referring to the outline I gave for this section, How has God blessed us? *In Christ.*

How has He chosen us? *In Christ.*

How has He predestined us? *Through Christ.*

Where is our redemption found? *In Christ.*

What is the mystery of His will revealed to us who are *in Christ*? *That* all things *are to be brought together under Christ.*

As we look into the later chapters of the book, it seems that Paul is speaking here, as he does in other places, of the great mystery of a spiritual Israel into which Gentiles have been invited (Ephesians 2:12–13). Much of chapter 2 points to this conclusion.

In the Old Testament, God promised Abraham there would be a land in which his descendants would settle and worship the Lord. Many people in that land presented a stumbling block to Israel's occupation. They would be judged by God, and Israel would be His instrument of wrath.

Yet even among those vessels fit for destruction, one woman, Rahab, responded to the sign of the sea and, in a statement of faith as robust as any prophet's, she affirmed that He was "God in heaven above and on the earth below" (Joshua 2:11).

The covenant by which Israel had become a nation had been ratified at Sinai (Exodus 19:6) and later reconfirmed at Nebo (Deuteronomy 7:6). An interesting thing happened when Joshua gathered God's people at Mount Gerizim to renew it. The new generation, ready to settle in the land, was called before God and given the opportunity to continue in that treaty relationship. After a passionate review of God's mighty acts on Israel's behalf, Joshua issued the challenge: "if serving the Lord seems undesirable to you, then choose for yourselves this day whom you will serve, whether the gods your forefathers served beyond the

River, or the gods of the Amorites in whose land you are living. But as for me and my household, we will serve the Lord" (Joshua 24:15).

This was no empty formality. It was the first of many times in Israel's history when the individual Israelite would be offered the choice of participating in the predestined people of God. The answer was not a foregone conclusion. If all the households of Israel except Joshua's had replied negatively, Joshua's household would have become that kingdom of priests, that holy nation.

Here's my point. If God decreed redemption through Christ before the earth was created, he also decreed Israel, Christ's nation, as Paul put it, *according to the flesh.* At no time in the history of that elect body were the people who called themselves Israel all God's people.

There were always some who were born of Israel who could, through their faithlessness, reject their place in that body to go after other gods. And there were always people from the Gentile world who, through their faith and faithfulness, could become part of the elect.

The mistake Israel made was in thinking that because the nation was elect, the individuals in the nation were also elect. That has never been true, as Paul argues persuasively in Romans 9–11.

The mistake Christians make is in thinking that our election is the result of some series of individual choices God made in primordial darkness before creation. But what God chose was Christ, not us. When we become part of Him, we share in the election of Him who was chosen from before the foundations of the world.

The Bible uses the discussion of election and predestination as an encouragement to believers. The plan of God, by which we become part of the Body of Christ, is fixed and eternal. We can trust the God who ordained it. His Son who died to make it happen will not change.

The plan by which we become *in Christ* will not change. He will not devise some new way to redemption, nor raise up some new mediator, nor cast off those who, through faith, have become *in Christ.*

In light of all this we cannot deny a biblical doctrine of predestination, but we can, and do, take issue with the way that biblical doctrine has been stated.

PRESDESTINED WITHOUT A PRAYER

Question 88   If God knows everything, and He's ordained everything, what is the purpose in our prayers? If God's will is going to be done anyway, why do we even have to ask (Ephesians 6:18)?

This passage in Ephesians makes a strong case for the effectiveness of prayer. It's the well known "whole armor of God" paragraph, and the direction to pray is its capstone.

Paul may have been treating prayer as the seventh weapon given the believer to stand against the world, the flesh, and the devil. Or he may have intended us simply to view prayer as the environment in which the weapons mentioned in verses 14–17 are effective.

In either case, it's unlikely that he intended us to understand that we were only praying for what was already determined. According to Paul, life for the believer was an ongoing guerrilla struggle in which they fought the good fight of faith, equipped with the whole armor of God. The life of continuous prayer made such a struggle possible for the individual soldier. I find nothing in the Bible's numerous references to prayer that suggests the fight has been fixed.

Yes I know. Jesus prayed for God's will to be done in the garden the night before His crucifixion, and some interpreters quote that as proof that our prayers are designed merely to bring our wills into line with the foreordained plan of God.

Remember, though, my caution against placing too much stress on doctrinal statements drawn from historical narratives. It's indisputable that Jesus prayed for God's will to be done. It's much less certain that we can make generalizations from that specific statement about all Christian prayer.

I see quite of bit of biblical evidence that prayer is much more than a mere realignment of our attitudes with the plan of God.

Abraham's prayers were both bold and impudent. He confronted God's stated purpose in the destruction of Sodom with the kind of counter offer he might have made in buying a donkey. "How can you even suggest such a thing?" Abraham seemed to ask God. "Would you sweep away the righteous with the wicked? That would be unjust. How can the one who will judge the world do what would be unjust?" (Genesis 18:16–33). That prayer has no hint of "nevertheless not my will but thine be done." It was an unvarnished attempt to move God to reconsider.

In the same way, Moses prayed for God's mercy for the people whose death sentence He'd just pronounced (Exodus 14:1–25). Whatever else we want make of this narrative, it's clear that Moses' purpose was to defend the name of the Lord before the nations. Verse 20 records God's words: "I have forgiven them, *as you asked."*

I fail to see a strong statement of immovable providence in that reply.

Isaiah delivered a solemn message to Hezekiah (2 Kings 20:1–6). He prefaced it by saying that it was God's utterance, not his own. The gist of the message was this: Put your house in order. You are about to die. Hezekiah met that news with weeping and prayer. After Isaiah left him, he turned to God and asked Him to remember the righteousness of his life and his devotion. Before Isaiah had left the palace, God's word came to him again. This time it cancelled the earlier word. God instructed him to speak with Hezekiah and tell him: "I have heard your prayer and seen your tears; I will heal you. . . . I will add fifteen years to your life" (vv. 5–6).

Jesus repeatedly instructed his disciples to ask for things from God. Did they desire the Holy Spirit? Jesus said ask, and God will give Him to you (Luke 11:9–13). Were they concerned about the loss of Jesus and the blessings they'd enjoyed at His hand? Jesus said that anything they asked in His name the Father would give (John 16:23–24). In the Sermon on the Mount (Matthew 7:7–8), Jesus said if they would ask, they would receive. If human fathers know how to give good gifts to their children, how much more the heavenly Father.

In all the places the Bible suggests, recommends, or orders prayer, I find nothing to hint that God has foreordained the answers or that He has foreordained the prayers as the means to the answers.

Here again we find ourselves beset by the problem of starting points. If we read the Bible from the starting point of absolute sovereignty and predestination, we are stuck with an obvious, though unstated, assumption in all the texts on prayer: that God has already ordained what will be.

If God has already ordained what will be, our prayers, likewise, are foreordained. The other side of that is that our prayerlessness, and the lack of answers, is also foreordained. Even more troubling is that prayers that go unanswered are also foreordained.

The answer to the question, then, depends on my starting point, just as the Calvinist's depends on his. Because I find the absolutist sovereignty of Calvinism, even that of "moderates," unacceptable on biblical grounds, I have to say our prayers do mean something. Prayer, it seems to me, is part of the larger whole we call the life of faith: a life of faith God designed to bring us closer to himself because we've learned to love Him more. To live that life, we need to understand what faith is. Faith itself is a combination of believing God and depending on Him. Believing is the easy part.

I have no trouble reading the Bible and seeing more than enough evidence to believe that God is and that He rewards people who seek and serve Him. None of the arguments about the fallibility of the Bible, its dependence on ancient mythologies, or its reliance on the supernatural to explain what was beyond the scientific understanding of the ancient writers carry any weight for me.

I believe in God.

It's even easy for me, on the basis of the biblical evidence for Jesus, to believe that He sent His son to die on my behalf and then raised Him from the dead.

I believe in Jesus.

But when it comes to living life day in and day out, the world is too much with me. It's much easier to depend on myself, whom I can see and touch, than to depend on God, whom I see and know only by faith. If there's any difference between faith that saves and faith that lives the Christian life, it's here. Living as if my success, not to mention my next breath, depends on God is harder than believing what I know is true about Him.

This is where prayer functions. Prayer is the active practice of depending on God. If "faith is being sure of what we hope for and certain of what we do not see" (Hebrews 11:1), then prayer is the act of putting that certainty to work.

I think God gave us prayer as a training ground for the active side of our faith. If we were limited to reading *about* God in the Bible, we might never come to know Him in His fullness. When we pray, we remind ourselves with every word that life and all other good things come from God. In prayer, we practice faith. If there were no other reason for praying, that would be enough.

But there is a class of prayer that specifically aims at getting something from God.

Christ has instructed us to "ask the Lord of the harvest . . . to send out workers into his harvest field" (Matthew 9:38). Jesus seemed to be placing the burden for evangelism and missions on the prayers of God's people.

He told the disciples to pray for the establishment of God's rule on earth, for the needs of daily life, and for protection from Satan (Matthew 6:9–13). The Lord's prayer implies that the coming Kingdom of God, our continued existence, and our protection from temptations from within us and the testings Satan hurls from without, are all accomplished through prayer.

The birth of John the Baptist to a mother long past childbearing was attributed to Elisabeth's prayers (Luke 1:13). Jesus told His hearers to pray for strength to persevere through tribulation.

All these passages, and dozens more, make it seem that our prayers do have impact on the course of events, both in our lives and in the advancement of the kingdom.

For me, it would take a powerful statement to the contrary to make me believe that prayer doesn't affect what happens in my life.

Everything I find in Scripture tells me the opposite, so I'll take my stand on the efficacy of prayer. Not foreordained, pre-answered prayer, but the effective, fervent prayers of righteous men and women accomplishing great things for the Kingdom of God (James 5:16).

THE QUEST FOR THE HOLY GUARANTEE

 uestion 89   How can I know God's will for my life? I'm never certain if what I'm doing is in His will or out of it (Ephesians 5:17).

When Paul talked about knowing God's will in Ephesians 5, he wasn't talking about some specific blueprint for each believer. He was talking about being filled with the Holy Spirit.

Paul had just admonished his readers to imitate God by living a life of love (5:1–2). Then he warned them about lives of immorality (5:3–7). Not content to leave them with a negative admonition, he reminded them of the darkness of their former lives (5:8) and the light of their new lives lived in Christ (5:9–14).

Having done all that, he warned them not to be foolish, but to make the most of every opportunity (5:15–16). This warning and admonition are followed by the important word *therefore*. As J. Vernon McGee used to say, "Whenever I see the word *therefore* I want to know what it's there for."

In this case, it's there to tell us that knowing the will of God is essential for carrying out the admonition to make use of every opportunity. It's followed by the command to be filled with the Holy Spirit. All those work together.

What we do in the Lord depends on the Lord's strength. The Spirit gives that. How we make use of the opportunities He gives depends on our sensitivity to God. The Spirit provides that. Understanding comes only when we are enlightened to know the hope to which God has called us (Ephesians 1:18). In 5:17 Paul seems to be coming full circle from his prayer in chapter 1, as if the commands issued in this passage hold the answer to his prayer. People filled with the Spirit will comprehend the riches of His calling. Called to be part of the new creation in Christ, the believer acquires a share in the glories of Christ's inheritance and in the incomparable power by which the Father raised Him from the dead.

This constitutes the mystery of God's will. People who were not God's have come to be called "My people." A wall of division between Jew and Gentile has been broken. The plan of God hidden from ages past has now been revealed. And the presence and power of the Holy Spirit makes it all possible and comprehensible.

Since before the foundations of the world, God has been preparing the people we call the church. It is, and always has been, God's will to do a new thing with us and in us. Out of that, all other aspects of His will radiate. An understanding of God's will begins with this truth.

God's will isn't a mystery. Nor is it a puzzle to be worked out. It is ours in the revealed word of God, interpreted by the Spirit of wisdom and revelation. The Bible is quite clear in laying out the nature of God's will, but Christians aren't usually talking about the same thing when we ask about God's will for our lives.

When we inquire after God's will, we're usually asking for direction in our decision making:

"Is it God's will that I take this job?"

"Is it God's will that I marry this person?"

"Is it God's will that I become a missionary?"

"Is it God's will that I witness to my friend?"

I could make a list several pages long that wouldn't exhaust the things people ask guidance for. What strikes me about all of them, though, is that those kinds of questions don't figure prominently in Scripture.

In the Old Testament there was a lot of "inquiring of the Lord" about such things as where lost donkeys were and whether it was a good time to go to war. But those were instances in which the *Urim* and *Thummim* were used. Cast like dice, they were given to Israel by God to use for making decisions of national importance, but people came to use them for lesser purposes. They're never mentioned after the coming of the Holy Spirit, however.

Gideon laid out his fleece (Judges 6:33–40), and his experience has led people to set up all sorts of tests to help God communicate with us. Looking at the text, though, Gideon had no need of a further sign. He'd already gotten his marching orders from an angel (6:11–22) and it had frightened him so much he was afraid God would strike him dead. So why did he ask for a sign? I've always suspected it was for the benefit of the army he'd gathered, who had not heard the orders. But if it was for his own sake, it was a remarkable example of lack of faith, not of approved behavior for a believer.

Paul received a vision (Acts 16:6–10) showing him his missionary work should go in the direction of Macedonia. He and his party had been blocked from entering the province of Asia, in the west of modern day Turkey, so they headed north through the province of Phrygia and tried to go northeast into the provinces of Bithynia and Pontus. They were blocked there as well. We don't know Paul's itinerary during that frustrating meander through Asia Minor. We only know that wherever he turned God blocked his way. I think he intended to turn eastward toward the third major concentration of Jews in his day: Babylon. That ancient city still held a sizable population of Jews, and it would have been in keeping with Paul's usual practice to seek out places where there were synagogues to preach in.

Imagine how different the world would be today if God had not intervened. Paul would have evangelized ever eastward. What impact might the gospel have had if Paul had ended up in India instead of Spain?

We can't know for sure, but I think it's likely that the history of the world would read differently today if he had.

Notice two things in this narrative.

First, Paul did not sit and wait for guidance. He worked while he waited. He didn't spend his time putting out a fleece or getting callouses on his knees praying for guidance. While he waited for God to direct more specifically, he occupied his time with what he knew God wanted him to do: preach. There was nothing passive about Paul's search for God's will.

Second, most of God's guidance came in a negative form. Paul wanted to go into Asia but was blocked. He worked his way north and tried to go east into Bithynia but was blocked. Moving back toward the west, he came to Troas. While there, on the threshold of Macedonia, God gave him clear direction.

The Macedonian call was not intended for all Christians everywhere. I don't mean God doesn't, or can't, do that again, but I think He reserves that kind of guidance for special cases.

My favorite passage on guidance is Exodus 3:12. God had just introduced himself to Moses, who was kneeling barefoot in front of an apparition. The Lord outlined His program of emancipation and explained to Moses what he was to do.

Moses whined, "Who am I, that I should go to Pharaoh and bring the Israelites out of Egypt?" (Exodus 3:11).

God responded with the promise of His presence and an unsolicited sign. It probably wouldn't have satisfied you or me, and it didn't satisfy Moses, but it was the sign God wanted to use. He said, "I will be with you. And this will be the sign to you that it is I who have sent you: When you have brought the people out of Egypt, you will worship God on this mountain" (Exodus 3:12).

Some sign.

How would that go over in an average testimony service or prayer meeting?

"God told me to go and do something for Him and said that, when I'm all done, I'll worship Him in the same place where He talked to me and that will be the sign that it was His will."

Right.

We want our signs and our guidance well before the first brick is laid. We want full assurance that once we set out we'll have God's favor and help.

But that wasn't the kind of sign God offered. He said, "Do what I've told you, and when you're done you'll know it was right."

I believe that what God told Moses is the essence of the life of faith. We want an ironclad promise that we won't make a fool of ourselves, lose our shirts, make a big mistake, or have anything bad happen. But God's way is to do it first and ask questions later.

What we do may not be as important as how we do it. To live a life that is open to and dependent on God, wherever we are and in whatever we do, is always God's will for us. In light of eternity, it doesn't matter whether I work in Denver or Chillicothe, or whether I am a mechanic or a computer programmer.

When it comes to knowing God's will, Jesus' instruction to seek the Kingdom of God first and let the rest take care of itself is still good.

My advice to my students, and to members of churches I've pastored, is to stop worrying about what we don't know about God's will and concentrate on what we do know.

God never intended for us to seek His will the way the ancients sought guidance with divination devices or "sophisticated" moderns seek it in horoscopes. He never intended for us to use the search for His will as a hedge against making a bad decision.

Like Paul, we should be doing, not seeking, God's will.

LOST, STOLEN, OR STRAYED

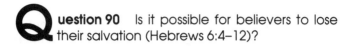 **uestion 90**   Is it possible for believers to lose their salvation (Hebrews 6:4–12)?

The answer is no. We cannot, by our own actions, be expelled from the Body of Christ. Only if we can be saved by works can our place in the body be lost through works.

One weakness in the Arminian position lies in its approach to the loss of salvation. The Calvinist is right to look with horror at the *saved today, lost tomorrow* idea that seems to be part of modern Arminianism. In fairness, I have to admit that those who call themselves Arminian give the impression that their salvation is that precarious.

Some who say that Christians are not eternally secure point to the "fruit" of a person's life as evidence. The kind of life we live reveals whether or not we have lost our salvation. After all, how can people who *act* like that be Christians? The flaw here is a preoccupation with behavior as the sign of salvation or lostness.

A book written earlier in this century had a title something like *Holes in Barroom Ceilings*. It was an attack on the doctrine of eternal security. Its title came from the question, "If eternal security is true will drunken 'saints' be taken up to meet the Lord in the air through the ceilings of the saloons in which they pursued their drunkenness?"

It sounds silly today, but in an era of temperance rallies and prohibition it was a serious concern. It remains so today, although it would probably be expressed somewhat differently.

We might ask, "Are Christians who fall into sin no longer Christians because of it?" Or are they Christians in need of the kind of loving reclamation Paul talked about in Galatians 6:1–5? Are they Christians whom the Lord disciplines, maybe even Christians who will suffer sickness and death as a redemptive antidote to their sinful behavior (1 Corinthians 11:30–32)?

Were the believers at Corinth, whose lifestyles would certainly rate expulsion from any evangelical church I've ever been in, still Christians or had they forfeited their place in the Kingdom by their actions?

I continue to struggle with the specific application of these and other biblical situations and passages to individuals today, but I think the principle is clear.

Bad actions call for reclamation, not rejection. In this holy Body to which we belong, God doesn't amputate, He heals, even when healing means physical death so the individual may be saved.

With the Corinthians, whose incest, drunkenness, prostitution, and pagan worship are well known, Paul appealed to their place in Christ as a reason to stop their behavior.

God's grace (i.e., His favor, love, and compassion) are so strong that nothing can wrench us away from Him. For me, my Arminian background takes this truth far too lightly.

Can we lose our salvation then? I think not. Losing implies a kind of witless misplacing. We can lose our car keys. We can lose a purse. We can lose our way and even carelessly lose our lives. But when we accept salvation we place ourselves in the hand of God, and He has promised to hold us secure.

But I think we can choose to give it back. To choose consciously and willfully to reject what we've received from God is not simply a sinful action. It is the premeditated assassination of faith. Placed in a position of honor and respect in the heavenlies, we grasp at the higher place of God for ourselves.

I believe this is what the writer of Hebrews was getting at. His sober warning in Hebrews 6 has been read in three ways.

The first group reads it as a hypothetical case. The writer described the condition of a person who had accepted Christ and then fallen away. According to this interpretation, it is a cautionary tale told for the admonition of young Christians. It assumes such a thing would never really happen. After all, the writer said he was "confident of better things in your case" (Hebrews 6:9).

The second group supposes a much more serious warning. Some people make profession of faith in Christ but never actually come to saving faith. It interprets the passage, with its references to enlightenment, sharing, and tasting, as a description of people who've dabbled at the edges of the faith but never become full partakers of the new life Christ offered.

The third group reads it as a description of real Christians who have turned away from their faith.

I honestly have to say that I find the first interpretation without merit. It's not that biblical writers can't use hypothetical situations to prove points. I simply see no evidence that the writer has that in mind here.

The second has more to recommend it, but I find it equally unconvincing. We need to be careful to take the language of a passage like this seriously. Those who have "tasted the heavenly gift" and have "shared in the Holy Spirit" must be Christians. To suggest otherwise is to trivialize the core of the New Testament teaching about who we are in Christ and how we get to be that way. The Holy Spirit cannot be shared by people who are still in Adam. These are people who walk after the flesh.

Which brings us to the third possibility. I find it difficult to read this text and not see people who have fallen, or are in danger of falling, into apostasy with dire possible consequences. They are, in other words, people who have known Christ and consciously rejected him. It seems that they are now beyond hope. It is *impossible* for such people to be brought back to repentance (vv. 4–6).

Most discussions of this verse revolve around whether or not it really means impossible. *Impossible* is one word in the larger family of words having to do with power. A slavish translation would say that there's no power to bring them back. I want to ask the text a different question: For whom is it impossible? The verse can't be referring to the one who has fallen away, because the verb is passive. The phrase "to be brought back" implies that someone other than the wanderer is doing the bringing. It's not an act that arises out of the will of the one who has fallen away.

Does that mean that other Christians are powerless to bring him back? It's true that Christians are powerless to bring a person back to repentance. But it's just as true that it's the work of the Holy Spirit, not believers, to convict and call to repentance. We have our place in the proclamation of the faith, but it is God's work to bring us to faith. Whether we're being born again or reclaimed, Christians have no power to bring anyone to repentance.

People in biblical times thought of God as the source of power. If there was no power to bring a person back to repentance, that meant God himself was powerless to bring the backslider to contrition. There are at least two reasons for making such an assertion.

First, perhaps there's only one repentance to a customer. The way God has set up the system, once we use up our repentance, we're not eligible for any more. If that is true, we have to rethink the relationship of law and grace, because that's a very legal formulation. Besides, the verse itself places the onus on the one fallen away.

I think the second reason is more likely: that the backslider was guilty of the same attitude that marked the religious leaders responsible for Jesus' crucifixion. They had observed many of the same miracles as the disciples. What they hadn't observed, they had heard about through the reports of people who had. There were men in the crowd at Bethany when Lazarus came out of the grave on the fourth day who rushed back to Jerusalem with the news (John 11:46).

When the Sanhedrin met to discuss their response to this noteworthy miracle there was no rejoicing. Neither was there debate over the truth of the reports. They assumed it was true. Confronted with that truth, the Sanhedrin, led by Caiaphas, determined it would be better for Jesus to die, regardless of His power and regardless of who He was, to preserve the status quo for Israel and to maintain the Sanhedrin in its place of power (John 11:49–53). From that day forward, they plotted to have Jesus killed.

The person who rejects Jesus, having known Him as Savior, re-enacts the treachery of the self-serving among the leaders of Judaism who thought it was better for Jesus to die than for them to lose their place of rule. This is the ultimate act of unfaith. For the one who knowingly rejects the love of God in the Son of Man, there can be no repentance.But I don't think that decision is made from God's side. I think it's made by a person willfully choosing death over life. But I don't think it need be permanent. Should that rebellion end, however, I see no biblical reason for assuming grace could not be offered again.

*All over the world, every minute
of every day, someone is
hurting, dying, suffering.
And most people ask,
at the height of
their suffering,
"Where is God
in all of this?"*

CHAPTER **8**

PRINCIPLES

27 Wisdom books are a specific type of biblical literature, and we must be careful to read and understand them on their own terms. Wisdom writing deals with life as it's lived and experienced. It makes no claim to be God's promises.

28 The proverbs collected by Solomon and Hezekiah have close parallels in practically every language and culture under the sun. They are principles, guidelines, good advice to live by and hand down to our children. But they are not absolute rules.

29 Old Testament wisdom is not God's wisdom. It's the best attempt of human reason to understand God's world and our place in it.

30 Old Testament saints saw only glimmers of the truth of the afterlife. The New Testament magnifies those glimmers into the light of a coherent doctrine.

QUESTIONS

91 The Bible says, "I was young and now I am old, yet I have never seen the righteous forsaken or their children begging bread" (Psalm 37:25). But what about believers who are persecuted behind the Iron Curtain or who starve in famines or are killed in natural disasters?

92 If we're supposed to think of God as our Father and Jesus as the firstborn of many brethren, why are we supposed to be afraid of God (Proverbs 1:7)?

HURTING PEOPLE, LOVING GOD

31 Old Testament wisdom is universal. It speaks plainly to non-believers about the well-ordered, moral life that is the basis of human conduct most people throughout history and across the globe agree makes for civilized conduct.

32 God inspired the writing of this human wisdom to provide a bridge into Scripture for people who are moral and good but have no commitment to God's more direct self-revelation. He did not inspire it as absolute truth (Satan's words in Job certainly are not). These books provide the common ground on which we can stand to open dialog with people in need of the Savior.

33 Whenever a troublesome passage forces us to choose an interpretation that contradicts other Scripture, the problem probably lies with our interpretation, not the Bible.

34 Wisdom literature's principles for successful living apply only in a sensible world.

93 How could Job insist that he was righteous when we know that no one is righteous?

94 How could a loving God allow Job to suffer when He knew Job didn't deserve it (Job 2:3, 6)?

95 The Bible says we will be healed if we have the elders of the church pray for us. Why doesn't God heal everyone we pray for (James 5:14–16)?

Years ago one of my daughters brought home a wooly bear caterpillar whose name, she informed me, was Wuzzle. She intended to raise and care for that insect as a full-fledged member of our family. Although Wuzzle would be no bother to anyone and would surely die when the winds of November blew in from the Arctic Circle, I quickly concluded that where Wuzzle was concerned outside was better than inside.

With all the hard-hearted resolution of a Simon Legre hurling a helpless orphan into the teeth of the gale, I insisted that she relegate Wuzzle to the harsh mercies of a Minnesota autumn. The caterpillar seemed unmoved by my heartless sentence, but it devastated his adoptive mother. Her mourning probably could have drowned a whole generation of Wuzzles in teary brine.

Although she has a bit of the tragedian burning within her, I have no doubt that her suffering over that proto-butterfly was genuine. I can remember enough of my own agonies over baby birds and adopted bunnies to know that children's attachments are immediate, fervent, and soul-wrenching. And their suffering over the loss of these fuzzy babies is profound, though usually short-lived.

Maybe this is why the problem of suffering is the basic, recurring question that has dogged the thoughts and the faith of believers since before Job cursed the day of his birth. We've all suffered. Maybe not in the cosmic, wrenching way that Job suffered. Maybe not in the staggering proportions we see in media coverage of natural disasters. But in the experimental mourning of a child for a bird or a puppy, or in the quiet, personal anquish that comes with the loss of a job, the death of a loved one, or in the diminished world so many experience in poverty, isolation, or old age, we all have known sorrow.

As I write, the world is shuddering over the massive destruction and the deaths of 60,000 in an earthquake in Armenia. Yesterday's news brought word that three commuter trains in London had crashed, killing dozens. A few years ago, 1700 people died in Cameroon. Toxic gases erupted from a lake bed in the northwest of that African nation, killing people in their sleep. That suffering hit home for me; the denomination in which I serve has several medical missionaries concentrated in that area, and hundreds of believers, some whose names I've read in prayer letters, died.

In 1985, the big story was the Mexico City earthquake. Before that we shuddered at the news that thousands had been buried in mud slides, drowned in typhoons, or died from numerous natural disasters that follow on one another's heels like soldiers marching in lock step.

Whether by earthquake, flood, fire, or the death of a neighbor, we're constantly reminded that this earth only seems solid, stable, and safe. None of us knows when the security of our private world will be shattered by disaster, natural or manmade. When it happens, we're reminded of a truth we suppress most of the time.

Pain hurts. Suffering hurts. Death hurts.

All over the world, every minute of every day, someone is hurting, dying, suffering. And most people ask, at the height of their suffering, "Where is God in all this?"

The question is a good one. From humanity's earliest moments, the notion of a good and loving God has foundered on the universal experience of suffering. The classic statement hurled at Christians by nonbelievers is, "If God is all-good and all-loving, he must not be all-powerful. If he were all-good and all-loving he wouldn't allow suffering. Since there is suffering, he's either powerless to stop it, or he doesn't care about it."

How do we deal with that question? If we spend more than fifteen minutes with a nonChristian talking about the faith, it's bound to come up. For some it's the ultimate argument against Christianity.

The way the question is stated makes some powerful assumptions about the nature of good and evil. It assumes that a God of love would want all people everywhere to be happy and prosperous. It also assumes that we finite humans should be able to understand God's workings. And, of course, that they should conform to our understanding of good.

Yet the most telling assumption underlying that question is the assumption that life is the ultimate good and death the ultimate evil. Life, and life lived to its fullest for all humanity, is what the questioner usually means by the word *good*. When people get anything short of that ideal, God must be absent, powerless, or uncaring.

These are important assumptions of the secularist world view, which considers man the measure of all things. According to this doctrine, health, lifespan, and bank balance are the units by which we measure happiness and good.

Another assumption here, that God controls everything, seems out of place among those who deny God's existence. Some of the most adamant unbelievers argue that, if there were a God, He would control every event with the paternalistic good will of a doctrinaire liberal.

We shouldn't be too hard on nonbelievers in all this, though. They argue against a God we Christians have taught them about. And they ask the same question most Christians have asked at some point in life.

For us, the question has double potency. Not only is it the nameless, faceless Somebody-Up-There who causes us to suffer. It's the one we know as Father. History demonstrates that being a Christian is no antidote to suffering. The grisly tales in *Foxe's Book of Martyrs* proves that. In fact, the Bible teaches that as well. It warns those of us who are true to the faith not to be surprised if we suffer for it. Is the servant greater than his master? If this world hated Jesus, why wouldn't it hate His followers? We're told to pray for our persecuters, so apparently we can't expect a life of ease. And if we're supposed to be rich, why didn't Peter say, "Of silver and gold I've got a bundle. Here's a ten spot. Keep the change."

In all this, where is the moral government of the universe? Where is justice when the just suffer with the unjust? Why should a Christian's righteousness be rewarded with poverty, sickness, and suffering? How can I love a God who acts this way?

TEARS ON THE TRAIN TRACKS

I could offer a hundred easy answers to those questions, but they don't satisfy anyone. At least we don't talk as though they satisfy. In times of suffering, we use our private Christian language to muffle the sound of our own quiet questions.

For example, our Christian catalog of euphemisms for death is staggering. We will talk about homegoings, graduations, and coronations. Christians never die, they're ushered into the presence of the Master. No bereaved Christians dare grieve openly because the funeral of their deceased loved one couldn't be victorious if they did. We like a victorious homegoing.

Euphemism is the language of avoidance. We use it to soften the harshness of words like death, to deflect the force of loss, and to lift our bruised faith. Even the strongest, in the anquish of suffering, find that right theology doesn't comfort as well as a familiar voice or a loving hand.

That doesn't deny the truth of the theology; it simply affirms the depth of pain. Victorious as we may be theologically, we are still lonely, and the loneliness of death will not be overcome in this life.

It is certainly true that Christ has conquered death. But, for us, not yet. It is certainly true that when someone dies they are no longer present in the body but are present with the Lord. But they're no longer here with us either.

The old Northwestern Railroad depot in downtown Minneapolis was always a melancholy place for me as a child. It always meant goodbye. After visiting my mother's family we were going back to whatever small town we happened to live in at the time. And we always cried when we boarded the train there. It wasn't because we thought there would be no reunion. We knew that next Christmas or Easter vacation or summer holiday, we'd be getting off the train and greeting our loved ones again. But we would miss them in between. And it was for that separation we wept.

Why then, if we can grieve over a separation of a few months, can't we admit the reality and depth of grief over a separation as long as life itself? Perhaps it is because we're afraid our faith isn't strong enough to stand in the face of a feeling that strong or questions that profound.

SUFFERING AND LIKING GOD

Some time ago I attended a seminar on how to counsel parents after the death of a child. I expected an academic presentation delivered by a psychologist or a pastor that would add another set of techniques to my pastoral toolkit. What I got was a wrenching three-hour session with two sets of parents whose children had died tragically.

One of the fathers, face red, voice trembling, and tears running down his face, spoke of the efforts of religious people to comfort him after the death of his daughter with answers we usually offer at times like that. "They said, 'She's with Jesus now' or 'God must have needed her more than you did' or 'We don't understand but it must have been God's will.' It made me so mad," he said. "How could God need her more than I do? Why would God will a beautiful child like that to die? If that's what God's like, I don't think I like God very much."

I suppose some would have been shocked to hear that confession, but I wasn't. I remembered a night several years before when I'd learned from the surgeon that my mother's cancer was incurable. And I remembered some of the rash, angry things I'd said to God. And the death of a child is far more traumatic.

I grieved for that father's pain, but I also grieved for the failure of his theology to offer answers that eventually would have allowed him to turn from his anger and back to God. I grieved because there are better answers to his questions than he'd gotten from well-meaning friends and clergy. It's possible to hurt and still love God, but it helps to understand something of the biblical answer to the problem of suffering.

THE "GOD-KILLED-GRANDMA" SYNDROME

No one ever says "God killed Grandma," but think of testimonies you have heard from people who've said it indirectly, without realizing it.

"The Lord took my grandmother home last summer. I really had a lot of questions after it happened. I couldn't understand what God was doing. But now I realize that the Lord needed to teach me an important lesson about commitment."

It may be true that the person who gave such a testimony needed to learn a lesson about true commitment. But if we pare away the euphemisms, that testimony clearly says that God killed Grandma to teach me a lesson. Whatever the purpose, and whatever the benefit to the person giving the testimony, it was pretty hard on Grandma.

I've heard variations on the theme countless times. A husband and father might say that God took his job away to teach him that everything he had belonged to the Lord. Perhaps, but why were the man's wife and family made to suffer while the husband learned an obvious lesson?

A student might suggest that her parents' divorce was to teach her the importance of fidelity. But would the God who prohibited divorce cause one to reinforce the commandment about adultery?

In the long list of actual statements I could record from my own pastoral and teaching experience, there's always a common thread: Purpose. There must be a purpose in suffering. It must accomplish something worthwhile.

But is this what the Bible teaches? Is all suffering designed for some specific purpose? Must all suffering come from the hand of God?

FOOL'S WISDOM

God's word speaks to us often of suffering. And of prosperity. But a lot of the message is garbled in transmission. Thinking we know God's will and God's way, we make the teaching of Scripture fool's wisdom by turning it on its head to make it say what we expect to hear. We do this easily when we read the three books in the Bible that speak most clearly about universal human experience. These books, Proverbs, Job, and Ecclesiastes, make up a collection that Old Testament scholars speak of as the wisdom books.

P rinciple 27   Wisdom books are a specific type of biblical literature, and we must be careful to read and understand them on their own terms. Wisdom writing deals with life as it's lived and experienced. It makes no claim to be God's promises.

Unfortunately, many people read these books as if they proclaim divine Law directly to American Christians in the twentieth century. These writers, however, speak more from the timeless vantage point of universal human experience than from a specific Christian perspective. These books make no appeal to law or, for that matter, to revelation. What they do speak of is their own observation of the created universe.

REVEALED FROM HEAVEN

Moses reports long conversations with God. The prophets thunder, "Thus says the Lord." The Gospels record the very words of Jesus. The books of Daniel and Revelation are based on visions. But the wisdom books say, "Go to the ant" (Proverbs 6:6), or "As I have observed" (Job 4:8), or "I devoted myself to study and to explore by wisdom all that is done under heaven" (Ecclesiastes 1:13).

In a sentence, the wisdom writing deals with life as it's lived and experienced. It makes no claim to be God's promises. It does rest firmly on a belief in God as the creator and governor of the universe, but it sees that governance operating through natural laws. We're not the first to miss that point, though. Back in the days of Job people held the mistaken idea that living by the rule of proverbs guaranteed a long life filled with success, happiness, and many children.

As C. I. Scofield observed in his introductory notes to the book of Ecclesiastes, "This is the book of man 'under the sun,' reasoning about life. It is the best man can do, with the knowledge that there is a holy God, and that he will bring everything into judgment. . . . Inspiration sets down accurately what passes, but the conclusions and reasonings are, after all, man's."

I would say "Amen" to that and extend the observation to include the rest of the Wisdom Literature. To speak to men or women away from God, it's important that there be inspired books that don't rely on a prior agreement that God has revealed himself.

Unlike the rest of the Old Testament, the wisdom books are universal in their application and appeal. That's why people so often choose Proverbs as their favorite book. Of course it is. It's a down to earth, religiously neutral, common sense approach to life. A Buddhist could read Proverbs and agree with much of it.

Principle 28   The proverbs collected by Solomon and Hezekiah have close parallels in practically every language and culture under the sun. They are principles, guidelines, good advice to live by and hand down to our children. But they are not absolute rules.

TO TEACH A FOOL

Look at Proverbs 26:4–5: "Do not answer a fool according to his folly, or you will be like him yourself. Answer a fool according to his folly, or he will be wise in his own eyes."

If those are both divine promises, or absolute rules, we're in real trouble. Which is correct?

Both. There are circumstances in which it's a mistake to be drawn into an argument with someone who's hostile, belligerent, and convinced, but there are other circumstances in which a fool's folly must be corrected to save the man from himself.

And that's my point. These two verses are guides for conduct, each appropriate under a different set of circumstances. The better part of wisdom is to know when to apply each proverb. As general principles, they apply across cultural and historical boundaries and establish a basis for moral human behavior.

As I mentioned, virtually all the proverbs have close parallels in other languages, cultures, and religions. We should expect them to. If they are sincere human efforts to understand the world God made and our place in it, then people everywhere should agree on certain rules of conduct. Even with the power of sin perverting our reason, it's amazing how universal this wisdom is.

IF IT'S BROKE, WE'D BETTER FIX IT

Because proverbs are general principles and not absolute rules, they apply generally and not absolutely. Sometimes you'll find godly parents whose children rebel against them and against the Lord. Occasionally you'll find a righteous person whose life is marked by sickness, poverty, and loss. Occasionally you'll find an industrious, hard working person who, no matter what he does, can't seem to keep two steps ahead of the bill collector.

What then? Has God broken His promises?

Only if proverbs are promises. Only when we treat proverbs as promises do they cause us problems. And under those circumstances they cause problems aplenty.

If we're the ones for whom the general rule hasn't worked, we question God's justice. If we're on the outside looking in, we become like Job's friends.

The great temptation attached to the idea that these guiding principles are really rules is to try to fix them when they don't work. We develop a way of thinking that turns all God's dealings with us into equations. Righteousness equals blessing. Sin equals suffering.

According to this way of thinking, if we follow the formula and live by the rules, God owes us prosperity. If we break the rules, judgment is sure to follow.

That's true, but not always in this life. We know from Hebrews 9:27 that "man is destined to die once, and *after that* to face judgment." But Old Testament believers didn't have that verse. Because the knowledge of a heavenly reward is so much a part of our Christian faith, we assume it was in the faith of ancient Israel. But that's not so.

The Old Testament has no well-developed doctrine of the afterlife. It talks about *sheol*, the place people go after they die, but Israel thought of it as the grave, the abode of the dead. An occasional Old Testament writer shows unusual insight into the existence of reward for the righteous after death, but nothing in the Old Testament even faintly resembles a description of the New Testament's heaven.

Why would God withhold such powerful and blessed knowledge from His Hebrew children? C. S. Lewis wrote:

> When God began to reveal himself to men, to show them that He and nothing else is their true goal and the satisfaction of their needs, and that He has a claim upon them simply by being what He is, quite apart from anything he can bestow or deny, it may have been absolutely necessary that this revelation should not begin with any hint of future, Beatitude, or Perdition. . . . Later, when, after centuries of spiritual training, men have learned to desire and adore God, to pant after Him "as pants the hart," it is another matter. For then those who love God will desire not only to enjoy Him but "to enjoy Him forever."[1]

Imagine what effect it would have on our faith and the way we live if God hadn't told us about heaven and hell. How would we deal with the problems associated with suffering and punish-

---

[1]
C. S. Lewis, *Reflections on the Psalms.*

ment on the basis of righteousness and evil. But they were sensitive to the suffering they saw all around them. They saw the wicked prospering and the righteous suffering. And there, as Shakespeare might say, was the rub.

The psalmist Asaph, who wrote Psalm 73, admitted to a near loss of faith over this problem: "But as for me, my feet had almost slipped; I had nearly lost my foothold. For I envied the arrogant when I saw the prosperity of the wicked" (vv. 2–3).

His doubt had become so profound he was ready to complain that righteousness offered no reward. "Surely in vain have I kept my heart pure; in vain have I washed my hands in innocence" (v. 13).

But as he met the Lord in worship (vv. 16–17) he saw the reality of divine justice: "Surely you place them on slippery ground; you cast them down to ruin. How suddenly are they destroyed, completely swept away by terrors!" (vv. 18–19).

So far, that's a pretty traditional answer for the Old Testament. But Asaph doesn't let it rest there. He rises above the conventional wisdom of his day to see a deeper truth. The Lord himself is the believer's reward: "When my heart was grieved and my spirit embittered, I was senseless and ignorant; I was a brute beast before you. Yet I am always with you; you hold me by my right hand. You guide me with your counsel, *and afterward you will take me into glory.* Whom have I in heaven but you? And earth has nothing I desire besides you. My flesh and my heart may fail, But God is the strength of my heart and my portion forever" (vv. 21–26).

In this Psalm, Asaph joins the elite of the Old Testament believers in his vision of a system that goes beyond the conventional. Notice the italics I added. Asaph saw that there was more to life than life. He was granted a glimpse of glory, but it was not this glimpse that settled his doubts. It was the knowledge that the answer to the problem of suffering is not simply an answer but a Person.

Sadly, too many of Asaph's contemporaries, and ours, look for the settling of accounts in the here and now with the what and how much.

When we do, we fall into the equation trap: righteousness equals prosperity; sin equals suffering.

On the surface, that looks good, but a deeper look reveals a serious flaw. One of the properties of the equal sign is that an equation can be read either way. If righteousness equals prosperity in this life, it is logical and consistent to assume that success equals righteousness. That part, by itself, isn't so bad. If a prosperous sinner is treated as if he were righteous on account of his prosperity, it probably won't hurt much. But the other side is a dark and evil perversion of God's truth. If we assume that sin equals suffering in this life, it is also logical and consistent to assume that suffering equals sin.

SHOOTING OUR WOUNDED

Someone has said that Christians are notorious for shooting our wounded. In spite of the clear biblical teaching that we should do all in our power to reclaim fallen brothers and sisters, we're quick to place the heel of our own righteousness firmly on the neck of a suffering sinner.

A girl who studied with me in several classes was a serious, intelligent, committed Christian. She was the kind of student I'd be proud to have as a daughter. During her senior year, she fell and hit her head, hard. As a result of that injury, she suffered excruciating headaches, dizziness, occasional blackouts, and a variety of other symptoms. Nothing the doctor did seemed to help; the symptoms wouldn't go away. For several weeks her friends supported her with sympathy and prayer, but when the symptoms persisted they began to press her about unconfessed sins. Sure that God owed her a healing if she were right with Him, they assumed she wasn't right with God because she wasn't healed.

That was exactly how Job's friends responded. Although we have had their sorry model around for almost 4,000 years we still haven't learned from their mistakes. Christians today, with the benefit of subsequent revelation, have no excuse for using that old equation.

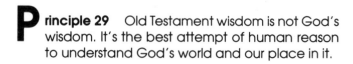

Principle 29   Old Testament wisdom is not God's wisdom. It's the best attempt of human reason to understand God's world and our place in it.

P rinciple 30   Old Testament saints saw only glimmers of the truth of the afterlife. The New Testament magnifies those glimmers into the light of a coherent doctrine.

P rinciple 31   Old Testament wisdom is universal. It speaks plainly to nonbelievers about the well-ordered, moral life that is the basis of human conduct most people throughout history and across the globe agree makes for civilized conduct.

P rinciple 32   God inspired the writing of this human wisdom to provide a bridge into Scripture for people who are moral and good but have no commitment to God's more direct self-revelation. He did not inspire it as absolute truth (Satan's words in Job certainly are not). These books provide the common ground on which we can stand to open dialog with people in need of the Savior.

The eight principles in this chapter will guide our study of the three Old Testament wisdom books as we explore the problem of suffering and God's response to it.

Q uestion 91   The Bible says, "I was young and now I am old, yet I have never seen the righteous forsaken or their children begging bread" (Psalm 37:25). But what about believers who are persecuted behind the Iron Curtain or who starve in famines or are killed in natural disasters?

Is the Bible wrong or are those "believers" not really righteous? These are the two options. Of course, if it's a choice between these and no others, then the answer must be that anyone who suffers must not be righteous.

Principle 33   Whenever a troublesome passage forces us to choose an interpretation that contradicts other Scripture, the problem probably lies with our interpretation, not the Bible.

The problem with Psalm 37 is our interpretation of it. This is one of a handful of psalms that fall into the category of "wisdom." David gives us a clue when he says "I have never seen." He does not say "Thus says the Lord." The observations and deductions of godly writers are the hallmarks of Wisdom Literature, but these are not the covenant promises of God.

Principle 34   Wisdom literature's principles for successful living apply only in a sensible world.

In other words, there are some implied prerequisites for its effective application.

First, it requires a stable society.

People must have the assurance that raiders won't swoop in at harvest season to destroy their crops; that their king is righteous and their judges are honest; and that what they plan this year won't be swept away next year by a coup, an invasion, or a greedy, dishonest ruler.

Many Christians around the world, who live lives of Christian piety and sacrifice that put most Americans to shame, don't have these assurances. They plant their rice, millet, or corn during planting season, never knowing whether or not they will be allowed to harvest it.

David's observation may have been largely accurate in the prosperous, peaceful Israel over which he ruled. However, I doubt if he'd have written the same psalm during the years of the Assyrian ascendancy.

A second prerequisite for this kind of writing is a unified, orthodox, God-fearing population.

One of the great fears of Christian parents today is that the power of outside influences will outweigh the spiritual teaching received at home when their children reach middle teens. We live in a pluralistic age, and we can't count on the nice couple next door to reinforce our Christian teaching.

The statement that a properly raised child will continue in the fear of the Lord as an adult is less likely to be true when some teachers see it as their duty to dispel "the dark religious mythology that keeps young people from attaining their highest intellectual development." Or when neighbors and their children consider standards of holiness, respect, and dependence on the Lord as quaint, antiquated, or even destructive.

Failing to recognize that Wisdom Literature presupposes like-minded citizens in a spiritually unified culture can lead to devastating and inaccurate conclusions.

When I was teaching I received a copy of a popular book about the book of Proverbs. The publisher wanted my comments. Actually, the publisher hoped I'd like the book and say something wonderful about it. I must have been a awful disappointment.

My comment, which I'm sure the publisher appreciated immensely, was that the book did everything I was trying to teach my students not to do with the proverbs. For example, the author glibly asserted that if children don't turn out the way parents wish, it is because the parents have failed.

Maybe it's true in some cases that bad children are the result of bad parenting. Maybe it's even true that some apparently devout people are secret child abusers, drunks, or dope pushers.

But not all turn from the Lord because of poor parenting. Imagine the impact that indictment would have on the Christian parent who has seen a fine Christian young person become a rebellious sinner because of a friend's influence.

Brandishing the proverb like a weapon, we might make theological protests about how that can't happen. But our practices say we're afraid it can. If we don't recognize the possibility of forces outside the home influencing our children for evil, why do so many Christians want their children in Christian schools from day one to keep them away from those influences?

David's observations are not about the working of God, but about the working of the world as God made it. As I mentioned in the introduction to this chapter, the wisdom writer looks at the world and, believing in a God who has ordered everything, sees a moral order in everything, from the industry of ants to the affairs of men. When human beings fear the Lord, that moral order prevails. When that moral order does prevail, there is no need for the children of the righteous to beg bread. If we push the Psalm beyond this, we risk inventing a world that doesn't exist, which we then have to live in.

Does this mean the Psalm is meaningless for us today? As Paul, in a tactful moment, might have said, "Don't be silly." But its meaning can't be found in the promise of never-ending prosperity. It can only be found in the righteous society Christ created to be His physical presence in the world: the church. No, David wasn't writing about the church, but if the church is alive to the moving of the Holy Spirit we can see his vision fulfilled there.

Where, in this soiled society of ours, should we be able to find justice and righteousness? Among God's people. Wasn't that where David was looking in the first place? God's moral government of the world was encoded in the Laws of Israel. Those Laws were written with significant provisions for the care of the poor. In fact, it was Israel's rejection of those provisions that roused Amos, Hosea, and others to holy anger.

If we want to take this Psalm as a promise, we can, but not in the world at large. It speaks clearly about our responsibility for stewardship among the people of God, of the privilege we have, as believers together, of caring for more than the simple needs and not so simple wants of our own family. When God's people, born of the Holy Spirit, saved by the grace of God, alive in Christ, live like who they are, we can expect to see that promise fulfilled, even in the midst of this present and evil age. Even among the poorest of people, the righteous will not need to beg because their brothers and sisters will rally round to supply their needs.

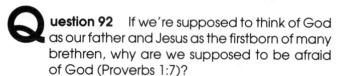

Q **uestion 92**   If we're supposed to think of God as our father and Jesus as the firstborn of many brethren, why are we supposed to be afraid of God (Proverbs 1:7)?

Most attempts to explain this question appeal to the Hebrew word for *fear*. It's argued that the fear we're to feel in God's presence is a sense of awe and reverence rather than a sense of dread. This is probably true as far as it goes, but I'm not sure it really solves the problem.

It sounds more like the kind of explanation we might come up with to calm the unrest we feel when we're commanded to fear our Father. There are times when we might be well advised to fear both our father and our Father, but there's much more to it than that. If we examine the way the Wisdom Literature uses the phrase we may gain some insight into its meaning.

The phrase "fear of the Lord" occurs, in a variety of forms, three times in Proverbs (1:7, 9:10, 15:33), once in Job (28:28), and once in Psalms (111:10). In each case, it is related directly to the acquisition of knowledge, or wisdom. The idea of dread is absent from these five verses. The demons know that God is, and they tremble with dread. They do not begin to know wisdom. Simple dread or awe is insufficient to explain the results that *fearing God* is supposed to achieve.

Fear of the Lord is much broader than is usually suggested. Certainly every believer has, at one time or another, been struck by the majesty and magnitude of God and His power. But that experience can have two quite opposite effects.

For the person who responds to God in faith, God's majesty and power are a tremendous source of comfort and reassurance. Even when we recognize how insignificant we are before Him, we're encouraged by the knowledge that such a one loves us and watches over us.

But what of those who respond with rebellion? Knowledge that they're at odds with the greatest power in the universe must be a terribly sobering and frightening fact.

A story that appeared in *Guideposts* illustrates the point. Without warning or invitation, a very large stray dog adopted a woman and her family. The woman fed it, and the dog followed her wherever she went when she was out of the house. She came to take the dog's presence for granted.

One day she was menaced by a stranger. She became aware of the dog at her side, and so did the man.

"Does that dog bite?"

"Yes," she replied, "I think he would."

The stranger beat a hasty retreat.

After that day the dog disappeared. Make of the story what you will, but she was certain the dog had been sent as a providential protector.

But imagine the different feelings the two people had about the dog's presence. To the one he was comfort, protection, a friend. To the other, he was a threat that awakened a sense of primal dread.

So it is with men and women who confront the holy and awesome God. He becomes either a comfort and a friend or a threat to sinful self-rule. In neither case is awe or reverence, or even fear, enough to explain the difference.

In the Old Testament, although people feared what God might do if they sinned, that wasn't the controlling emotion toward God. To the contrary, the great men and women of Israel seemed to enjoy a rather cordial relationship with Him. Only those who stood afar off seem to have been cowed by His presence.

We hear a lot about Sarah's laughter when God announced she would have a son. But Abraham laughed so hard he fell on the ground (Genesis 17:17). When God announced the planned judgment of Sodom and Gomorrah (Genesis 18:20–32), Abraham dickered with Him as he might have with a merchant. When God declared His intention to destroy Israel and start over with Moses and his family (Numbers 14:10–25), Moses countered by suggesting that God's reputation would be damaged by such an action. On the eve of Babylon's capture of Judah, Habbakuk challenged God to show how He could do such a thing and be called just (Habakkuk 1:12–2:1).

Something more profound is at work in these people than fear, or even reverence. They and others like them were God's friends, and they knew it. Certainly they felt reverence in His presence. And certainly His mighty acts on Israel's behalf, or in judgment against Israel, called forth feelings of awe. But they were moved beyond that to love and obedience. As used in the Old Testament, the *fear of the Lord* contains elements of reverence, awe, even fear at times. But it's a broad term that encompasses so much of what it means to be a believer that we might define it as *the totality of a person's relationship with God*. It is love, reverence, awe, obedience and more, all rolled together. We might also speak of it as true religion.

Proverbs sets out to teach young men how to get along in the world (1:4). It's filled with practical advice ranging from how to behave if the king invites you to dinner (23:1–3) to the value of parental discipline (13:24). It warns against drunkenness (23:29–35), pride (16:5), gossip (26:22), deceit (12:19), and co-signing loans for friends (11:15). It reminds us of the virtues of discipline (12:1), humility (25:27), honesty in business (20:23), and self-restraint (17:27).

In the mastery of all this practical advice lies the danger of believing that the wisdom of the world is sufficient. Then, as now, temptation dogged the ambitious young person trying to climb the ladder. It was the temptation to exchange the relationship with God for the more easily manipulated techniques of the wise.

The wise compiler of proverbs reminds us that true wisdom is found in our relationship with and obedience to the Lord. The truly wise know Him. Knowing everything else, but rebelling against the Lord, a person becomes a fool. The recurring reference to the *fear of the Lord* in the Wisdom Literature was a reminder that wise men, like Job's friends, who limit their wisdom to what may be seen, observed, and deduced, become the worst kind of fools.

If we want to know wisdom, we should study. We should learn all the wisdom of the ancients and apply it. But we should realize that the wisest of the wise is the person who knows, and obeys, the Lord.

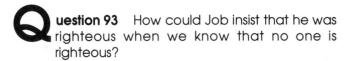

Q **uestion 93**   How could Job insist that he was righteous when we know that no one is righteous?

Actually, Job was not the only one in the book who proclaimed him righteous. The very first verse of the prologue (1:1) describes him as blameless and upright, a man who "feared God and shunned evil." The writer knew that Job's innocence, indeed his righteousness, was a foundational truth of his story.

What's more, God himself identified Job twice in the first two chapters with much the same words (1:8; 2:3). The second time He repeats the same words but adds that Satan is ruining him without reason. This makes it clear that Job, at least in the prologue, is a man whose suffering is not the consequence of sin.

Some argue that Job deserved his "punishment" because he was proud. Otherwise he wouldn't have made such an issue over his innocence. And he was certainly guilty of blasphemy for the way he spoke of God during the argument with his friends. Many Christians understand Job in this way, but in the epilogue (42:7), written after all the shouting has died down, God tells the three friends how angry He is with them and how pleased He is with Job. In fact, He contrasts the friends' seemingly orthodox and pious remarks with Job's seemingly blasphemous statements and accuses the friends of speaking falsely while He praises Job for truth!

We need to be careful not to read modern Christian theology into this work. Job was a sinner as all men are sinners. But that wasn't the point. The point was that Job's suffering was not deserved punishment.

Furthermore, no one is righteous apart from the grace and forgiveness of God. Job, who had called upon God in better days and had walked with God before his catastrophes overtook him, was a man whom God had declared innocent. That's the only innocence or righteousness the Christian can claim. How then can we make Job guilty when God has pronounced him guileless?

The whole book of Job deals with the problem of suffering, but not in general terms. It deals with the suffering of the righteous. If we don't acknowledge that Job was righteous, we miss the whole point. Job deals with what happens when the conventional wisdom of proverbs doesn't work.

Job and his experiences don't fit into the neat explanations we construct for why people suffer. Job's friends attempted to justify God by arguing that Job's suffering came from God and that he deserved everything he suffered. Job, on the other hand, argued throughout the book that he had done nothing to deserve his suffering; in the concluding chapter, God approved his argument. In God's own words, Job suffered without reason.

God wants us to know that there is often no direct correlation between suffering or prosperity, guilt or innocence. We have to appreciate that conventional wise men like Job's friends looked to the *sin equals suffering* equation as an absolute rule.

The death blow to this thinking comes in Job 28, the Hymn to Wisdom. The writer looks throughout heaven and earth for the source of wisdom, which, in the Old Testament context, was the formula for a happy life. He inspects the depths of the sea, crawls through the subterranean tunnels in which men have sought gold and diamonds, inquires of the spiritual powers, death and the grave, and finds that wisdom is not to be found or bought.

As with Proverbs, or Psalm 73, Job tells us that true wisdom is not to be discovered in this world, but in a relationship with the living God. Indeed, when God revealed himself to Job after the arguments had ceased, He offered himself to Job in place of the wisdom of men and general revelation. He says, in effect, that He is the answer to the question of suffering and asks, "Now that you've seen me, Job, will you trust me?" And Job's response is yes.

For the Christian, that's the only answer possible. Even when we can see no purpose, even when there may be no purpose, in a specific tragedy or loss, can we trust Him? When we realize that so much in this world and beyond resists our best efforts at understanding or wisdom, we must ultimately come back to the one who put us here and say, "I don't understand, but I trust you, Father."

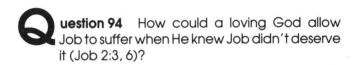

Q **uestion 94**   How could a loving God allow Job to suffer when He knew Job didn't deserve it (Job 2:3, 6)?

Here we find ourselves at the very heart of the problem of suffering. Really, the question is not how can a loving God allow a righteous man to suffer, but what kind of God do we worship, anyway.

The issue bristles with possibilities, most of them unacceptable. If we nose around it like an inquisitive hound around a porcupine, all we'll get for our troubles, more often than not, is a snoot full of quills.

Is God loving but powerless? Rabbi Harold Kushner, in his popular book *Why Bad Things Happen to Good People*, offers that as the solution. The God of the Bible does indeed love us deeply, the author concludes, but He must not be able to do anything about the predicaments in which we find ourselves. That solution preserves God's love at the expense of His Omnipotence.

On the other hand, it's common to hear Christians answer that our trials are evidence of God's love. This preserves His Omnipotence, but for the sensitive soul it's hard to see how the deaths of Job's seven children can be called a loving act. It is of no use to assert that the purpose behind the disasters that befell the patriarch and his family, regardless of how it may seem so to us, was good.

If we used this argument to excuse questionable human activity, Christians would respond immediately that the end doesn't justify the means. But, it would seem, in God's case the pointless deaths of Job's seven children were justified if the end is the perfection of Job's spirit, or his education and purification. When our theology leads us into traps like that, it may be time to examine our theology.

The solutions offered to this problem almost all make a common and erroneous assumption: that God is the author of suffering. This is apparently what Job believed: "Naked I came from my mother's womb, and naked I will depart. The Lord gave and the Lord has taken away; may the name of the Lord be praised" (Job 1:21).

It's also the assumption behind the arguments of all four of his antagonists. "Blessed is the man whom God corrects; so do not despise the discipline of the Almighty. For he wounds, but he also binds up; he injures, but his hands also heal" (Job 5:17–18). Although they argue their case long after uttering these two verses, they never really go beyond them.

Some believe the speeches of Elihu (Job 32–37) advance the idea that suffering is redemptive, but Elihu does little more than restate the arguments of the friends and the complaints of Job. His contribution is heated and contains much that is generally true, but in Job's case he misses the mark altogether (especially in such verses as 36:15–17).

He returns to the idea that Job's suffering is deserved, only softening his argument by allowing that the punishment was redemptive and not merely punitive.

I would be the last to deny that God disciplines believers. All of Job's tormentors were right, as far as they went. But all their arguments founder on the clear statement that Job was ruined without cause.

The first mistake we make in reading the book of Job is to read it as if the events of the prologue (chapters 1 and 2) were known to the characters we meet in chapter 3. In reality, no human participant in this tragedy was given the glimpse into heavenly deliberations that readers of the book share. If Job had known that Satan, not God, was his tormentor, would his pain have been so great? Would the three friends, or Elihu, have been so certain of their understanding and wisdom if they had access to the simple statement of Job's innocence found in 2:3? The second mistake is theological. We import an understanding of God's absolute sovereignty into an Old Testament text that is not at home there. In fact, the book is quite specific that neither God's plan nor purpose is being carried out. Rather, Job is a pawn in the hands of Satan. Satan's purpose, not God's, is at work in Job's life.

It is neither necessary nor desirable to see God's hand at work in all suffering. In fact, it's possible to find at least four different reasons in Scripture why a person might suffer. And God's discipline is only one of them.

It would be foolhardy to deny that some suffering is at the hand of God and has redemption as its goal. Paul attests to this in 1 Corinthians 11:30–32. The sickness and death experienced by some members of the Corinthian church was attributed to God's disciplinary judgment. But when we extend this to cover universal suffering we do so at great peril.

Also inescapable, in light of what Job 1–2 teaches, is that some suffering is the result of satanic activity. When the New Testament teaches so clearly that this world is the domain of Satan, the prince of this world (John 12:31; 14:30; 16:11), the prince of the powers of the air (Ephesians 2:2), it is difficult to understand why we're so reluctant to admit that he is the source of much suffering.

The fallenness of the world is clearly taught in Romans 8:18–25. We live in an age that thinks of nature as pure; honey and oat bran are a sure ticket to back-to-nature heaven. But the Bible teaches that the world is tainted by the fall of Adam.

If the ground, which brought forth the good food God ordered for Adam, brings forth thorns and thistles because of the Fall, what other perversions of nature are we overlooking? Mosquitoes and woodticks are two that spring to the mind of a native Minnesotan. Bacteria and viruses are others. And tornadoes, hurricanes, earthquakes, volcanoes, floods, and other natural disasters that insurance companies glibly call "acts of God" would be too.

In other words, do we take the doctrine of the Fall seriously enough? We hear a lot about original sin in us, but what about the impact of the Fall on the world around us? To understand the full consequences of the Fall, we must recognize that this beautiful world with all its wonders is really booby-trapped (Romans 8:19–22). Creatures and features of creation that God designed to be good and purposeful have become time bombs waiting to go off. Some are triggered by seemingly harmless movements of air currents or the sliding of the plates of the earth's surface. The earth is a dangerous place to live. And countless innocent people fall victim every year to the fact of a fallen creation.

Then what about our own decisions? Romans 1 seems to paint an ugly picture of human decisions run amok. Knowing God, these people turned from worshiping Him and took up the worship of the things He'd made. As a result of that decision, God "gave them over" to its degrading consequences.

To me, this is a forceful argument for the freedom of the will and human decision making power. If that's not what Romans 1 is talking about, then Paul's hypothetical antagonist in Romans 9:19 has a case. If God decreed that those people should do evil, by what standards of justice does God condemn them?

It's interesting that Job accuses God of exactly that sort of might-makes-right approach to justice. The gist of Job 9 is that God is certainly all powerful, but He acts in a way that may not be honorable or just. Job's innocence, which God himself has attested, is no protection from God's wrath (9:14–31).

Can you sympathize with Job's anguish? What level of suffering makes a man like Job talk like that? For Job, the belief that God is the author of his suffering is the greatest burden of all.

With the greater insight provided by the prologue, we know that the agent of his suffering was Satan, not God. We also know that he's not being punished for his sins. If his suffering has any purpose, it is to provide countless generations of believers with the knowledge that suffering does not equal divine punishment.

But if we grant that Satan is the agent of Job's suffering, why did a loving God allow it? Why didn't He intervene to thwart Satan?

Here's where I appeal to the idea of divine sovereignty. God's sovereign decisions to create humanity with a will, and to give Satan jursidiction over the domain of fallen man, are not to be treated lightly. If God decided to allow the devil to rule, and to allow humanity to have a will, His willy-nilly intrusion on that system would be a violation of His own sovereign decision.

The high point of the end time will come when Satan is dethroned. It will be the prelude to a time when there will be no sorrow, no tears, no death, no parting. God has ordained this as His final way of dealing with the problem of suffering. In the meantime, to those who trust Him, He has given the Holy Spirit as a comforter and the promise of that day as our hope.

Question 95   The Bible says we will be healed if we have the elders of the church pray for us. Why doesn't God heal everyone we pray for (James 5:14–16)?

As a pastor, there's nothing so perplexing as praying diligently over long periods for the healing of a friend, a child, or an accident victim and then seeing that person die. In my experience with the families of the bereaved, the question why is always present, even when they do not voice it.

I'd like to suggest a semi-radical explanation for this verse, and then spend time trying to unravel the problem in more general terms.

There seems to be an assumption in this section of James that sin and sickness are somehow related. Prayer, confession, forgiveness, and healing all figure prominently in James's admonition. I think sickness that comes from the Lord is statistically rare, but I can't deny that the Bible gives many examples over 2,000 years where God used sickness to bring people to repentance.

The book of James is often pointed out as the New Testament's contribution to the Wisdom Literature, so it's reasonable to expect James's treatment of sickness to reflect that background. It's also reasonable to expect James to state a lot of principles, or general rules, that we can count on in specific settings.

I believe that James was dealing with situations where sickness was the result of sin and healing was to be expected when the sin had been dealt with.

In the opening of this chapter, I cited three other biblical reasons for sickness: Satan, human decision, and a fallen order. Can God heal when one of these is the source of sickness?

The general topic of divine healing divides Christians today. Some want to relegate any reference to healing to the apostolic age or the Millennium. Others acknowledge God's freedom to heal if He chooses, but advise us not to look for it. Still others assume healing as the right of believers, the "children's bread" as one evangelical writer put it.

As with so many of the questions I've tried to answer, the reason for so many positions is that each camp treats the subject as if it were an isolated problem with no necessary connections with other biblical doctrines.

In fact, the question of why some are healed and not others involves us in a discussion of the nature of faith, the purpose of miracle, and the justification for expecting healing at all.

GREEN STAMP FAITH

Some of us remember the day when grocery stores and filling stations lured us with the promise of Green Stamps. Sheets of these stamps, when collected, licked, and placed in stamp books, could be turned in for prizes. You could leaf through the Green Stamp catalog and pick what you'd like to get for nothing. The premiums that called for 125 books of stamps were out of reach, so you usually settled for the eight- or nine-book premiums. My mother collected stamps for years, and the only premium I remember was a hassock she probably could have bought (back in 1965) for ten or twelve dollars.

Some Christians have what I call Green Stamp faith. They treat it as a commodity. When they collect enough, they take them to God for a miracle. Think about the language we hear applied most often to faith. It has to do with quantity. "I didn't have enough faith for . . ." This is very similar to what my mother used to say. "I didn't have enough stamps for . . ." Green Stamps didn't create this view of faith, but they illustrate it nicely.

But faith is like manna. We can't collect it. God gives the faith we need when we need it.

Jesus talked about having faith as insignificant as a mustard seed, which seems to introduce the idea of quantity into the discussion. But look at what He said about it. Faith like a mustard seed would move a mountain. In simple, literal language, Jesus said faith is so powerful that, if we liken it to the smallest common seed, it could move the biggest imaginable object. It is, in other words, a force that no one at any time in history could understand. Even in our age of fission, fusion, solar, geothermal, and garbage fired energy, there's nothing in our experience like faith. Except faith.

Lamentably, though, faith has become the object of faith for far too many people. During my years in Christian work I've run into more people, unbelievers mostly, who face crises in their lives with the bland assertion, "You have to have faith."

In what? Faith is nothing without its object. The concept of faith and the person of Christ are so tightly bound together that if we lose one, we lose the other. Faith-as-belief is a weak substitute for the real thing. *The Little Engine That Could*, that ultimate statement of the gospel of positive thinking written for children, illustrates this aspect. The theological Little Engines that run around inciting people to "just believe" have created a laughable parody of Christian faith. Convincing ourselves to really believe in something is not true faith.

Faith-as-works is a cruel illusion. We can no more win a healing by doing works of law than we can win a marathon by being good at needlepoint.

Faith, as defined in the Old Testament, is more an act than a condition. The word translated *faith* in the older versions is better understood as *faithfulness*. It is a brass-bound commitment to one in whom we believe.

The New Testament word for faith partakes of this same element. To believe means more than just thinking something is true. Try this test. Lay a solid 2-by-10-foot plank on the ground. Put a concrete block under each end, raising the plank about eight inches. Now walk the length of the plank. Easy isn't it?

Now take that same plank and put it on a construction scaffold sixty feet off the ground.

I'll never forget the first time I worked on a construction job and was sent to the top of a scaffold about three stories above the sidewalk. All I had to do was move a bunch of widgets from one end of the scaffold to the other. I knew that plank was strong. I'd been carrying its brothers around on my shoulder for weeks;

it was as solid as a plank can get. I knew the scaffolding was strong. I'd watched several concrete pours, from ground level, and seen tons of wet cement held perfectly well by the scaffolding. All I had to do to accomplish the job I'd been given was commit myself to the plank and the scaffold and walk about twelve feet across that wonderfully strong plank. After much hesitation, I made my first trip . . . on hands and knees. I tried walking, but my feet wouldn't move. After a couple weeks, I was tip-toeing across the tops of steel joists barely two inches across, but that first twelve-foot voyage of exploration took all the resolution I could muster.

You might say my faith was weak. It had nothing to do with believing. I had firm belief in the safety of the equipment. I just wasn't ready to commit myself to it.

That's the element of faith I think we need to keep in mind when we talk about healing. The question isn't whether we believe God can heal us, but it's whether we're prepared to commit ourselves to Him for healing.

The faith involved here is the act of giving ourselves to God for His care. It's not a question of quantity or strength of faith. It matters only that we're ready to leave the resolution to Him.

That's why I question people's understanding of faith when I hear them say they have faith so they know God will heal them or has healed them. I'd rather hear them say they know God can heal them, but they will trust Him to do what's right. Which brings us to the next question. Why wouldn't it be right to heal a person, end suffering, and save family and loved ones from the grief of impending death?

The answer to this part of the question looks back at the purpose of miracle in the New Testament. The most common word translated *miracle* in the KJV was the Greek word *semeion* (sem-ee-OWN). It was translated *sign* fifty-one times and *miracle* twenty-two times. That makes seventy-three times the New Testament writers used that important word. Whether it's translated "sign" or "miracle" the Greek word never gives up the idea of a wondrous act that shows the hand of God at work.

John, for example, said the making of wine at Cana was the beginning of *semeion* (John 2:11). The lame man's healing in Acts 3 was judged by the Sanhedrin to be "an outstanding *semeion*" (Acts 4:16) and they were afraid to punish John and Peter because the people had seen it. It was indeed a great sign, since it brought another 2,000 into faith in Christ. When Jesus performed *semeion* at the Passover (John 2:23) many people believed.

Healings seem to be chief among the signs. More than just the sign that the Holy Spirit was in the world or that Jesus was the Messiah, the signs of New Testament times spoke of a whole new order we can call the Messianic Age.

Jesus himself identified His healings this way when He answered John the Baptist's question, "Are you the one?" The messengers from John had reached Jesus when He was healing many. Was that a coincidence? When Jesus heard their question, He reminded them of what they had seen, of the signs they had witnessed: "Go back and report what you have seen and heard: The blind receive sight, the lame walk, those who have leprosy are cured, the deaf hear, the dead are raised, and the good news is preached to the poor" (Luke 7:22).

Of course Jesus' answer was not just a reference to current events. He, and certainly John, knew that He quoted from Isaiah 29:18–21, 35:5–6, and 61:1. These were signs that the Messiah had come.

Although the healings, exorcisms, and resuscitations done by Jesus and the disciples were certainly motivated by pity and love, they were not just acts of kindness. They were the clarion call to faith among people expecting the Messiah.

This is probably the reason that Jesus performed only a few healings among His own neighbors at Nazareth (Matthew 13:53–58). He taught them in the synagogue, and they wondered at His wisdom. The stories of His signs reached them, but they saw only a power. The man who had grown up in their midst, whose mother, four brothers, and some sisters lived among them, had acquired some source of power somewhere, but they saw only the power, not the sign.

I think that's why people who pray for healing are often left in their sickness. The power to heal is there. The pity and love that Jesus displayed when He healed during the days of his earthly ministry are there. But the sign isn't.

I've seen healings that would make the most hard-headed skeptic falter. I've even prayed for healings in impossible situations and seen those prayers answered on a few occasions. But

I've prayed for far more when God's sovereign answer was, "Not yet, but in the Kingdom."

Healing is a sign of an age that has already dawned, but its light comes from beyond the horizon. We are granted glimpses into the coming age when God graciously touches the body of a sufferer and makes it whole. But we haven't yet reached the place where "there will be no more death or mourning or crying or pain."

Some argue that healing has been promised in the atonement (Isaiah 53:4) and, like salvation, should be ours for the asking. That's not what the New Testament says, though. It promises a future when sickness and death will be vanquished and wholeness and health will rule as they did in Eden. In that day we'll rest in the shade of the tree of life and bask in the Light that is the presence of God.

Until that day, the Holy Spirit provides the foretaste (2 Corinthians 1:22, 5:5; Ephesians 1:14) of life in the world where death has died and sin is no more. Until then the healing of the body will be the sign God gives, when He sees the larger purpose, that the day is real and is coming.

*There are times when
dying for a cause
is easier than
living for it.*

CHAPTER 9

PRINCIPLES

35 Do not use historical narrative to develop doctrines.

36 Ask yourself why the writer included this event and not some other.

QUESTIONS

96 Are tongues the sign that a person is filled with the Holy Spirit? (Acts 2:4; 8:14–17; 10:46–48; 19:6–7)?

97 How could the Ephesian "disciples" have been Christians when all they knew was the baptism of John (Acts 19:6–7)?

98 How could Paul say there shouldn't be any tongues without interpretation (1 Corinthians 14:27–28) when on the Day of Pentecost all the disciples spoke in tongues and the crowd understood them as if they were speaking in their own language (Acts 2:4)?

99 Paul used different lists of spiritual gifts. Why did he do that and does it mean that some gifts are not for today (1 Corinthians 12:7–11; Ephesians 4:7–13; Romans 12:1–9; 1 Corinthians 13:8)?

100 If the Bible teaches that drinking is a sin, why did Jesus turn water into wine, and why did Paul tell Timothy to drink wine for his stomach? Was it alcoholic wine (John 2:1–11; 1 Timothy 5:23)?

HOW SHOULD
WE LIVE, THEN?

37 Don't bend and twist the meaning of the biblical text to avoid an unpleasant conclusion.

38 Don't formulate doctrine on the basis of problem passages.

101 Didn't Paul say everything was lawful for the Christian? If so, isn't it legalistic to judge other believers for things they've done if the Lord doesn't convict them (1 Corinthians 6:12)?

102 If Paul wouldn't let women teach or have authority over men, why do some people today want to ordain women (1 Timothy 2:11–14)?

103 Paul said women should be subject to their husbands. What does that mean (Ephesians 5:22–33)?

104 Does the Bible condemn all homosexuality or only homosexual promiscuity (Genesis 18:21–22; 19:1–10; Romans 1:21–27)?

On the twenty-fifth anniversary of the assassination of John F. Kennedy, Daniel J. Boorstin wrote a thoughtful retrospective on his career. In it he pondered what impact an additional five years in the presidency might have had on America's perception of the man who has become one of its most idealized leaders.

Had Kennedy lived, things like the Bay of Pigs, the war in Viet Nam, or his promiscuous personal life would certainly have tarnished his public image, for his was a presidency of almost messianic dreams, but all too human accomplishments. Kennedy has, said Boorstin, been judged more by his speeches than his deeds. The harsh critiques of a fading Camelot that were beginning to make themselves heard in the autumn of 1963 were permanently hushed by the echoes of the assassin's rifle, and history's assessment of America's thirty-fifth president is overshadowed by his sudden and tragic death. Although later generations may cast a more jaundiced eye at his record, as history looks back on this century it is likely that "Jack" Kennedy will still be remembered as fondly as he is today. His memory is fixed in time, undimmed by later, lesser feats.

We remember Martin Luther King, Jr. for his leadership in the civil rights movement, but it is his "I Have a Dream" speech that has become representative of the man's life. From a historical perspective, it was the zenith of King's career.

When he was assassinated in 1968, the movement King had birthed was starting to fragment. Younger, more militant leaders were beginning to shoulder him aside. King died a martyr to a great cause, but his premature and tragic death fixed his place permanently and positively in American memory. Nothing can change that now.

Most Americans would see Abraham Lincoln as the greatest of our presidents, surpassing even the Father of Our Country, George Washington, in national affection. But Lincoln's successor, Andrew Johnson, was impeached by a Senate that was hostile to the Great Emancipator's magnanimous plans for reconstruction. If Lincoln himself had lived, would he have been the first president brought before that legislative body for judgment? And would we remember him today as we do—with awe and reverence as a man who was somehow more than just a man?

Here's a point every Christian should remember: There are times when dying for a cause is easier than living for it.

For centuries the church has honored its martyrs, and there is great truth in the saying that the martyrs' blood is seed for the church. From Stephen onward, those believing heroes who have died for the cause of Christ have been the most potent of witnesses to the Gospel.

I remember as a child thinking how wonderful it would be to be a martyr. I didn't really like the idea of getting there, but *being* a martyr seemed very noble and courageous and altogether pious. I don't know if I was hopelessly idealistic or just morbid.

What I do know now, from the vantage point of two-score and then some, is that living for Christ also calls for faith and courage, albeit a different, but no less heroic kind.

Is there a Christian alive who hasn't thought, at least once, how good it would be if the Rapture were scheduled for today? Usually for me that thought comes when I'm facing a deadline I'm about to miss again, or when yet another car demands several days of my presence under its hood. I think, "Today would be nice, Lord." And looking at the state the world is in, who could deny having at least a slight desire for the Lord to put an end to it all and take us home?

Most of us are called to a servant's life, not a martyr's death. But the problem with a servant's life is that you're always on call. You are always moving from today's success to tomorrow's new responsibility. And there's where it becomes terribly tangled.

Living the Christian life is easy—in the abstract. "I am crucified with Christ" we say with Paul. "Not my will, but thine be done," with Jesus. "I am a new creation, with old things passed away," and "I'll take up my cross and follow," we add.

But, as the saying goes, it's hard to soar with the eagles when you're surrounded by turkeys. And harder still when you recognize yourself as King Gobbler. It's not that we haven't become new creations or been crucified with Christ. It's just that we'd like a few more rest areas on the long, long road.

And the church isn't very helpful at times. Instead of being a place of healing, the body is often torn apart over issues of right and wrong. We can disagree almost to the point of violence over practically every facet of Christian living.

Scripture has become the battlegrounds over which we fight when we talk about these things. They are so numerous, in fact, that I won't pretend to try to deal with even a tenth of them. So what I've done in this chapter is select a few issues that I've seen dividing people in places where I've served. Then I have offered the answers that have helped me understand these matters and cope with fallout.

I have no illusions about the impact these answers will have on the larger debate. For those whose minds are made up, these will either call forth a hearty amen or send the blood pressure up about thirty points. For those with genuine questions, however, I hope I can offer a sober assessment of the issues and a reasonable explanation of the text. I won't guarantee I'll be right, but then that kind of guarantee is offered only by the ignorant or the arrogant.

TONGUES OF FIRE UNDER FIRE

Few issues divide the modern church as thoroughly or as acrimoniously as the issue of tongues. As a pastor I've stood with one foot in each of the opposing camps during most of my ministry. I've lamented the hostility of some toward a phenomenon the Bible labels a gift of grace. I've also lamented the unbridled emotionalism and hucksterism practiced in many of the Pentecostal/charismatic groups. Frankly, I'm not comfortable with either camp. One seems offended that other believers have received a gift that doesn't fit neatly or manageably into the structures of their rational theology, while the other seems constantly on the verge of skittering over the thin line dividing truth from heresy, the power of the Spirit from the arrogance of Gnosticism.

If I never hear another anti-charismatic catalog the obvious excesses of the movement, and if I never hear another charismatic tell me how God needs to short-circuit our minds to let us really pray or worship, I'll know I've died and gone to heaven.

The scriptural material on the subject falls somewhere between the two extremes. Peter spoke in tongues; Paul spoke in tongues. At the same time, Paul spends most of the chapters he devotes to the gift of tongues—he does deal with them as a genuine gift from God—trying to rein in the overexuberance of its recipients.

If there were a way to disprove most of the central teachings of the charismatic movement from the Bible, I'd be the first to argue against them, but there isn't. The kind of special pleading that tries to remove the gift of tongues from the Christian's arsenal has to work overtime to make the Bible cooperate with its agenda. There's no legitimate argument from Scripture that says a Christian today can't speak in tongues.

I wish that some of the most rabid anti-tongues groups could be infected with the genuine zeal for the Lord I've known in Pentecostal and charismatic fellowships over the years. At the same time, I wish the zeal of the latter could be tempered with knowledge.

Unfortunately, the very fervor that comes with the intimate, personal experience of the Holy Spirit that marks charismatic practice is subject to excesses of almost unspeakable proportions. The problem is that these people are unprepared or unwilling to go to Scripture in a systematic way to find out what it really says about their experience. And any approach that uses experience to interpret the Bible, rather than using the Bible to interpret experience, leaves itself open to error. Paul had good reason for warning the Corinthians to guard against the spirits at work among them lest they fall subject to those that would move them to make Jesus a curse.

While the number of possible questions on this difficult subject is almost endless, we'll look at four that I think help to lay the groundwork for a biblical understanding of what God has been doing among His people.

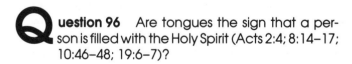

Q **uestion 96**   Are tongues the sign that a person is filled with the Holy Spirit (Acts 2:4; 8:14–17; 10:46–48; 19:6–7)?

That's what I was taught as a teenager. I remember praying one night to be filled with the Spirit. My grandfather took me to his prayer closet in the attic and knelt with me while I prayed. Before we started he read these four passages to show me that tongues were indeed the sign that the Holy Spirit had come.

In spite of my profound respect for my grandfather, and in spite of the fact that many Christians believe as he did, I have to say no to this question. These verses do not teach that tongues are a sign that a person is filled with the Spirit.

I know someone is bound to ask, "Then what do you do with the Day of Pentecost?" I could add to that, "What about the Samaritans, or Cornelius, or the Ephesians?"

What I do is try to understand what the texts are saying. To do this, I need to ask some questions. I need to know certain things before I can say anything about what these texts mean.

The first question is, "Is the gift of tongues in these passages intended as a sign?"

The obvious answer is yes. In all four instances tongues are recorded as a sign that the Holy Spirit had come. In fact, Peter says as much about the incident at Cornelius's house: "God, who knows the heart, showed that he accepted them by giving the Holy Spirit to them, just as he did to us. He made no distinction between us and them, for he purified their hearts by faith" (Acts 15:8–9).

But to say that tongues served as a sign that the Holy Spirit had come on these four occasions is a far cry from saying that tongues serve as the sign of a person's encounter with the Holy Spirit at all times.

Principle 35   Do not use historical narrative to develop doctrines.

History can be valuable in the illustration of doctrine, but doctrine itself must be developed from teaching passages.

Of course people within the Pentecostal/charismatic sphere dispute this. With the heart of the doctrine of tongues as the initial evidence of baptism in the Holy Spirit found in historical narratives you'd expect that. "Where does Scripture say that you shouldn't use history as doctrine?" they are apt to say. "That's just a rule made by men."

The question is valid. Why not use historical narrative as a doctrinal base?

Because the purpose of historical narrative is the transmission of events, not doctrine. Historical narrative records events without explaining the motivation behind them. Historical narrative may be used to illustrate or support a doctrine, but as with figurative language, doctrinal propositions lie a step beneath their surface. While biblical history sometimes tells us something happened for certain reasons, we usually are not informed directly of the purpose of an event. This leaves us free to exercise our sanctified imaginations without biblical restraint.

One of the great challenges facing historians, biblical and secular alike, is how to deduce the motivation behind an action. For example, it's usually agreed that Lee Harvey Oswald shot John Kennedy. But why? It's usually agreed that John Wilkes Booth shot Abraham Lincoln. But why? There is no evidence that the curiosity of history has been satisfied in either case. We will probably never know the answer to either question, but we will continue to rework the same events, reshaping and reinterpreting in an effort to find out.

Even the simplest actions often fail to reveal the motivation behind them. Let me illustrate.

A woman who was preparing dinner while her young daughter watched unwrapped a ham, cut it in half, and put the pieces in a roasting pan.

"Mommy, why did you cut the ham in half?"

The mother thought a moment and replied, "Because my own mother always did that."

"Why did Grandma cut the ham in half?"

The mother thought a moment and realized she did not know. She had always assumed there was some good reason why her mother always cut hams in half before cooking them, so she did the same.

At her first opportunity, the woman asked her mother what the reason was.

"No secret," her mother answered. "When you were little I never had a roasting pan large enough for a whole ham, so I cut them in half and cooked half at a time."

Another mystery solved!

But do you see my point? An observer may record an event. We read the details and know what happened. But knowing what happened doesn't explain why it happened or why the historian chose those specific details to build his account.

It would be foolish to deny the sign element in these four incidents recorded in the book of Acts. It would be just as foolish to assign a particular purpose to the sign without first examining the text carefully for clues to its purpose.

Principle 36   Ask yourself why the writer included this event and not some other.

In this case, a second principle for reading historical narrative comes into play. Historians, by the very nature of their work, always have more material than they can record. This means they have to decide what to leave out. So the second principle I always apply to the text is, "Why this event and not some other? Is some purpose in the larger narrative served by this account?"

To discover that, we need to look at the book of Acts and its place in New Testament revelation. Easier said than done.

While Luke carefully explained his purpose for writing the gospel of Luke (Luke 1:1–4), he didn't say a word about his purpose for writing Acts. So we must make some deductions.

Some argue that he wrote the book as a defense of Paul and his Gentile ministry on the eve of his trial. Others see this as a straightforward attempt to record the early days of the spread of the Gospel; miraculous events had taken place and they deserved preservation. Or we might argue that Luke intended to demonstrate the universality of the faith by describing its ready acceptance in every quarter.

From a more pragmatic perspective, we might theorize that Luke desired to show that Roman authorities had seen and examined the Christian faith at practically every level. As the hostility grew, evidenced by encounters in Ephesus and Corinth, it would have been valuable to be able to cite numerous official decisions that had found the work of the church without fault.

All these are plausible and commendable purposes, and all may have contributed to the writing of the book. But I see still another motivation.

The growing church described in Acts is an institution none of the early Christians could have predicted. While they looked for a Jewish political ruler (Acts 1:7), the kingdom of God took form as a multi-ethnic, multi-lingual, multi-national conglomerate drawn from every tribe and nation. This was a major affront to the expectations and sensibilities of devout Jews.

The Messiah was to be a Jew! He was to save the Jews from their enemies. The prophets may have talked about the nations beating a path to Jerusalem, but it would certainly be to pay tribute to the Jewish king. These were expectations held by the majority of Jewish people.

Luke, the early church's most famous Gentile believer and Paul's close associate in the Gentile mission, took aim at the Jewish exclusivism that plagued the church throughout Paul's ministry, and Acts is the result. Acts 1:8 is a key to understanding this: "But you will receive power when the Holy Spirit comes on you; and you will be my witnesses in Jerusalem, and in all Judea and Samaria, and to the ends of the earth."

This verse is usually treated as a mere repetition of the Great Commission, but it is not.

The Great Commission (Matthew 28:18–20) is the last command Christ gave His church. Acts 1:8 is both a rebuke and a promise that Jesus gave in response to the question: "Lord, are you at this time going to restore the kingdom to Israel?" (Acts 1:6).

The men who followed Jesus were patriots, men who had at first followed Jesus in hope of political freedom. While their love for the Lord came to overshadow their earlier desire for power, the political motivation continued to percolate just beneath the surface, even after the resurrection.

But Jesus had His own strategic plan for the world, and it didn't fit into the expectations of his followers at all. He laid out that plan in Acts 1:8. There are no imperatives here, no voice of command. The rebuke is gentle, but no less real. The disciples wanted power. It would come, but it would be unlike any power they had ever envisioned.

These power-hungry disciples would have to go back to Jerusalem and wait. Then in God's own time the Holy Spirit would give them real power, and they would be witnesses for Christ in Jerusalem, Judea, Samaria, and to the ends of the earth. Nothing less than the whole world is the objective.

How would you feel if you were a disciple who expected some really great things to happen to Israel and then found out those things were going to happen to the whole world? It would be like showing up for a National Guard weekend only to be told you were off to invade Europe. What a shock it must have been to those good Jewish men to learn they would preach the Gospel of the Jewish Messiah to a Gentile world. And that is the strategic plan underlying the whole book of Acts.

In the Old Testament the book of Joshua shows how God was faithful to His promise to provide a land for Israel. Acts plays the same role in the New Testament. Jesus promised He would build His church. The advance of the Gospel, following the pattern Jesus laid down in Acts 1:8, would be the fulfillment of that promise.

These four accounts of tongues must be understood in that context. They were essential signs for a church that resisted the master plan once it reached beyond the borders of their own nation; they overruled objections to each new group Christ added.

Peter and John's ministry in Samaria (Acts 8:14) was among a group of people no Jew would have considered suitable for the Messiah's kingdom. They hated the Samaritans, looking upon them as half-breed turncoats who had departed from the worship of the true God hundreds of years before. Because of this prejudice against the Samaritans, God demonstrated the coming of the Holy Spirit with an outward sign, indicating that Christ would have them in His church.

No doubt the believers in Jerusalem were skeptical about the conversion of the hated Samaritans under Philip's ministry. After all, Philip was only a deacon, and not even one of the inner circle of Hebrew-speaking believers. Peter and John were sent to verify the reports they'd heard that Samaritans had believed. The Lord validated their conversion in the same way He'd witnessed to the birth of the Jerusalem church—with the sign of tongues. That way there would be no mistaking the message.

Peter's visit to Cornelius's house was another matter, yet in a similar vein. Cornelius was a Gentile, and most of Peter's peers would not have believed there was a place for Gentiles in Messiah's kingdom. Even Peter needed a vision from heaven before he would accept Cornelius's invitation!

Notice (Acts 10:45) that the Jewish believers with Peter were astonished that Gentiles, too, could receive the Holy Spirit. This incident, so difficult for the original Christians to accept, is recorded as the first real move of the Spirit away from the church's Jewish roots. The groundwork was laid for Paul's great

Gentile mission at the home of an officer of the army that oppressed Israel.

Even with the testimony of Peter's vision and the unassailable evidence of the Spirit's presence, Peter had to defend himself before the leadership of the Jerusalem church!

The reason for the tongues spoken by Cornelius and his household may be deduced from his defense (10:34–48). "If God poured out His Spirit on Gentiles, just as He did on us," Peter argued, "who was I to oppose Him?"

It would seem that God had carefully chosen the recipient of this outward sign. Of all Gentiles, Cornelius would have been the least objectionable. Palestine was a hotbed of sedition, and only the finest of men were trusted to command in that difficult area. Cornelius was an officer in the Italian Cohort, an elite unit of men. He was, to paraphrase Paul, a Gentile of the Gentiles.

Like many of the noble Romans, Cornelius had grown weary of the immorality of the new Rome and the debauches that were becoming more and more a part of the life of the capital. The old gods and the stories of their wars, loves, jealousies, and immoralities held no promise for him. Cornelius was a man living a good, moral life, and he was attracted to the holiness and justice of the Jewish God.

That Cornelius's conversion created a problem for Peter is evidence of the hostility of the leadership at Jerusalem toward the Gentile world. When Peter brought his report that the Holy Spirit had also come upon the Gentiles, the church accepted it grudgingly. You can hear echoes of Jonah in their praises.

After this, Peter is no longer at the center of activity in Acts. Except for the story of his imprisonment and release (Acts 12) and his defense of the Gentile mission (Acts 15), he is not heard from again. Many New Testament scholars believe his influence declined because he championed the first Gentile convert.

Then there was Paul and his band of disciples in the pagan city of Ephesus. These people were not only Gentiles, but they had come to faith in Christ without benefit of the preaching of the apostles. Their faith was based on the most basic understanding of the message of Christ. Yet the Spirit fell here too.

Let's ask ourselves this question: "Why have these four accounts of tongues, and no others, been included in the inspired record?"

First of all, this descent of the Spirit at the birth of the church—the first instance of the preaching of the Gospel in Jerusalem—was a magnificent sign of the power of the age to come, the power Joel had prophesied (Joel 2:28–29). Just as certainly the descent of the Spirit on the Samaritans was evidence that the promised power had been extended to Judah's cousins, indicating that the Jewish Messiah was also to be Lord of the Samaritans. When the Lord sent the Holy Spirit to the household of Cornelius, He opened the door of the kingdom to the Gentiles. And with the Ephesian disciples, we come face-to-face with the fulfilled reality of Jesus' promise in Acts 1:8: the Gospel had gone to Jerusalem and Judea and Samaria. Now the last place on the earth fell open to the Gospel when the unlearned, uncircumcised Ephesians were admitted into the kingdom with the seal of God's ownership.

God used tongues as a sign, not to the new convert nor to the world at large but to a reluctant church, that even these were His people. Because each incident is recorded as a unique sign, for a specific purpose, we can learn much from them, but we cannot generalize from them for all people at all times.

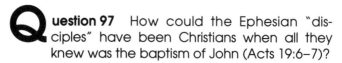

Q **uestion 97** How could the Ephesian "disciples" have been Christians when all they knew was the baptism of John (Acts 19:6–7)?

These were people whose knowledge of salvation was pretty skimpy, but they were believers. When Paul first met with them and questioned them, he referred back to the time "when you believed." And Luke, in his narration, called them "disciples." They were not merely disciples of John the Baptist who had been stashed away somewhere in Asia Minor since the time when John was beheaded in Jerusalem some twenty years earlier. Neither were they simply followers of the eloquent Apollos (18:24–28).

Some may ask how they could have been true Christians if they didn't know anything but John's baptism of repentance and were completely ignorant of the work of the Holy Spirit. I'd reply by asking: Did any of us have to pass a theological exam to be accepted into the kingdom?

We have to be careful not to apply some lofty theological standard to new believers. God doesn't.

It is grace, not the whole counsel of God, that saves. The ability to recite and define every divine attribute only proves you have a good memory. It doesn't say anything about the state of your soul. Take the case of a man who came to Christ and began to attend a church I once pastored. Early in his Christian life he told me he could believe in Jesus, but he couldn't accept the Bible. For him it was still a collection of folk stories, legends, and wishful thinking, riddled with error. Yet his conversion was undeniably real.

I didn't immediately push him to subscribe to a fully developed doctrine of revelation, inspiration, and inerrancy. After all, we don't expect two-year-olds to understand calculus. God, in His grace, was willing to wait for this earnest believer to grow enough to understand how important the Bible really is—and he did. My friend's salvation was as real as it gets, but his spiritual growth took time and teaching.

God granted the disciples at Ephesus the same grace, and He sent Paul to bring them into a knowledge of the whole truth of the Gospel.

John the Baptist had prophesied that the Coming One would baptize with the Holy Spirit and with fire. If they knew John's baptism, I can't believe they didn't know that promise or didn't know about the One who would fulfill it. What they probably knew was that judgment was coming and that Jesus had come to save them from judgment. What they probably didn't know was the kind of life God had in store for those who accepted Jesus.

The thief on the cross was promised a place in Christ's kingdom and all he knew of Jesus he got by observing Him die by his side. These believers knew more than that.

Q **uestion 98** How could Paul say there shouldn't be any tongues without interpretation (1 Corinthians 14:27–28) when on the Day of Pentecost all the disciples spoke in tongues and the crowd understood them as if they were speaking in their own language (Acts 2:4)?

Most people look at Pentecost in one of two ways. Some remember it as they remember the landing of the Pilgrims at

Plymouth Rock or the discovery of the New World. Celebrated and memorialized, it remains a long-ago day frozen forever in time. For others, it is not just a part of biblical history. It's a part of their personal history. The mere words "the second chapter of Acts" bring knowing nods and smiles of understanding. There's no mystery here. They know just what it was like.

Neither approach sees the whole picture. One gives theological assent to the historical reality of the Holy Spirit, while almost ignoring the Spirit's presence today. The other focuses on present reality, evidenced in individual personal experiences, while ignoring the whole sweep of history.

It's not enough just to celebrate the birth of the church with the coming of the Holy Spirit on Pentecost. The church must live in the power of that same Spirit today. Nor is it accurate to read the particulars of Acts 2 into any subsequent event.

The birth of the church is an historical fact leading to a present reality, but the present reality draws its meaning from that single historical fact. We have to look back into the original significance of Pentecost to understand that meaning.

First, let's get it clear that the events of Pentecost were unique. There is only one Pentecost. It will not be repeated.

Let's also get it clear that Pentecost is not unique because the Holy Spirit came for the first time on that day. Jesus' statement in Acts 1:8 did not mean that the Holy Spirit would be coming on them for the first time. He had already given the Holy Spirit to His disciples right after the resurrection (John 20:22). What He meant was that on that day the Holy Spirit would anoint them with the power to become the body of Christ active in the world. Pentecost is unique because, until then, believers had not been empowered to be the church.

Ten days earlier Jesus had told His disciples to return to Jerusalem and wait for the gift God had in store for them. That gift was the baptism of the Holy Spirit. The wind, fire, and tongues were signs that the power Jesus had promised was theirs.

The word "baptized" implies an immersion in something. The classical Greek writers talked about warriors baptizing their swords in wine. This makes a good argument for baptism by immersion, but in this instance it makes a better argument for what Jesus meant.

According to John the disciples had received the Holy Spirit between the resurrection and the Ascension; but the manifestation and power of that gift were yet to come. On Pentecost they would be immersed in the Spirit of God in a way they had never known before.

This raises another question, however. Was this a second work of grace? (That is, as the term is generally understood, did the disciples only receive the Holy Spirit after they had gotten their hearts right and emptied themselves of all hindrances to becoming a suitable dwelling place for the Holy Spirit?) Did Jesus send the disciples back to Jerusalem to become spiritually ready for the power before He sent it?

No. The disciples had to wait because God wasn't ready to demonstrate His power, not because they weren't ready to receive it.

Jesus didn't commmand His disciples, or us, to tarry until their hearts were right so the Spirit could come. After all, the simple meaning of the term grace is "unmerited favor." So if we somehow have to get our hearts right, it's hardly grace at all, is it?

So why the delay?

God chose the Day of Pentecost for the birth of the church for the same reason He chose Passover for the crucifixion—because of the meaning it held for the Jewish people.

Most Christians are familiar enough with Passover to recognize why it was the chosen day for the crucifixion. Jesus is prefigured in the perfect Passover lamb whose blood turned the angel of death away from the homes of the Israelite slaves in Egypt. But few Christians know enough about Pentecost to fathom the marvelous message God had in store for the world on that second select day.

Pentecost was one of the three great pilgrim feasts in Judaism. These feasts—Passover, Pentecost, and Tabernacles—were unique in that they required all men to be present at the temple. Hence the name "pilgrim." This also explains why there were great crowds from all over the Roman Empire in Jerusalem on the occasions of Passover and Pentecost described in the New Testament.

Pentecost comes from the Greek word for "fiftieth," since the date for the festival was fifty days from the Passover Sabbath. It was an agricultural festival, celebrating the completion of the harvest. Fifty days earlier, during the Feast of Unleavened Bread, they had offered God the first sheaves of barley. At the end of the season they offered two loaves of leavened bread. This marked the beginning of the offering of firstfruits.

Think of the events of Acts 2 and you'll see why God chose this day for the birth of the church in the power of the Holy Spirit.

On Pentecost Jews from all over the known world were gathered at Jerusalem to celebrate the goodness of God in the harvest; then God, in the person of the Holy Spirit, appeared to them to begin the new celebration of even greater firstfruits.

Gathered from every nation, these pilgrims were themselves the first of God's harvest. As the church was born, it was born in the hearts of people who would take the Gospel of Jesus back to villages and cities around their world. In them was planted the seed of the modern missions movement.

But if the purpose of Pentecost was to make people think of the harvest, why did God use tongues as His sign?

Because the church was to reverse the alienation that had been the lot of humanity since Adam—not only from God, but from one another as well. Nowhere in the Bible is that alienation seen as clearly as in Genesis 11: the story of the Tower of Babel. Speaking gibberish, unable to communicate, terrified at the spectacle of friends and neighbors turned into grunting, babbling beasts, humanity scattered into its thousand warring camps.

But when men spoke in their strange tongues on Pentecost, listeners heard not gibberish but the Gospel of Jesus Christ, and each heard it in his own language.

This new union in Christ was one in which there was neither Jew nor Greek, neither slave nor free, neither male nor female. And the gift of tongues that so dramatically marked the birth of the church was the sign God used to demonstrate that in Christ the dividing wall of hostility was at last destroyed forever

Long before we ever thought of the idea of a global village, God knew the church had to be built for export, living stones from all the earth.

It was to be a body that in spite of linguistic, social, ethnic, and sexual divisions would span the globe in the unity of the Spirit.

uestion 99   Paul used different lists of spiritual gifts. Why did he do that and does it mean that some gifts are not for today (1 Corinthians 12:7–11; Ephesians 4:7–13; Romans 12:1–9; 1 Corinthians 13:8)?

ROMANS	1 CORINTHIANS	EPHESIANS
	Apostles	Apostles
Prophesying	Prophecy	Prophets
Teaching	Teachers	Teachers
		Evangelists
Serving		
Encouraging		Pastors
Contributing to needs of others	Able to help others	
Leadership	Administration	
Mercy		
	Speak with Wisdom	
	Speak with knowledge	
	Faith	
	Healing	
	Miraculous Powers	
	Distinguish between spirits	
	Tongues	
	Interpretation	

Look at the above comparison list of spiritual gifts. At first glance they seem to have little in common. In Romans Paul lists seven gifts; in 1 Corinthians 12 he talks about nine gifts in one place and eight in another (combined here); and in Ephesians he gives only five.

By combining gifts from the three sources you come up with a total of seventeen different gifts. Six gifts are mentioned at least twice: prophecy, teaching, apostleship, pastoring, helps, administration. And prophecy and teaching are mentioned in all three of Paul's lists.

Why are the lists so different?

Paul obviously had a reason for the diversity of his lists, and I suggest that the significance can be found in the people he was writing to rather than in the gifts themselves.

In Romans, where he has just spent three chapters talking about the place of the Jew in God's plan and the relationship of the Gentile believer to the Jewish believer, Paul is concerned with the peaceful coexistence of two potentially hostile segments of the church. To them he wrote about (emphasized) gifts of serving, encouraging, contributing to the needs of others, leadership, and mercy because those were the gifts they needed to see in practice among them

The church at Corinth had a problem with spiritual pride and placed an excessive emphasis on a type of self-centered giftedness. It was a church where everyone seemed to compete over the quality and quantity of their gifts. Paul wrote to this church about the need to channel an enthusiasm that was running away with them and about the particular gifts that were dividing them. How better to deal with the problem than to talk about the gifts involved and their need for the additional gifts of wisdom, knowledge, faith, interpretation, and the ability to distinguish between spirits. And, of course, to insist that all the gifts be exercised for the benefit of the church at large.

Ephesians is a general letter to churches in Asia Minor. It was a circular, or, as we'd say today, a form letter. This is why it doesn't reflect a specific set of church problems and why it reflects a heavenly, triumphal view of the church. If Ephesians is a general letter about "the" church and not just a church, then it makes sense that Paul mentions those gifts that are essential for church life everywhere. The five gifts in Ephesians are those most essential for preparing the members of the church for the work of ministry.

Does this imply that some of the gifts were exclusive to the early church? Some people make a case for this, based on the verb forms in 1 Corinthians 13:8, claiming that the Second Coming will abolish prophecy and knowledge but that tongues will already have disappeared somewhere along the way.

The only reason for this suggestion is to deny the continuation of the gift of tongues beyond the apostolic age. But Paul's argument is quite clear: Love will never cease, but the time will come when all the gifts the Corinthians valued so highly will have lost their purpose.

Some use the argument of history against the presence of tongues today. Tongues, they say, were very prominent in the apostolic church. But they began to diminish toward the end of the first century, and by the fourth century were all but gone. Only fringe groups continued to speak in tongues after that. Therefore, tongues were intended to die with the apostles.

I'll agree with this pattern of history. But so what? Personal piety also tended to diminish at certain periods of history, and sound theology was almost dead during the latter years of the middle ages. Does that mean personal piety and sound theology were only intended for the apostolic age?

None of the many arguments proposed to deny the validity of the modern Pentecostal/charismatic experience would convince anyone who doesn't already agree that the modern experience is invalid.

However, this brings us to another matter raised by these passages. If tongues are still a valid gift today, does that mean they serve as a sign of baptism in the Holy Spirit?

They can't be—because they are too easily counterfeited. This is at the root of Paul's problem with the Corinthian church.

The Corinthians believers, who were relatively new Christians from backgrounds hardly conducive to piety, sobriety, or orthodoxy, had been swept up in a false assessment of the gifts of the Spirit. Paul knew it was a problem because he had two sources of information.

First, a delegation of believers had come to him with facts about church life there (1 Corinthians 1:11; 5:1; 6:1); and second, he had a letter from the Corinthians themselves in hand in which the question was raised (1 Corinthians 7:1).

The first three verses of 1 Corinthians 12 lay out the nature of the problem, although we're never told its specifics. We can only deduce those from the book itself, but there are some strong clues. The church had come under the influence of teachers with tendencies toward the Gnostic heresy, a syncretistic, philosophical religion which believed there was a small, elite group that had received supernatural knowledge from God. This is why Paul wrote so much about knowledge and wisdom in the first few chapters.

The church was divided over teachers and the members were even taking one another to court with lawsuits. There was a dispute over the resurrection and another over eating meat offered to idols. Sexual immorality also seemed to be a real problem. These are the people whom Paul said were too immature to treat as spiritual. But they are also the people whose dispute over their experience of spiritual gifts gives us the only in-depth discussion of the topic in the New Testament.

The problem in Corinth was that these were people who were barely removed from paganism and yet were spiritually proud. They were used to religions that manifested some elite, ecstatic supernatural experience. (anthropologists have observed that most of the world's religions recognize some sort of control by the supernatural world that, among other things, leads to speaking in tongues) Yet in their ecstasy some of the Corinthian believers were saying and doing things that simply did not glorify the Lord. That Paul had to begin the discussion at all rests on the fact that there were signs and wonders taking place at Corinth that were not the result of the working of the Holy Spirit.

Interestingly enough, there's one spiritual gift Paul mentioned in his catalog in chapter 12 that is all but ignored today, and that is the gift that allows a person to discern the spiritual source of signs and wonders.

I've talked with missionaries who have seen spectacular examples of demonic activity where people do such things as levitate. One of my missionary friends calls this sort of thing "pre-rapture flight." These people are acting under the power of a spirit all right—the power of "a" spirit, not "the" Spirit.

If we believe the Lord is active in the world today through the power of the Spirit, we need to take Paul's teaching on the discernment of spirits much more seriously. It's a tragic situation when the church of Jesus Christ, claiming direct knowledge from the Spirit and manifestations of power, disregards the very clear biblical warning that there's more than one spirit that can provide religious experiences.

I suspect there will always be Christians who fear the loss of control and decorum that sometimes comes when the Spirit moves. For them nothing can make the more spectacular gifts of the Spirit, such as tongues, palatable.

I also suspect that there is a much larger group of noncharismatic believers who are repelled because the Lord gets the credit, or blame, for everything that comes down the pike brandishing the label "miracle."

Paul told us to assess the spirits carefully and exercise the gift of discerning which spirit was responsible for each dramatic act. As long as believers are willing to take the gift without examining the giver, the Holy Spirit will be held in disrepute by sober Christians for whom God is not the author of disorder but of peace (14:33).

Question 100   If the Bible teaches that drinking is a sin, why did Jesus turn water into wine, and why did Paul tell Timothy to drink wine for his stomach? Was it alchoholic wine (John 2:1–11; 1 Timothy 5:23)?

I've read all the arguments about unfermented grape juice and how fermentation doesn't take place naturally in the climate of Palestine, and I have to tell you—they're based more on wishful thinking than on linguistic study or scientific understanding. Jesus turned the water into real wine.

I know this makes some believers nervous. I know it makes some hostile. "How can I counsel alcoholics not to drink if you're telling them drinking isn't a sin?" they ask.

I wish the Bible did teach that drinking is a sin, but it doesn't. It contains numerous warnings against the abuse of alcohol, but nowhere does it say it's a sin. And we are not free to make the Bible say what it doesn't say just to make our decisions easier. For me there's a very profound principle at work here.

Principle 37   Don't bend and twist the meaning of the biblical text to avoid an unpleasant conclusion.

If we convolute the meaning of a text to avoid a conclusion that we find unpleasant, we might as well give up the doctrine of inerrancy. If we reject the clear meaning for an interpretation that is more palatable, we render such a doctrine irrelevant.

We have good reason, of course, for our strong feelings about alcohol. In our day alcohol is used as a means to an end. The societal pressure to drink to excess is monumental. It's as old as time: "Eat, drink, and be merry, for tomorrow you die." Every year the cost in dollars and lives lost to alcohol is in the billions, if you can put a price on life. Lost work hours or non-productive hours cost our economy more millions.

Christians in my situation have an even stronger reason for avoiding alcohol. I'm the son of an alcoholic, which means that if I were to drink, my odds of becoming an alcoholic would drop from one in ten to one in two. It's not worth the risk.

But despite all this, the Bible does not say that the drinking of alcohol is a sin.

Let's look at the evidence.

There are two main words used for wine in the Bible: *yayin* (YAH-yin) in Hebrew and *oinos* (WEE-noss) in Greek. Both refer to an intoxicating beverage.

The word *wine* occurs 214 times in the NIV. The word *yayin* is used 131 times in the Hebrew of the Old Testament, and *oinos* 33 times in the Greek of the New. That leaves only 58 places in all 66 books where these two words are not used.

Some argue that the next most common word (*tirosh*), translated new wine, is the non-alcoholic variety Jesus made. Unfortunately, it's a Hebrew word and isn't even used in John. What's more, in the two places in the Old Testament where context gives any indication of its nature, it is clearly intoxicating.

Joel 1:5 says:

> Wake up you drunkards, and weep!
>   Wail, all you drinkers of wine;
> wail because of the wine,
>   for it has been snatched from your lips.

When Hosea uses the word, he mentions it in connection with prostitution and old wine. If new wine really meant grape juice, would the prophet place it in that kind of company?

Did the overseer at the banquet think mere grape juice would dull the wedding guests' taste buds? Did Paul warn against overindulgence in grape juice (Ephesians 5:18)? Did Noah drink too much grape juice (Genesis 9:21)? Is grape juice a mocker (Proverbs 20:1)? Did Jeremiah liken himself to a man overtaken by grape juice (Jeremiah 23:9)?

In the New Testament passage about Jesus putting wine in new wineskins, translators have translated *oinos* as "new wine." Unfortunately for the argument, wine was put into the skins after the first stage of fermentation had already taken place.

The other references contain no contextual clues to what the word means. They are passages about the promise of plenty in Canaan (Deuteronomy 7:13), offering of produce (Deuteronomy 14:23; 18:4), or the cutting off of blessing (Isaiah 24:7; Joel 1:10).

People assume that new wine must be unfermented, but that isn't necessarily so. Fermentation requires only sugar, some micro-organisms, and time. The sugar is in the grape, the yeasts that produce fermentation cling to the skins of the grape, and the time begins the minute the skin is broken and the two are brought together. It can happen with grapes still on the vine.

In unrefrigerated liquids the process begins within hours and can produce noticeable alcoholic content in a very short time. From a book on wine-making I learned that "new" wine can be put into bottles after the second day. By that time it's already fermented.

The strength of wine is determined by the sugar content of the fruit used to make it. In biblical times, wine had a practical alcohol content of 10–11 percent. A higher alcohol content would have killed the micro-organisms that make the process possible. When rainfall was sparse, the alcohol content declined. Today's wines have alcohol added to increase their kick. That wasn't possible in biblical times.

What's more, biblical wine was often watered down. Or, more precisely, their water was "wined" down. As in many places in the world today, water was unsafe. People may not have known about bacteria and viruses, but they made good, practical observations and they understood the dangers of untreated water. The alcohol in the wine served as a very good disinfectant in water, and the water rendered the wine much less potent.

In most wine the fermentation process continued until the wine became vinegar. Without refrigeration or an underground wine cellar, it couldn't be stopped. This was the same bitter stuff that Roman soldiers received as part of their daily ration and that Roman soldiers offered Jesus on the cross.

Paul counseled Timothy to take some wine for his stomach's sake. He probably knew that plain water often led to perpetual stomach upset. The wine would probably have been the watered wine that could be drunk without much danger of intoxication or addiction but which rendered the water safe.

This points to a situation in which wine played a very different role in the culture than it does today. Those of us who enjoy the luxury of a consistently wholesome water supply should be careful in our assessments of the "sin" involved in the use of wine in biblical times. But it isn't enough to be able to demonstrate that the wine of the Bible was alcoholic. We also need to know why Jesus made 120 gallons of the stuff. Even as disinfectant, that seems excessive.

Let's look at John 2:1–11 and see what was involved in this, Jesus' first miracle. John's gospel records only seven miracles, and each was a *sign*. We tend to disregard the sign element in Jesus' miracles in John and the other Gospels as well. We usually think of miracles as a display of power, which diminishes our understanding of these seven signs. More than demonstrations of power, each miracle was a mighty parable pointing to the nature and purpose of Christ.

John is the most mature of the Gospels, written around A.D. 90. Christ and the nature of the gospel had been discussed and clarified for decades when John wrote. Therefore, his gospel is the most sophisticated of the four, and we should ask more sophisticated theological questions of the text than "Was the wine alcoholic?"

John said, "This, the first of his miraculous signs, Jesus performed in Cana of Galilee. He thus revealed his glory, and his disciples put their faith in him" (v. 11).

This was no garden variety display of power Jesus performed to humor his mother. John placed it at the beginning of a line that runs through five subsequent miracles, climaxing in the raising of Lazarus from the dead.

The seven signs each point to Christ as the replacement of some aspect of the old religious ways. How is that so in the miracle at Cana?

Jesus called for the containers that held water used in the rite of purification. Instead of water, He filled them with wine. Some see that as a shift from the external purification of washings to the internal purification of regeneration through the Holy Spirit. At the very least, Jesus showed His disciples that the old was passing away. It wasn't just the wonder of it that won them to belief. It was the sign that Jesus, the Messiah, had come to fill them with the new wine of the Spirit.

The reason for so much wine was not to provide for the excessive drunkenness of a wedding crowd, but to demonstrate, in the same way He did by multiplying the loaves and fishes, that the promised bounty of the age of the Messiah had come (Amos 9:13–14; Jeremiah 31:12).

 uestion 101   Didn't Paul say everything was lawful for the Christian? If so, isn't it legalistic to judge other believers for things they've done if the Lord doesn't convict them (1 Corinthians 6:12)?

Legalism has been a curse among the religious since before the Pharisees. We need to be on guard that legalism doesn't define our practice of the Christian faith, but first we need to know what legalism is and isn't.

Trying to live a godly life is *not* legalistic. As we attempt to fit our faith into the world, we sometimes find things we must abstain from. It's not legalistic for me, for example, to abstain from the recreational use of mood altering drugs. It is one example of my understanding of what it means to live a holy life before the Lord.

Recognizing when another Christian slips into a style of life that violates clear biblical commands and prohibitions is *not* legalistic. The one who's been caught by sin needs our concern and our correction (Galatians 6:1–2). It's not legalistic to give it.

Going to Scripture to find God's way for our lives is *not* legalistic.

Trying to win God's favor by adopting and living by a set of rules carried out without love *is* legalistic. Legalists lick their chops at the chance to condemn sin in another. The sense of hurt that comes when a loved one falls is seldom felt by the legalist.

The difference in attitude can be characterized this way.

If a brother in Christ falls, we recognize that we are capable of the same sin. If we live by godly precepts we respond with sorrow and a powerful desire to see him brought back into fellowship with the Lord and His church.

If we live by the codes of legalism, we respond with outrage, because our law is more important than the people who break it. Unable to see ourselves in the place of the fallen one, we point an accusing finger and demand the person's removal to avoid contamination.

Paul railed against the legalism, and he was not soft on sin. His letters are filled with help for believers who had fallen into sin. It wasn't just the Corinthians, it was everybody. Paul might not have written more than a handful of letters if there hadn't been so many sinners in his churches.

His dealing with them, though, was instructive. He pointed first to their shared faith in Christ and the life their faith called them to live. Then he called them back to living it.

The man who refused to acknowledge his sin of living with his mother-in-law was treated sternly, but notice the purpose for the harsh treatment: "so that the sinful nature may be destroyed and his spirit saved on the day of the Lord" (1 Corinthians 5:5). The punishment was to be redemptive.

Was Paul afraid to tell people what was right and what was wrong? No.

Would the man who wrote so extensively to correct errors in thought and behavior have written, "All things are lawful"? No.

But the Corinthians would have. Remember the letter Paul quoted from? Remember the delegation from Chloe's household? They both contained serious questions about the lifestyle and teaching of various factions at Corinth.

One of those factions shouted slogans to prove they could live any way they chose. "All things are lawful" (1 Corinthians

6:12). "Food for the stomach, the stomach for food" (1 Corinthians 6:13).

Sounds contemporary, doesn't it? This faction seemed to wave these slogans like red flags of revolution, declaring their freedom from the law. Paul quoted the sayings, but didn't agree with them. Paul wasn't a bull. He didn't paw and snort and bellow. He didn't attack blindly. Doing so would have destroyed other believers. He could have said, "That is the dumbest slogan I ever heard." Instead, he qualified it.

"Maybe so," he said, "but certainly not everything is useful."

"Maybe so," he continued, "but you wouldn't want to become the slave of any of these things you're using to flaunt your freedom. Yes, food was made to fill the stomach, and the stomach was made to receive the food. But you must remember that these are temporary." Here's a lesson for all of us. Paul knew he could catch more flies with honey than vinegar. He began his response tactfully and gently. It didn't take long for him to get at the heart of the matter, though.

The Corinthians weren't really talking about food at all. They were talking, in a way that's painfully reminiscent of the sexual revolution of the sixties, about continuing the immorality they had practiced before they knew Christ. Paul zeroed in on sexual immorality almost immediately.

Was he legalistic about it?

No. He simply called it sin and condemned it as unworthy of one who had become a new creation in Christ.

Today, as in Paul's day, we need to be brought back to the Bible and reminded that our salvation puts us under obligation to our Savior. We are, after all, not our own. We've been bought, and what a price was paid for us. To say that people bought by the blood of Christ should live up to the price paid for them is the furthest thing from legalism.

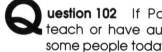 **uestion 102** If Paul wouldn't let women teach or have authority over men, why do some people today want to ordain women (1 Timothy 2:11–14)?

Sometimes I wish the translators had left this passage in the original Greek—not because I'd like to see it eradicated from our consciousness, but because translation masks the difficulty of the text.

As mentioned elsewhere in this book, we should not use problem passages to formulate doctrine unless that doctrine is supported elsewhere in Scripture.

Well, this is a problem passage and then some—not just because the issues it raises are hot in today's world, but because the language of the passage is remarkably obscure.

Beginning with Paul's statement that he doesn't permit a woman to teach, we ask: Why did he say it that way? Why didn't he just use the imperative and prohibit women from teaching? And if he didn't permit women to teach, what can we make of the role of Priscilla in instructing Apollos (Acts 18:26)?

A growing number of evangelical scholars accepts the idea that Paul was stating his personal custom rather than putting the church under a straightforward prohibition. It was the custom, not the law, in other words.

What about a woman learning in quietness and full submission?

The word translated *quietness* is rare in the New Testament. It was used in only two other places: Acts 22:2 and 2 Thessalonians 3:12. In Acts, the mob in the temple court that had been stirred up against Paul became very *quiet* when they heard him speak to them in their own language. In 2 Thessalonians Paul ordered a group of busybodies who were stirring up the congregation to *settle down* and get back to work.

Both examples came from situations where a group of people had been involved in some disorderly conduct and quietness was seen as the opposite of their undesirable activity.

This doesn't prove anything, but consider this: we're dealing with a word that's used only three times in the New Testament, and two of those times it describes the quietness that follows disorder. Without evidence to the contrary, we expect it to have that same meaning in the third. Therefore, I understand it to refer to some kind of furor in the church that these women were causing or participating in.

Then there's "full submission."

I'm not sure it meant the same thing for Paul that it means for us. Our conception of submission is to surrender to someone stronger and say "uncle." Little boys who inflict pain on other little boys today probably don't require that particular word, but they probably require something like it. When I was young I endured all sorts of unpleasantness to avoid saying *uncle.*

Submission was shameful. It denoted weakness and the admission that someone else was stronger than I. No American raised on the Horatio Alger myth of rugged individualism, that we all could lift ourselves by our own bootstraps, would ever willingly submit to anything or anyone.

But Paul willingly submitted himself to Christ, becoming His bond servant, and so do we. Without that kind of submission, we can't come to Christ. For the Christian, submission is a word that has to take on a different meaning. It's not grovelling with our faces in the dirt and a bully sitting on our backs and twisting our arms. To submit to Christ is a noble thing, and to be in submission, in that context, is ennobling.

Paul used a relatively rare word. It appears only in Paul's letters, and then only four times.

In 2 Corinthians 9:13, Paul praised the Corinthians for the "*obedience* that accompanies your confession."

He asserted that when the Judaizers attempted to have Titus circumcised, he "did not *give in* to them for a moment. . ." (Galatians 2:5).

One of the qualifications for "overseers" in the church was that "his children *obey* him with proper respect" (1 Timothy 3:4).

The larger family of words from which this noun comes has a couple of threads running through it: law and order, often military order. The context usually includes one or both of those senses.

We are to *submit* to governing authorities (Romans 13:5). Jesus was *obedient* to His parents (Luke 2:51). The church is to *submit* to Christ (Ephesians 5:24). The Corinthians were asked to *submit* to people like Stephanas and his household (1 Corinthians 16:16).

In all these examples, and others I could cite, the emphasis was on maintaining order by submitting to some person or authority.

Paul went on to say he didn't permit women to teach or "have authority (*authentein* [Awe-then-tane]) over a man."

This is the only place in the New Testament where *authentein* is used. This is important for two reasons. First, there's another perfectly good word (*exousia* [ex-OO-see-ah]) that means authority. It's the word we might expect in a sentence like this. Paul must have had a very good reason to use a rare word when a common one was available. Second, *authentein* isn't used anywhere else in Scripture, so we have no other contexts to verify its meaning, so any translation or comment on the word must be tentative.

A. T. Robertson, one of the great American Christian New Testament scholars of this century, defined *authentein* as a compound word meaning "self-doer, master, autocrat." He also suggested that the verb form means "domineer." If he was right, simple authority is a somewhat misleading translation.

Putting all this uncertainty together in two verses, we can only go so far toward understanding them by studying the verses themselves. It does seem, however, that the verse is saying something slightly different than we usually understand.

Here's my understanding of the text. Paul told the women in the church to learn with a spirit quieted from turmoil. They were to recognize that there was an order into which they should fit. A part of that order was that Paul did not allow women to teach nor to play the autocrat over men in the church.

The question that comes to mind immediately is whether or not this was an order Paul intended to impose on the church for all time, or a practice he instituted because of conditions the church had to deal with in the first century.

Paul obviously let Pricilla teach (Romans 16:3, Acts 18:26). Nothing in these verses implies that her husband, Aquila, invited people home and Priscilla made coffee and cookies while he did the teaching. And 1 Corinthians 11:5, by saying that women should pray and prophesy *with their heads covered,* implies that women will be involved in prayer and prophecy.

When Paul urged Euodia and Syntyche to agree, he did not address them as bickering old women who were disrupting the church with their disagreements. It was as women who had "contended at my side in the cause of the gospel" (Philippians 4:3). Does that mean they washed the table cloth after communion?

Paul was the man who said there is neither male nor female in Christ (Galatians 3:28). If his statement of principle negates the impact of gender on those in the kingdom, and if Paul worked side by side with women in the defense of the faith, what unspoken conditions might have existed to make him tell women to learn in silence and prohibit them from teaching?

Since this apparently was a prohibition Paul practiced in all his churches, the condition wasn't simply local. It must have been a local expression of a widespread condition or set of conditions.

One of these conditions might have been a widespread cultural acceptance of women as prophetesses and rejection of women as teachers. Both were common in the Greek world. Women were generally involved in pagan prophecies, but there was a general hostility to women as teachers.

There was also a very nasty element in women's religious experience in the Greco-Roman world. Their devotion to their particular gods was accompanied by unbelievable acts of violence, sex-role reversals, ecstatic cries during worship, and other elements that made their religious experience seem strange and repellent to men.

Paul stated a principle that I think helps us understand why he might have forbidden women in general from full participation in public worship and teaching. He claimed to have become a slave to all people in order to win some of them (1 Corinthians 9:19). In other words, he customized his practice to avoid hostility so he could present the gospel more effectively.

In a world where religious women are given to violence, dominance, and shrieks, wouldn't it be wise to restrict women's participation in areas that would confuse the basic issues of the gospel? Using the principle Paul stated, it makes sense, in a world where women were accepted as prophets, to permit prophecy. And in a world where women were not accepted as teachers, it makes sense to restrict them from teaching. If, on the other hand, the prohibitions of 1 Timothy 2:11–12 are universal, it's inconsistent for modern Christian men to pray without raising their hands and for Christian women to braid their hair or wear jewelry and expensive clothes.

If they are universal, why don't we require young widows to marry and organize a welfare role for widows over sixty? Are Christian slaves supposed to serve with diligence today as in the first century? Since Paul proposes guidelines for the conduct of slaves, does that mean he affirms slavery as an institution?

In other words, is the exclusion of women from teaching or "having authority" over men different from the other instructions Paul gave Timothy? It is both inconsistent and hypocritical to insist on one while ignoring the other.

In practice, the American church would not function without women. As a pastor my experience has been that men make decisions, but nine times out of ten women do the work. I've been awed by the spiritual insights and biblical literacy of women with whom I've studied and served. I've seen women in ministry whose gifts far exceeded their husbands'. From a purely pragmatic point of view, why would the Holy Spirit give a woman a gift if He didn't intend her to use it?

As is the case with most people who write about these verses, I've decided that one set of biblical information ranks above another set. My understanding of 1 Timothy 2:11–12 is controlled by my understanding of Galatians 3:28.

Others see Galatians 3:28 as an ideal formulation that will not prevail until the final realization of Christ's rule on earth. For them, 1 Timothy formulates a rule that applies until then.

P rinciple 38   Don't formulate doctrine on the basis of problem passages.

There is probably no ultimate resolution to the debate, this side of the Second Coming. But the one principle I come back to is this: *Don't formulate doctrine on the basis of problem passages.* Ample biblical evidence argues that there is indeed no male nor female in Christ when a woman has gifts and is in a situation where those gifts are needed.

We're faced with two alternatives here. On the basis of a limited number of texts, all ambiguous in one way or another, we have to decide whether it's right for women to minister. On the evidence of Scripture, women have ministered. On the evidence of church history, women have ministered. On the evidence of most people's personal experience, women have ministered.

On the basis of my understanding of the text, and the evidence of the working of the church over time, it would be a serious mistake to deny the validity of all that ministry.

Should women be ordained?

Why not?

Ordination is a human act affirming the church's identification of an individual's giftedness and calling. In a world where women can run major corporations, there's no cultural reason not to recognize their calling and giftedness in ministry. And I cannot see how this passage forbids it.

Q **uestion 103**   Paul said women should be subject to their husbands. What does that mean (Ephesians 5:22–33)?

The question begins in verse 22, but the text begins in verse 21. Before Paul said women should be subject to their husbands, he told husbands and wives they should be subject to one another.

I suggest that we look at that command as the setting for the other. The order of mutual submission seen here echoes throughout the New Testament. Jesus' emphasis on servanthood, on taking the lower place, of meekness, and of loving our neighbors as ourselves all teach submission. When Jesus says those things, no one makes them gender specific.

Both men and women are to be servants. They are to respond to others with gentleness. They are to forsake leading positions in favor of subordinate ones. They are to love their neighbors as themselves. None of those requires a particular set of genes or hormones. The commands are binding on all believers.

In that context we shouldn't be surprised that Paul told husbands and wives to submit to one another. That's yesterday's news. Any believer who knew the sayings of Jesus should have known that. Marriage wouldn't negate any of it.

Why did Paul command women to submit when he didn't do the same for men?

I suspect it has to do with the tendencies of humanity since Adam blamed Eve for his sin. The cryptic statement of God in Genesis 3:16 hints at those tendencies. He said to Eve, "Your desire will be for your husband and he will rule over you."

A lot of nonsense has been written about that sentence in Genesis, but let me review what I think is being said there.

Your desire will be isn't simply the normal physical desire of a woman for her husband. It's the same expression used of sin crouching at the door (Genesis 4:7). Sin's desire is to overpower, not love.

The *Theological Dictionary of the Old Testament* defines the word *desire* in Genesis 4 as "hungering, intent upon."

The Hebrew phrasing of Genesis 4:7 is so like that of 3:16*b* that it can't be coincidental. The meaning of both sentences is somewhat obscure, but they both imply conflict.

Since Genesis 3 describes God's statement of the consequences of the Fall, the condition of male domination is the result of sin, not the plan of God.

The mutual subjection principle stated by Paul in Ephesians 5:21 is yet another reversal of the effects of sin among people of the Lord.

The condition that has brought disharmony, divorce, and division into countless homes since the beginning is set aside by the work of Christ in making us new creatures.

What follows corresponds to what I think Genesis 3:16*b* says about the hostility between the sexes. Paul said woman, whose condition since the fall has been to be *intent upon* or *hungering* for her husband, is now to learn to submit to him, as to the Lord.

Paul's illustration looks back to the beginning, too. Those who see this as a statement of a divinely instituted hierarchy within the home and the church point to the word *head* to prove that men will have authority over their wives. Here again, the use of a word in Greek does not correspond well to our use of a similar word in English.

For us, head means authority. But Greek has a very common word for authority that Paul used elsewhere, but not here. Here he chose a word that Jewish scholars, who translated the Old Testament into Greek a couple of hundred years earlier, rejected as a proper translation of the Hebrew for *authority*.

Paul used the word head in chapter 4, and by comparing the two usages we may learn something about what it means in chapter 5.

Paul started chapter 4 by telling the recipients of his letter to be humble, gentle, and patient, bearing with one another in love (Ephesians 4:1–2).

In other words, he started a section on unity in the church with a set of instructions that bear a striking resemblance to the intent of the submit to one another out of reverence for Christ statement.

Chapter 4 describes the unity of the body in terms of giftedness which will lead to growth "into him who is the head, that is Christ" (4:15). Here, Christ is not described as the authority over the church but as both the source (v. 16) and the goal (v. 15) of Christian growth. On this basis, Paul tells the Ephesians how they should live as His body in the world (4:17–5:20).

The theme of the passage is summarized in the saying: "For you were once darkness, but now you are light in the Lord. Live as children of light (for the fruit of the light consists in all goodness, righteousness, and truth) and find out what pleases the Lord" (Ephesians 5:8–10).

In verse 22, the focus shifts to the Christian home, with verse 21 serving as a summary of what's gone before and an overarching principle for what follows.

As is so often the case, Paul goes back to the Old Testament to make his case. For women, whose darkness includes the desire to master their husbands, submission is the command. If the husband is the head, as Christ is head of the church, the analogy has nothing to do with power. How can mutually submissive people exercise power within their relationship?

According to Genesis, woman had her origin in man, just as the church had its origin in Christ. Just as the church is Christ's body, Adam's response to Eve was to call her "bone of my bone, flesh of my flesh."

The focus of the wife's submission in this setting is the recovery of the relationship that existed before the Fall, a relationship so selfless and unself-conscious that the man and woman were naked before one another without shame. They were one in spirit, so their bodies were not yet a source of shame.

For husbands, whose desire will be to domineer, the rule is to love the wife as Christ loved the church.

Paul used the categories familiar to his world to describe that love—feeding and caring for—but those categories are summed up under the heading of Christ's self-giving on behalf of the church.

It was no accident that Paul quoted Genesis 2:24. Becoming one flesh, a reference to physical union that pictures spiritual union, is the goal of the instructions in this section. If there's room here for dominance and subjection, I can't see it.

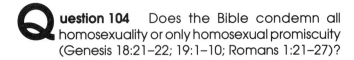

Q **uestion 104**   Does the Bible condemn all homosexuality or only homosexual promiscuity (Genesis 18:21–22; 19:1–10; Romans 1:21–27)?

A concerted effort in the last twenty years has tried to remove the Bible's condemnation of homosexuality. Psychiatrists no longer consider it a disorder. Society is increasingly concerned that "gays" be accorded every consideration. Politicians seem to feel their political lives are at stake unless they do everything in their power to protect people from discrimination over "sexual orientation."

Even people who profess faith in Christ have attempted to find some pro-homosexual way to interpret Scripture. We are reminded, rightly, that homosexual feelings are no more a barrier to faith in Christ than heterosexual feelings. Homosexual activity, wrong by its very nature if we believe Paul, is a barrier, just as promiscuous heterosexual behavior is.

In other words, I think it's important to recognize that homosexual people are no more repugnant to God than the rest of us. He saved homosexuals in Corinth, He can save homosexuals in Minneapolis, Dubuque, or Portland. But their salvation requires a turning away from things God calls sin. And homosexual behavior is one of those things.

The laws of the Old Testament and Paul's statements in Romans 1 assert this, and the story of Sodom and Gomorrah is a historical narrative that illustrates it.

Leviticus 18:22 says, rather bluntly, "Do not lie with a man as one lies with a woman; that is detestable."

This prohibition uses the same word as the prohibitions of the Ten Commandments. "Do not" may not sound as impressive as "Thou shalt not," but it means the same thing.

The verb has clear sexual connotations. Leah bought a night with Jacob with a bunch of mandrakes (Genesis 30:15–16). The verb *to lie with* is used three times in those two verses, and there's not much doubt about Leah's intent.

Exodus 22:19 places the penalty of death on anyone who "lies" with an animal. Deuteronomy 22:22 places the same penalty on a man who "lies" with another man's wife.

It would take some pretty creative interpretation to make Leviticus 18:22 say anything except that homosexual behavior is detestable.

First Corinthians 6:10 lists "homosexual offenders" among the wicked ones who will be excluded from God's kingdom. The Greek word here is quite specific in denoting a male homosexual.

Paul described the depths of depravity that are inevitable when humanity rejects God's sovereignty over it in Romans 1. Idolatry is the great sin, and homosexuality is its result. When people are willing to substitute the creature for the creator, there's no limit to where they might go.

This, by the way, is why I think homosexuality is so rampant today. We no longer measure ourselves against God's standard, but against our own. Unfortunately, our measure is warped and erratic, flexible beyond belief. No carpenter would build a house with such a rule, but we seem quite content to build a culture with it.

Homosexuality is so obviously unnatural that it makes a good example of the kind of life the God-rejecter will eventually come to. People throughout history have championed the perversion as natural and wholesome, but for Paul, the obvious facts of human biology argue against homosexual behavior (1:26–27).

Sodom and Gomorrah present a case study of Paul's contention. Even here, though, we need to be careful not to overstate our case. In the only divinely inspired statement of God's purpose for judging those sorrowful cities, homosexual behavior isn't even mentioned. Ezekiel 16:49–50 says: "Now this was the sin of your sister Sodom: She and her daughters were arrogant, overfed and unconcerned; they did not help the poor and needy. They were haughty and did detestable things before me."

On the basis of Romans 1 we might deduce that the idolatrous Canaanites, because they would not acknowledge God, were subject to every range of wickedness. We're burdened with a narrative of their homosexual lust, but that is only one of the full range of sins into which they had fallen. God's judgment was triggered by something else, but I don't think it's stretching too far to say that the detestable things they practiced included sodomy.

Recently, some have argued that the sin of Sodom was inhospitality. The men of Sodom were pretty inhospitable, all right. They called to Lot asking him to send out his visitors so they could have sex with them (Genesis 19:5), and then threatened Lot with worse (Genesis 19:9). But the text doesn't emphasize their inhospitality; it emphasizes their depravity.

It would be easy to give a ringing denunciation of the homosexual sins of Sodom and modern day homosexuals, but it might be more beneficial for Christians to be reminded that both are guilty of the ultimate sin: the rejection of God. We often recoil in horror from homosexuality, but we are quite at home with ease, arrogance, and plenty, which were included in God's assessment of Sodom. Homosexuality was a symptom of their deepest sin.

If some city in today's world were destroyed by brimstone from heaven, we might also be tempted to point our fingers in condemnation of a particularly noteworthy sin of which it might be guilty. But today, as then, sins like homosexual practice are the evidence of the deeper, root sin: rejection of God.

Part 4 ALL THREE

Most of the Bible isn't puzzling. The core truths of Scripture are repeated and repeated and then repeated again so that no reader seeking to know God can escape them.

MY MOTHER, THE PHILOSOPHER

I never thought of my mother as a philosopher when I was a child. She was just Mom. But now I'm realizing how much I learned about the world and my place in it at my mother's knee.

She taught me that a penny saved is a penny earned; that rolling stones gather no moss; that a bird in the hand is worth two in the bush; and, of course, that we can't have our cake and eat it too.

There were times, I admit, that I thought she was out to lunch without dessert when she talked about me not being able to have my cake and eat it. I initially rebelled at that notion because I was, and am, a committed cake eater. Some kids were born with silver spoons in their mouths. Not me. I had a stainless steel cake server.

But incipient preadolescent cake addiction aside, my little mind knew that I couldn't eat my cake until I had it. And when I finally learned that the proverb meant I couldn't keep it *and* eat it, I couldn't understand why anyone would want to keep a piece of cake.

Without realizing it, I was caught on the horns of the logicians law of non-contradiction. Whether the topic is cake or biblical revelation, the axiom that nothing can *be* and *not be* at the same time governs our lives.

As philosophers are fond of putting it, *a* cannot be *a* and non-*a* at the same time and in the same relationship.

Now that's a mouthful, or a mindful, even for a philosopher. Personally, I prefer "you can't have your cake and eat it too"; but no matter how we state it, we all operate on that basis every day of our lives.

On Friday nights we may ask, "Will it rain or will it be sunny this weekend?" We know we can't have it both ways. If we're on a jury, we must find a suspect innocent or guilty, never "sort of guilty but not really." The light in the garage is either on or it's off. The law of non-contradiction is an unseen companion in the orderly conduct of our everyday lives. We don't have to be philosophers to agree with that.

Nowhere does the law of non-contradiction figure more importantly than in the study of Scripture. If God has inspired the Bible, it must present a cohesive, unified picture of God and His dealings with humanity.

What is said at one point must correspond with what's said at another. If God has spoken, it must be in a voice so coherent and consistent that every believer can listen without fear of being misled. The Word of God is open to serious challenge if anyone can prove it contains contradictory teachings. Skeptics delight in citing examples of why the Bible is no more reliable than other ancient literature.

Even those who approach the Bible as believers will encounter occasional passages that seem out of sync with the broader teachings of Scripture. When this happens, it's good to know that someone, somewhere has probably thought about how the history, language, and culture of Bible times can explain various difficult passages.

*If God has inspired the Bible, it must
present a cohesive, unified picture
of God and His dealings with humanity.
If God has spoken, it must be in a voice
so coherent and consistent
that every believer
can listen without
fear of being
misled.*

CHAPTER 10

Principles

39 When two or more passages contradict each other, make a distinction between immediate responsibility and ultimate responsibility.

40 God deals with His people at their level. Theologians call this progressive revelation. When God spoke to His people in their infancy, He spoke simply.

41 Look at the text as a whole and see how seemingly contradictory statements might fit together into a complementary picture. We call this *harmonization*.

42 Whenever a passage from an early period of biblical revelation seems at odds with a passage from a later period, we should consider the later passage a more complete statement of the truth.

43 Do not overinterpret figurative language.

Questions

105 Did God incite David to number Israel, or did Satan?

106 Don't statements in Judges and elsewhere in Joshua contradict the description of the conquest as it appears in Joshua 11:16–20?

107 How could Jacob and Job claim to have seen God when John says no one has seen Him?

108 Does God prohibit the taking of any life?

CAKE CRUMBS
AND CONTRADICTIONS

44 When interpreting the Gospels, keep in mind that they were written from four different vantage points.

45 Don't look for mathematical precision in wording. Different writers will record the same conversation using slightly different wording, omitting things another writer would include and vice-versa.

46 Don't argue from silence. Christians do this as often as non-Christians, and it always weakens our position in the eyes of perceptive non-believers. And don't fall for this argument when others use it.

47 Learn to distinguish between passages that are didactic, or teaching, and those that are illustrative, or metaphorical. Parables should never be used as the primary basis for doctrine because they require too much interpretation.

109 How can the God of the New Testament, of whom Peter says, "He is patient with you, not wanting anyone to perish, but everyone to come to repentance" (2 Peter 3:9) also be the God of Joshua who commanded the annihilation of every living being in the city of Jericho (Joshua 6:17–18)?

110 What were the precise words of Jesus at the Last Supper?

111 Who actually carried Jesus' cross to Calvary? Was it Jesus or was it Simon of Cyrene?

112 Does Jesus command persistence in prayer, or does He see lengthy prayers as being like the pagans' vain repetition?

Most of us already know whether we're Calvinists, Arminians, Charismatics, Dispensationalists, or a combination of the above. But other issues, smaller in scope, still puzzle us, as the questions in this last chapter indicate. No book has all the answers. Even if it did, it would take a golf cart to carry it home from the bookstore. Besides, believers are better off when they don't have all the answers. They have a responsibility to know the Bible for themselves. Giving them principles for handling difficulties, which I tried to do in this book, makes more sense.

Many possible ways may exist to solve a biblical difficulty. This doesn't disturb me. We are only responsible for plausible explanations. Absolute proof of our explanations is usually not possible and certainly not necessary.

After all, we see our reflections in a tarnished mirror; our understanding is distorted by the power of the world around us and the vestiges of Adam still in us. What we see is recognizable, but not until God finishes his grand plan of redemption will our understanding be complete.

 uestion 105   Did God incite David to number Israel, or did Satan?

2 Samuel 24:1
Again, the anger of the Lord burned against Israel, and he incited David against them, saying, "Go and take a census of Israel and Judah."

1 Chronicles 21:1
Satan rose up against Israel and incited David to take a census of Israel.

These verses represent one of the most difficult types of apparent contradiction. They're simple, declarative sentences describing the same event and giving radically different information. The one verse says God was responsible for David's census and the other blames Satan. How could two statements be more opposite?

 rinciple 39   When two or more passages contradict each other, make a distinction between immediate responsibility and ultimate responsibility.

Immediate is a word related to *mediate* and *mediator*. First Timothy 2:5 says, "There is one God and one *mediator* between God and man, the man Christ Jesus." The emphasis in this verse is on Christ as the one who mediates or goes between God and man. *Im*mediate means without a go-between.

Immediate responsibility for creation belongs to God and immediate responsibility for the Fall belongs to Adam because each was the cause of the effect in question.

On the other hand, we can trace ultimate responsibility backward through any number of mediating forces. For example, we say, "For want of the nail, the shoe was lost. For want of the shoe, the horse was lost. For want of the horse, the man was lost. For want of the man, the battle was lost."

Here we're dealing with ultimate responsibility. One of the jobs historians perform is the untangling of complex networks of cause and effect to arrive at ultimate causes. It's never easy, because immediate causes camouflage ultimate causes.

God was the ultimate cause of what 1 Samuel reported. No such temptation of David could have taken place without God's permission.

But it's also correct to say, as 1 Chronicles does, that Satan was responsible as the immediate cause. A portion of the problem in these texts involves confusion of immediate cause with ultimate cause.

But it isn't the whole story. Why would the writer of 1 Chronicles intentionally imply that he's contradicting the writer of 1 Samuel? He's not. He's only amplifying and clarifying the information in 1 Samuel.

AN IDOL MIND IS THE DEVIL'S WORKSHOP

Principle 40   God deals with His people at their level. Theologians call this progressive revelation. When God spoke to His people in their infancy, He spoke simply.

Like a good father or a good teacher, God takes His people where they are and begins training them for what He wants them to be. Any parent will remember the thrill of baby's first steps or first words, though neither was really anything to shout about. The steps were inefficient, unsteady, and without discernible direction. The first "Da-da" or "Ma-ma" fit in the same category. It sounded wonderful to the loving ears of a parent, but the neighbors may have had trouble catching the message.

And yet letters and long distance phone calls document the event, every time it happens, hundreds and thousands of times a day, as surely as if it were the successful launch of a space satellite or the completion of an international summit meeting.

None of us would think of entering that novice walker in the next marathon or that new talker in an oratory contest. Despite all our excitement over the achievement, we know they're not ready. We celebrate the accomplishment, not because of its importance on a global scale, but because it's a small miracle every time a new baby takes its first step or utters its first word.

If a human parent has the wisdom to appreciate the first step, knowing that normal growth will assure monumental advances, how much more does God recognize the abilities of His infant people, presenting them with challenges and instructions that they're able to meet and follow, knowing that the day will come when they're ready for bigger things.

What I've rather lightly dubbed the "Please, don't spit on the furniture" principle in an earlier chapter is at work here. Simply put, when God spoke to His people in their infancy, He spoke simply, as to children. For this reason, many doctrines are incomplete in the Old Testament. They don't reach their fullest development until "the time had fully come" (Galatians 4:4).

As much as we value the Old Testament as God's revelation, we must remember that the fullness of revelation comes, not in the words of the prophets, but in the person of God's Son (Hebrews 1:1–2).

The doctrine of Satan was one that had to wait for fuller development. The Old Testament reveals that Israel's ancestors, and that includes Abraham and his family, were idol worshipers before they left Ur. The long road from idolatry to true monotheism began when God called Abraham to follow Him away from his homeland and his father's people.

The next fifteen hundred years of Israel's history are ones of constant backsliding to the idolatrous faith of their fathers. Abraham was the first generation removed from idolatry, and his background was so steeped in the worship of multitudes of gods that it would be hard for any westerner today to appreciate it.

The attraction of the competing gods from Egypt, Canaan, Mesopotamia, and the smaller neighboring nations must have been intense. In fact, Israel's history is salted liberally with flirtations with other gods. We know that Jacob buried the idols of his household before reentering Canaan following his twenty-year sojourn with his father-in-law (Genesis 35:2–5). David's wife Michal was able to use the household gods of her father, Saul, to buy time for her escaping husband (1 Samuel 19:13). Moses' own grandson hired himself out as a priest, first to an Ephraimite named Micah and then to the whole tribe of Dan, to serve at the shrine of an idol made of silver (Judges 18:30). It wasn't until after the exile that God's baby people weaned themselves from the false security of their gods.

First Samuel is an old work, based on older records, probably official court records from the actual years of David's reign. First Samuel 24:1 (cf. 1 Chronicles 21:1) comes from a time when the virus of idolatry was still virulent and infectious.

What would the people who were willing to worship Baal and the whole host of heaven alongside their covenant God have done with the full doctrine of Satan? Can you imagine the leaders of Israel telling the people that there was a powerful spiritual force whose armies stood in opposition to the plan of God? They'd have been falling all over themselves in their rush to get the construction contracts out on temples to this new god. Anything that powerful had to be worshiped.

God, however, shielded His people from that temptation. Only in works from the later years, following the exile, does the word Satan begin to appear as a proper name and not just a title. God allowed Israel to become aware that there was an *adversary* (the literal meaning of Satan), but God spared them fuller knowledge of his precise character until they were able to cope with that knowledge.

The author of 1 Chronicles wrote after the return from exile, some 500 or more years later than 1 Samuel. God granted him the knowledge of the work and power of Satan because, whatever other failings postexilic Israel may have had, the temptation to sink back into idolatry wasn't one of them. So when he chronicled the life of David, he could tell the whole story. Although God assumed ultimate responsibility in 1 Samuel, He did so to protect the children. In 1 Chronicles, when the children were adolescents capable of dealing with the information, He then pointed the finger of immediate responsibility at Satan. His existence could be explained to the almost grown children of that age. Loving parents withhold certain information from children until the children are old enough to cope.

If we understand the principle of progressive revelation, know something of the historical settings of these two biblical books, and appreciate the distinction between immediate and ultimate responsibility, apparent contradictions evaporate.

Q **uestion 106**   Don't statements in Judges and elsewhere in Joshua contradict the description of the conquest as it appears in Joshua 11:16–20?

Is the whole Old Testament a hodgepodge of contradictory, cut-and-paste fragments of ancient and inaccurate tribal legends? Were these ancient Jewish "editors" so inept that they took all these stories and slapped them together willy-nilly without even noticing the contradictions?

If you were one of these imaginary editors and you were trying to make a theological point by compiling a book about Israel's ancient conquest, would you include all sorts of material that contradicted everything you'd set out to prove? If the original authors didn't see any contradictions here, and we seem to, it probably means we're missing the point.

P **rinciple 41**   Look at the text as a whole and see how seemingly contradictory statements might fit together into a complementary picture. We call this *harmonization*.

In harmonization we take the separate notes of the biblical symphony and put them together so we can listen to their music more clearly.

Admittedly, harmonization is often misused, but that does not make it invalid. Understanding the reason Joshua and Judges

Joshua 13:1

When Joshua was old and well advanced in years, the Lord said to him, "You are very old, and there are still very large areas of land to be taken over."

Joshua 18:3

There were still seven Israelite tribes who had not yet received their inheritance. So Joshua said to the Israelites: "How long will you wait before you begin to take possession of the land that the Lord, the God of your fathers, has given you?"

Judges 1:19

The Lord was with the men of Judah. They took possession of the hill country, but they were unable to drive the people from the plains, because they had iron chariots.

Judges 2:2c–3a

Yet you have disobeyed me. Why have you done this? Now therefore I tell you that I will not drive them out before you; they will be thorns in your sides and their gods will be a snare to you.

Judges 2:14–15

In his anger against Israel the Lord handed them over to raiders who plundered them. He sold them to their enemies all around, whom they were no longer able to resist. Whenever Israel went out to fight, the hand of the Lord was against them to defeat them, just as he had sworn to them. They were in great distress.

(Also compare Judges 3:1–4.)

Joshua 11:16–20

So Joshua took this entire land: the hill country, all the Negev, the whole region of Goshen, the western foothills, the Arabah and the mountains of Israel with their foothills, from Mount Halak, which rises toward Seir, to Baal Gad in the Valley of Lebanon below Mount Hermon. He captured all their kings and struck them down, putting them to death. Joshua waged war against all these kings for a long time. Except for the Hivites, living in Gibeon, not one city made a treaty of peace with the Israelites, who took them all in battle. For it was the Lord himself who hardened their hearts to wage war against Israel, so that he might destroy them totally, exterminating them without mercy, as the Lord had commanded Moses.

were included in Scripture in the first place is a key to harmonizing the apparent contradictions.

Most Christians know there are sixty-six books in the Bible, thirty-nine in the Old Testament, twenty-seven in the New. But how many other books might have been written by Jewish people during the same periods of time? We can only guess at the number of books produced during the two-thousand years from Abraham to Christ. But the evidence suggests that there were many. The Bible itself makes direct reference to Jewish books like the *Book of Jashar* (Joshua 10:13), the *Acts of Solomon* (1 Kings 11:41), the *Annals of the Kings of Judah* (1 Kings 15:23) and the *Annals of the Kings of Israel* (1 Kings 14:19).

Luke talked about many other accounts of the life of Christ (Luke 1:1) produced before his gospel was written. Even if Mark and Matthew were written earlier than Luke, the two wouldn't qualify as "many other accounts." Jude quoted from two separate non-canonical works popular during the first century. It's even likely that the apostle Paul wrote additional letters besides those in Scripture.

With all the hundreds of books written in Israel and Judah and in the early church, only the sixty-six books of our Bible are considered authoritative. Each of those sixty-six books contributes something unique to our understanding of God and His dealings with humanity. Together, these books make up all there is of written revelation. Each book occupies a special place in the ongoing march of revelation. Lose one book and we lose something irreplaceable. Add one book and we add something redundant.

Joshua and Judges both have forceful messages. Joshua demonstrates God's faithfulness to His promises. Judges dramatizes the consequences of not living up to God's covenant, as ratified at Sinai and confirmed at Shechem (Joshua 24).

Without the clear statement of these two principles found in Joshua and Judges, much of what follows in the rest of the Old Testament becomes obscure.

The history of the Old Testament is recorded to teach the general lesson that Israel's obedience as a nation resulted in God's blessing. The opposite lesson is also taught. Disobedience resulted in God's judgment. The writings of the prophets assume the continued validity and force of the contract that God entered into with Israel. Their pronouncements of judgment are based on the promised consequences of violating that contract (Deuteronomy 27:9–26; 28:15–68).

God is always careful to show himself in action. His revelation isn't an abstract set of theoretical formulations about himself, but a concrete set of historical events demonstrating who He is and how He works.

Joshua is the biblical record of God's actions in conquering the Promised Land. Not Israel's actions, but God's.

Judges, on the other hand, is the dismal record of Israel's failure to abide by the terms of the covenant. Not God's failure, but Israel's.

Although this may seem like a roundabout way of resolving the problem of the contradictory verses in Joshua and Judges, we can't deal with it unless we remember the different purposes of these two books.

Joshua 11:16–23 is a theological reminder of what God has accomplished in history. The entire land falls before Joshua, God's servant. At the end of Joshua, the land is ready for occupation. Just as God had promised Moses and Abraham before him, He made the Promised Land available to His people in its entirety.

The main opposition to Israel, important coalitions of powerful city-states, had been swept aside in Joshua's three campaigns, all by miraculous means. All that remained was the occupation of the land. As the summary statement of Joshua 11 asserts, God had been faithful (v. 23). Joshua had fulfilled his commission faithfully. Now it remained for the individual tribes to act as faithfully in the appropriation of their tribal allotments.

Joshua 13:1 and the attached list of unoccupied territory make it clear that God, Joshua, and the writer of Joshua, were all well aware of the great gap between what God had provided and what Israel actually took.

In many ways, this passage stands as an indictment of the believer who, knowing the fullness of the riches available in Christ Jesus, is content to live in the beggar's rags of frustration and spiritual retardation. God has provided, but "there are still very large areas of land to be taken over."

When the tribes gather at Shiloh in chapter 18, we become aware of a failure of nerve in seven of the tribes. Joshua chided them for their fearful procrastination. The country lay open before them, but they were afraid to go ahead and possess it.

Here's how these three passages work together to make the point. For all practical purposes, the conquest is complete in Joshua 11. God had kept his side of the bargain. But in chapter 13 we see that the occupation still lies in the future. God's provision, no matter how freely and completely given, must always be appropriated.

Chapter 18 gives us our first hint of Israel's failure to obey. Because the purpose of Joshua is to demonstrate God's faithfulness, Israel's failure isn't emphasized. But neither is it swept under the rug.

When we come to Judges, where the primary focus is on Israel's faithlessness, the "contradictions" come into sharper focus. Whereas Joshua 11 told us that Joshua took the entire land, the passages in Judges show the numerous ways in which the promise of God has gone unclaimed.

Judges 2:2–3 indicates that the Israelites did not conquer the whole land because of their broken covenant with Yahweh. As a result, God pronounced a richly deserved punishment. The divine army that drove the Canaanites ahead of Joshua would no longer fight on Israel's side. Up to this point, all the conquests of Israel had been God's victories. From this point on, all their defeats would be their own. With God no longer fighting on their side, the men of Judah were unable to conquer the plains people with their chariots (Judges 1:19). Chariots had presented no great obstacle to the earlier conquest of Hazor and its allies (Joshua 11:6–9).

The impact of God's judgment is repeated in Judges 2:14–15. God handed all of them over to their enemies for their disobedience. It wasn't only the men of Judah who faltered before their enemies, but all of the people. They were no longer strong in the Lord and, reduced to their own strength, they proved hopelessly weak.

Even here, though, God shows His mercy by using the Canaanites to teach warfare to this new, weak, generation of Israelites. More importantly, God would use Canaanite oppression as a tool to turn Israel to repentance (Judges 3:1–4).

With God's help, Joshua could provide a rest from war. But only obedience could assure a continuation of that rest. Rather than contradictions, these passages indicate Israel limited God's plan for them by their disobedience and lack of commitment.

 uestion 107   How could Jacob and Job claim to have seen God when John says no one has seen Him?

John 1:18
No one has ever seen God, but God the One and Only, who is at the Father's side, has made him known.

Genesis 32:30
So Jacob called the place Peniel, saying, "It is because I saw God face to face, and yet my life was spared."

Job 42:5
My ears had heard of you but now my eyes have seen you.

These three statements are quite different in tone. John, whose gospel contains some of the most sophisticated theological statements in the Gospels, stresses Jesus' role as the incarnation of God.

The incarnation reveals God in human terms. In its context, the emphasis isn't on the kind of experience Job and Jacob report. It's more than a simple declarative statement that no one has seen God. More completely, it's a statement that anything we may have known about God before Christ is now as if we'd never known it. It completes the thought in Job's statement, a poetic exclamation of Job's heightened awareness of God's nature.

In a set of statements like this, we need to let the later, more developed passage set the standard for understanding the other two.

P **rinciple 42**   Whenever a passage from an early period of biblical revelation seems at odds with a passage from a later period, we should consider the later passage a more complete statement of the truth.

John's gospel has priority, both as a later statement and as a statement that fits well with Jesus' own description of God as a spirit (John 4:24). But the statement of John 1:18 is also the statement of a more profound truth.

John's purpose is to describe the magnitude of the incarnation. The greatest man in the history of Israel's covenant experience was Moses. Even he was not allowed more than a glimpse of the afterglow of the passing glory of God (Exodus 33:18–23).

In contrast with that experience of Moses, John tells us that those who believe have seen, "his glory, the glory of the One and Only, who came from the father, full of grace and truth" (John 1:14).

The gospel writers have a particular interest in the verb *to see*. For them, seeing is not restricted to the eyes. Indeed, the seeing of the spirit is true seeing. The meaning of John 1:18 may lie more in that direction.

No human being may "see" God unless he or she first "sees" Jesus. Having said that, we may also justify the simpler meaning of the text. At least, and this is inherent in the passage, no human being has ever seen God until God made himself visible and manifest in the human flesh of Jesus.

If John, and Jesus himself, are right in their pronouncements, how should the Old Testament passages be understood?

The account of Jacob at Peniel is a strange one. It's one of the events in the Old Testament that theologians call a *theophany* or a manifestation of God in physical form. Sometimes that form is human, but not always.

In Exodus 3:1–4, for example, the Lord spoke to Moses out of a burning bush. In this instance, He chose a form that would catch Moses' attention from a distance. Although there was no human figure present, many still consider this a *theophany* because God appeared in physical form to a human being.

God made an even stranger appearance in a vision to Abraham in Genesis 15:17. In affirming the Abrahamic covenant with an oath, God manifested himself in the form of common household articles. Again, this is a *theophany*.

Seeing a *theophany*, however, is not the same as seeing God in His true form. If He is spirit, He has no "true" form.

People frequently see the story of Jacob at the river Jabbok as a refinement of the idea of theophany. Not *theophany*, they say, but *Christophany*, or a preincarnate manifestation of Jesus.

If the "man" of Genesis 32 is in fact Christ, there's no possibility of contradiction. It is, after all, in Jesus that we see God who is a spirit. But if this mysterious "man" was not a Christophany, who was he?

In the ancient Near East, messengers of the king spoke with the king's authority. They spoke in the first person, as if the king had spoken through them. In fact, when people heard the king's messenger, they might as well say they had heard the king himself.

In Hebrew, the word for "angel" also means "messenger." If this man of the river was not a manifestation of Christ, it was at least an angel from the Lord speaking for God in the first person. Both human and supernatural messengers did that.

A human messenger might say, "I will say to those called 'not my people, you are my people'; and they will say, 'You are my God'" (Hosea 2:23*b*).

A supernatural messenger might say, also in the first person, "Lift the boy and take him by the hand, for I will make him into a great nation" (Genesis 21:18).

In either case, although the messenger was not God himself, the words were His.

We also need to remember that, although Jacob may have thought he had seen God, he wasn't necessarily right. The text records his reaction accurately and correctly, but that doesn't insure that his reaction was either accurate or correct. This was, after all, the man who thought peeling willow branches could produce spotted sheep! Although Jacob's encounter with the "man" at the river Jabbok introduced him to the God of Abraham and Isaac in a personal way for the first time, Jacob was still a man of limited religious sensibilities.

In light of all the biblical data, the "man" of the Jabbok was probably one of God's messengers acting on His behalf and with His authority, an angel and not God himself.

P **rinciple 43**   Do not overinterpret figurative language.

Job's claim to have seen God (Job 42) is far easier to explain. Recent translations set the passage as poetry, and poetry frequently uses figurative language.

The only manifestation of God mentioned in the text is the voice that spoke from inside the whirlwind. There's no reference to a physical form at all. Just as God spoke to Moses out of the burning bush, He spoke to Job out of the whirlwind. Job uses the verb *see* symbolically to show his heightened awareness and understanding of God. Prior to this experience his knowledge and experience of God had been secondhand, but in his encounter with God in the whirlwind they became personal and firsthand.

Q uestion 108   Does God prohibit the taking of any life?

Exodus 20:13 (KJV)
Thou shalt not kill.

Deuteronomy 20:16–17
In the cities of the nations the Lord your God is giving you as an inheritance, do not leave alive anything that breathes.

If you've ever talked sincerely about murdering a mosquito, this question probably keeps you up nights. If, on the other hand, you understand that all languages give you a variety of words for the taking of life, you're well on the way to understanding.

I know, from years spent under attack by midwestern Kamikaze Mosquitoes, that few creatures in God's creation excite such a desire to slay, slaughter, massacre, murder, execute, put to death, and otherwise terminate as they do. Most of us just swat, though. The only good mosquito is a flat mosquito.

Those other verbs are colorful, but for most people they're just metaphors. Except for animal rights activists, we don't think in terms of murdering mosquitoes, chickens, or other livestock. Even when dealing with human deaths, we don't speak of deaths in an automobile accident as murder, either, unless a driver is totally reckless or totally drunk.

Unfortunately, the King James translators selected the wrong word to translate Exodus 20:13 and created a misunderstanding of the text that's been with us ever since. A comparison of recent translations should clear up the problem. Almost without exception, modern translators have replaced the more general "kill" with the more specific, and accurate, "murder."

In fact, the other laws of the Old Testament give ample evidence that God meant murder as murder, not simply the taking of any human life. For example, the regulations for the cities of refuge (Numbers 35:6–34) were laid down to protect people who took human life unintentionally. The elders of the cities of refuge were responsible to determine whether the man-slayer was guilty of murder. The greater problem here isn't related to the Hebrew word for murder, though.

 uestion 109   How can the God of the New Testament, of whom Peter says, "He is patient with you, not wanting anyone to perish, but everyone to come to repentance" (2 Peter 3:9) also be the God of Joshua who commanded the annihilation of every living being in the city of Jericho (Joshua 6:17–18)?

The resolution to this dilemma is that God is both a God of love and a God of justice. The two exist in a fine balance through-out biblical history, for which we can be infinitely grateful. We can be glad that God's justice is tinged with mercy, for if any of us got what we truly deserved, we'd be, as my kids like to put it, dead meat.

We can all cope with the notion of God's judgment at the end of time, but the notion of God judging in the here and now somehow sets us back on our heels. It's almost as if we don't think He ought to be trespassing into our territory while we still have time left on the clock.

But God has been intervening since the beginning of time. The Bible opens with an act of divine love in creation, moves almost without pause to an act of human sin, to be followed by the first act of divine judgment. From that point on, human history is a litany of sin punctuated by periodic judgments.

Although God sometimes used natural forces as His tools of judgment (the Red Sea is about as natural as you can get) and sometimes supernatural, as often as not He arranged the affairs of nations to coincide with His plans for blessing and judgment.

While pestilence and famine accompanied the fall of Samaria and the fall of Jerusalem, they were natural companions of siege warfare. God used human armies to judge Israel and Judah.

Is it any surprise then that He also used a human army to judge the Canaanites? The conquest of Canaan was no afterthought with God. Some time around 2,000 B.C. He promised that land to Abraham. But even though He spoke about the land as if it had already been delivered, Israel wouldn't take delivery until generations had passed.

It used to trouble me that God's promise wouldn't be fulfilled until long after Abraham was dust. But the delay was necessary. God used the time to help the patriarchs to grow in their faith. But the interval had another side to it; to give the land to Israel, God had to first throw out the Canaanites.

He wouldn't arbitrarily evict His current tenants, even to give a gift to His chosen people. That would be unjust. Instead, He waited because "the sin of the Amorites [a name sometimes used for the residents of Canaan] has not yet reached its full measure" (Genesis 15:16).

Even in judging the Canaanites, God was gracious and patient. His justice demanded that their sinfulness be punished, but by His grace the punishment could not come until there was no other alternative. God was not willing that any should perish. But when the fullness of their iniquity had come, the armies of Israel were the tool God used to enact judgment.

THE LIFE OF CHRIST IN QUADRAPHONIC SOUND

When I was a teenager, I listened to news reports of hit and run accidents and holdups with bewilderment. The police in our town always seemed to be looking for a late model blue (or brown or green) sedan. I couldn't understand why witnesses couldn't give a detailed description of the getaway car just by listening to the sound of the engine and the transmission.

As you might guess, I was a car fanatic. My brother and I challenged each other to identify by sound alone the makes of cars stopped at the intersection outside our duplex. We prided ourselves on being able to identify anything on the road. If either of us had witnessed a holdup or a hit and run accident, our testimony to the police would have included a detailed description of the car, including year, make, model, precise color, hubcap style, hood ornaments, and whether or not fuzzy dice were hanging from the rear view mirror.

Now that I'm middle aged, I ask my teenage son if I want a car identified. Now all I really care about cars is what they cost and if they have room for all six of my family and their assorted paraphernalia. My perspective has changed radically, and with it my perceptions.

Likewise, different observers of the same scene will describe it in terms of their own interests, expertise, and motivation. Ask the fans of opposing football teams whether a close interference call on the defender's ten-yard line with thirty seconds left to play in a scoreless playoff game was justified, and you'll see what I mean. This doesn't mean that one is wrong and the other right. Even with instant replay, officials themselves can't always agree on the call. What it does mean is that each person, with his or her own interests at stake, watches a football game from a different vantage point, and that vantage point determines what the person sees.

P **rinciple 44**   When interpreting the Gospels, keep in mind that they were written from four different vantage points.

If each of the writers had exactly the same perspective, there would be no reason to have four accounts. Unfortunately, their differences in viewpoints have been the cause of claims that they contain all sorts of contradictions.

Although interpreting them is sometimes difficult, the realization that each account of Christ's earthly existence was written by a human being with a particular audience in view, a particular purpose in mind, and a particular set of information and abilities to work with goes a long way toward resolving the problems.

Having two eyes allows us to see in three dimensions. We enjoy the richness of depth and perspective only when our two eyes work together, each seeing the same scene from a slightly different angle. If we lose one eye we are plunged into a two-dimensional world, where simple distinctions of depth and distance are all but lost to us. The richness and depth of the gospel account depends on the separate perspectives of the four evangelists. A gospel written by a former tax collector from Judea (Matthew) can hardly be expected to cover exactly the same ground as one from the quill of a doctor from Greece (Luke). John's introspective, theological interpretation of the life and ministry of Jesus is necessarily different from the active narrative of the overthrow of world history by the Kingdom of God that came from the hand of Mark.

Mark 14:22–25
While they were eating, Jesus took bread, gave thanks and broke it, and gave it to his disciples, saying, "Take and eat; this is my body." Then he took the cup, gave thanks and offered it to them, and they all drank from it. "This is my blood of the covenant, which is poured out for many," he said to them. "I tell you the truth, I will not drink again of the fruit of the vine until that day when I drink it anew in the Kingdom of God."

1 Corinthians 11:23
The Lord Jesus, on the night he was betrayed, took bread, and when he had given thanks, he broke it and said, "This is my body, which is for you; do this in remembrance of me." In the same way, after supper he took the cup, saying, "This cup is the new covenant in my blood; do this whenever you drink it, in remembrance of me."

(Also compare Mark 15:21; Luke 23:26)

Matthew 26:26–29
While they were eating, Jesus took bread, gave thanks and broke it, and gave it to his disciples, saying, "Take and eat; this is my body." Then he took the cup, gave thanks and offered it to them, saying, "Drink from it, all of you. This is my blood of the covenant, which is poured out for many for the forgiveness of sins. I tell you, I will not drink of this fruit of the vine from now on until that day when I drink it anew with you in my Father's Kingdom."

Luke 22:15–20
And he said to them, "I have eagerly desired to eat this Passover with you before I suffer. For I tell you, I will not eat it again until it finds fulfillment in the kingdom of God. And he took bread, gave thanks and broke it, and gave it to them saying, "This is my body given for you; do this in remembrance of me." In the same way, after supper he took the cup saying, "This is the new covenant in my blood, which is poured out for you."

Together they paint a portrait of Jesus that provides us with a clear idea of the total impact of His earthly ministry. Any one of the four Gospels by itself would leave too much of value unsaid.

In this variety of perspectives, however, a surface reading leaves us with an uneasy feeling. The accounts sometimes seem to disagree with one another. This is especially true when we compare the first three Gospels with John. Matthew, Mark, and Luke (called the *synoptic* Gospels—from the Greek meaning "to see together") present a remarkably unified vision of Christ, even given their different emphases. John, on the other hand, seems almost oblivious to the other Gospels. A large part of John contains material unique to that Gospel, and a great deal of material found in the other three Gospels is not mentioned in John. Even in the synoptic Gospels, there are puzzling differences. Because of this, they present a particular set of problems in New Testament studies. They all tell the same story, but not always in the same way. Here are some specific examples of three different types of problem passages found in the Gospels.

Q **uestion 110**   What were the precise words of Jesus at the Last Supper?

Comparing different gospel accounts of the words Jesus spoke at the Last Supper from any translation will show striking differences. In the case of Luke, the order of the cup and bread is even reversed. The problem here is not so much a problem with the biblical text as it is with the question of perspective.

P **rinciple 45**   Don't look for mathematical precision in wording. Different writers will record the same conversation using slightly different wording, omitting things another writer would include and vice-versa.

Our twentieth-century attachment to tape recorders and quotation marks is out of place in the study of the Gospels. Exact quotations were difficult, if not impossible, to record in Jesus' day. Judas was treasurer for the disciples, but we have no record that anyone was recording secretary. It's unlikely that anyone sat in a corner of the upper room recording in shorthand the conversation at the Lord's Supper. And a secretary, had there been one, probably would have tried to record precise meaning, not precise wording.

That sounds odd to us because we are programmed to think that the only way to know meaning is through direct quotations. But meaning can be expressed in a variety of ways. An almost infinite number of sentence structures, synonyms, and variant wordings can be used to say the same thing.

Abraham Lincoln said, "Fourscore and seven years ago our fathers brought forth on this continent. . . ," and that line has become one of the most famous in American history. He could have said, "Eighty-seven years ago the first American patriots introduced to North America . . ." Or other words such as "America's founders, eighty- seven years ago, initiated . . ." Some of these phrases are more poetic, but the essential meaning is the same in all of them. Lincoln's words could hardly have been more powerful, but they could have been very different and still have conveyed the same sense. I wonder how we would remember the speech if Lincoln hadn't left behind a manuscript.

Jesus left no manuscript behind, and there was no secretary working quietly in the corner of the room. For these reasons, we should read the parallel accounts for equivalent meaning and be less concerned over precise wording. If that's what we're looking for, we find no problem here. In its essentials, the Lord's words tell us that His body would be broken, and broken bread would symbolize it. His blood would be shed to establish a new covenant, and the cup would be its symbol.

In some circles the authors of the four Gospels were called evangelists. They were preachers of the gospel who told the stories of Jesus' life and death the way a good preacher would. They didn't recite the stories like a school boy at an open house. With complete respect for the meaning of the words, they wrote them in the way that would communicate most effectively with their readers. The reliability of Scripture doesn't depend on slavish, word-for-word reporting. If their purpose for writing had been a word-for-word account of what Jesus said, one gospel would have been sufficient. Instead God used the foolishness of the evangelists' craft to paint four distinctive, individualized portraits of the Savior.

 uestion 111   Who actually carried Jesus' cross to Calvary? Was it Jesus, or was it Simon of Cyrene?

Matthew 27:32
As they were going out, they met a man from Cyrene, named Simon, and they forced him to carry the cross.

John 19:17
Carrying his own cross, he went out to the place of the Skull (which in Aramaic is called Golgotha).

Like the recorded words of Jesus, His recorded acts some-times raise questions because they appear to disagree on details and sequence. This particular action is recorded in all four Gospels.

Matthew, Mark, and Luke all say that Simon, a Cyrenian, was pressed into service to carry the cross to Calvary. Only John says that Jesus went out carrying His own cross.

Artistic renditions show it as a whole cross, but Roman custom probably involved something different. In a troublesome province like Judea, where crucifixions were a common event, the upright post of the cross was left standing as a constant reminder of executions, past and future. The condemned man would be led to his death with the cross beam strapped across his shoulders.

I've had some experience carrying wood, both as a construc-tion worker and as the owner of a wood-burning stove. Believe me, carrying a beam heavy enough to serve the purpose of the Roman executioners from Pilate's judgment hall all the way to Golgotha would be an endurance test for a strong man in excel-lent physical condition. For a man who hadn't slept since the previous morning and who had spent the last several hours being beaten and tortured within an inch of his life, the task would have been a physical impossibility.

The Roman decision to draft a cross-carrier was not an act of kindness. It was a simple, practical act governed by the need to get their victim to the place where he would die.

Simon the Cyrenian, a man the synoptic Gospels say was coming in from the country, was pressed into service. After this solitary mention, Simon drops out of sight in the biblical record.

Principle 46   Don't argue from silence. Christians do this as often as non-Christians, and it always weakens our position in the eyes of perceptive non-believers. And don't fall for this argument when others use it.

John omits reference to Simon altogether. For some, this suggests a contradiction, but John can't be proved wrong on the basis of what he didn't say. To argue otherwise is to fall into the all-too-frequent trap known as the *argument from silence.*

Debaters know that arguments from silence are the weakest type. Those who use it examine their evidence and assume, if they find no mention of a particular person, thing, place, or event, that it doesn't exist.

The most despicable use of such an argument I've heard in a long time cropped up shortly after the release of the pro-life film *The Silent Scream*. Through the use of ultra-sound technology, the film graphically depicted an abortion, showing the unborn victim thrashing and fighting to escape the abortionist's instruments.

Pro-abortion forces, recognizing a powerful force against their practice, moved quickly to discredit it. They promptly trotted out a battery of house experts who proclaimed, with great feeling if not great sense, that there is no evidence that the nerves of infants in the first trimester of pregnancy are developed well enough to record pain. This, of course, ignores the evidence of the film, but it's also logically indefensible. The absence of evidence can't be displayed as evidence. In its simplest form, this argument says, "We're ignorant. We don't know. What we don't know doesn't exist."

To argue that John is wrong, as some have done, because he doesn't mention Simon, is to argue from silence. When a writer chooses not to record an event, or a detail involved in an event, he hasn't made a mistake; he's made a decision.

I believe John omitted reference to Simon because he didn't want anything to distract his readers from the awful sacrifice Christ was about to make. Even if he ignored Simon because he wasn't aware of his role, John's account wouldn't be mistaken. The only way we could prove John guilty of error or contradiction would be if he had specifically said *no one* helped Jesus.

Some argue that John's wording indicates a denial of help: "Carrying his own cross, he went out to the Place of the Skull." If He carried His own cross, doesn't that mean no one else carried it for Him? Not really. John accurately records the Roman custom that required the condemned man to carry his own cross. I don't believe the soldiers had any intention of allowing the suffering Jesus to escape that last torment before crucifixion. But on the way there, Jesus' strength failed. The soldiers, with orders to obey, got Simon to carry the cross.

Simon's role in this incident adds color and personal understanding to the synoptic Gospels. Its omission by John keeps our thoughts in sharp focus on the ordeal of the Lamb of God, about to be slain as God's Passover sacrifice for the sins of the world.

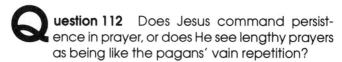

Question 112 Does Jesus command persistence in prayer, or does He see lengthy prayers as being like the pagans' vain repetition?

Matthew 6:7–8
And when you pray, do not keep babbling on like pagans, for they think they will be heard because of their many words. Do not be like them, for your Father knows what you need before you ask him.

Luke 18:6–8a
And the Lord said, "Listen to what the unjust judge says. And will not God bring about justice for his chosen ones, who cry out to him day and night? Will he keep putting them off? I tell you, he will see that they get justice, and quickly."

The problem in these two passages is with our misreading of Jesus' use of language. The statement in Matthew, a part of the Sermon on the Mount, is an example of a simple, straightforward *didactic* (teaching) statement. These type of statements have priority over parables.

Principle 47 Learn to distinguish between passages that are didactic, or teaching, and those that are illustrative, or metaphorical. Parables should never be used as the primary basis for doctrine because they require too much interpretation.

Parables are stories Jesus used to illustrate truth. Didactic sections are statements of the truths that parables sometimes illustrate. Because of this, we should never go to parables to formulate theology, only to clarify or illustrate theology based on didactic sections.

We tend to think, rather uncritically, that a sentence is a sentence is a sentence, especially if we find it in the Bible. But that's simply not so. Different kinds of sentences bear different weights of meaning.

For example, God is variously described in the Old Testament as having an eye that roves to and fro in the land, an arm that is not shortened to save, and wings under which His people take refuge. Each of those sentences makes a point, but the point is one step removed from the didactic statement. They have to be interpreted.

Even those who claim most vigorously that they read the Bible literally, will explain such verses symbolically. Metaphorical language always has more than one possible interpretation.

Not all language is like this. If I say, "Jesus died for our sins," we may argue over the truth of the statement, but the statement itself is clear. "Jesus died for our sins" is a didactic sentence. "The Lord is my shepherd" is metaphorical. When Jesus uses the language of likeness, or metaphor, it is, by its nature, less certain than His teaching.

The clear teaching of Jesus in Matthew is that God, who knows everything, doesn't need to be told what our needs are. Because He knows our needs, the "many words" of the heathen are nothing but "babbling."

By taking this teaching in isolation, we might get the impression that all our praying should be in quick bursts to avoid empty repetition or babbling, but this isn't the point of the teaching. The application of this teaching to the Christian's prayer life is that the length of a prayer doesn't guarantee its success or failure. Quality is what matters.

That isn't to say there's no reason to spend great amounts of time in prayer. I'm inclined to feel that quality prayer comes only when we spend quantity time with the Lord. The great prayer warriors of Christian history have devoted countless hours to prayer, not to increase their effectiveness but because they loved the Lord.

When we equate prayer only with getting things from God, we've missed the whole purpose of prayer. We're not told to pray to get our way. We're told to pray because prayer is the communion of dependent children with the Father. Jesus himself spent hours in communion with God because for Him prayer was intense fellowship with His Father.

Often in that communion we express our needs, wants, and desires. When God gives us what we ask for He does so because He knows what we need, not because we've asked. We are to give ourselves to prayer, not simply to get, but to enjoy the presence of our Lord.

In Matthew, Jesus criticized both pagan and religious abuses of prayer. Then He offered a model for prayer that begins with adoration and worship and proceeds to petition.

To summarize, Jesus removed the emphasis on duration, which was common among pagans and religious people as well. He diverted our attention from the amount of time we spend with the Lord and redirected it toward the goodness and Omnipotence of God.

Jesus' parable in Luke, on the other hand, has nothing to do with how long we pray.

Some have been defined parables as earthly stories with a heavenly meaning. That's a pretty good definition as far as it goes. But we need to remember that the point of contact between heaven and earth in a parable is normally only in one place. In other words, parables are illustrations used to illuminate a single spiritual truth.

Unfortunately, parables are often confused with allegories. In an allegory, every detail in the story has a hidden meaning. In a parable, the details function together to point our thoughts toward a single, central truth. Even in the parable of the sower, where there are four types of soil and each type represents a different type of person, the central meaning is that the gospel will be received in different ways by different people. The parable of the sower was offered to explain to the disciples why everybody didn't fall to their knees and worship Jesus, which apparently was puzzling them.

The parable of the unjust judge uses a technique the rabbis called "the light and the heavy," which argues that if something unimportant is true, something important is much more true. In this parable, Jesus told a story about a poor widow who went before a dishonest judge to ask for justice. After the widow nagged him half to death, the poor man finally caved in and gave her the justice she deserved just to get her off his back.

Was Jesus telling us God is like that? The relationship between the Father and the judge is one of contrast, not comparison. God is not like the judge. In fact, Jesus says He's just the opposite. Look at verses 7–8 again.

Jesus asked if God would put off His people the way that judge had done. The answer, of course, is no, He won't. In fact, when God responds He responds quickly.

In this story the judge is unimportant. He is unjust and can be reached only through uncommon pleading. God is just and can be reached without pleading.

I might paraphrase here and say, "If an unjust human judge will give justice just to get a little peace, how much more will a just God respond to His children, whom He loves."

The "light to heavy" nature of this parable should be obvious when it's stated this way. Jesus never suggested we should try to wear God down with our prayers. Rather, He encouraged us to bring our needs before the Father because He hears and cares.

AND THAT'S THE WAY IT IS

I could wish that none of these biblical difficulties existed. I could wish that the Gospels said things in such a way that no doubts were ever raised by apparent contradictions. I could also wish that our understanding of Scripture never required the slightest bit of mental exertion.

But that doesn't seem to be the way God set it up. I've discussed three types of apparent contradictions found in the Gospels. That doesn't mean there aren't more. It just means that I chose three different kinds to illustrate three different approaches to a better understanding.

There are many principles throughout this book. Try to keep them in mind whenever you read the Bible. Many seemingly difficult passages can be simplified by applying sound interpretive principles. No single principle will work with all problems, but the more we know the better we can understand the Bible.

*Many possible ways may exist
to solve a biblical difficulty,
but we are only responsible
for plausible explanations.*

EPILOGUE

WHO CAN KNOW?

Some people might ask, "If all you say in this book is true, how can the ordinary Christian, with no time for formal Bible training or seminary, ever understand the Bible?" We need to remember that problem passages are the exception, not the rule. Most of the Bible isn't puzzling. The problems of history, language, and culture do not obscure the clear realities of God's revelation. The core truths of Scripture are repeated and repeated and then repeated again so that no reader seeking to know God can escape them. The shadow of some confusing words, verses, or concepts shouldn't blind us to the overwhelming clarity of divine revelation.

The stumbling blocks on the path to biblical understanding are well scattered throughout the Bible. We can easily walk around them, as we would walk around a large rock on an otherwise smooth path. Problem passages of Scripture need not keep us from our goal of knowing and serving God. But even the simplest biblical passage has depths of meaning and edification that yield themselves only to study. There's a new layer waiting to be uncovered every time we read.

In archeology, there are two ways of looking at a site. For mapping or selecting a site for excavation, the team will simply walk over an area and pick up whatever artifacts they see on the surface. They call this a *surface survey*. It gives archeologists an idea of the different levels of occupation they might find if they were to excavate. But it takes the arduous and expensive task of excavation to unlock the secrets of the cities buried one on top of the other.

If our reading of the Bible is limited to surface survey, we will collect an impressive array of verses and ideas. But to really know, there's no substitute for careful digging. Even John 3:16, that simplest of gospel statements, contains depths of truth and inspiration that give up their meaning only to the student who carefully digs for it.

What does John mean by the word *love*?

What does he mean by the word *world*?

Does *only begotten son* resonate with other biblical harmonies? What is the definition of *believes*?

What would I discover if I examined the words *perished* and *eternal life?*

Each of these questions has been the subject of numerous books and sermons. A simple reading of this verse can lead us to salvation, but a deeper look greatly enriches our lives.

HOW DO I KNOW? THE BIBLE TELLS ME SO

The current stress on experience in American Christianity has nearly silenced those who challenge us with our responsibility to study Scripture. People warn one another against "head" knowledge, commending "heart" knowledge instead, because the world of biblical scholarship is filled with people whose intellectual understanding of Christianity is profound but whose hearts have never yielded to the lordship of Christ. Furthermore, didn't Jesus say that the Holy Spirit would "teach you all things" (John 14:26)? Didn't Paul warn that the "natural man receiveth not the things of the Spirit of God: for they are foolishness unto him: neither can he know them, because they are spiritually discerned" (1 Corinthians 2:14, KJV)? And weren't Jesus' disciples "unschooled, ordinary men" (Acts 4:13)?

These passages seem to imply that study is unnecessary, so why am I suggesting the opposite?

To begin with, that conclusion is drawn from an inadequate survey of the texts in question. In this case, skimming over the surface ignores context, which is always important. For example, to understand Acts 4:13, a reader needs to know that it was the leaders of the Sanhedrin, the men persecuting the disciples and leading the drive to crucify Jesus, who viewed the disciples as unschooled laymen. Acts 4:13 expresses the biased opinion of men educated in what they considered the "right schools." The ability of outsiders like Peter and John to engage them successfully in theological debate was blowing all their circuits. It was only in their narrow, limited understanding that the apostles were unschooled and ordinary.

Jesus spent three intensive years preparing His disciples, and in the course of those three years He taught them all they needed to know to carry the gospel to the entire world. They had the best seminary education any twelve preachers ever received. They *lived* the language, culture, customs, and history that so often baffle us. They had daily access to the Great Teacher, and we know from Scripture they took advantage of that. Like good inquistive students, they questioned teachings they didn't understand. The fact that the leaders of Judaism never won an argument with the disciples proves that they learned their lessons well. The teaching method Jesus used was practiced widely in his world. Teachers took on students who lived, ate, slept, traveled, and learned with them. They walked about, carefully observing everything they saw, using every day experiences to drive home their lessons. For those who have some knowledge of education in the ancient world, the Gospels provide a clear picture of twelve men undergoing a high level graduate education.

The work of the Holy Spirit, as promised by Jesus, was not to give the disciples new information, but to remind them of everything Jesus had taught them. "But the Counselor, the Holy Spirit, whom the Father will send in my name, will teach you all things and remind you of everything I have said to you" (John 14:26).

Too often, people read the first half of the verse and ignore the second. This is a mistake because Hebrew, and its cousin Aramaic, rely on repetition. It's a mark of the best Hebrew literature. Jews of Jesus' day, like the prophets of earlier centuries, emphasized and clarified their statements by recasting them in different words. In this verse, the second half of Jesus' promise clarifies the first. Teaching and reminding are two aspects of the same process. Jesus promised that the Holy Spirit would keep what Jesus had taught them fresh in their minds, calling it forth when needed.

RICHER THAN KING TUT

What do you see in the first instant after you enter a dark room and flip on the light? Unless you're a little overactive in the hallucination department, you'll never see more in the room than is already there when the light comes on.

This is how the Holy Spirit works to fulfill Jesus' promise. Theologians call the process *illumination*. It's our responsibility to fill our minds with the truth of Scripture. The Holy Spirit won't illuminate verses or passages that we've never read.

The tomb of Pharaoh Tutankhamen was one of the most spectacular finds in the history of archeology. After years of hard work and frustration, archeologist Howard Carter discovered the partially intact door of the lost tomb in the Valley of the Kings. In his memoirs he describes the electric moment when the tomb was opened.

> On the morning of November 26th, 1922 the inner door of the tomb was broken open and Carter thrust a light through the hole. The shimmering jumble of treasures that emerged from 3,000 years of darkness into the shimmering light of Carter's lamp was so magnificent he stood speechless at the sight.
>
> When Lord Carnarvon, his patron, could stand the suspense no longer, he broke the silence and asked Carter if he could see anything.
>
> Carter's reply was a simple, "Yes, wonderful things."
>
> What no one knew until months later was that the treasures of the room they came to call the "antechamber" had not been placed there by careless mourners in the moments before the tomb was sealed. It was the work of tomb robbers who had stacked the treasures for removal.
>
> While the greatest wonders of the tomb still lay hidden in other rooms, those anonymous grave robbers from millennia ago had prepared the antechamber for the moment when Egypt's New Kingdom met the twentieth century in the yellow glow of Howard Carter's light.
>
> And only those pieces placed in that room by the tomb robbers were illuminated.

In much the same way the Holy Spirit brings to mind all those things that belong to Christ. When the Holy Spirit illuminates us during our study, He casts light on those objects carefully collected from all of Scripture and beyond. He picks out a piece here and there, shines His light on them, and thereby puts them together in our thoughts to bring to light a truth we've never seen before.

To reveal the treasures of Scripture to the marketplace of life, we must search the storehouse diligently, collect the artifacts of truth in the antechambers of our minds, and await the illuminating light of the Spirit. What a sad thing to have Him come to shed light on our collection and find only a tiny stack of favorite verses and stories that have satisfied us over the years while the real treasure still lies buried beyond our reach.

FOR MEMBERS ONLY

As Paul said, the things of God are spiritually discerned, which means that Scripture yields its true meaning only to those who approach it as believers. He wasn't suggesting that some super-spiritual Christians could receive the things of God while the rest were left unenlightened. Neither was he proposing that knowledge of Scripture came only from some mystical, spiritual experience. In fact, that's the nature of the teaching he was combating in Corinth. Like Peter, Paul had to deal with Gnostics who claimed special spiritual knowledge available only to themselves. Peter, Paul, and John all condemned this approach as heresy, as did the councils of the early church.

Others at Corinth were swept away by teachers long on presentation but short on content. These teachers, known as sophists, valued rhetorical form and delivery and used it without much concern for the truth or actual meaning of what they argued for.

Paul put distance between himself and this group of opponents by saying he taught the testimony of God without "eloquence," like the sophists, or "wisdom" like the Gnostics. Paul was not criticizing good preaching or solid thinking. Rather, he was warning Christians against the abuses that come when persuasive preachers have nothing worthwhile to say or claim to have special revelation not available to the "average" Christian.

If we study Paul's life we learn that he was both a dynamic preacher and a gifted scholar. He was such an eloquent speaker that the people of Lystra confused him with Hermes, the spokesman of the gods (Acts 14:8–13). He was such a gifted student that the great Gamaliel, a man still revered by Jews as one of the brightest and best rabbinic scholars, accepted him as a student. The apostle Paul is our best example of a balance between the power of the Spirit and the love for intellectual inquiry. In his zeal for the gospel and his commitment to excellence in study, Paul advised Timothy: "Do your best to present yourself to God as one approved, a workman who does not need to be ashamed and who correctly handles the word of truth" (2 Timothy 2:15).

Here, then, is a more accurate picture of the men who turned the world upside down. All were well educated. Most studied in the Lord's school, but Paul was a graduate of the Harvard of his day as well. All were gifted in the proclamation of the gospel. All were filled with the Holy Spirit and power. And among those things the Holy Spirit used to make them such a potent force for Christ's kingdom were the treasures of the knowledge of Scripture.

Study is not at odds with the working of the Spirit. Proverbs 19:2 cautions, "It is not good to have zeal without knowledge, nor to be hasty and miss the way." Today, we stand in danger of ignoring that clear cut biblical advice. There is a high level of zeal in the evangelical church in America, but our mistrust of study has made much of it zeal without knowledge.

THE LITTLE CHRISTIAN THAT COULD

The kind of study and knowledge I'm talking about is not beyond the abilities of the lay person. Everyone copes with complex problems unimagined by past generations. We possess more information on more topics than any people in human history. It takes more technical skill to set a digital watch than most people in history had to exercise in a lifetime.

When confronted with the complexities of the modern world that threaten our livelihood, we knuckle down and learn to deal with them. When confronted with the complexities of Scripture, though, some Christians retreat to an anti-intellectual refuge and leave them to the "experts."

As the knowledge explosion sweeps over us, the church can't afford to be weak in its knowledge of Scripture. In all of the armor of the Christian, our only offensive weapon is the Word of God (Ephesians 6:13–17). We may talk about defending the faith, but the best defense is always a strong offense.

We don't need a *Ph.D, D.D, Th.D, St.D.* behind our names to receive God's grace, or to grow in Him. Small children can understand that God made all there is and that Jesus loves them. Very young children can understand that they sin and need forgiveness, that Jesus loves them and has come to offer it. We don't need a Ph.D. in biblical languages to understand God's commands to live holy lives, to evangelize and disciple the world, or to share our faith with an unbelieving neighbor.

But there are truths in God's Word that only a lifetime of study will unlock. The longer I preach and teach, the more convinced I become of the unplumbed depths of Scripture. After years of full time ministry and ten years of formal instruction in the Bible and its world, I can honestly say that I'm just beginning to understand a part of what God has revealed.

It's good to know that no matter how much I learn about God, there's always more to learn. Even if I could understand all the theologies and languages and stories of Scripture, which I never will, there would still be the experience of walking with God and coming to say, with Job, "My ears had heard of you but now my eyes have seen you" (Job 42:5).

The God who inspired our Bible has also made himself known through it. We need to know its contents with our minds, and to know it that way we need to study. But the depths of God are beyond the reach of the greatest intellects. None of us should give up because there are portions of the Word we don't understand. Many of those puzzling passages are accessible to us. This book has shown how they might be understood, but it can't answer every question. Only continued study will pay the dividend of deepened understanding.

None of the roadblocks to understanding that we've talked about in this book are insurmountable. Anyone who can read and truly loves the Bible will be able to find the way around or over the majority of them. I hope this book has helped you make your own detours around some, and that your own curiosity and commitment will clear out many more.

APPENDIX

WORKERS
AND THEIR TOOLS

My grandfather, Rev. H. S. Thomasson, was a mechanic, a printer, a writer, an inventor, and a man of God whose influence on the lives of others was profound. His tools were simple, many of them of his own manufacture, and he never considered a job finished until they'd been cleaned, oiled, and carefully returned to their proper place.

His library also was filled with tools, the tools of study. In a day when Pentecostal preachers were looked down on as aisle-rolling, babbling backwoods idiots by the ecclesiastical hierarchy, Grandfather used a remarkably diverse set of tools. He kept his keen mind honed by reading widely among authors who were his theological opponents as well as those who were his allies. He has always been a model for me. I've had the benefit of formal education, but he had a curiosity and capacity for seeking that humbles me.

How do we hone our minds? Where do we go to seek answers to our questions? In other words, what tools can the Christian acquire in the quest for increased biblical knowledge?

For those who can't afford years of formal study, books are the best tools. Christians, as a group, are avid book buyers, but we tend to shy away from the kinds of books that make the most effective tools. I often encounter dismayed believers who can't believe they need to buy books to understand the Bible. Not long ago I was describing the basic Bible study tools that every serious Christian should own. One man in the seminar looked increasingly troubled as I went on with my recommendations of all the books that belonged in his library.

He finally blurted out the question I'm sure everyone wanted to ask, "How many books can you expect us to buy?"

My answer was another question. "How important is understanding your Bible to you?" Our answer to this question determines how much we're willing to invest in time and tools to study Scripture.

A more specific answer to the man's question would have been "six."

That's a minimum of six: three good Bible translations (not paraphrases); an analytical concordance; a Bible dictionary; and a single-volume commentary on the whole Bible. That's a respectable beginning. Beyond these basic six books, the only limit is your interest and income.

Here are some personal suggestions about books to enrich your study life.

BIBLE TRANSLATIONS

Because only a few people can read the Bible in the original languages, good translations are essential. The particular words of the translation we used when we first came into the Lord's family usually become especially precious to us. If we were saved using the King James and our Christian nurture, memory work, study, and devotional reading have marched to the measured cadences and sonorous harmonies of Elizabethan English, the minimal vocabulary and self-conscious simplicity of the Good News Bible doesn't even sound like the Bible. On the other hand, many new Christians today are coming to maturity using the *New International Version* and the *New American Standard Bible*. They have no patience for the archaic language and obscurities of the venerable KJV.

C. S. Lewis, in the introduction to the Phillips paraphrase of Paul's epistles, observed that continual changes in language and usage make it necessary for each new generation to have its own translation. Because of the incredibly high cost of translation work, that ideal is impractical, but it shows why a multitude of new translations confront the Bible reader today.

On the following pages I'll review the strengths and weaknesses of most of the major translations and suggest uses for each.

King James Version (also known as the Authorized Version)

For those not raised with it, the complex sentence structures and obscure vocabulary of the *King James Version* reads almost like a foreign language. We who have known it since childhood find its language familiar and comforting, but it's no longer the language people—even Christians—speak. This is not to say that the King James has lost its value.

Just before Easter some years ago I heard a Christian actor perform the entire book of Mark from the *King James*. It was a magnificent two-hour presentation that rates among the finest I have ever seen. It was more than just a dramatic performance, though. The powerful words of Mark's action-packed account of the life and death of Jesus, spoken by a skilled interpreter, took on a life that made the modern translations sound ordinary.

Not a "thee," a "thou," or a "straightaway" had been deleted. The story of Jesus presented on that stage took on power that it seldom displays from the pulpit. And no one in the audience objected that it came to life in that hoary, Elizabethan tongue.

The actor who held us spellbound that night had devoted two years to learning and understanding that language. No wonder he made it live.

We can transform the archaic language through the artist's craft, but most readers aren't willing to spend two years just to understand Mark!

The power of its language gave the *King James* supremacy over several other translations that competed with it when it was new and still gives it stature over its younger competitors. Some English scholars give the *King James Version* credit as the most powerful agent in the shaping of our English language. Its first readers probably would be astonished at that.

The *King James* originated from the sectarian controversies that raged through England at the end of the 1500s. At that time two different versions were used by the clergy, and a third, the Geneva Bible, was the favorite of the laity.

King James, who was more interested in a stable kingdom than in biblical knowledge, believed that uniformity in religion was the key to political stability. To achieve that uniformity, he commissioned the translation of a new version, one *authorized* for use in the church, to replace the competing versions. This new translation would be based on the Bishop's Bible, but the Tyndale, Coverdale, and Geneva versions, along with several others that are less well known, were also consulted.

The *King James Version*, or *Authorized Version*, was released in 1611, but it took forty years before it won popularity over the Geneva Bible. Major revisions were undertaken in the 19th Century (*The English Revised Version* and the *American Standard Version*) and the 20th Century (the *Revised Standard Version* and the *New King James Version*). It has also undergone five minor revisions.

Its long life alone argues for the high quality of the *King James*. But English is a living language, and it has undergone massive change in the past 350 years. Also, our understanding of the biblical languages, especially Hebrew, has grown dramatically since 1611. These two changes alone have made new translations a necessity. A third reason new translations are necessary is that the translators of this majestic version were simply inaccurate in a number of places.

In spite of these problems, however, no edition of the Bible in English can compare with the beauty of its language. While the archaic vocabulary and sentence structure make understanding difficult, the rhythms of Elizabethan English lend themselves much more easily to memorization than does the choppy modern English of most contemporary versions. There is also no version that can compare with the power of the *King James* when read aloud by a skillful reader.

In some pastoral settings I use the *King James* simply because its familiar words speak biblical comfort in a way that touches hurting hearts at a level that transcends intellectual comprehension.

Revised Standard Version and American Standard Version

These are the most venerable of the contemporary translations. Both are in the Tyndale tradition, tracing their roots back through the KJV to the work of William Tyndale. Both have attempted to retain the flavor of the KJV while making use of the advances in knowledge of biblical languages and conforming more closely to modern usage. Both are older versions, the ASV completed in 1901 and the RSV in 1952. Both versions are still well respected translations, often used as study texts in colleges and seminaries. Both provide a good compromise between the KJV and the newer independent translations.

APPENDIX

The RSV still commands respect. It's accurate, reasonably up to date, and still retains some of the majesty of the *King James*. The ASV, which is older, has less to recommend it. Its primary value lies in detailed textual study, but some recent translations are more valuable in this area. Its translators aimed at achieving an extremely close rendering of the original text and succeeded, as much as it's possible to translate "literally." It also attempted to retain the flavor of the *King James*, but in this it failed.

If you're looking for a translation that is older and more majestic to complement the KJV, I'd recommend the RSV. The ASV has been superseded by a revision of its own.

New American Standard Bible

This popular version is based on both the ASV and the KJV. It has enjoyed wide usage in the evangelical community. The scholars who produced it held the "conviction that the words of Scripture as originally penned in the Hebrew and Greek were inspired by God." The finished product leans heavily in the direction of adhering closely to the original languages, making its use of English less than fluent. The language of the NASB is what some call "translation English," a hybrid form in which word order and grammar from the original language are super-imposed on English. The result is no longer Hebrew or Greek, but it isn't quite good English either. Because of this, the NASB is often clumsy to read. But if you want a translation that brings you into close contact with the original languages, I recommend the NASB. I use it in teaching my Bible clases, and I still use, value, and preach from my NASB. But for public reading, memorization, or devotional reading, I'd look elsewhere.

The Living Bible

This popular paraphrase is also based on the ASV. While it's not a translation, and shouldn't be treated as one, its wide readership requires that I deal with it. *The Living Bible*, in any of its many incarnations, is a remarkable undertaking. It represents the efforts of a single man and therefore is a monument to his commitment and self-discipline. However, we shouldn't overlook the fact that the impetus behind it was to produce a Bible that his children would understand. The author checked with evan-gelical authorities when handling difficult passages, but the final work, nevertheless, reflects the interpretations of the man doing the work. Some have stressed its value for children and the unchurched, with which I agree. But it's not a Bible to use for study. It is better read as a one-man commentary, not as Scripture itself.

This doesn't mean I'm opposed to *The Living Bible*. In fact, let me suggest a use for it that you might not have considered.

Its rendering of biblical narratives, especially in the Old Testament, is more readable than any of the more accurate translations. Because people often find themselves bogged down in the Old Testament, I often recommend that they try *The Living Bible*. Here's how it works.

Imagine that you've never read the Bible before and you've just picked up a copy of *The Book* (as it is also called) from the book rack at the supermarket. Start reading it as if you've never heard of any of those people or events. Read about Abraham, Moses, and David for the sheer enjoyment of it. Don't look for anything profound and don't search for spiritual enlightenment. Just enjoy.

We often forget that the Bible contains some of the world's greatest stories. People are more likely to read books they enjoy, so it is not surprising that God wrote an enjoyable book. Even the most difficult passages have a literary beauty and grace that entices readers into their depths.

Sometimes I think we're so intent on hearing the Lord speak that we muffle the Word in our expectations. When we set out to find something that speaks to our specific situation, we'll probably find it, even if it isn't there, just because we're looking so hard. If, on the other hand, we read to enjoy God's Word, we will know it more thoroughly and liberate the Spirit to surprise us with what we've never seen before.

Come to the Bible fresh and let it surprise you. When I read the Bible for pleasure, instead of from duty, the Lord speaks more often and more powerfully.

New King James Version

Most Bible translations are well intentioned, and the NKJV is no exception. It's an attempt to bring its venerable parent into the twentieth century by preserving its language while upgrading its translation. Its appeal is obviously to the person for whom the

KJV is still the only acceptable version. But if you fall into that category, I'm afraid the NKJV will probably prove a disappointment. It retains enough of the 1611 language to sound old fashioned, but not enough to preserve its richness. My opinion is that it preserves all the weaknesses of the *Authorized Version* but none of its strengths. It's an adequate translation, at best. If you're devoted to the *King James*, stick with it. In the case of the NKJV, new doesn't necessarily mean better.

New International Version

There's a good chance that the NIV is destined to become the translation of choice for the majority of American conservatives. Produced by a group of evangelical scholars committed wholeheartedly to the inspiration of Scripture, the NIV could very well be the best general purpose translation produced anywhere in the Twentieth Century. It is carefully done, scholarly, and readable. There hasn't been a translation in modern times that has involved such a significant number of first-rate conservative scholars. The broad range of denominations and positions represented on the translation committees guarantee an even and usually unbiased translation.

There's no such thing as a perfect translation, however, and that includes the NIV. I've already come across a number of verses I wish they had handled a bit differently, and I've noted several instances where it seems that theological considerations have overruled good translation. But on balance, I can't think of a Bible available that will be as satisfactory to as many different people.

THE MAKING OF TRANSLATIONS

These translations represent only a fraction of those available, and they are not the only versions with features to recommend them. I enjoy the *New English Bible* for its language, but I use it with caution. And *Today's English Version* is a first-rate translation based on the principle of dynamic equivalence. The *Phillips* paraphrase of the letters of Paul is a pleasure to read, and the *Jerusalem Bible* does a good job of translating at a fairly high literary level.

I keep two leather-bound Bibles to use in the pulpit or lectern and I have fifteen assorted translations on my bookshelves, all in inexpensive bindings, to use for comparison.

Because of the difficulties involved in translating from two ancient languages, all translations are imperfect. People who can't go back to the original languages should at least use several English versions for study. For this purpose there are several excellent parallel translation editions available. With as many as eight different translations in one book, these volumes are both valuable and convenient for study.

BIBLE DICTIONARIES AND ENCYCLOPEDIAS

A great variety of reference works use these titles, but don't ask me what the difference between them is. Theoretically, a dictionary defines biblical words and concepts while an encyclopedia deals with a wider selection of material. In practice, some dictionaries are more encyclopedic than some encyclopedias, and most works tend to cover the same ground regardless of title.

Dictionaries and encyclopedias are available in different formats as well. Some call themselves "Illustrated" or "Pictorial" because they contain photos, drawings, and maps, but I think you'd have to look very hard to find one that doesn't have some of those features.

A more important difference has to do with the number of volumes. Obviously, a reference work done in four or five volumes will cost more, but you also get more. The added investment required for multiple volume sets is justified by the added information and detail they offer.

Price is the primary advantage of single volume works. Their articles tend to be concise and focused, but they can only say so much. A few years ago I was assigned to write 110 articles for a new Bible dictionary. I got to explain things like cheese, furniture, and scum. Those were fairly easy to handle in my allotted one hundred and fifty words, but I almost stripped my gears when I tried to explain science. As is so often the case in a one-volume work, the problem was not so much what to put in, but what to leave out. For some people a thirty- or forty-word explanation might be enough, but I am often frustrated with an abbreviated definition that does little more than pique my curiosity. If you have more than a superficial interest, you might want to consider the greater depth of a multi-volume set.

Caution. Whenever you buy a reference work, check the copyright date. In dictionaries and encyclopedias, newer is always better. Advances in archeology, history, and language study since the 1940s have proven a real bonanza for biblical studies. Our knowledge of biblical life and times has expanded so greatly that any work published before 1950 is almost certainly out of date. Some publishers have acquired the rights to dictionaries compiled early in this century or late in the last century and released them without revision. Their copyright dates might be in the 1980s, but they are seriously flawed.

Don't buy a dictionary or an encyclopedia based on an older work unless it has been updated, because articles presenting historical or archeological information will be inaccurate, incomplete, or wrong. I don't deny the value of the spiritual insights of the older commentators. In fact, their devotional value is lasting. But for serious study, it's good to have the benefit of up-to-date research. For up-to-date research at a bargain price, there are many fine single-volume works available. I recommend the following.

The serious student of Scripture who is on a tight budget would do well to consider the *New Bible Dictionary* (2nd Edition) from Inter-Varsity Press. As I write, this is the most up-to-date work of its type available. The articles are written by some of the world's best evangelical scholars.

Although it's called a second edition, it's almost completely new. If you're up to detailed and fairly technical treatments of a carefully selected range of topics, NBD is for you.

If you can only afford one book from this category, though, you might want to consider something a bit more general. The editors chose to cover selected topics in considerable depth; consequently there are a number of words and subjects of interest that aren't covered at all.

A work that covers a lot more ground and is written specifically for the non-technical reader is *Nelson's Illustrated Bible Dictionary*. Released in 1986, it's one of the most recent entries into the dictionary/encyclopedia competition. Nicely illustrated with color photos, this book is new from the ground up.

Bethany House's slightly older *Today's Dictionary of the Bible* is a revision of an older work, but covers the same ground as Nelson's. For the beginner on a tight budget, this might be a good choice. Though it lacks the color photos, its information is updated and complete. Written for the lay reader, it's a non-technical explanation of most of the words used in the *King James Version*.

STRENGTH IN NUMBERS

When it comes to books, the more, the merrier. Nowhere is this more true than in the purchase of reference books. Single volumes are good, multiple volumes are better. The only drawback to the multiple volume sets is expense. You have to decide how much the information in a set of encyclopedias is worth to you. If it isn't worth a lot, stick with the single volumes. If the information is worth the hefty price, here are some multiple volume sets to consider.

If you've looked at the *New Bible Dictionary* and liked it, you're going to love the Tyndale *Illustrated Bible Dictionary*. The NBD text has been stretched out over three volumes with the additional pages given to marvelous illustrations, maps, and photographs. Of all the reference works described as illustrated, none deserves the description more than this excellent set. If you like pictures but can't afford to pay for all the pictures, this would be your best buy. If you want a broader range of topics and can live without all the pictures, you might want to look elsewhere.

Fortunately, there are some excellent alternatives. *The Zondervan Pictorial Encyclopedia of the Bible* is old enough that it doesn't reflect some of the latest archeological discoveries, but still new enough to be useful.

You may wonder why I chose 1950 as the oldest copyright date for good reference works. The reason has to do with archeology. We're so used to talking about archeology that we forget it only began to make itself felt in a positive way in the years between World Wars I and II.

Most of the discoveries in the Near East during those years didn't get into publication until years later. Even today, with all the furor that has swirled around the discovery of the ancient city of Ebla, most of what's been written since has been speculative. Every new text and reference makes some reference to Ebla and its remarkable library, but the actual new knowledge of life in Syria around 4300 years ago is still only microscopic. During the first 10 to 20 years following a major discovery, scholars argue over the find. Not until decades later, when the scholarly publications have appeared and detailed comparative study of the documents has begun, do we really know what's been found.

The Zondervan Pictorial doesn't reflect the most up to the minute digs in Jerusalem or the discovery of Ebla, but don't worry. There's no telling how long it will be before that material will be sufficiently analyzed and understood to have any real impact, and longer before any of the existing reference works will be revised to reflect that impact. In the meantime, *The Zondervan Pictorial* is a fine collection of articles by respected conservative scholars. It is illustrated, but for this five-volume work you will be paying for information, not pictures.

My third recommendation is probably the best. It combines the timeliness of the Tyndale with the breadth of the Zondervan. For years the original *International Standard Bible Encyclopedia* (ISBE) has been the standard reference work for evangelicals. Though badly outdated, the original still commands the respect of many. Its revision has been undertaken by the best of evangelical scholars and in the same spirit as the original.

Any of the multiple volume sets will cost you a lot of money. At today's prices, most of them live somewhere in the neighborhood of one hundred dollars. But compared to what it costs to buy the latest best-selling novel that is read once and then forgotten, this is still one of the best possible book buys.

To provide some different points of view for your personal study, you might want to buy one multiple-volume set and supplement it with a single-volume dictionary.

TRACKING THE ELUSIVE GIRGASHITE

If you've been reading through the Bible and midway through Joshua you decide to find out who all those "ites" are, how do you find out? You begin by looking them up in a concordance. There you will find every strange name, anonymous tribe, and theological key word in the Bible listed in alphabetical order. Simply look up the word in question and the concordance will tell you every place in both Testaments where it's used. I haven't known too many people for whom the in-depth study of the Girgashites awakened dreams of discovery, but I have known quite a few people who have used their concordances to trace every use of words like *righteous*, *saved*, *Messiah*, and so on.

For careful independent study of the Bible, you need a good concordance. Be careful in your choice. If you grew up memorizing from the *King James*, as I did, the newer concordances, keyed to such versions as the NIV or NASB, may be confusing. If you cut your Christian teeth on one of the newer versions, you may want to try one of the newer concordances. But none of them will provide the range of features that the good old standbys do. Some bright computer whiz may correct this situation any day, but at the moment there are only two concordances in English that serve the purposes of the serious student: *Young's Analytical Concordance* and *Strong's Exhaustive Concordance*. With over 300,000 entries each, these two giants cover every significant word in the Bible, and then some. They also both provide the reader with a limited access to the original languages.

Some say that "Young's is for the young and Strong's is for the strong." I've always felt that Young's was for the young at heart and Strong's was for those who wanted to become exhausted.

As you may guess, both concordances have their followings. Young's greatest advantage is that each English word is subdivided by the various Greek and Hebrew words it translates. This subdivision occurs right in the body of the text rather than in a series of indexes at the back of the book. Because many English words are used to translate a variety of Greek and Hebrew originals, it helps to know which original lies behind the English word you're studying. This saves time and introduces a degree of precision to basic concordance work that is missing if you depend on separate lists like those found in Strong's.

Strong's is more tedious to use than Young's because its entries use a reference number in the body of the concordance with corresponding word lists at the back of the book. But it has one major advantage over Young's. Because Strong numbers each word from the biblical languages, his word lists have become the springboard for the use of more advanced reference works. In recent years, more and more books have adopted

Strong's numbering. After finding your word in this concordance, you can look up the original in a broadening range of dictionaries. This expands the value of the concordance immeasurably. Instead of the usual one- or two-word concordance definition, you can follow the numbering into other reference works that may give you pages of explanation on the usage and meaning of the word. This use of Strong's numbering seems to be a continuing trend. This feature might tip the balance in favor of Strong's concordance for the serious lay reader.

Several resources take advantage of this feature, but there's no single volume to turn to. W. E. Vine's *Expository Dictionary of New Testament Words* is a good beginning point. Of the numerous editions available, I would rate the *Expanded Vine's* as the best buy. The fact that some editions include a list of Hebrew words does not make them more valuable, since the Old Testament sections of these versions are too incomplete to be of much use.

Bethany House's edition, in addition to the helpful linkage with Strong's, also leads into the excellent *New International Dictionary of New Testament Theology* (Zondervan) and Walter Bauer's *Greek-English Lexicon* (usually referred to as *Arndt and Gingrich* for the two Americans who translated it). These will open whole new vistas on the meaning of New Testament words, but you'll probably want to borrow rather than buy them.

For the Old Testament, Strong's will get you into the *Theological Wordbook of the Old Testament* (Moody Press), which also uses Strong's numbering. This is a very up-to-date, scholarly, and readable book. That's an unusual combination, but this conservative work offers understandable and informative articles on the use and meaning of most important Old Testament words.

TAKE THE FIRST LEFT PAST THE PLAINS OF MOAB

Sometimes the "what" of biblical history is obscured by the "where." The geography of the ancient world is a welter of strange names, sometimes two or three different ones for the same place. A good Bible atlas is necessary for building mental images of the places and events of Scripture. But not all atlases are created equal. And they don't all set out to do the same thing. Some contain far more pages of text than of maps, some have no text at all, and some use a combination of text and graphics to teach everything from military movements to average annual rainfalls. In the last few years the market has been deluged with specialty atlases.

The most elaborate, and expensive, is the *Carta Folio* atlas. This is the Rolls Royce of atlases. Its lavish and detailed maps aren't even bound into book form. They are carefully folded and sold in a wooden box. If you have more money than sense, or if you're the purchasing agent for a research library, there's nothing better.

For most of us, the next best thing will have to do. In atlases, there are lots of next best things. It's almost impossible to recommend just one because they are such a diverse and impressive lot. Having no clear favorite, I will throw out the names of several excellent atlases and allow you to make your choice.

The *Oxford Bible Atlas* is a recently revised classic. It offers excellent maps and explanatory text on topography, climate, and the major historical periods. With numerous black and white pictures of biblical locales and artifacts, and with valuable introductory articles on biblical history and archeology, this is an excellent general purpose atlas. It's also available in paperback, which helps those on limited budgets. Few others can make that statement.

A historical atlas uses geography to teach history. The best of this class is the *Macmillan Bible Atlas*. It boasts 265 detailed maps of specific periods and events in biblical history. If you've ever puzzled over battle descriptions in Joshua, or Abraham's migrations, or Jesus' movements in the Gospels, you'll find separate maps to solve each problem. Each is accompanied by explanatory text retelling the biblical account with added insights from ancient history and archeology. Just one note of caution. The authors are Jewish scholars who sometimes present a position that most evangelicals won't accept, but don't let that frighten you off.

Zondervan's *Student Map Manual* is nothing but maps with ample room to make study notes. There's no explanatory text, no introductory text, in fact, no text at all. This is the best, most detailed collection of maps covering the whole range of biblical history that I'm aware of. It is by far the most difficult to use, but if you're willing to invest the time and money, it can also be the most rewarding. There's a supplementary manual that goes with the collection of maps, but the purchase of both could put a severe strain on a limited book budget.

Moody and Zondervan both have new atlases that I've never had the opportunity to use. The reviews I've read of them have been positive enough that I'd recommend you consider them before you buy.

NO SHORTAGE OF OPINIONS

Dictionaries and encyclopedias will usually reflect the bias of the editors who compiled it. There's no getting around that. Even atlases, if read carefully, will reveal something of the stance of their compilers. But concordances are value free. There's not much possibility of theology intruding into the kind of word lists found in concordances.

In commentaries, it's essential that you know the theological stance of the commentator. That doesn't mean that you should only read commentators you agree with. Far from it. In some cases, the insight of those outside your theological persuasion is dazzling. When dealing with commentators, it's not so important whether or not they agree with your position but whether or not you know theirs. If you do, you'll be able to compensate for their biases.

When buying commentaries, the problem will be how to choose between a bewildering variety. They offer more choices than any other biblical reference work. Like dictionaries and encyclopedias, commentaries are available in single and multiple volume works. They're also available as single or multiple author works.

As a rule of thumb, avoid single author sets. No single human being, no matter how committed or well prepared, has the depth of understanding that a team of commentators has. The task of becoming an expert on just one biblical book is so great that I don't know of a single contemporary scholar qualified to deal with the whole Bible with consistent quality.

Specialists are important. A surgeon showed up at the bedside of a man about to undergo exploratory brain surgery. Just before the man was put under the anesthetic, the surgeon said to him, "My knowledge of the human brain is limited, but I have a good general knowledge of how the body works."

The man did not stick around to give the doctor experience.

If biblical study, like brain surgery, is a life or death matter, we shouldn't settle for general practitioners. We need to go to specialists. Laypeople need, and deserve, the same breadth and depth of understanding applied to what they read as the most advanced specialist does. There's no reason for the non-technical or "layman's" commentary to be any less accurate, insightful, or up to date than those written for a scholarly audience.

A good single volume commentary written by a first-rate team of British evangelicals is the *New Bible Commentary: Revised*. If I could afford only one single commentary, this would be it. Although a one-volume commentary must leave many questions unanswered and many details unexamined, this one deals with the Word as accurately, reverently, and as completely as we could expect one book to do.

If you can afford more, my choice of commentary sets for a basic library would be the Tyndale Old and New Testament commentaries. These books originated in the Tyndale Fellowship for Biblical Research in England. The twenty-two volumes of the New Testament series are available, and the Old Testament set, when finished, will have twenty-four volumes. Both sets are conservative, scholarly, and well-written.

The two-volume *Bethany Parallel Commentary* breaks all my rules of thumb, but I feel confident about recommending it as a valuable commentary innovation. They combine the classic commentaries of Matthew Henry, Adam Clarke, and Jamieson, Fausset, and Brown in parallel columns. I like the format, and having these three classics side by side for comparison has some real advantages.

All three are one hundred years old or older, so they don't give any of the new insights that archeology and recent linguistic study have provided. But they have immeasurable value as a part of the history of the interpretation of the Bible. They provide access to Christian voices from recent church history that are rich in devotional and interpretive insight. Some of the ideas, based as they are on erroneous historical assumptions, will have to be rejected. But their broader understanding of God and His dealing with humanity is timeless. The parallel format reduces the tendency of some Christians to become too dependent on a single commentary, and the three works disagree often enough to remind us that no single commentator will always be right.

Numerous other commentaries are readily available. I've listed only those that I think fit well into a layperson's budget and interest level. The American Christian community enjoys an embarassment of riches when it comes to the availability of good Bible study resources. Your pastor or Christian bookseller can certainly recommend other books that don't fit into my limited scheme of things.

A good reference library is a must for the serious believer. Each of us encounters God in His Word for ourselves, but the questions we ask about Scripture have all been asked before. Answers to those questions can be found in the accumulated wisdom of generations of believing scholars. To insist that we need a fresh approach to Scripture every generation, only to rediscover truths that past believers have already unearthed, is foolhardy.

There's nothing unspiritual or dishonest about consulting the experts. The writer Flannery O'Connor gave a student a piece of good advice. She said, "To find out about faith, you have to go to the people who have it, and you have to go to the most intelligent ones if you're going to stand up intellectually to agnostics and the general run of pagans that you are going to find in the majority of people around you."

I hope you'll explore this broad and fertile field of biblical understanding as it's been mapped out by earlier pilgrims. Use their maps as guides, but make the trip on your own. Never rely on the comments or interpretations of others as a substitute for your own study, understanding, and insight.

PRINCIPLE INDEX

Principle 1   The more ancient manuscripts we have, the more certainty we have about the true nature of the text.   **43**

Principle 2   The more ancient the text is, the closer it is to the original; and the closer it is to the original, the more accurate it is likely to be.   **44**

Principle 3   The quality of the text is as important as the age of the text.   **44**

Principle 4   The more we know about the world in which the Bible was written, the better we understand the Bible itself.   **53**

Principle 5   The Bible may accurately record sinful acts without wholeheartedly applauding them.   **54**

Principle 6   An understanding of the prophetic prototype can help open up some of the more troublesome prophetic passages. Looking back at the known biblical world can help us gain a better appreciation for the shape of unknown things to come.   **76**

Principle 7   To understand apocalyptic literature we need to understand that it is symbolic and that it has its own rules.   **76**

Principle 8   To understand apocalyptic literature we need to determine what the text meant to the people it was written to.   **79**

INDEXES   443

Principle **46** Don't argue from silence. Christians do this as often as non-Christians, and it always weakens our position in the eyes of perceptive non-believers. And don't fall for this argument when others use it.   **409**

Principle **47** Learn to distinguish between passages that are didactic, or teaching, and those that are illustrative, or metaphorical. Parables should never be used as the primary basis for doctrine because they require too much interpretation.   **411**

QUESTION INDEX

INDEXES

SUBJECT INDEX

Jesus
    age at crucifixion 61
    anger at money changers 56
    baptizing with Holy Spirit 150
    building church on Peter 131
    camel through needle's eye 137
    days of Noah 100
    explanation of forgiveness 135
    hating mother and father 136
    how to determine age 61
    Morning Star 142
    prayer for anything 139
    Second Coming 100
    Son of Man 153
    water into wine 365
    who carried cross 408
    words at Last Supper 407
Jesus ben Sirach 41
Jews
    and Samaritans 57
Jezebel 218, 239
Joab 65, 66, 67, 243, 266, 267, 268
    killing of Absalom 266
    why he disobeyed David 266
Job 17, 18, 19, 75, 181, 313, 314, 319, 320, 321, 324, 325, 331, 332,
    333, 334, 335, 336, 388, 399, 401, 402, 423
    claim of righteousness 331
    his suffering 333
    seeing God 399
Joel 356
John 61, 72, 73, 76, 77, 78, 79, 83, 92, 104, 121, 143, 156, 157, 158,
    260, 340, 341, 354, 356, 368, 388, 399, 400, 405, 406, 407, 409,
    410, 411, 418, 421
John Mark 64
John the Baptist 61, 62, 121, 150, 151, 274, 302, 341, 344, 356, 357
    baptizing with fire 150
Johnson, A. 346
Johnson, J. W. 165
Johnson, L. 239
Jonah 33, 54, 55, 260, 355
    reason for going to Tarshish 54
Joppa 54
Jordan River 218
Joseph 198, 212
Joseph of Arimathea 137

Questions
  See **QUESTION INDEX**
"Quietness" 372
Qumran 143

Rachel 253
Rahab 287, 289, 297
Rain 185, 220
Rainbow 220
Ramses II 28, 287
Rapture 101, 104, 105, 347
Rebekah 128, 285
Redemption 77, 105, 195, 199, 200, 201, 223, 226, 228, 283, 295,
    297, 298, 335, 390
Reflections on the Psalms 322
Reformation 38
Regeneration 369
Reliability of Scripture 116, 408
Repentance 73, 191, 212, 213, 265, 288, 289, 309, 310, 337, 356,
    398, 403
Requiem 188
Rest 184
    God's after creation 184
Resurrection 29, 49, 141, 295, 296, 353, 358, 359, 364
Revelation 19, 41, 78, 89, 125, 166, 169, 172, 178, 182, 195, 201,
    212, 283, 320, 324, 333, 352, 357, 385, 392, 396, 397, 417, 421
Revelation, the book 72, 75, 76, 77, 83, 102, 103, 104, 226
Revised Standard Version 212, 428, 429
Rich
    salvation of 137
Righteousness
    and hunger 325
Rizpah 266
Rockwell, N. 224
Romans 91, 92, 97, 355
Romans, the book 280, 282, 296, 361, 362
Rome 33, 38, 59, 60, 83, 87, 88, 91, 92, 104, 226, 355
Rosh 80, 81
Russia in prophecy 68, 71, 79, 80, 82

Sabbath year 247
Sacred pillars 272, 273
Sacrifices

SCRIPTURE INDEX